THE GUINNESS
FOOTBALL
ENCYCLOPEDIA

David Platt of England, Italy 1990

THE GUINNESS FOOTBALL ENCYCLOPEDIA

EDITED BY GRAHAM HART

GUINNESS PUBLISHING

First published in 1991 by
Guinness Publishing Ltd
33 London Road
Enfield, Middlesex

This book is a product of FORSTER books

Designed by Graham Mitchener

Text copyright © 1991 by Guinness Publishing Ltd

Illustrations copyright © 1991 as credited

A catalogue record for this book is available
from the British Library

Typeset and page-planned by
Systemset Composition, London NW2

Printed and bound in Great Britain by
Butler & Tanner Ltd, Frome, Somerset

'Guinness' is a registered trademark
of Guinness Publishing

ISBN 0-85112-998-6

Alastair Maxwell of Motherwell, Scottish Cup Final 1991

Kevin Keegan, in front of Liverpool's Kop

INTRODUCTION

When I was asked to compile this Encyclopedia 'my' team had just gained promotion to Division 3. They were a shade lucky to do so. As I write this introduction, some thirteen months later, they have just started training for the 1991/92 season . . . their first ever in Division 2! Football, as they say, is a funny old game.

I hope this Encyclopedia reflects this glorious unpredictability of soccer – but also puts matters in their overall context. It has taken a long time for fans to accept that Burnley are no longer a top flight club, and it may take decades of success before a team like Halifax or Hartlepool could pretend to senior status. That's the way things are.

Clearly an encyclopedia of soccer could consist of ten volumes and still not claim to be comprehensive. These 200 or so pages have entries on all the League clubs of England and Scotland (excluding Barnet because the editor has a certain affection for the '92', and at the time of writing Barnet have yet to play a League match). Also included are a number of great players, entries on international soccer and a selection of themes of interest and importance. Several items are not here – and I make no apology. I didn't have the space. Also some things will be out of date, but we did our best.

Anyway, no more apologies or explanations. I hope that the writers' love of the game shines forth from the pages. The contributors, quite simply, are all fans and I'm sure the book demonstrates that.

In the role of both editor and contributor (a sort of publishing player/manager) I have the happy task of thanking the 'team'. Importantly, I must express sincere thanks to all the writers:

Moira Banks
Bob Ferrier
Guy Hodgson
Derek Hodgson
Simon Inglis
Ken Jones
Peter Lovering
Sean MacSweeney
Kevin McCarra
Tony Morris
Ivan Ponting
Phil Shaw
Andy Ward.

They did a great writing job and answered scores of questions and enquiries from me. Additionally, the following have also helped significantly in other ways in the compilation of the Encyclopedia: Chris and Jo Forster, Moira Banks, Janine Drake, Alison Paris, Graham Mitchener (responsible for the excellent design), Ken and Jeanne in King's Lynn (fact checkers), fellow Southend United fan Nick, all at Colorsport, especially Hugh Godwin (sorry about Barnet) and Andy Cowie, and David Webb for leading 'my' team. All the photo agencies contacted were extremely helpful as were the typesetters and staff at Guinness. Good on you all.

And of all the above, I must single out Alison Paris as my 'Player of the Year'. Without her help the book would not have been completed at all. Thanks.

Graham Hart

Gary Lineker hurdles a challenge during England's
1–0 win over Switzerland in Lausanne in May 1988.

ABERDEEN

Founded 1903

Joined League 1904
(Division 2)

Honours Scottish
League Championship,
Division 1, 1955; Premier
Division, 1980, 1984,
1985; Scottish Cup, 1947,
1970, 1982, 1983, 1984,
1986, 1990; League Cup,
1955/56, 1976/77,
1985/86, 1989/90;
European Cup-Winners'
Cup, 1983

Ground Pittodrie Stadium

Aberdeen have done far more than win trophies. In the 1980s they did not just come through to take silverware, they repeatedly trounced both Celtic and Rangers. It was the greatest disruption to the status quo in the modern history of Scottish football.

The confidence and pugnacity seemed to originate in the personality of manager Alex Ferguson. A marvellously blended side deployed the rigour of defenders Willie Miller and Alex McLeish as well as the deft skills of Gordon Strachan, Mark McGhee and Peter Weir in attack.

Their finest two hours came in the extra-time victory over Real Madrid in the 1983 Cup Winners' Cup final. The 2-1 scoreline masked the annihilation of the celebrated opposition. Now managed by Alex Smith, Aberdeen remain likely contenders for honours in Scotland.

Their prominence is aided by remoteness (fans cannot be wooed away to watch the Old Firm) and the fact that they are their city's only senior club. Shrewd administration down the years, seen in the fact that Pittodrie was all-seated long before the Taylor report, has also been significant.

There had been celebrated figures before such as goal scorer Benny Yorston between the wars and Martin Buchan who, as a 21-year-old, captained them to the Scottish Cup triumph over Celtic in 1970. Despite memories of them and of other trophies Aberdeen's present utterly eclipses its past.

ABERDEEN Perhaps the most popular victory for Aberdeen during their period of success in the early 1980s was that in the 1983 European Cup Winners' Cup Final when they beat Real Madrid in Gothenburg. They won 2-1 in extra time. The photograph shows Eric Black's opening goal of the game, tucking the ball past Real's 'keeper Augustin. John Hewitt scored the winner when it looked as if the Spanish club would be happy to wait for penalty kicks. The game, played in pouring rain, was watched by only 17,804 spectators, but the massed Scots supporters minded neither the weather nor the low attendance.

AFRICA

To describe a competition appearance in which 14 goals were conceded in three successive defeats as a basis for optimism might seem far-fetched, but in 1974 Zaire became the first non-Arabic-speaking African state to appear in the World Cup finals; to compete at world level was significant in itself and the confidence and self-belief of that continent's other teams were raised. Sixteen years later, Cameroon, with a style that might euphemistically be termed robust, reached the quarter-finals, and that, plus Morocco winning their first-stage group in 1986, prompted FIFA to increase Africa's contingent for 1994 to three teams.

Football in Africa, as might be expected, has colonial origins, and ironically the political, economic and cultural consequences of post-imperialism are among the many things holding up the sport's development in that part of the world. To a European, the words Congo, Biafra, Uganda, Ethiopia, Zimbabwe and Mozambique represent not so much countries as disasters: famine, drought, civil war. A 1989 survey showed that, in almost every country in a broad band sweeping across central Africa from Mozambique in the south-east to the western Sahara, economic growth was negligible and the average income less than 500 dollars per head.

The climate and attendant disease are also not to be underestimated as problems. It is against such a background that African soccer is trying to make its mark on the world.

Football, a school as well as a street sport, is tremendously popular throughout the continent, but it is in north Africa, particularly the Franco-phone states (France arguably having done more to promote world soccer than the game's mother nation), that the game's traditions are strongest. Algeria rival Cameroon as the continent's strongest side. In the 1982 World Cup, with Lakhdar Belloumi, they beat West Germany 2-1 and, but for that team settling for a mutually beneficial draw

players for their club - and national - teams. France's record-holding Just Fontaine was Moroccan. Benfica of the 1960s had three Angolans in their team including goalkeeper Alberto Costa Pereira, and two famous players from Mozambique who also represented Portugal - skipper Mario Coluna and Eusebio. Such signings are still a rarity in England but continue in France.

Since the 1950s, countries south of the Sahara, notably Cameroon, Zaire and Ghana, have emerged as football powers. The Confederation of African Football (CAF) was formed in 1957 with four member nations - today there are some fifty. Almost their first act was to expel South Africa because of its system of apartheid. FIFA suspended the South Africans in 1964 and did the same to Rhodesia in 1970. Among South African whites, football comes a poor second to rugby union. The national league was disbanded in 1978 despite the enrolment of stars such as Ian St John and Francis Lee. But the game is hugely popular among the non-white population. Formal structure, facilities and coaching are all lacking, but recent moves towards racial integration, in particular the formation in late 1990 of one ruling body, the SAFA, have led CAF and FIFA to reconsider South Africa's position. CAF's influence in FIFA has grown and in 1985 Africa staged the first Junior World Cup.

As well as the African Cup of Nations there are continental club competitions based on European models, and, wisely for a continent larger than South America, regional international tournaments. No east African country has ever won the Nations Cup; rivalry between Kenya, the region's top team, and Uganda is intense but the two sides do not experience enough competition with north African and European sides to improve - a replication in miniature of one of Africa's main

problems. The average Kenyan footballer has an excellent physique for the sport but his country's approach often emphasises individual excellence at the expense of teamwork.

Idi Amin, a football enthusiast, brought Uganda financial ruin and civil war - conditions which make sport seem trivial. Tanzania lost her best players of the 1970s and 1980s to Europe, the Middle East and the USA - another disadvantage experienced by most African nations. Malawi, with their tough brand of football, and Zambia, a nation boasting home-grown coaches and staff, also exhibit keen rivalry.

The lowly status of a small, under-resourced country such as Gambia is understandable; more puzzling is Nigeria's lack of success. Football is widely played in this populous country but the league, established in 1972, took some years to get off the ground and the national team rarely live up to expectations. The Biafran war was obviously a hindrance. Less apparent is the disturbing effect of emigre stars returning and trying to adapt to the national style. Ghana, on the other hand, has a proud record. As the game took hold, European administrators were phased out until, strangely enough, independence in 1957. Then a commemorative tour by Stanley Matthews so inspired the national association that European coaches were brought over to increase their players' technical skills and tactics. In 1963 the national side toured Europe, holding Real Madrid to a 3-3 draw. The following year they beat Italy. Ghana's four victories in the Cup of Nations is a record.

Although various styles exist in African soccer, with greater or lesser European influences, the climate to a large extent determines the basic approach. Individual dribbling skills, accurate passing and willingness to take direct, long-range shots are at a premium in slow, patient build-ups.

This is as true for Cameroon as Algeria; British footballers admired the poise and fluent passing of the central Africans – players such as M'bouh, Makanaky and Omam-Biyik spring to mind.

In 1994 Africa will have a chance to set out her stall; her representatives will want to do well but it is equally important that, meanwhile, the main

AFRICA African football, although well served in World Cup finals by representatives such as Tunisia (1978) and Morocco (1986), finally came of age in the international arena with the appearance of the 'Indomitable Lions' of Cameroon in 1990. Their first match was the opening game of the tournament in which they beat the holders and 1990 finalists Argentina 1-0 with a goal by François Omam Biyik (pictured during the match). Cameroon also had two men sent off, perhaps dispelling the idea that African players were merely tricky ball artists. Biyik's goal was the first of seven they scored in the tournament, before going out 2-3 to England in a match they were unlucky not to win.

problems within African football are tackled. Political, economic and ecological issues are, of course, beyond the power of sporting bodies, but work can be done in other areas. Professionalism needs to be established to encourage Africa's best players to stay at home. National and club sides must gain more experience abroad; CAF might try to persuade other FIFA countries to help finance tours.

The 1990 World Cup made Cameroon, with goalkeeping strength in depth and the remarkable Roger Milla, the best-known African team of recent times. But other teams such as Ghana, Libya, Senegal and Nigeria are itching to get on the world stage. Players such as George Weah (Liberia), Charles Musonda (Zambia) and Stephen Keshi (Nigeria), not to mention countless unknown South Africans, are waiting in the wings to show what they can do.

AFRICAN CUP OF NATIONS

Set up in 1957 with the establishment of the Confederation of African Football, this competition has taken place every two years, almost without exception - no small

with Austria, might have achieved more. In colonial Morocco and Tunisia, football became identified with nationalist sentiment. (Today, in central and eastern Africa, regional pride is greatly in evidence, many national teams taking on nicknames which celebrate the power of African fauna: the Green Eagles, the Lions, the Elephants, the Scorpions.) Egypt joined FIFA in 1923 and was one of the first African states to organise a league and gain international recognition. It still is a power, having won the 1986 African Nationals Cup.

Unlike Britain, France and Portugal maintained links with the football scene in their former colonies, often poaching the best

AFRICAN CUP OF NATIONS

Year	Winner	Runner-Up	Score
1957	Egypt	Sudan	
1959	Egypt	Sudan	
1962	Ethiopia	Egypt	4-2*
1963	Ghana	Sudan	3-0
1965	Ghana	Tunisia	3-2*
1968	Congo	Ghana	1-0
1970	Sudan	Ghana	1-0
1972	Congo	Mali	3-2
1974	Zaire	Zambia	2-2*
	Zaire	Zambia	2-0
1976	Morocco	Guinea	
1978	Ghana	Uganda	2-0
1980	Nigeria	Algeria	3-0
1982	Ghana	Libya	1-1**
1984	Cameroon	Nigeria	3-1
1986	Egypt	Cameroon	0-0**
1988	Cameroon	Nigeria	1-0
1989/90	Algeria	Nigeria	1-0

* after extra time ** on penalties
In 1957, 1959 and 1976 the tournament was decided on a league basis.

achievement in a huge Third World continent. The range of winners is testimony to a healthy competitive element in African football. Ghana emerges as the most consistent nation.

AIRDRIEONIANS

Founded 1878 (as Excelsior, renamed Airdrieonians 1881)

Joined League 1894 (Division 2)

Honours Scottish League Division 2 Champions 1903, 1955, 1974; Scottish Cup Winners 1924

Ground Broomfield Park

Industrial Lanarkshire is footballing heartland but Airdrie, like Motherwell, lose potential support to nearby Celtic and Rangers in Glasgow. None the less they are a durable club.

Their fine side of the 1920s, which won the 1924 Scottish Cup, included Bob McPhail, who became a Rangers legend, and Hughie Gallacher, one of the 'Wembley Wizards' who defeated England 5-1 in 1928.

Airdrie survived only two seasons in the Premier Division (1980-82) but returned to it in 1991.

ALBION ROVERS

Founded 1882

Joined League 1903 (Division 2)

Honours Scottish League Division 2 Champions 1989

Ground Cliftonhill Stadium

Overshadowed even in Lanarkshire, by nearby Airdrie and Motherwell, life has always been trying for Albion Rovers. Their principal moment of national celebrity came in 1920 when they outlasted Rangers to win the second replay of a Scottish Cup semi-final. The final was lost all the same.

Jubilation of a more contemporary nature came with their Second Division Championship in 1989, although relegation followed a year later. The club can boast of service from future internationalists such as Tony Green (Scotland) and Bernie Slaven (Republic of Ireland).

ALDERSHOT

Founded 1926

Joined League 1932 (Division 3/S)

Honours None

Ground Recreation Ground

Aldershot have achieved little during their 65-year history, but at least there is still hope - and that was a commodity which had all but disappeared at the Recreation Ground in the summer of 1990. The Shots were deep in debt and on the verge of extinction when, at the eleventh hour, an injection of cash saved the day - for the time being.

In terms of tradition and stature in the game, investors in Aldershot get precious little for their money. For 41 years after being elected to the League, they remained one of the handful of clubs never to have won promotion. When the big step-up finally came in 1973, it was the prelude to only three years in the higher grade before a return to the Fourth Division. There was a second escape in 1987, but this time there were but two campaigns in the Third and then the basement beckoned once more.

Perversely, there was a time when Aldershot - whose best FA Cup runs ended in fifth-round knockouts in 1933 and 1979 - could boast the strongest side in the land. Of course, there was a catch. It was during the war, when some of Britain's finest players were stationed at Aldershot barracks and the likes of Tommy Lawton, Wilf Mannion and Frank Swift turned out for the local team. May the 'Shots', without the assistance of any new conflict, one day bring players of that standard back to the Rec.

ALDERSHOT Aldershot are certainly not noted for any domination of English football — and they probably never will be while they remain at their quaint Recreation Ground site. The single policeman outside the ground, and the flower beds inside, contrast dramatically with some of the large old stadia found in Britain's industrial cities. Clubs of this size remind the fan of the continuum that exists — from park team to top league giants.

ALLCHURCH, Ivor

1929	Born in Swansea
1947	Joins Swansea Town
1949	Makes first-team debut
1951	Wins first of 68 Welsh caps, v England
1958	Transferred to Newcastle United for £27,000; World Cup quarter-finalist, 0-1 v Brazil
1962	Transferred to Cardiff
1965	Returns to Swansea
1967	Retires

Grace and touch were the hallmarks of Ivor Allchurch. A wonderfully skilful inside-forward, he always seemed to have plenty of time on the ball, a sure sign of a good footballer. He could pass brilliantly with either foot, dribbled perceptively and was a prolific scorer for a midfield player, getting more than 250 goals in an 18-year career. His tally of 160 is still a club record at Swansea.

National Service delayed Allchurch's first-team debut until he was 20 but almost immediately he stood out. Tall and blond, he drew attention like a magnet and throughout the 1950s his elegant skills were coveted by many First Division clubs. Swansea managed to resist all offers until Newcastle paid £27,000, then a consider-

IVOR ALLCHURCH

Ivor Allchurch in his Swansea Town (later to be called Swansea City) strip during the 1953/54 season. This was during the first part of his career, and during his first spell with his home town team. Having made 330 League appearances, he went off to Newcastle United and rivals Cardiff City before returning home for a further 116 outings. Ivor's younger brother Len was at Swansea during the first sojourn; Len also returned to the home-town team following excursions to Sheffield United and Stockport County.

able sum, in 1958.

His four years at St James's Park were probably his best. Ron Greenwood, the former West Ham United and England manager, said: 'You could do nothing but admire him. He was a great prompter, a creative player who could always find his centre-forward with a great through pass.'

Allchurch, whose brother Len also played for

his country on 11 occasions, won 68 caps for Wales between 1951 and 1966, which stood as a record for 20 years until overtaken by Joey Jones.

ALLOA

Founded	1883
Joined League	1921 (Division 2)
Honours	Scottish League Division 2 Champions 1922

Ground Recreation Park

Since League reconstruction (1974) Alloa have oscillated between the First and Second Divisions. The experience of modest success which has proved difficult to sustain is typical of the club.

Their Second Division Championship of 1922 (Alloa's first season in the League) was the most spectacular with 49 goals coming from diminutive centre-forward Willie Crilley who was soon to join Celtic. Then, and often since, the club has had to take pride in simply grooming stars for others' benefit. In more recent decades they have nurtured fledglings such as the late John White and Tommy Hutchison who went on to play for Scotland and who had considerable success south of the border.

AMATEUR CUP

The FA Amateur Cup was the major knock-out competition for amateur teams bewteen 1893 and 1974 (when the distinction between 'amateurs' and 'professionals' was made obsolete by the Football Association). From 1949 the Final was held at Wembley. Bishop Auckland's record ten wins include three in succession in the mid-1950s.

AMATEUR CUP In another 10 years an encyclopedia of soccer will probably not mention the FA Amateur Cup – it will have passed into history. However, it is still (in the early 1990s) remembered by many for crowds of 100,000 at Wembley and an important place in the sporting calender. The 1954 final featured the two sides who won it most times, Bishop Auckland (10 wins) and Crook Town (5 wins, equal with Clapton). The captains, J. Major of Bishop Auckland and R. Davison of Crook Town, lead out their teams for the second replay at Middlesbrough. Davison's side won this match 1-0 following 2-2 draws at Wembley and Newcastle. In 1990/91 Crook lined up in Division 2 of the Skol Northern League and Bishop Auckland in the Premier Division of the prestigious HFS Loans League – a direct feeder into the GM Vauxhall Conference.

AMATEUR FOOTBALL

Amateurs were responsible for the emergence of many of football's most important features: the early laws, national Football Associations in Britain, the FA Cup and Scottish Cup, international matches and the network of local associations. The power of amateurism has dwindled since 1885, when the FA legalised professionalism, but amateur football is still the foundation on which the game is based.

Top amateur teams competed with professionals until well into the twentieth century. The Corinthians, for instance, thrashed Cup winners Blackburn Rovers and double-winning Preston North End in their heyday in the 1880s. They also beat 1903 Cup winners Bury 10-3 and achieved good FA Cup results until the late 1930s. As late as 1974, Hendon held Newcastle United to a 1-1 draw at Newcastle. Hendon, then an Isthmian League amateur team, lost the replay, and Newcastle went on to reach the FA Cup Final.

The Amateur Football Association was formed in 1907 to ensure the distinction between the increasingly popular professional game and the 'old school' of amateurism. The AFA stated: 'It is essential for the good of the game of Association football as played by amateurs that an Amateur Football Association be formed.' (The title was changed to the Amateur Football Alliance in May 1934.)

An example of amateur-professional conflict was the penalty-kick, introduced in 1891. Those in the public-school tradition believed that the penalty-kick law was not needed, and the Arthur Dunn Cup, inaugurated in 1902/03 as a competition for old boys' teams from Eton and elsewhere, refused to recognise the penalty kick until reprimanded by the FA. Even in the 1920s some amateur teams were so appalled at conceding a penalty that they instructed their goalkeeper to stand aside and permit the just punishment of a goal into the empty net.

The Scottish Amateur FA was formed in 1909, but it was a combined United Kingdom amateur team that won the first two football tournaments in the Olympic Games - in London (1908) and Stockholm (1912).

In 1914 the breach between the Football Association and the breakaway Amateur Football Association was

When Britain returned to FIFA in 1946, 'broken time' payments were still contentious and 'shamateurism' remained an issue in Britain. 'Shamateurism' was the payment of expenses and compensation to amateurs, some of whom played in the Football League. The debate was finally ended in 1974 when the FA classified all footballers as 'players'. The problem of deciding whether or not a player was paid was therefore passed to the tax authorities. A notable exception is the Olympic Games football tournament, which, under the jurisdiction of the Olympic Committee, has continued to be plagued with problems of defining who are truly amateurs.

The 1974 decision effectively ended the FA Amateur Cup and the home internationals amateur tournament introduced in 1953/54. Some famous amateur leagues have adapted to survive the new legislation. These include the Northern League (formed in 1889) and the Isthmian League (1905). The Athenian League, formed in 1912, lasted until 1984.

Many amateur players have ranked alongside professionals in their contribution to the game. G.O. Smith, who scored 12 goals in 20 full England games at the turn of the century, was an outstanding centre-forward of any era. Bernard Joy was an amateur when capped for the full England team in 1936. Jim Lewis, who achieved 49 England amateur international caps, played in Chelsea's 1954/55 Championship team, and the 1948 Great Britain Olympic team included Queen's Park's Ronnie Simpson, who later played as a professional for Newcastle United, Celtic and Scotland.

Today, amateur football is still the grass roots of the game. There are far more amateur players than professional, and most professionals start as amateur, even if only in schoolboy football. The development of the Sunday game in the 1960s helped

healed. They had fallen out over the acceptance of professional clubs to local football associations.

In 1928 the four British Football Associations resigned membership of FIFA over problems of defining 'amateurism' and 'broken time' (the payment of wages lost by amateurs while absent from work playing football). The British bodies were in favour of 'broken time' payments but FIFA voted against them, with the exception of part payments in special circumstances.

increase the number of teams, leading to the inauguration of the FA Sunday Cup in 1965. The number of clubs continued to grow in the 1980s.

ARBROATH

Founded 1878

Joined League 1921 (Division 2)

Honours None

Ground Gayfield Park

A club founded by rugby enthusiasts produced a football score to match. The world record victory in senior football – 36-0 against Bon Accord (an Aberdeen club) in a Scottish Cup tie on 12 September 1885 – still stands. Perhaps they felt that was sufficient impact, for they have scarcely troubled the statisticians since.

Arbroath, though, have often possessed an air of diligent stability. Albert Henderson was manager for 17 years until 1980, during which period the club twice won promotion to the old Division 1. Earlier times saw the rapid-fire achievements of Dave Easson, who notched up 45 goals in season 1958/59.

ARDILES, Osvaldo

1952 Born in Cordoba, Argentina

1978 June – takes the eye as his country wins the World Cup on home soil, July – joins Tottenham Hotspur from Huracan of Buenos Aires for £325,000

1981 Plays prominent role in Spurs' FA Cup Final victory over Manchester City.

1982 April – helps Spurs beat Leicester City in FA Cup semi-final, then misses final because of Falklands War; June – plays for Argentinian side knocked out in second phase of World Cup in Spain; starts season on loan with Paris St Germain while Falklands furore dies down

1983 January – returns to White Hart Lane

1984 Comes on as substitute to earn UEFA Cup Winner's medal against Anderlecht

1988 March – joins Blackburn Rovers on loan; July – moves to Queen's Park Rangers, but makes only a handful of appearances.

1989 Succeeds Lou Macari as Swindon Town manager

1990 Swindon qualify for Division 1 in play-offs, but stay down because of financial irregularities.

1991 Takes over Newcastle boss

The purchase of 'Ossie' Ardiles, and fellow countryman Ricardo Villa, represented a brave gamble by Spurs manager Keith Burkinshaw. After dazzling displays in the World Cup, the players' talent was not in question but many critics were sceptical about their ability to adapt to the hurly burly of the English League. Both men laid such doubts to rest, but Ardiles in particular was a revelation.

A slightly-built, nimble midfield general blessed with glorious all-round skills and deceptive strength, he was a masterful passer and intelligent reader of the game whose experience and enthusiasm proved a spendidly positive influence at White Hart Lane.

Ardiles became one of the most popular overseas footballers to come to these shores, and a testimony to his stature was the way in which British fans, not always noted for tact or tolerance, continued to accept him in the wake of the Falklands conflict when Britain was at war with Argentina. As manager of Swindon Town he transformed a lacklustre side into an attractive one, and was desperately unfortunate to see his first season's work count for nothing.

ARSENAL

Founded 1886

Joined League 1893 (Division 2)

Honours Division 1 Champions 1931, 1933, 1934, 1935, 1938, 1948, 1953, 1971, 1989 1991; FA Cup Winners 1930,

1936, 1950, 1971, 1979; League Cup Winners 1987; European Fairs Cup Winners 1970

Ground Highbury

Arsenal are an institution throughout the soccer-playing world. Even when their fortunes dip alarmingly, as they did throughout most of the 1950s and 1960s, the 'Gunners' retain their eminence. Such is the weight of achievement, the sense of tradition and sheer splendour exuded by Highbury's marble halls, that a fall from grace seems unthinkable. It was not always the case.

After winning election to Division 2, Woolwich Arsenal, as they were then known, experienced several decades of dour consolidation and financial struggle. Indeed, during this unimpressive interlude the Gunners were relegated for the only time in their history – in 1913, when they chalked up only one home win, a wretched record (that no other League club has matched).

The turning point was the arrival of Herbert Chapman in 1925. The brilliant Yorkshireman, who had just led Huddersfield Town to the first two legs of their League Championship hat-trick, predicted that he would need five years to transform Arsenal from non entities to a power in the land, and so it proved. The darkness began to lighten with the lifting of the FA Cup in 1930, and there followed the club's most successful period, which saw five League titles and another FA Cup triumph before the Second World War ended the bonanza.

Stars of that era included deadly marksman Charlie Buchan (who missed out on the trophies but helped lay the foundations of a great team), visionary play-maker Alex James, goal-scoring wingers Cliff Bastin and Joe Hulme, prolific forwards David Jack and Ted Drake, and a posse of defenders and half-backs including George Male, Eddie Hapgood, Wilf Copping,

Jack Crayston, Bob John, Tom Parker and Herbie Roberts.

When peacetime soccer resumed, Arsenal were no longer the same all-dominant force, although with Tom Whittaker at the helm they collected more silverware, thanks to the likes of wing-half and skipper Joe Mercer, schemer Jimmy Logie, and gifted brothers Les and Denis Compton. There was also Welsh international goalkeeper Jack Kelsey, who helped the Gunners take the title in 1953 and then proved their only truly top-class performer throughout a period of distressing mediocrity. Despite acquiring skilled individuals such as inside-forward George Eastham and striker Joe Baker, a succession of managers - including former England captain Billy Wright - failed to effect a revival.

The glory days were not to return until club physiotherapist Bertie Mee took command. Then, with on-the-field drive from centre-half Frank McLintock, the creative ability of George Graham and Charlie George, devoted and accomplished service from forwards such as John Radford and George Armstrong, and a seemingly iron-clad defence, Arsenal won the League and FA Cup double in 1971. Mee's side was functional rather than exciting, and the feat received but grudging acclaim, an unfair reflection on a magnificent season's work.

The rest of the 1970s and the first half of the 1980s - though enlivened at times by the contributions of sublimely talented midfielder Liam Brady and stylish defender David O'Leary, among others - were something of an anti-climax, and it was not until the appointment of George Graham as manager in 1986 that deeds to rival past successes again appeared possible. The Scot has led the side to the Championship in both 1989 and 1991, an achievement they could repeat.

ARSENAL The double of 1970/71 will live in the record books as one of Arsenal's great achievements. It was wrapped up in a few days at the end of the season with a League victory over Spurs (third in the League) and a Cup Final win against Liverpool. It is often remembered for flamboyant Charlie George's winning goal, and his prostrate celebration, in the Final. This picture, however, is of the first goal in that Final, with Eddie Kelly forcing the ball past Ray Clemence on a hot afternoon at Wembley.

ARSENAL Top right: The Gunners en route to Islington Town Hall with the 1990/91 League Championship trophy. Their title triumph, was ground out during a season of travail which saw the club docked two points for their part in a brawl at Old Trafford, and their captain Tony Adams jailed for drink-driving. Below right: Anders Limpar is stopped by Everton's Stuart McCall, but the Swede managed to elude the opposition on enough occasions during the season to make him a bargain at £1.3 million.

THE ARTS AND FOOTBALL

In *The Good Companions*, J.B. Priestley implied that football was itself one of the Arts: 'For a shilling Bruddersford United AFC offered you Conflict and Art, it turned you into a critic, happy in your judgment of fine points, ready in a second to estimate the worth of a well-judged pass, a run down the touch line, a lightning shot, a clearance kick by back or goalkeeper'.

Football has certainly produced music from Kop choirs, boardroom drama and 'artists' on the field, but it has never been a particularly fertile source of artistic achievement. Classic football fiction is limited to a small number of writers who grew up in football hotbeds and could hardly ignore the game. Priestley was writing about an amalgam of Bradford and Huddersfield, and Arnold Bennett, from the Staffordshire Potteries, left a legacy of early football culture in *The Matador of the Five Towns* and *The Card*.

In the 1960s Brian Glanville added to football fiction with novels like *The Rise of Gerry Logan* and collections of short stories. Two of Glanville's books have remained in print,

Goalkeepers are Crazy and *Goalkeepers are Different*. Bill Naughton's short story *The Goalkeeper's Revenge* is a classic from the same era, and *The Blinder* by Barry Hines remains in print. One-off football novels in the past two decades have included some with footballer collaboration. Jimmy Greaves (with Norman Giller), Terry Venables (with Gordon Williams) and Derek Dougan all have their names on covers, not to mention Pele with *The World Cup Murder*. Dick Morland's *Albion! Albion!* (Faber & Faber, 1974) is an interesting look at hooliganism which may

appear occasionally in second-hand shops, and J.L. Carr's *How Steeple Sinderby Wanderers Won the FA Cup* is a delightful fantasy.

Football also earns many passing references in literature. George Blake's *The Shipbuilders* provides insight into life as a Scottish spectator in the 1930s. In *A History of the World in 10½ Chapters,* Julian Barnes describes heaven in terms of Leicester City winning the FA Cup (among other things). Collections of football fiction appear in *Joy of Football* (edited by Brian Glanville) and *The Faber Book of Soccer* (edited by

Ian Hamilton). There are a number of examples of football on canvas, summarised by Mary Ann Wingfield in *Sport and the Artist (Volume 1)*. Perhaps the most famous painting is Lowry's *Going to the Match*, a scene of matchstick supporters and northern factories. The FA celebrated its 90th anniversary with a sponsored competition for artists, and this led to a football-as-art exhibition in late 1953. Ten years later the FA centenary was commemorated by a painting of the 1962 FA Cup Final, and this hung in many club boardrooms. More accessible to the

public is a sculpture of Sir Stanley Matthews in Hanley town centre. Unveiled in 1987 to commemorate the pedestrianisation of one of Stoke-on-Trent's five towns, Colin Melbourne's sculpture captures Matthews with a ball at his feet in 1930s style. The maestro appears to be dribbling towards Millett's but could easily swerve across the street to Woolworth's.

Many people have mixed music and football. Top violinist Nigel Kennedy makes no secret of his support for Aston Villa, the song 'You'll Never Walk Alone' is associated more

with the Anfield choir than it ever was with Gerry and the Pacemakers, and eight football teams have made the top ten, the England World Cup Squad's 'Back Home' even reaching number one. The others were another England World Cup Squad ('This Time' in 1982), Liverpool ('Anfield Rap' in 1988), Chelsea ('Blue is the Colour' in 1972), Scotland ('We Have a Dream' in 1982), Spurs ('Ossie's Dream' in 1981), Manchester United ('We All Follow Man United' in 1985) and Leeds United ('Leeds United' in 1972). Glenn (Hoddle) and Chris (Waddle) made number 12 with 'Diamond Lights' in 1987. There is also a wealth of underground music which carries cultural messages for football. Dennis Alcapone's *World Cup Football* directed reggae lyrics at Ron Greenwood's 1982 England team selection: 'Forget yo pride and prejudice; and carry the man Cyrille Regis.'

There are a few soccer movies, but many themes are still unexplored. Pre-war films included *The Arsenal Stadium Mystery*, based on a novel by Leonard Gribble - worth watching on one of its occasional television showings. Leslie Banks puts in a splendid performance as the detective, and Arsenal players and manager George Allison are in the cast. *Escape to Victory* (1981), John Huston's remake of the Hungarian *The Last Goal,* is memorable mainly for a football-match sequence with Bobby Moore, Pele, Ossie Ardiles, Sylvester Stallone and Michael Caine. British soccer movies include *Yesterday's Hero* (1979) and *Gregory's Girl* (1980). The latter, directed by Bill Forsyth, is

a delightful Scottish story about boys' reactions to a girl winning a place in the school team. In addition, there have been World Cup films with more artistic footage, e.g. *Goal! World Cup 1966.*

Poets such as Roger McGough and Alan Bold have written classic football poems, and there is also a rich minor vein of television drama and theatre focusing on the game.

ASIA

FIFA and a geographer would not agree on their identification of Asia. For administrative purposes the International Federation includes the countries of the Middle East in the continent. This does pose problems with regard to Israel, something of a nomad in the football world because of boycotts by Arab countries, and at different times her teams have contested World Cup qualifiers in Asia, Europe and Oceania. In 1970 Israel competed in the finals of the competition, and held both Italy and Sweden to draws.

Politics has often interfered with sport in the East. In 1991 Iraq's

ASIA The exuberant celebrations of the South Koreans after scoring to secure victory against Saudi Arabia in a 1990 World Cup qualifying game. The days of a curt handshake, a word of congratulation and a brisk job back to the centre circle seem certain to have vanished forever – hard to believe that, in the 1960s, television and the press received countless complaints about players hugging and kissing. Modern displays fall into two broad categories: team efforts, which include scrums as seen here – also popular in ice hockey – and embraces; and solo exhibitions – somersaults, dance movements (the best known being Roger Milla's corner-flag shimmy) and frenzied directionless sprints. Some players are said to run faster after scoring than while actually playing. It's surprising more injuries aren't caused by the whole business. On the way to Italy, South Korea scored 30 goals and

conceded only 1 in 11 games. The goal against them was scored by the United Arab Emirates, who also qualified for the finals. Once there, however, neither country had much to celebrate. They both failed to progress beyond the first stage.

national and club teams were suspended from FIFA competitions following the invasion of Kuwait and the subsequent war. Japan and China have both been expelled from FIFA in their history, although they are now well-established members. China was readmitted to FIFA in 1975, and three years later West Bromwich Albion became the first Western club to tour communist China. In 1976 Taiwan and

Israel were expelled from the Asian Football Confederation, which in turn found itself threatened with a FIFA ban for its actions. The Confederation was formed in 1954 to promote the sport and it set up much-needed coaching schemes and instigated the Asian Cup for national teams in 1956.

It was North Korea, beneficiaries of Soviet coaching, who first put Asia on the football map with their spirited performances in the 1966 World Cup in England. Their Group games were played in Middlesbrough where the crowd took to the small Asians. They drew against Chile and played intelligently against Italy to win 1-0. Their quarter-final at Goodison Park against Portugal was even more of

a sensation. They led 3-0 before their opponents scored five goals (four from Eusebio). The North Koreans were fit, dedicated and played a lively, short-passing game, but, like so many nations new to the international arena, lack of tactical understanding was their undoing. Their outstanding footballer was the playmaker Pak Seung Jin who set up their attacks, and Pak Doo Ik will be remembered for his goal against Italy. South Korea had played in the 1954 World Cup but they didn't win a single point and in 1986 they were also unimpressive; however the country has a good record in Asian competitions.

Korea, before the Second World War and before the division created by its own civil war, had been occupied by the Japanese who appreciated their subject people's footballing skills and made them represent Japan in the 1936 Olympic Games. Japan's FA was formed in 1921 and they were admitted to FIFA eight years later, although their national league didn't start until 1965, after failure to qualify for the 1960 Olympics prompted them to bring over a prominent West German coach who trained new coaches. After the war American influence was strong, so that baseball is now more popular than soccer - except in Hiroshima, where British troops were based.

In Pakistan, British traders and military personnel brought hockey as well as soccer and it was the former which proved more popular. In other Asian countries, traditional sports prevailed. However, the increasing popularity of football is evident; India's amateur game was strong in the 1950s and early 1960s and the game has a great following in Hong Kong, Malaysia and Bangla Desh. Chinese students played international games in the early years of this century and the game's roots might be stronger if political events had turned out differently.

Forms of football existed in the Far East in ancient times. In Japan this was mainly as a type of ball juggling, although there is evidence from 1004 BC and AD 611 of a competitive game played on a pitch, and in 50 BC there was an international between Japan and China! A game known as *tsu chu* (kick-ball), played two and a half thousand years ago on the Chinese Emperor's birthday, involved kicking a ball through a hole in silk netting; there was physical punishment for the losers.

In the Middle East, however, the British Imperial influence is more apparent. Iran (Persia at the time) formed its national association in 1920 and Afghanistan in 1922; Arab countries were to follow in the course of the next three decades. Iran, coached by former Manchester United boss Frank O'Farrell, reached the 1978 World Cup finals. The following year the Ayatollah banned the sport, but today there are 300,000 registered players compared with 43,000 in 1980 and Iran is one of the strongest teams in the area. Since 1980 football's position in the Middle East has been stable. The number of clubs ranges from 8 in Qatar to 96 in Saudi Arabia, 155 in Iraq and 6226 in Iran.

Most of the countries in Asia and the Middle East play their international football in the Olympics, the Asian Games and the Asian Cup, which means they do not get enough experience of top-flight competition. To this are added well-publicised political and economic problems.

ASTON VILLA

Founded 1874

Joined League 1888 (founder member)

Honours Div. 1 Champions 1894, 1896, 1897, 1899, 1900, 1910, 1981; Div. 2 Champions 1938, 1960; Div. 3 Champions 1972; FA Cup Winners 1887, 1895, 1897, 1905, 1913, 1920, 1957; League Cup Winners 1961, 1975, 1977; European Cup Winners 1982

Ground Villa Park

Although the bulk of Aston Villa's honours were won during the reign of Queen

ASTON VILLA Quite a parade of silverware for Aston Villa following the 1898/99 campaign. Although other Birmingham sides may not agree with the assessment, Aston Villa were probably favourites to win most of the trophies — indeed, any tournament for which they entered at that time. They are: *(left to right, back row)* the Walsall Cup, the Sheriff of London Charity Shield, the Mayor of Birmingham Charity Cup; the Birmingham Challenge Cup, the League Championship Cup, the Staffordshire Cup. Villa won the League by two points from Liverpool that year and went on to win again, by two points from Sheffield United, in the following season.

Victoria, they remain one of the leading clubs in the land, a status they have every prospect of maintaining into the next century. It does seem unlikely, however, that they will ever outstrip those early achievements. After being formed at a meeting under a street-corner gas-lamp, the Birmingham club made rapid strides. Doubtless inspired by the fact that one of their officials, William McGregor, had founded the Football League, Villa proceeded to place considerable strain on their trophy cabinet. In the seven seasons leading to the turn of the century they won five Championships and lifted the FA Cup twice, with the coveted double being secured in 1897.

As the standard of competition grew, the rate of success slowed, but Villa continued to be Division 1 bastions. Stars included combative centre-forward Harry Hampton, who scored 242 goals for the club between 1904 and 1920, and England's Sam Hardy, who guarded Villa's net on either side of the First World War. Then, in the 1920s and 1930s, it was masterful inside-forward Billy Walker and the prolific Pongo Waring - he once notched 49 League goals in a single campaign - who held sway. It was not until 1936 that Villa slipped into the Second Division for the first time. They soon regained their seniority, but then began a lengthy period of mediocrity. The 1950s, mostly disappointing, offered brief hope of revival with an FA Cup triumph over Manchester United - albeit a controversial one in which two-goal match-winner Peter McParland was involved in a sickening collision with the United 'keeper. But relegation followed and although new boss Joe Mercer soon achieved promotion and saw his side become the first winners of the League Cup - which at that time attracted entries from few top clubs - there was worse to follow. England marksman Gerry Hitchens

SUNDAY·PIC

SALE MORE THAN DOUBLE THAT OF ANY OTHE

No. 424. Registered at the G.P.O. as a Newspaper. SUNDAY, APRIL 29, 1923

WEMBLEY STADIUM STORMED BY EXCIT

A striking aerial photograph of the scene at Wembley Stadium yesterday after the gates had been closed. All accomm flood the playing pitch, while thousands clustered outside are clamouring for admittan

headed for Italy, and an inexorable slide began. Successive managers, including the tempestuous Tommy Docherty, failed and Villa sank to the Third Division. After much boardroom upheaval, it was left to former wing-half Vic Crowe to rebuild.

It was not until Ron Saunders arrived in 1975 that the glory days returned. His side restored Division 1 status, won two League Cups and then lifted the League Championship for the first time in 71 years. With

midfielders Dennis Mortimer and Gordon Cowans outstanding, Villa went on to win the European Cup a year later, but even that did not signal ultimate consistency, and there was another one-season sojourn in Division 2 before the decade was out. Now, with Graham Taylor having left to guide England the appointment of extrovert Ron Atkinson as manager may herald a new era; he certainly brings a hint of the 'big time' with him.

ATTENDANCES

The paying customer provides the life-blood of professional football, so it is not surprising that a great deal of interest is shown in the numbers of supporters who attend matches. Even beyond the professional game, a large crowd can be important in lifting a team and elevating an occasion.

The British game, although generally enjoying increasing attendances in the late 1980s and early 1990s, is still poorly supported when compared

with the halcyon days immediately after the Second World War. The record for one day's English League matches was set on 27 December 1949 when 1,272,185 spectators attended the 44 matches. That day 70,000 saw Aston Villa lose at home to Wolves, while 56,000 watched Sheffield United draw with Preston North End in the Second Division.

Apart from falling interest, nearly all Football and Scottish League teams have current ground

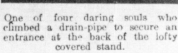

One of four daring souls who climbed a drain-pipe to secure an entrance at the back of the lofty covered stand.

packed, spectators

capacities well below their record attendances. Improved facilities and safety regulations account for this trend that produces such examples as Blackburn Rovers (capacity 17,819 - record 61,783) and Aberdeen (capacity 22,568 all seated - record 45,061).

The record English League match attendance was set at Maine Road (Manchester City's Ground) where 83,260 saw Manchester United play Arsenal in 1948, although this falls well short of

Rangers' 118, 567 for the 1939 New Year League match with Celtic at Ibrox Park. Glasgow's Hampden Park has been the scene of enormous crowds such as the 135,826 that saw Celtic v Leeds United in the second leg of the European Cup semi-final in 1970, and the 146, 433 for the Celtic v Aberdeen Scottish Cup Final of 1937.

Cup matches have often accounted for individual club records throughout Britain. The 1923 FA Cup Final between West Ham United and Bolton

ATTENDANCES The 1923 FA Cup Final has gone down in history for the overspilling crowd and the white police horse that helped clear the ground. This is how the *Sunday Pictorial's* front page covered the event, showing that aerial photography is nothing new . . . and neither is gatecrashing. The back pages gave a full match report of Bolton Wanderers' 2-0 win over West Ham, explaining that the presence of people right along the touchlines certainly had an effect on the play and the players.

Wanderers had an official figure of 126,047, but these were only the paying customers; gatecrashers are estimated to have put the final figure up to 200,000. A far cry from the 2000 who witnessed the first Final in 1872.

That 1923 figure compares well with the recognised world record of 199,854 who saw the 1950 World Cup Final between Brazil and Uruguay at Rio's Maracana Stadium.

Over the years there have been small crowds too, records that have been added to by the occasional instructions to play a match 'behind closed doors' as a punishment for a club's misdemeanours. A British example is the European Cup Winners' Cup match (second leg) between West Ham United and Castilla of Spain. Each team was permitted a 70-man delegation (including players) and 16 ballboys manned the empty terraces. The official attendance figure was 262; 500 police were outside the ground!

AUSTRALASIA

Australia and New Zealand have failed to make an impact on the World Cup to rival that of North Korea in 1966 or the African countries in the 1980s, but both have reached the finals and Australia ended the 1980s with some excellent results which promised well for the future.

In Australasia soccer has

had to compete with rugby league, rugby union and, in Australia's southern states, Australian Rules football. Progress has been slow. The first Australian soccer club was formed in Sydney in 1880, but the Australian Football Association was not formed until 1920 and the first World Cup entry was as late as 1964. The Australians celebrated 100 years of soccer in 1980, when England won 2-1 in Sydney and Northern Ireland won two out of three, the game in Melbourne being drawn.

Australia gave Scotland a fright in a two-leg qualifying play-off for the 1986 World Cup finals: Scotland won 2-0 in Glasgow but only drew 0-0 in Australia. This was undoubtedly an improvement on some of Australia's earlier showings against British international teams such as the 17-0 defeat by England in Sydney in 1951.

The variety of ethnic origins of Australian soccer, with players and supporters having roots in Europe and elsewhere, add a touch of volatility to the National League and regional leagues, and there have been recent bans on national flags, emblems and ethnic names such as Croatia, Juventus and North End. The names of many minor-league Australian teams are known in Britain through their appearance on football pools coupons during the British summer, but top Australian teams play during their own summer, the British winter.

The catalyst for one of the biggest booms in Australian soccer came when Jim Mackay's goal against South Korea brought a 1-0 win in a qualifying play-off for a place in the 1974 World Cup finals. In West Germany, Australia held Chile to a goalless draw; otherwise, there were predictable defeats against East Germany and the West German hosts.

In 1981 Australia staged the FIFA Youth Championship. Around the same time, the New Zealand team was working towards

the 1982 World Cup finals. For a few minutes, in their first game of the finals, New Zealand threatened an upset, having pulled back from 3-0 down to 3-2, but Scotland eventually won 5-2. The Kiwis also lost to the USSR and Brazil - it wasn't an easy group - but the World Cup finals provided a boost for the New Zealand FA, which was formed in 1891.

In 1988 there was a double success for Australian soccer. The national team beat world champions Argentina 4-1 in a four-nation tournament to celebrate the Australian bicentenary. Australia lost 2-0 to Brazil in the final, watched by 28,161 people. The other success came in the 1988 Seoul Olympics. Wins against Yugoslavia and Nigeria brought a runners-up place in a group won by Brazil. Australia's quarter-final was lost 3-0 to the Soviet Union, the eventual gold medal lists.

Australasia has always been a popular place for touring club teams. In addition, players have been recruited from the area for the British leagues. An example is Craig Johnston, who played for Middlesbrough and Liverpool in the 1980s.

AYR UNITED

Founded 1910

Joined League 1910 (Division 2)

Honours Scottish League Division 2 Champions 1912, 1913, 1928, 1937, 1959, 1966; Second Division Champions 1988

Ground Somerset Park

Ayr United achieved their highest profile under the exuberant Ally MacLeod (the first of three spells as a manager) in the late 1960s and early 1970s. They were then a frequent threat in cup competition.

Of earlier feats the most remarkable was Jimmy Smith's tally of 66 League goals in season 1927/28.

Ayr United take pride in having produced three players on the current international scene: Steve Nicol, Bobby Connor and Alan McInally.

B

BANKS, Gordon

1937	Born in Sheffield
1955	Turns professional with Chesterfield
1959	Joins Leicester City for £6,000
1961	Takes home FA Cup runner-up medal as Tottenham Hotspur clinch League and Cup double
1963	Another FA Cup Final defeat, this time by Manchester United; England debut, against Brazil at Wembley
1964	At last, a club honour; League Cup Final victory over Stoke City
1966	The ultimate glory: World Cup triumph
1967	Moves to Stoke City for £52,000
1970	Performs World Cup heroics in Mexico
1972	Helps Stoke City to beat Chelsea and win the League Cup; voted Footballer of the Year by the Football Writers' Association; car accident ends career.

At his peak, Banks was regarded as the greatest goalkeeper in the world, yet he never played for a 'fashionable' club. After learning his trade for four seasons with Chesterfield, he moved into the top flight and it soon became apparent that Leicester had unearthed a rare gem. Brave, strong and blessed with an acute positional sense, he was not an habitually flashy custodian, but at times his natural elasticity between the posts was astonishing.

Accomplished though it was, Bank's club career was overshadowed by his international exploits. He was an ever-present member of Alf Ramsey's team which won the 1966 World Cup, conceding only three goals during the finals. But the moment for which he is lionised most came four years later in a World Cup confrontation with Brazil in Mexico. The incomparable Pele rose above the England defence to send an apparently unstoppable header arrowing towards the unguarded corner of Bank's net. The 'keeper dived but seemed to have been beaten by the bounce when he somehow managed to twist upwards and divert the ball over his crossbar. Sadly, illness forced him out of the subsequent quarter-final

GORDON BANKS
Wearing the colours of England, Gordon Banks will always be remembered as an international rather than a club 'keeper. He was between the sticks when England enjoyed World Cup success and began a period when English goalkeepers really did seem to be better than those from the rest of the world. In this shot he is looking to clear his lines while receiving the attention of Welsh striker Ron Davies in a match in Cardiff in 1972.

against West Germany, and his deputy, poor Peter Bonetti, will be forever vilified for his part in England's 3-2 defeat.

Banks, who had been allowed to leave Leicester for Stoke due to the emergence of the young Peter Shilton, went on to win 73 caps before damaging his right eye in a road accident and being forced to quit the game. Though 35 at the time, Banks, whose popularity was fuelled by a natural dignity and amiable disposition, was still in majestic form.

BARNES, John

1963	Born in Jamaica
1981	Turns professional with Watford
1982	Hits sparkling form as 'Hornets' win promotion to Division 1
1983	Makes England debut as substitute against Northern Ireland in Belfast
1984	Takes home FA Cup runner-up medal after Wembley defeat by Everton; dribbles through Brazil's defence in Rio to score one of the most breathtaking England goals of modern times.
1987	Moves to Liverpool for £900,000
1988	Holds centre stage as 'Reds' lift title but becomes two-time Wembley loser as Wimbledon win FA Cup; receives Player of the Year awards from football writers and his fellow professionals; June - disappoints for England in European Championship finals in West Germany
1989	Helps beat Everton to claim FA Cup winner's medal at last
1990	Wins a second Championship medal;

JOHN BARNES A typically thrusting run between two Everton players, Ratcliffe (4) and Watson, by John Barnes. His game at domestic level has been marked by both prolific goal-scoring and superb support play. At national level he has shone less brightly, but nonetheless has collected more than 50 England caps and put in some memorable performances. His strength, if not his poise on the ball, is well illustrated in this picture.

Breathtakingly brilliant for Liverpool, frustratingly inconsistent for England. Barnes was arguably the supreme soccer artist of the late 1980s and early 1990s.

Whether patrolling the left flank or adopting a free-roaming role, he was, at his best, well nigh unstoppable when he ran at defences. Big, strong and blessed with magnetic ball control, Barnes boasted the intricate wiles to trick his opponents and deceptive pace which left them stranded in his wake. He was also a lethal finisher, with a particularly wicked free-kick technique which made him a 'keeper's nightmare anywhere within 30 yards of goal.

Perhaps Barnes's greatest achievement was in bringing, almost instantly, a new dimension to Liverpool after his move from Vicarage Road. For all their success, the 'Reds' had been sometimes described detrimentally as 'machine-like', and it took the West Indian-born winger to bestow on them the panache and glitter that had traditionally been the preserve of Manchester United and Spurs.

The mystery of his fluctuations of form remains. But even after his World Cup anti-climax in Italy, there was no one on the football fields of England – and certainly not the over-exposed Paul Gascoigne – to match John Barnes.

BARNSLEY

Founded 1887

Joined League 1898

Honours FA Cup winners 1912; Division 3 (N) Champions 1934, 1939, 1955

Ground Oakwell

Located in the coal-mining area of South Yorkshire, Barnsley has a very strong football tradition. The club has promised more than most small-town clubs, but First Division soccer has always proved elusive. The greatest honours have come in the FA Cup. Barnsley lost to Newcastle United in the 1910 FA Cup Final, but won the 1912 FA Cup Final replay against West Brom, the only goal of the two games coming in the last minute of extra-time when Harry Tufnell ran from the halfway line to score

brilliantly. The 1912 Cup-winning team was nicknamed 'Battling Barnsley', partly for their long, 12-game battle to the trophy – six 0-0 draws, five odd-goal victories and a 3-1 win over Birmingham – and partly because of the team's rugged approach.

The club had a rough time through the late 1960s and 1970s, spending ten seasons in the Fourth Division and surviving financial crises, but the 1981/82 season saw Barnsley restored to what many would see as the club's rightful place, the

ENGLISH CUP-TIE. BARNSLEY v. QUEEN'S PARK RANGERS. FOURTH ROUND, MARCH 5TH, 1910.
BARNES (Capt., Q.P.R.) Mr. F. HEATH (Referee). BOYLE (Capt., Barnsley). Photo by A. W. Feasby.

BARNSLEY Just to prove that football cards are not new, here are two photographs of Barnsley adapted for use as postcards in the early part of this century. The FA Cup-winning line-up includes directors, trainer Will Norman (flat cap and moustache) and the man who scored the only goal in the last minute of extra time in the Final replay (after a 0-0 draw); he's Harry Tufnell (*cross-legged, left of front row*). The cup was the new FA Cup. This was the second time it was awarded and the first time it had left Bradford. It had been made there and the first winners were Bradford City (1-0 after a 0-0 draw).

The handshake between Barnes (Queen's Park Rangers) and Boyle (Barnsley) took place at Oakwell under the gaze of referee F. Heath. Barnsley won 1-0 and reached the Final, where they were beaten 2-0 in a replay by Newcastle United after a 1-1 draw. Note the open side, typical at the time.

BARNSLEY ENGLISH CUP WINNERS 1911–12.

Second Division. In fact, Barnsley's strange League record is that they have spent more seasons in Division 2 than any other club, seven more than Leicester City.

As befits many smaller town clubs, Barnsley have often transferred star players for large fees. Post-war examples include Danny Blanchflower (Aston Villa), Tommy Taylor (Manchester United), Mick McCarthy (Manchester City), David Hirst (Sheffield Wednesday), John Beresford (Portsmouth) and David Currie (Nottingham Forest). Barry Murphy holds the club appearance record with 514 League appearances between 1962 and 1978.

BAXTER, Jim

1939 Born in Hill o' Beath, Fifeshire, Scotland

1957 Raith Rovers pay Crossgates Primrose £200 to sign Baxter as a part-timer.

1960 Signs for Rangers (£20,000); first of 34 Scotland caps (v Northern Ireland)

1963 Scores two goals (one a penalty) to defeat England 2-1 at Wembley

1964 Suffers broken leg in away-leg of Rangers' European Cup tie with Rapid Vienna

1965 Signs for Sunderland

1967 Plays brilliantly in Scotland's 3-2 defeat of world champions England at Wembley; signs for Nottingham Forest at a new record fee for a half-back (£100,000)

1969 Leaves for Rangers on a free transfer after only 48 games for Forest

1970 Retires to become a Glasgow licensee

In five years at Rangers, Baxter helped the club win three Scottish League Championships, three Scottish Cup Finals and

JIM BAXTER Hard to spot the man behind the net, but Scottish hero Jim Baxter has just taken the perfect penalty against England at Wembley in 1963. By putting the ball past Banks (on the goalkeeper's debut) Baxter helped his team to a 2-1 victory and gave Scottish fans a great deal to celebrate. Baxter and Scotland had even more to celebrate when they returned to Wembley in 1967 and won 3-2. Baxter had an exceptional game and, following England's 1966 World Cup victory, the Scots not unnaturally assumed the title of the 'best team in the world'.

four League Cup Finals. In contrast, his English clubs were always worried more about relegation from the First Division than winning honours. Baxter himself never justified his big fees. Known as 'Slim Jim' in Scotland, he put on weight in England and his autobiography describes his liking for 'bets, birds and booze.' Altogether he played 347 Football and Scottish League games.

North of the border Baxter was a cult hero, as much for his style of play as for his achievements. He was an unhurried attacking wing-half whose lazy-looking left-footed skill somehow left him with time to spare. He could torment opponents and was never more cocky than when teasing England at Wembley. His most outrageous taunts were during the 1967 Wembley international when he kept the ball in the air with a juggling exhibition and then, on another occasion, calmly walked away from the ball knowing a team-mate would probably reach it first. In 1963 he walked off the Wembley pitch with the ball stuffed up his jersey at the end of an eventful victory.

BECKENBAUER, Franz

1945 Born in Munich, Germany

1958 Joins Bayern Munich

1963 Makes first-team debut

1965 First full cap, West Germany v Sweden

1966 World Cup finalist, 2-4 v England

1967 Wins European Cup winner's medal, 1-0 v Rangers

1970 World Cup semi-finalist, 3-4 v Italy

1971 Appointed captain of West Germany

1972 Wins European Championship, 3-0 v Soviet Union; European Footballer of the Year

1974 Wins European Cup, 4-0 (replay), v Atletico Madrid; leads West Germany to World Cup, 2-1 v The Netherlands

1975 Wins European Cup, 2-0 v Leeds United

1976 Leads Bayern to a hat-trick of European Cups, 1-0 v St Etienne; European Footballer of the Year

1977 Transferred to New York Cosmos

1982 Transferred to Hanover

1983 Returns to New York Cosmos

1984 Retires from playing; appointed manager of West Germany

1986 World Cup runners-up, 2-3 v Argentina

1990 Becomes the first man to captain and manage a World Cup-winning team, 1-0 v Argentina; appointed coach of Marseille, but later demoted to technical staff

Beckenbauer's influence on football over the three decades from the 1960s cannot be overstated. Credited as the inventor of the modern, attacking sweeper, and hence 'Total Football', his *curriculum vitae* since graduating into management could scarcely be more impressive: two World Cup Finals, one won, one lost.

An admirer of Giacinto Facchetti, the overlapping Italian and Internazionale left-back, Beckenbauer wished to practise the art of attack from defence in a more central position but had to wait until he had won half his 103 caps before the German manager, Helmut Schoen, was persuaded. The rest of the world has won over more quickly, Germany winning the European Championship in 1972 and the World Cup on home soil two years later.

A wonderfully elegant footballer with faultless distribution and a bewildering change of pace, Beckenbauer won international honours at schoolboy, youth and full level as an attacking right-half, having outstanding World Cups in 1966 and 1970 before switching to sweeper where his influence on the national side became absolute. His club Bayern

BECKENBAUER The 1970 World Cup, Mexico, and Franz Beckenbauer, on the ball, moves away from the England number 4 Alan Mullery to launch another West German attack. West Germany came from behind to win 3-2 and put England out of the tournament. After a hugely successful playing career and then, as manager, leading West Germany to their third World Cup victory in 1990, Beckenbauer turned to a new challenge. He signed a two-season contract as technical director of top French club Marseille. Despite the title, it is a tracksuit rather than pin-stripe suit job. However, it has not all been plain sailing. Beckenbauer speaks excellent English but no French (something he is in the process of amending, in his usual thorough way) and has had to communicate with his players in the language of his old enemies, England. Indeed, recent disappointments at the club meant a 'demotion' upstairs – the the suits.

was similarly dominated by the man whose nickname, 'The Kaiser', was worn with the comfort of a favourite sweater, and they dominated German football, winning a hat-trick of European Cups in the mid 1970s.

A superb strategist, Beckenbauer's zenith was

probably the European Championships of 1972 after which he became more cautious, much less ready to foray upfield. He carried this more defensive attitude into management where the Germans, for all their success, established a reputation for efficiency rather than flair. The 1990 World Cup Final against Argentina was commonly condemned as a disgrace and it was with respect rather than affection that Beckenbauer was regarded as he bowed out of international management immediately afterwards. He announced his intention to work in football promotion and administration but was lured back to management for a brief spell in France.

BERWICK RANGERS

Founded 1881

Joined League 1951 (C Division)

Honours Scottish League/Second Division Champions 1979

Ground Shielfield Park

Berwick Rangers were in no hurry. It took 70 years for them fully to enter Scottish football. Appropriately for a club on English soil, they spent their early years in the Northumberland Association.

There was nothing peripheral about their role in Scottish football one Saturday in January 1967. In the Scottish Cup's most remarkable result of modern times they beat Rangers 1-0 at Shielfield through a goal by Sammy Reid.

Feats such as Ken Bowron's 50 goals in 1963/64 do not disguise the fact that Berwick have sometimes been competing merely for survival.

BEST, George

1946 Born in Belfast

1961 Homesick youngster arrives at Old Trafford

1963 Turns professional with Manchester United

1964 Makes Northern Ireland debut, against Wales in Swansea

1965 Wins first club honour, a League Championship medal

1966 Earns the nickname 'El Beatle' by destroying Benfica in Lisbon

1967 Helps United take another League title

1968 Footballer of the Year; scores in Red Devils' European Cup Final triumph December — European Footballer of the year

1970 Nets six times in FA Cup tie against Northampton Town, first game after suspension following clash with referee

1971 Withdraws from international match after threats on his life

1972 Announces retirement after repeated brushes with authority

1973 Makes short-lived United comeback

1975 Joins Stockport County on loan, then Los Angeles Aztecs and Cork Celtic

1976 Moves to Fulham

1977 Wins 37th and final cap, against Holland in Belfast

1978 Switches to Fort Lauderdale strikers

1979 Plays briefly for Hibernian

1980 Signs for San Jose Earthquakes before seeking treatment for alcoholism

1983 Appears five times for Bournemouth, then retires.

GEORGE BEST
Thousands of photographs of George Best exist — so why choose this one? Because it shows every aspect of the player: the hips ready to swivel, the left leg ready to swing, the ball apparently glued to his boot and not an opponent anywhere near him! And if you look closely, there's even a hint of a smile under the beard and mane of dark Irish hair. A packed house watched Best and Manchester United lose 3-0 against Queen's Park Rangers.

Few would dispute that George Best was the most naturally gifted British footballer of the modern era. Most, however, would bemoan the fact that the Irish genius allowed the second half of his career to be wasted in a self-destructive maelstrom of personal problems.

With the perspective that time brings, it is more pertinent to dwell on the seven or eight of his eleven campaigns at Old Trafford in which Best was a purveyor of sheer delight. He was at his peak during the mid and late 1960s, in harness with fellow greats Bobby Charlton and Denis Law, when his irresistible ball skill created countless undying memories. He was quick, too, could tackle like a full-back, and there wasn't a more deadly finisher in the First Division. Sometimes he infuriated team-mates by holding the ball too long, but he more than paid for such self-indulgence with magical match-winning interludes of sublime beauty. Eventually he became a victim of the goldfish-bowl existence that was thrust upon him, and his subsequent fall from grace was profoundly distressing. But no one can take away from George the knowledge that, for a time, he entertained more royally than any other player in the world.

BINGHAM, Billy
1931 Born in Belfast

1950 Leaves Irish League club Glentoran for Sunderland

1951 Debut for Northern Ireland against France in Belfast

1958 June - plays a leading part in Northern Ireland's progress to the World Cup quarter-finals in Sweden; July - moves to Luton Town for £15,000

1959 Stars in Luton's progress to the FA Cup Final, where the 'Hatters' are beaten by Nottingham Forest

1960 Joins Everton for £20,000 plus two players

1963 Helps Everton win League title and then moves

to Port Vale; November - wins last of 56 caps, against England at Wembley

1965 Takes over as Southport Manager

1968 Becomes boss of Plymouth Argyle and Northern Ireland

1970 Assumes control of Greek national side

1973 Succeeds Harry Catterick as Everton boss

1977 January - gets the sack; April - returns to Greece to run PAOK Salonika

1978 Takes over at Mansfield Town

1980 Starts second spell as manager of Northern Ireland

1982 His team reach last 12 of World Cup in Spain

1986 Northern Ireland qualify for World Cup Finals in Mexico

Bingham has enjoyed two illustrious careers at soccer's top level, and his subsequent success as a manager should not obscure the peaks he scaled as one of Britain's most gifted wingers throughout the 1950s and early 1960s.

A fast, slightly built raider possessed of intricate skills and a deceptively powerful shot, he first came to prominence with a brilliant display for the Irish League against the

BILLY BINGHAM
Perhaps feeling ill at ease in the limelight (although his tie matches the razzamatazz), the softly spoken and earnest Billy Bingham pictured during the elaborate draw for the 1982 World Cup finals in Spain. Northern Ireland's group included hosts Spain and fancied Yugoslavia — yet Bingham's men topped it before losing out to a powerful French side in the second-round matches. Always a popular manager, he kept his small squad highly motivated despite an apparent quietness of nature.

Football League in 1950. After Sunderland snapped him up, he became one of the First Division's star attractions and a key member of the Irish side, although his talents were more unpredictable than those of team-mates Danny Blanchflower and Jimmy McIlroy, with whom he often linked so effectively.

As a manager, Bingham seemed to have reached his zenith when he took the Everton job, but he failed to bring glory to Goodison and it was not until his second stint in charge of his country that he found his most productive niche. He

is a genial, shrewd character who has served Northern Ireland with rare distinction.

BIRMINGHAM CITY
Founded 1875

Joined League 1892 (Division 2)

Honours Division 2 Champions 1893, 1921, 1948, 1955; League Cup Winners 1963

Ground St Andrews

For a long-established club which carries the name of England's second city, the Blues have a dreadful record. They have never won either the League Championship or the FA Cup, and even though they boast a spacious stadium and can tap vast support - in 1972/73 their average gate exceeded 36,000 - they have offered but token resistance to the superiority of neighbouring Aston Villa.

Birmingham, originally named Small Heath, made a bright start to League life, topping the inaugural Second Division table but staying down because they failed in promotion test matches. There was to be no lack of movement between divisions, however. At the end of their second season they rose to the top flight, the first of nine such ascents in

90 years; depressingly, of course, there was an equal number of journeys the other way.

It wasn't until the 1920s that City showed real mettle, with centre-forward Joe Bradford and England goalkeeper Harry Hibbs claiming most headlines. During this period the Blues remained in Division 1 for 18 years - still their longest stay - and reached their first FA Cup Final, losing to West Bromwich Albion in 1931.

But they were demoted in 1939 and after the war, with the excellent Gil Merrick replacing Hibbs, they resumed their ups and downs before enjoying another short spell of relative success. In 1955/56, newly promoted City finished sixth in the First and lost to Manchester City at Wembley. Building on this - thanks to a defence in which Jeff Hall, who was soon to die of polio, and Trevor Smith were outstanding - Birmingham became the first Britons to reach a European final, that of the Fairs Cup. In fact they did so twice, losing to Barcelona in 1960 and Roma the following year.

But stability vanished, they were relegated in 1965, and even former Wolves boss Stan Cullis could not achieve revival. His successor in the 1970s, Freddie Goodwin, did better, discovering precocious goal-scorer Trevor Francis and fellow

BIRMINGHAM CITY
A big-city club, but overshadowed by neighbours such as Aston Villa and Wolves, Birmingham City have rarely challenged for top honours. One of their most popular, and gifted, players was Trevor Francis who, during his time at City (1970-79), often seemed to carry the side on his own. They achieved First Division status at that time, but struggled in the top flight. Francis moved to Nottingham Forest in February 1979; the Blues were relegated to Division 2 three months later.

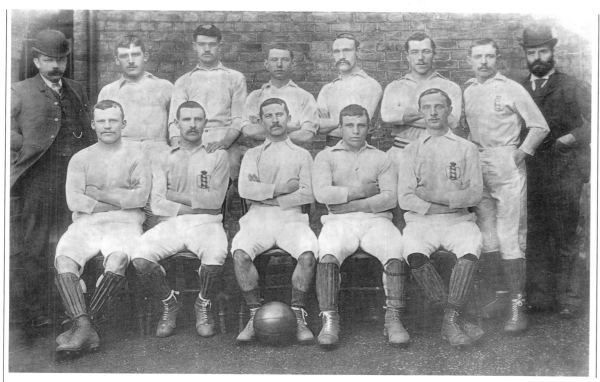

striker Bob Latchford, but when the manager left the yo-yo tendency returned, and in 1989 the Blues reached their lowest ebb, tasting life in Division 3. A club with so much potential should surely not remain in the depths for long - though with Birmingham City it is difficult to tell.

BLACKBURN ROVERS

Founded 1875

Joined League 1888 (founder member)

Honours Division 1 Champions 1912, 1914; Division 2 Champions 1939; Division 3 Champions 1975; FA Cup Winners 1884, 1885, 1886, 1890, 1891, 1928

Ground Ewood Park

Blackburn Rovers' impressive tally of trophies is enough to put the achievements of most clubs firmly in the shade; sadly for the current generation of Ewood Park fans, however, nearly all those honours were won before the First World War.

Towards the end of the nineteenth century, Rovers were among the game's giants, and they are the only surviving club with a hat-trick of FA Cups to their name. With play-maker Jim Forrest prominent, they were at the forefront of the northern professionals challenge to the southern amateurs who had dominated in pre-League days. Such glory came too early for Bob Crompton, but the great full-back and captain, the most revered figure in Blackburn's history, made up for it by playing a major role in lifting two titles before the conflict intervened.

Despite an isolated FA Cup victory, there was a gradual decline between the wars which culminated in a first ever relegation in 1936. Rovers soon climbed back, only to sink again, and it was not until Johnny Carey became manager in 1953 that a revival began. He led a side which included such stars as wing marvel Bryan Douglas, constructive wing-half Ronnie Clayton, full-back Bill Eckersley and centre-forward Tommy Briggs back to the top flight in 1957, and then celebrated by reaching Wembley three years later.

Defeat by Wolves proved the prelude to major changes, and promising youngsters such as defenders Mike England and Keith Newton and striker Fred Pickering were introduced. Blackburn consolidated encouragingly but key players were sold and 1966 brought a

demotion from which they have yet to recover.

Since then Rovers have remained mostly in Division 2, although there have been two stints in the Third. Notable personalities of this lack-lustre era have included long-serving defender Derek Fazackerly, the club's record goal-scorer Simon Garner, and managers Howard Kendall and Don Mackay. A series of failures in the late 1980s in the promotion play-offs did little to dent the notion that times are likely to remain hard for all but the giants in crowded Lancashire - however glorious their traditions may be.

BLACKPOOL

Founded 1887

Joined League 1896 (Div. 2)

Honours Div. 2 Champions 1930; FA Cup Winners 1953

Ground Bloomfield Road

One golden era dominates the history of Blackpool. From the late 1940s to the mid 1950s, the 'Seasiders' were one of the most entertaining sides in the land, and in Stanley Matthews they boasted arguably the finest player in the world.

Their beginnings were

infinitely more modest. After three campaigns in the Second Division Blackpool failed to gain re-election, although one year later they were back in the League to stay. There followed three decades of consolidation before they reached the top grade, inspired by 45 goals from Johnny Hampson. After suffering relegation in 1933, Blackpool rose again four years later to signal their arrival as a footballing power. With shrewd manager Joe Smith now in command, they settled quickly and topped the table as war broke out in 1939. When normality returned, Blackpool were ready to compete with the best. Between 1948 and 1953 they reached three FA Cup Finals, finished runners-up in the title race in 1956 and throughout the 1950s were rarely out of the League's leading group. The highlight was the legendary 'Matthews Final' of 1953, which ended in victory after the great winger inspired a stirring comeback. Stan Mortensen scored a hat-trick that day, with other leading lights including half-back and skipper Harry Johnston, goalkeeper George Farm, and inside-forwards Jackie Mudie and Ernie Taylor.

Ron Stuart replaced Smith in 1958 and, with the lifting of the maximum wage shifting the balance of power ever more towards the big clubs, Blackpool began a gradual decline, despite the sterling efforts of England captain and full-back Jimmy Armfield, England World Cup hero Alan Ball, goalkeeper Tony Waiters, defender Roy Gratrix and centre-forward Ray Charnley.

When the Seasiders were demoted in 1967, only Arsenal could boast longer consecutive membership of Division 1, but alas, such heady days were not to return. A brief resurgence, in which schemer Tony Green was outstanding, produced one more promotion before Blackpool plunged, reaching Division 4 in 1981 and returning there, after brief relief, in 1990.

With cheap overseas holidays the town is no longer so popular with travelling fans, and, beset by the usual financial difficulties under which many clubs labour, Blackpool face a mammoth task to achieve sustained resurgence.

Blanchflower ranks as one of the outstanding British

DANNY BLANCHFLOWER Not a man to be trifled with, Danny Blanchflower took his football and his later work very seriously. Leading out the Spurs side in 1956, ahead of goalkeeper Ron Reynolds, Blanchflower was crucial to the success of the Spurs sides of the era. One incident worth repeating (a point with which Blanchflower would almost certainly disagree) concerns the attempt to get him to appear on the TV programme *This Is Your Life;* Blanchflower was surprised at the last minute (as the show's format demands) but refused to appear, leaving a lot of embarrassed guests and a television company without a programme.

sporting personalities since the Second World War. After richly promising years with Barnsley and Aston Villa, he blossomed as the leader and creative hub of Tottenham Hotspur's greatest side. Playing at right-half, he forged two constructive midfield partnerships; first with Tommy Harmer as the north Londoners emerged as challengers to the dominance in the late 1950s of Wolves and Manchester United; then with the subtly brilliant Scot John White, as manager Bill Nicholson moulded the team which was to become the first this century to win the League and FA Cup double, before going on to further triumphs.

The Irish play-maker dominated Spurs' approach with his vision, ball control and cultured long-distance passing, and he was equally influential when on duty for his country. During the course of a 56-cap international career - a record at that time - he was an inspirational figure in the 1958 World Cup campaign.

As eloquent off the field as he was elegant on it, Blanchflower - whose brother Jackie played for Manchester United until injuries sustained in the Munich air-crash put him out of the game - was an intellectual, far removed from the normal run of professional footballers, and his forcefully expressed opinions sometimes led him into conflict with authority. Some 14 years after retiring, a brief fling with management ended badly, but his glory days at Tottenham had already assured him a place in soccer's hall of fame.

BLOOMER, Steve

1874 Born in Cradley Heath, Staffordshire

1891 Signs for Derby County for 7s 6d a week

1895 First of 23 England caps (scores twice against Ireland)

1906 Signs for Middlesbrough (£750)

1910 Returns to Derby County (£100)

1912 Derby County's leading League goal scorer for the 15th season, he helps the club to the Second Division Championship

1914 Plays his last game for Derby County five days after his 40th birthday

1915 Coaches in Germany, where he is interned during First World War

1938 Dies in Derby

Steve Bloomer's goal-scoring achievements set the standard for British football. He scored 331 League and Cup goals for Derby County, 63 for Middlesbrough and 28 international goals for England, the latter an England record until Nat Lofthouse improved upon it in 1956. But Bloomer scored in each of his first ten internationals and played only 23 England games – a phenomenal scoring ratio. He played 524 League and Cup games for Derby County and 130 for Middlesbrough, yet his only honour was a Second Division Championship medal with Derby. With Derby County he played in eight FA Cup semi-finals (six goals), including two replays against Sheffield United, and two finals (one goal), but never in a Cup-winning team.

Bloomer, along with Welshman Billy Meredith, was the star of the period up to the First World War. He appeared physically deficient, being pale and slender, but had underlying strength and ability. His goal-scoring secret lay in sudden, surprise shots with either foot. He used hardly

STEVE BLOOMER Steve Bloomer, working as a coach on the Derby County staff, making a point to *(from left)* Sid Wileman, Sammy Crooks, Dally Duncan, Jack Nicholas, Jack Barker and Jack Bowers.

any backlift when shooting. He was a strong, skilful runner with the ball, but, like Jimmy Greaves half a century later, he was dedicated to one task only in the opposition penalty area – scoring goals.

BOLTON WANDERERS

Founded 1874

Joined League 1888 (founder member)

Honours Div. 2 Champions 1909, 1978; Div. 3 Champions 1973; FA Cup Winners 1923, 1926, 1929, 1958

Ground Burnden Park

Bolton Wanderers are a club of proud tradition whose star began to fall with the abolition of the maximum wage in 1961. Since then top players have left - understandably - for richer pickings, all but the most loyal fans have been drawn inexorably to Manchester and Liverpool, and life has been a struggle for the 'Trotters.'

It wasn't always easy, either, in the 1880s, when Bolton were at the forefront of the battle to legalise professionalism. They prevailed but reaped no immediate dividend in trophies, losing one early FA Cup Final. Around the turn of the century, League consistency also became elusive and they suffered four demotions to Division 2 in 12 years.

Success came in the 1920s, when they won the FA Cup three times and twice finished third in the First Division. Stars of the day included prolific inside-forwards David Jack and Joe Smith and winger Ted Vizard. There followed a descent into mediocrity, with the Wanderers' only national headlines being of the unwelcome kind, when 33 supporters died following the collapse of a barrier at Burnden Park in 1946. But Bill Ridding took over as manager in 1951 and built a competitive side around England centre-forward Nat Lofthouse and a formidably physical defence, in which Malcolm Barrass and Tommy Banks were outstanding. They reached the celebrated 'Matthews Final' of 1953, which they lost to Blackpool, but, after recruiting accomplished 'keeper Eddie Hopkinson, made amends five years later against a Manchester

BOLTON WANDERERS With the 1923 FA Cup, following the famous (White Horse!) 2-0 win over West Ham in the first Wembley final, Bolton Wanderers line up with their prize: *(back row, left to right)* **Nuttall, Howarth, Pym, Seddon, Jennings, Rowley; Butler, Jack, J. Smith, Joe Smith, Vizard, Finney. Jack, with an early goal, and J. Smith were the scorers. The Cup run obviously distracted the Bolton team that year as they finished 13th in Division 1, the only time in a sequence of nine seasons in which they finished outside the top eight.**

United side ravaged by the Munich air crash.

The Wembley triumph was well deserved, yet it did not presage further glories. Harsh economic realities forced the sale of strikers Wyn Davies and Francis Lee and, despite the delightful prompting of schemer Freddie Hill, the team were in the Second Division by 1964 and the Third by 1971.

Enterprising boss Ian Greaves, ably assisted by stalwart midfielders Roy Greaves and Peter Reid, hauled them back to the top flight in 1978, but new horrors awaited. They kicked off the 1987/88 campaign in Division 4, and although Phil Neal lifted them one rung up the League ladder a year later, Bolton were still a world away from their former eminence.

BOOKS

The cliche that football literature lags far behind cricket literature is becoming dated. In the past two decades there has been a rise in the wealth of published material: reference books, statistical histories of clubs, academic contributions and fanzines. 'Football has rediscovered its history,' says John Gausted of Sportspages, London's specialist sports bookshop. His shop sells more literature on football than on cricket, but this may not represent the national picture.

Rothman's Football Yearbook, first published in 1970, has become football's equivalent to cricket's *Wisden*, with an annual summary of clubs, games, teams and records. Several smaller reference books - *The Football Association Yearbook, The News of the World Football Annual* and the *Playfair Football Annual* - have a much longer history than

Rothman's Football Yearbook, however.

For a true feel of the sport, there are several entertaining books. Two 1960s classics, John Moynihan's *Soccer Syndrome* and Arthur Hopcraft's *The Football Man*, have recently been republished. Two from the 1970s, Eamon Dunphy's *Only A Game?* and Hunter Davies's *The Glory Game*, have also reappeared, the former still the most illuminating autobiographical comment on life as a professional footballer, the latter a journalist's insightful observations on Tottenham Hotspur's 1971/72 season. Two easy-to-read books from the 1980s are *The Book of Football Quotations* by Peter Ball and Phil Shaw, and *One Afternoon in Lisbon* by Kevin McCarra and Pat Woods, an account of Celtic's 1967 European Cup triumph based on evocative interview material.

Autobiographies are abundant, some more famous for their titles than their insight, a favourite being Ian Ure's *Ure's Truly*. Good biographies are very limited, but Tony Francis challenged this with *Clough*. The 1980s also saw classic biographies of

Stanley Matthews (by David Miller), Jock Stein (by Ken Gallacher), Billy Meredith and Alex James (both by John Harding).

The encyclopaedia tradition began with Pickford and Gibson's four-volume *Association Football and the Men Who Made It* in 1906, and the same publisher repeated the enterprise with *Association Football*, edited by A.H. Fabian and Geoffrey Green, in 1960. The 1906 set was recently republished by the Association of Football Statisticians in photocopied form. This association has a big publication list, much of it original material on the statistical history of the game.

Almost every club has its history documented. One of the best is *The Glory and the Dream : The History of Celtic FC, 1887-1987* by Tom Campbell and Pat Woods. A Derby firm, Breedon Books, has become a market leader in club statistical histories. Their 'Complete Record' series covers almost 40 Football and Scottish League clubs, giving team records for every game in the club's history and background text on players and club. Many individuals have also taken initiatives to publish club histories.

For sound historical background to the game, the best starting point is Tony Mason's *Association Football and English Society 1863-1915* and Nick Fishwick's *English Football and Society*. Richard Holt's *Sport and the British* is strong on football history, while Simon Inglis, a journalist with architectural experience, is the author of *The Football Grounds of Great Britain* and *The Football Grounds of Europe*, the former one of the most popular books of the 1980s. Many other books are mentioned elsewhere in this encyclopaedia, but the best place to browse through new books is Sportspages, Caxton Walk, 94-96 Charing Cross Road, London. Out-of-print books are available through John Whittaker, 51 Western Hill, Durham City while general information can be obtained from the Association of Football Statisticians, 22 Bretons, Basildon, Essex.

BOURNEMOUTH

Founded 1899

Joined League 1923 (Div.3 S)

Honours Div.3 Champions 1987

Ground Dean Court

Anyone curious to find out about life in the Third Division could hardly do better than study the history of Bournemouth. Between their election to the League in 1923 and their relegation in 1970, the 'Cherries' chalked up a record number of campaigns in the Third Division, a statistic which points, with reasonable accuracy, to decade upon decade of mediocrity.

Such predictability - enlivened by the occasional FA Cup run, notably that of 1957 when stirring victories over Wolves and Spurs preceded a plucky quarter-final exit against Manchester United - ended in the year of their demotion with the appointment of John Bond as manager. The extrovert newcomer changed the Dean Court club's staid image, found a hero for the fans in goal merchant Ted MacDougall, and soon won promotion.

Alas, Bournemouth were not destined for a fairytale rise. Bond departed, a seven-year sojourn in Division 4 ensued and it was not until the arrival of another enterprising boss, Harry Redknapp, in 1983 that real hope for the future blossomed anew. Redknapp took his team into the Second Division in 1987, but then came the unexpected disappointment of a return to the Third after three years. The Cherries were back once more in the shadows of south coast neighbours Southampton and Portsmouth.

BRADFORD CITY

Founded 1903

Joined League 1903

Honours Div.2 Champions 1908; Div.3 (N) Champions 1929; Div.3 Champions 1985; FA Cup Winners 1911

Ground Valley Parade

Despite hailing from a city with a 300,000-plus population, and losing their closest competition when neighbours Park Avenue failed to gain re-election to the League in 1970, Bradford City have continued to make little lasting impact in the modern era.

In fact, they must look back to the days before the First World War for evidence of real success. Then, just three years after climbing out of Division 2 - to which, remarkably, they had been elected in the year of their formation - the 'Bantams' finished fifth in the top flight, capping their campaign by winning the FA Cup. Sadly that victory, gained after a replay against then-mighty Newcastle United, still represents the peak of their achievements.

After being relegated in 1922, City spent the next 15 years to-ing and fro-ing between the Second and Third Divisions before settling at the lower level until 1961. The remainder of the decade was spent in the Fourth, and they did not succeed in escaping the lower reaches for another 24 terms. Bradford's playing fortunes finally took a turn for the better in 1985 when manager Trevor Cherry led them to the Second Division, although the promotion celebrations were eclipsed by horror when a fire in the main stand during an end-of-season Valley Parade encounter with Lincoln City cost more than 50 lives.

City overcame the shock of the disaster to remain in Division 2 for five years but, after selling outstanding midfielder Stuart McCall and sacking Cherry's worthy successor Terry Dolan, they were demoted in 1990. More support - never overwhelming, even when nearby Leeds United are in a trough - is essential before real progress can be made.

BRADFORD CITY
Unfortunately, Bradford City's place in football history will long be remembered for the terrible fire at their Valley Parade Ground in 1985. A new stand, shown here, was built to replace the one destroyed and officially opened with a match between Bradford City and an England XI. Shilton is defending the England goal.

BRECHIN CITY

Founded 1906

Joined League 1924 (Div.3)

Honours Scottish League Division 2 Champions 1983; Second Division Champions 1990; Division C Champions 1954

Ground Glebe Park

Survival will always be Brechin's most remarkable achievement. The city's population is 7000, giving them the smallest catchment area of any senior club in Britain.

No player has ever won international honours while with them (although Davie Duncan did play for the club towards the end of his career in the late 1950s) but they have manoeuvred well in the transfer market and, remarkably, won the Second Division in 1990.

Local astuteness has been recognised in the career of chairman David Will. He has been President of the SFA and is a vice-president of FIFA.

BREMNER, Billy

1942 Born in Stirling, Scotland

1959 December - turns professional with Leeds United

1960 January - makes League debut at Chelsea

1965 May - wins first Scottish cap against Spain at Hampden Park

1968 Plays crucial role in League Cup and European Fairs Cup triumphs

1969 Skippers Leeds to League Championship

1970 Footballer of the Year

1972 Lifts the FA Cup at last, as Leeds beat Arsenal

1974 Wins second League title medal

1975 September - plays 54th and last game for Scotland, against Denmark in Copenhagen

1976 September - moves to Hull City for £35,000

1978 Becomes manager of Doncaster Rovers and plays for his new club

1985 Succeeds Eddie Gray as Leeds boss

1988 Sacked by Leeds

1989 Takes over at Doncaster for the second time

Bremner was the dynamic little fireball at the heart of Don Revie's successful sides of the 1960s and 1970s. Together with Johnny Giles, whose subtle guile was the perfect counterpart to Bremner's all-action style, he formed one of the most memorable midfield partnerships modern football has seen.

The pale-faced, red-haired Scot hurled himself into every game as if his life depended on it and, especially early in his career, he was often in trouble with referees. He was sometimes criticised for being over-physical, yet there was far more to his contribution than mere combativeness. Bremner was an astute reader of the game, a skilful passer and, often in important matches, a fine finisher. But above all there was the boundless energy, which made him a vital member of both attack and defence for the Leeds and Scotland teams he captained with such passion.

As a manager he twice led Doncaster to promotion from the Fourth Division.

BILLY BREMNER
Reminded yet again that you get 'nowt for coming second', Billy Bremner pictured with Don Revie at the end of Leeds United's 1-0 shock defeat by Sunderland in the 1973 FA Cup Final. Bremner did, of course, win plenty of honours during his career as a Leeds player, but also figured in five campaigns as a Division 1 runner-up as well as playing in losing FA Cup and European Cup Final sides. Perhaps his extreme determination to win made the disappointment all the keener.

BRENTFORD

Founded 1889

Joined League 1920 (Div.3)

Honours Div.2 Champions 1935; Div.3 (S) Champions 1933; Div.4 Champions 1963

Ground Griffin Park

There was a time when Brentford were the rising stars of English football. After joining the Football League as founder members of Division 3, the Bees showed indifferent form in the 1920s but took flight with an exhilarating surge in the subsequent decade. After topping the Third and then the Second Division with only one season between their triumphs, they enjoyed three campaigns in Division 1's top six and, for good measure, reached the FA Cup quarter-final in 1938. Griffin Park luminaries in those heady days included manager Harry Curtis, goal-scorer John Holliday and winger Idris Hopkins.

After the war, however, Brentford's fortunes took a turn for the worse from which they have never fully recovered. Two more runs to the last eight of the FA Cup did nothing to obscure disappointing League displays and they were relegated in 1947, slumping to the Third Division – despite a brief interlude with Tommy Lawton in the managerial chair, and the doughty efforts of long-serving defender Kenny Coote - in 1954.

Since then the 'Bees', who came close to merger with Queen's Park Rangers during a financial crisis in the 1960s, have endured three spells in the Fourth Division, but from 1978 onwards they stabilised in the Third. In 1989 their fourth appearance in an FA Cup quarter-final brought some hope, and if they could somehow claw their way into the Second Division (as they nearly did in 1991), there should be enough support in West London on which to build a winning team.

BRIGHTON AND HOVE ALBION

Founded 1900

Joined League 1920 (Div.3)

Honours Div.3 (S) Champions 1958; Div.4 Champions 1965

Ground Goldstone Ground

For a club as old as a century in which the world has witnessed staggering upheaval, Brighton and Hove Albion can point to a remarkably tranquil history - but they have had their moments. In 1910, as Southern League champions, they beat Aston Villa to win the Charity Shield, but perhaps

their most exciting hour came in 1983 when the 'Seagulls', already relegated from Division 1 in that same season, were within an ace of winning the FA Cup. With the end of extra time looming and the scores level, midfielder Gordon Smith muffed a fabulous chance and mighty Manchester United breathed again. Predictably, Jimmy Melia's men were eclipsed in the replay and quickly returned to their familiar place in the football world, far removed from such unaccustomed limelight.

The 'Shrimps', as they were first nicknamed, had entered the League as founder members of Division 3 and remained there for the next 38 years. When they finally climbed out as champions in 1958, they must have wondered if it had been worth the effort, going down 9-0 at Middlesbrough - their record defeat - in the opening Division 2 encounter. Brighton stabilised and hung on for four campaigns before entering a slump which saw them plummet to the Fourth Division. Recovery was swift, however, and the next decade and a half was divided between Third and Second Divisions before manager Alan Mullery, the former England wing-half, led them into the top flight. While never looking secure in Division 1, the south coast club competed pluckily both on the pitch and in the transfer market, with £900,000 being garnered from defender Mark Lawrenson's sale to Liverpool, and £500,000 being invested in Manchester United striker Andy Ritchie.

Sojourns in both Second and Third Divisions followed, and with the big London clubs an all too convenient alternative for supporters, another century of unspectacular, if worthy, activity may be in prospect.

BRISTOL CITY

Founded 1894

Joined League 1901 (Div.2)

Honours Div.2 Champions 1906; Div.3 (S) Champions 1923, 1927, 1955; Welsh Cup Winners 1934; Freight Rover Trophy Winners 1986

Ground Ashton Gate

Bristol City are a club with vast unrealised potential. Blessed with a splendidly appointed stadium and a wide, fairly affluent, largely untapped area from which to draw support, the 'Robins' should by now have established themselves as a major long-term power in English soccer. Indeed, there have been periods in their history when City seemed to have arrived, but consistent success has always eluded them. Their most prosperous playing era coincided with their first decade of League competition, in which they won the Second Division title, were runners-up in the top flight, and lost the 1909 FA Cup Final to Manchester United. Their leading light in those halcyon days was Billy Wedlock, a dominant centre-half who won 26 England caps and around whom City built their side.

Somehow, though, the impetus slipped away and for more than half a century the West Country-men made regular journeys between the Second and Third Divisions. In the 1950s and early 1960s even the prolific goal-scoring of England international John Atyeo, who found the net 350 times in more than 600 City appearances, was not enough to propel the 'Robins' back among the elite.

It wasn't until 1976 that a First Division place was reclaimed by manager Alan Dicks' workmanlike team but, sadly, that hard-won status was lost after only four seasons. Then began an alarming nosedive which saw the Robins plumb the Fourth Division depths and teeter on the very brink of oblivion during a financial crisis in 1982. Since then there has been a steady rebuilding process and now Bristol City, back in Division 2, seem equipped once more for greater things.

BRISTOL ROVERS

Founded 1883

Joined League 1920 (Div.3)

Honours Div.3 (S) Champions 1953; Div.3 Champions 1990

Ground Twerton Park, Bath

Bristol Rovers, a club of indomitable spirit, are used to taking setbacks in their stride. The ill-advised sale of their Eastville ground to a greyhound racing company in 1940, a bribes scandal that resulted in two players being suspended for life in 1963, a fire that destroyed their main stand in 1980, another blaze which severely damaged their temporary Bath home a decade later, and a cash crisis which never ends - somehow the 'Pirates' have risen gloriously, if at times precariously, above the lot.

Having joined the League as founder members of Division 3, Rovers settled into something of a rut, but the appointment of Bert Tann as manager in 1950 changed all that. A dedicated believer in the long-ball game, he produced a side which reached the FA Cup quarter-final against Newcastle in 1951 - bowing to the 'Magpies' only after a replay - and lifted the Division 3 (S) title in 1953. Star of the side was free-scoring Geoff Bradford, who remains the club's sole England international, and when he was partnered later in the 1950s by the richly gifted Alfie Biggs, the club had a strike force to be envied.

Since then, homely Rovers - less grand than neighbours City, yet always endowed with more larger-than-life characters - have split their time between the Second and Third Divisions, never really threatening to join the elite but always avoiding the drop to the basement. From winger Harold Jarman in the 1960s to Nigel Martyn, who became Britain's first £1 million goalkeeper when he joined Crystal Palace in 1989, there have been plenty of heroes.

Under enterprising manager Gerry Francis, Rovers - currently tenants of non-League Bath City – stepped up their bid to find a new ground. When Francis left in 1991, the future clouded, but one thing is certain - the 'Pirates' will fight on.

BURNLEY

Founded 1882

Joined League 1888 (founder member)

Honours Div.1 Champions 1921, 1960; Div.2 Champions 1898, 1973; Div.3 Champions 1982; FA Cup Winners 1914

Ground Turf Moor

The plight of Burnley in May 1987 was enough to make any genuine lover of English soccer weep. The 'Clarets', their history studded with heady triumphs, were bottom of the Fourth Division and had to win the last match of

BRISTOL CITY
John Atyeo, more than any other player, is associated with Bristol City. A local lad, he made over 600 appearances for City in all competitions between 1951 and 1965. Despite playing most of his football in Divisions 3, 3 (South) and 2, he still managed six full England caps in 1956 and 1957. A prolific scorer, he recorded 350 goals in 647 games for City.

BURNLEY Burnley line up for the 1959/60 season: *(back row, left to right)* Talbut, Cummings, Miller, Blacklaw, Seith, Scott, White; Harris, Connelly, McIlroy, Pointer, Adamson, Robson, Pilkington, Fenton. In those days mention of the 'claret and blue' would probably bring to mind Burnley before either West Ham or Villa. They won the First Division title in the 1959/60 season and reached the sixth round of the FA Cup. The back row offers a strange picture of under-fulfilment as Talbut, Cummings, Miller, Blacklaw and Scott all played represent-ative football ('B' internationals, schoolboy matches, under-23 and League representative matches) yet only managed four full caps between them. The front row contains Burnley's most capped players, McIlroy (55 for Northern Ireland) and Connelly (20 for England).

the season to stand a chance of retaining League status. Burnley survived - just - but their fans were left to rue a sad decline.

Not that the Lancashire cotton-town club were accustomed to undiluted success. Their earliest years saw several journeys between divisions before they won their first trophy, the FA Cup. But just as they threatened to become a real power, the First World War intervened and it was the early 1920s before the title landed at Turf Moor. The honour was due largely to a majestic half-back line of George Halley, Tommy Boyle and William Watson, with 'keeper Jerry Dawson also outstanding. A slump soon ensued, however, culminating in demotion as the decade closed.

Revival came after the Second World War when new manager Cliff Britton assembled a competitive side in which two future Burnley bosses, defender Alan Brown and forward Harry Potts, took the eye. In 1947 they won promotion and reached Wembley, where they lost to Charlton Athletic. Expectations ran high, but it was not until Potts assumed control in the late 1950s that the 'Clarets' reached their peak. Backed vociferously by contro-versial chairman Bob Lord, Potts led the club to the Championship in 1960 and an FA Cup Final defeat in 1962. The stars were midfield creators Jimmy Adamson and Jimmy McIlroy, winger John Connelly and centre-forward Ray Pointer.

Talented youngsters replaced the old guard, but Burnley had always had to sell to survive, and against a background of departures - winger Leighton James and midfielder Ralph Coates were two of many released reluctantly in the 1970s - the slide began. At first it was slow, with relegation in 1971 being followed by promotion after two terms, but by 1980 Turf Moor was hosting Division 3 matches and by 1985 Burnley, unthinkably, were in the basement.

Yet the ground is well-equipped and, as gates for important games have shown, there is still plenty of potential support. There is still hope for the Clarets.

BURY

Founded 1885

Joined League 1894 (Div.2)

Honours Div.2 Champions 1895; Div.3 Champions 1961; FA Cup Winners 1900, 1903

Ground Gigg Lane

Which club won two FA Cup Finals, only three years apart, by an aggregate of ten goals to nil? Might it be Liverpool? Or Manchester United, perhaps? No, it was their unfashionable neighbours, gallant little Bury, who beat Southampton 4-0 in 1900 and three years later

BURY Bury Football Club, FA Cup winners in 1903: *(left to right, back row)* Johnstone, Linsay, Thorpe, Montieth, Ross, McEwan; Richards, Wood, Sagar, Leeming, Plant. Their 6-0 success over Derby County followed a 4-0 drubbing of Southampton in the Final of 1900 – still the only two major honours for the club. The margin of the 1903 victory would have been hard to predict as both finalists finished the season with records of played 34, won 16, drawn 3, lost 15, points 35. Perhaps the vital factor was that Bury has scored more goals, 54 to Derby's 50.

set the record for the biggest victory margin in the Final with the 6-0 annihilation of Derby County.

That, of course, was in the days when the 'Shakers' enjoyed far greater standing in the game than today. Until 1929 most of their football had been played in the First Division, and they did not taste Third Division fare until 1957. Since then, they have divided their time between the three lower flights, having constant difficulty in competing for support with the north-west giants, as well as the other League clubs which proliferate throughout Lancashire.

In consequence, talented young players – 1960s

midfielder Colin Bell, who went on to win 48 England caps, was a prime example – have had to be sold so small-town Bury can survive. But there are few grounds with more character than Gigg Lane, and the Shakers appear endearingly ready to carry their unequal struggle into the next century.

BUSBY, Sir Matt

1909 Born in Lanarkshire mining village of Orbiston, Scotland

1928 Signs for Manchester City

1933 Wins sole Scottish cap, against Wales at Cardiff

1934 Helps City beat Portsmouth to win FA Cup

1936 Joins Liverpool for £8,000

1945 Takes over as Manchester United manager

1948 FA Cup victory over Blackpool, first trophy of Busby era

1952 United take League title

1953 Birth of the 'Busby Babes' as youth is given its head

1956 First of two successive Championships; September – pioneers British clubs' continental challenge as United enter European Cup

1957 FA Cup Final defeat by Aston Villa costs United the double

1958 Busby narrowly survives Munich air disaster, which claims the lives of eight players

1963 His rebuilt team lift the FA Cup, beating

MATT BUSBY The year is 1958 and Sir Matt Busby (then just Matt Busby) watches as his Munich survivors lose the FA Cup Final, 2-0 to Bolton Wanderers. To his left is assistant manager Jimmy Murphy. The nation had prayed for Matt's recovery following the air crash, and for a United win in the Final; their prayers were answered on the first count only.

Leicester City

1965 United win first of two League titles in three years

1968 Receives knighthood in wake of European Cup triumph against Benfica

1969 Relinquishes team control to Wilf McGuinness; continues as general manager

1970 Resumes charge of side as McGuinness is sacked

1971 Frank O'Farrell is new United boss; Busby takes seat on board and later becomes club president.

1980s Remains quiet but authoritative voice in background at United

Matt Busby is the man who made Manchester United. Admittedly the 'Red Devils' already had six decades of history behind them when he arrived at Old Trafford; but the United the world knows today, that magical institution whose appeal somehow transcends its periodic traumas, is essentially the creation of the visionary Scot.

After the Second World War, Busby, a benevolent figure with a core of steel, took on a club with no money and a bombed-out ground. Before long he had breathed life into the place, built the first of his three magnificent sides and was soon lifting soccer's most glittering prizes. The flair and charisma Busby had shown in his own career as a constructive wing-half was evident in each team. His creed was to entertain and, crucially, he had the priceless ability to communicate it to his players.

But despite all the triumphs on the field, his most awesome achieve-ment was fighting back from the brink of death after Munich to bring further glories to Old Trafford.

On retirement Busby was criticised for letting his stars grow old together. But this could not detract from his momumental career.

CARDIFF CITY

Founded 1899

Joined League 1920 (Div.2)

Honours Div.3 (S) Champions 1947; FA Cup Winners 1927

Ground Ninian Park

Cardiff City's first decade of League life was enough

CARDIFF CITY A place in the record books as the only team to take the FA Cup out of England. Could this Cardiff City side of 1926/27 have known that their record would remain intact? They had lost a Final, 1-0 to Sheffield United in 1925, before beating Arsenal by the same scoreline in 1927. Successive Cardiff teams have rarely threatened to repeat these feats, despite winning the Welsh Cup on numerous occasions. The line-up (back row, left to right) Latham (trainer), Nelson, Farquharson, Watson, McLachlan; Sloan, Irving, Keenor, Hardy, Davies; Curtis, Ferguson. It was Ferguson who got the all-important goal in the Final win over Arsenal.

to make the opposition tremble. By the end of their opening campaign they had gained promotion to the top flight; three years later, in 1924, they missed the League Championship only on goal average; the next term ended with a single-goal Wembley defeat; and in 1927 they became the first (and still the only) Welsh club to win the FA Cup.

Unfortunately for the 'Bluebirds' the success of that golden era, when half-back Fred Keenor was their driving force, was not to continue. By 1931 they had slithered ignominiously to the Third Division and were not to reappear in the First until 1952. This time they lasted for five years, with goal-scorers Trevor Ford and Gerry Hitchens making key contributions. Since then, apart from two campaigns in the early 1960s, they have not joined the elite.

As that decade progressed, the exertions of manager Jimmy Scoular and striker John Toshack did much to ensure Cardiff's security, and sometimes prosperity, in the Second Division. But by the late 1980s the team – who have had to labour hard to survive in a rugby

CAMBRIDGE UNITED

Founded 1919

Joined League 1970 (Div.4)

Honours Div.3 Champions 1991, Div.4 Champions 1977

Ground Abbey Stadium

Relative newcomers to the League, Cambridge United have achieved their successes on limited budgets in a town not noted for its fervent support of soccer.

United joined Division 4 in 1970, beating both Bradford Park Avenue (applying for re-election) and neighbours Cambridge City in the voting for

League status. The side that took them to the Division 4 Championship in 1976/77 held together and went on to win promotion to the Second Division in the following season; they achieved their highest placing of eighth in Division 2 in 1979/80. Stars of that era included Alan Biley and George Reilley, both of whom went on to bigger clubs, and skipper Steve Spriggs who made a club record 417 League appearances.

Following the League's longest ever run of games without a win (31), Cambridge finished bottom of Division 2 in 1983/84. Their return to Division 3 in 1990 was via a play-off final against Chesterfield

CAMBRIDGE UNITED

A little piece of history. The first play-off final to be played at Wembley was at the end of the 1989/90 season when Cambridge United, having finished in sixth place in Division 4, beat Chesterfield 1-0 to win promotion to Division 3. The Cambridge goal-scorer Dion Dublin is seen showing the award to fans (many watching the team for the first time) who made the trip to Wembley for a good day out.

and they repeated their two-promotions-in-two-seasons feat in 1991 by winning the Division 3 Championship.

fastness – had grown accustomed to floundering in the lower reaches, and a financial crisis in 1991 nearly brought about their downfall.

The Welsh Cup, which they have won 20 times, continues to offer the greatest chance of glory through entry to the European Cup Winners' Cup. Indeed, fans with modest memories still talk of 1968, when they lost the semi-final to SV Hamburg, and 1971, when they beat Real Madrid in a quarter-final first leg only to bow out by one goal.

CARLISLE UNITED

Founded 1903

Joined League 1928 (Div.3 N)

Honours Div.3 Champions 1965

Ground Brunton Park

After three matches of 1974/75, Carlisle United sat proudly at the head of Division 1. It was a supremely satisfying experience for the unfashionable Cumbrians, but not a lasting one. After being relegated at the end of their sole campaign at the top level, they have slipped all the way to the Fourth Division where they

entered the 1990s faced with the problem common to most small clubs – that of flourishing in the face of widespread public apathy.

United's moment of glory was all the more sweet in view of their lacklustre past. Thirty years of frugal Third Division existence were followed by two sojourns in the newly created Fourth before they began their climb to that lofty pinnacle of the mid 1970s.

Achievements in knockout competition have been few, though Carlisle did reach the FA Cup quarter-finals during their season among the elite and the League Cup semi-finals five years earlier.

Outstanding performers in the Cumbrians' blue shirts have been schemer Ivor Broadis in two spells after the Second World War; 1950s centre-forward Alan Ashman, who as manager led them into the First Division; inside-forward Stan Bowles in the early 1970s; and striker Peter Beardsley nearly a decade later. Notable bosses have included Bill Shankly (1949-51) and Bob Stokoe (three stints between 1968 and 1986).

CELTIC

Founded 1887 (first match: 1888)

Joined League 1890 (Division 1, founder club)

Honours Scottish League Championship, Division 1, 1893, 1894, 1896, 1898, 1905, 1906, 1907, 1908, 1909, 1910, 1914, 1915, 1916, 1917, 1919, 1922, 1926, 1936, 1938, 1954, 1966, 1967, 1968, 1969, 1970, 1971, 1972, 1973, 1974; Premier Division, 1977, 1979, 1981, 1982, 1986, 1988; Scottish Cup, 1892, 1899, 1900, 1904, 1907, 1908, 1911, 1912, 1914, 1923, 1925, 1927, 1931, 1933, 1937, 1951, 1954, 1965, 1967, 1969, 1971, 1972, 1974, 1975, 1977, 1980, 1985, 1988, 1989; League Cup, 1956/57, 1957/58, 1965/66, 1966/67, 1967/68, 1968/69, 1969/70, 1974/75, 1982/83; European Cup, 1967

Ground Celtic Park

Celtic are a club of distinctive origins. They were formed to support soup kitchens operating among the impoverished Irish Catholic immigrants of Glasgow's East End. Celtic, however, were also intended to reinforce that community's self-respect by providing a focal point of pride and achievement.

They and their fans have drawn sustenance from the questionable notion that they are romantic rebels. Despite the considerable resources they have always enjoyed, the club likes to cast itself as underdogs to arch-rivals Rangers as representatives of a Protestant Establishment in Scotland. The reality has

never been quite so simple.

In the early years Celtic were guided by aspiring middle-class businessmen who sought success single-mindedly. They utterly ignored the rules of amateurism (under which Scottish football supposedly operated before 1893) and were even able to take defender Dan Doyle from openly professional Everton. In Scotland Celtic plundered the ranks of the other clubs, tempting away their best players.

The effect was to rouse the domestic game. Attendances boomed and Rangers, especially, grew in strength by way of response. Before long Celtic moved on to a new policy of producing home-grown sides. The

CELTIC As player and manager – and then suffering the axe to make way for Liam Brady – Billy McNeill's contribution to the Glasgow side has been quite phenomenal. A record 486 League appearances between 1957 and 1975 saw him in the heart of the team during one of the most successful periods in their history. Pictured here in one of the scores of Old Firm matches in which he competed, the 1971 1-1 Scottish Cup Final draw (Celtic won the replay 2-1), McNeill played and managed firmly and singlemindedly; a Celtic man through and through.

development was nurtured by Willie Maley, who served the club first as player and then as manager from its foundation until 1939. The best of his teams won six League Championships in succession from 1905 to 1910.

Perhaps, though, the most cherished memories in Celtic's history are associated with Cup competition. Victories in the all British Empire Exhibition Cup of 1938 and the Coronation Cup of 1953 are bedded in the club's folklore. Celtic have always had men capable of the explosive moment which decides a Cup-tie.

The individualistic Patsy Gallacher equalised in the 1925 Scottish Cup final by somersaulting out of a goalmouth melee and over the line with the ball wedged between his feet. Celtic's great centre-forward of the 1920s and 1930s, Jimmy McGrory, scored the winner that day. Probably the club's greatest-ever player, he hit a British record 550 goals in first class football, mostly for Celtic, including eight in one match against Dunfermline in 1928.

Despite an extraordinary 7-1 victory over Rangers in the 1957 League Cup final Celtic were a club in decline over the years following the Second World War. That changed with the appointment of Jock Stein, a former captain, as manager in 1965. With very few excursions into the transfer market he built a team which possessed the athleticism, skill and tactical know-how to match the Continent's best.

They produced overwhelming attacking football to become the first British club to win the European Cup in 1967, beating Inter Milan 2-1. The aerial power of centre-half Billy McNeill, the playmaking of Bobby Murdoch and the trickery of winger Jimmy Johnstone were especially significant in that period. From 1966 to 1974 Celtic won nine successive Championships, equalling the world record of the time.

Towards the end of that run a new generation of talent appeared but men like Kenny Dalglish, David Hay and Lou Macari were sold to English clubs. World-class full-back Danny McGrain, who stayed, was an exception. The trend continued with Charlie Nicholas' move to Arsenal in 1983.

The club continued to discover gifted players, such as Paul McStay, but were surprised by the boom in Rangers' ambitions and fortunes. Celtic now need to win significant change from a period of turmoil if they are to recover past glories.

CENTRAL AMERICA

Central American countries are often underrated by European observers. Costa Rica's progress to the last 16 of the 1990 World Cup finals at the expense of Scotland and Sweden was not surprising to those who knew that Costa Rica had dominated the region's international football competition. Mexico's record of nine appearances in World Cup finals is better than many European countries, including England, Scotland and Spain. Mexico has also hosted the tournament on two occasions (1970 and 1986).

Cuba (1938), Haiti (1974), Honduras (1982) and El Salvador (1970 and 1982) have also reached the final stages of the World Cup. The last two made world news in 1969 in the so-called 'Soccer War' game. It took three games to decide that El Salvador rather than Honduras would meet Haiti in a play-off for a place in the 1970 World Cup finals. Shortly after the final game, played in neutral Mexico, a four-day war broke out, but diplomatic relations between the two

CENTRAL AMERICA
Cayasso of Costa Rica (*dark shirt*) is tackled by Dave McPherson of Scotland in the 1990 World Cup. Costa Rica won the game 1-0 and Scotland did not progress to the second phase, thus continuing their poor record in World Cup finals competitions. Costa Rica came second in their group with four points, having also beaten Sweden 2-1; but in the second round, Schiravi of Czechoslavakia scored a hat-trick against the Costa Ricans and the 4-1 scoreline signalled their departure from the tournament.
Costa Rica are probably the most successful side in CONCACEF. This affiliation is still growing, the latest additions being Aruba, Santa Lucia, and St Vincent and the Grenadines. The oldest national associations are to be found in Guyana (1902) and Haiti (1904). The size of the member states varies greatly, from the Bahamas (14 clubs, 700 players registered) and Grenada (15 clubs, 200 players) to Mexico with some 14 million registered players. Despite the popularity of the game in that country and the fact that it has twice hosted the World Cup – in 1970 and 1986 – Mexico has had little international success. Her top players often move to Europe, the best known being ace goal-scorer Hugo Sanchez (98 caps), who played for Athletico Madrid before signing for rivals Real in 1985. In 1989/90 he won the European Golden Boot with 38 league goals and enlivened the game by his celebrating style.

countries were already strained over land problems.

The association responsible for soccer in North and Central America is the Confederation Norte-Centro-Americana y del Caribe de Futbol (CONCACEF), founded in 1972.

CHAPMAN, Herbert

1875 Born at Kiveton Park, Sheffield

1897-1901 While working as a mining engineer, plays as an amateur for Stalybridge, Rochdale, Grimsby, Swindon, Sheppey United and Worksop

1901 Signs professional for Northampton

1903 Moves to Notts County (£300)

1905 Transfers to Tottenham Hotspur

1907 Becomes player-manager of Northampton Town

1909 Helps Northampton to the Southern League Championship

1912 Takes over as secretary-manager of Leeds City

1917 and 1918 Leeds City win the Football League (Midland Section) in successive seasons

1919 Temporarily suspended by an FA Commission enquiring into pre-war illegal payments at Leeds; Chapman denies involvement

1921 Takes over as Huddersfield Town manager and helps the club to win the FA Cup (1922) and the first two of three consecutive First Division Championships

1925 Becomes manager of Arsenal, where he manages another Cup-winning team (1930) and two Championship teams (1930/31 and 1932/33)

1934 Dies while still in office at Arsenal, the club half-way through a run of three consecutive League Championships

Herbert Chapman raised the status of football club

management. At both Huddersfield and Arsenal he built teams which won three consecutive Championships, and his Arsenal team of the 1930s dominated English soccer in the manner of Liverpool in the 1980s. Despite his early death in 1934, Chapman won a considerable haul of major managerial honours: four League Championships and two more for the taking when interrupted by migration (at Huddersfield) and death (at Arsenal), two FA Cup wins and two other FA Cup Finals.

After a modest playing career Chapman displayed managerial showmanship, persuasion, discipline and innovation. He arrested spectator interest with gimmicky signings such as 5 ft 2 in Fanny Walden (later an international) at Northampton and Charles Buchan (£2000 plus £100 for each goal) at Arsenal. He successfully persuaded the London Passenger Transport Board to change the name of the Gillespie Road tube station to 'Arsenal'. A regular churchgoer, he commanded authority, and the inter-war period became the 'Chapman era'. His innovations included

HERBERT CHAPMAN
A legend in British football, Herbert Chapman's reputation is for building the Huddersfield and Arsenal teams that each won the League Championship three times in a row. His style was a strange blend of solid authority and innovative thinking. Although never really a 'tracksuit manager', he thought seriously about team tactics and individual skills.

experiments with a white ball, rubber-studded boots, all-weather pitches and floodlights, but his biggest impact was tactically. He was one of the instigators of the 'stopper centre-half' system to deal with the new offside law. At Arsenal he paid big fees to attract players like Alex James (£9000), David Jack (£11000) and Wilf Copping (£6000), but he also signed players such as Eddie Hapgood and Cliff Bastin for bargain fees.

A bust of Chapman was erected in the entrance hall at Arsenal. He is also the subject of a biography by Stephen Studd and a poem, 'The Lost Captain', by Thomas Moult.

CHARITY SHIELD

The FA Charity Shield competition was introduced in 1908, when League Champions Manchester United played Southern League Champions Queen's Park Rangers at Stamford Bridge. This format, Football League Champions against Southern League Champions, was used for the next four years, but the FA refused to sanction the game in 1913 (and again in 1923) because they considered the FA Cup Final so unsporting.

In the 1920s it was common for a team chosen from Amateurs to play a team of Professionals, and the games were evenly balanced. In 1920 Spurs (Second Division Champions) lost to West Bromwich (First Division Champions), and in 1927 Cup winners Cardiff City beat crack amateurs Corinthians 2-1. In 1928 the Shield settled into the more familiar contest between FA Cup winners and League Champions. In post-war years this has been interrupted on five occasions: when Spurs (1961), Arsenal (1971) and Liverpool (1986) won the 'double'; in 1950, when two representative teams were chosen from summer touring parties; and in 1972 when Manchester City (fourth in Division 1) and Aston Villa (Division 3 champions) took up an invitation. Although the FA Cup winners beat the League Champions in both 1921 and 1922, the League Champions have won far more of the games.

Since 1959 the game has been played as a curtain-raiser at the start of the season. In the 1967 game Tottenham Hotspur goalkeeper Pat Jennings scored a goal against Manchester United at Old Trafford with a clearance from his own penalty area. The contest was switched to Wembley in 1974 in a match (decided by penalties) in which Keegan (Liverpool) and Bremner (Leeds) were sent off for fighting.

The neutral setting of Wembley has helped to attract large crowds and raise extra money for charity, for instance the record 92,500 to see the 1979 Liverpool-Arsenal game, and the FA reverted to a system of sharing the trophy (six months each) in the event of a draw. Liverpool have a record 13 wins (including shares of the trophy), followed by Manchester United (10). Liverpool have contested the Shield 16 times since 1964.

CHARITY SHIELD

Year	Winners	Runners-up	Score
1908	Manchester United	Queen's Park Rangers	1-1
	Manchester United	Queen's Park Rangers	4-0
1909	Newcastle United	Northampton Town	2-0
1910	Brighton and Hove Albion	Aston Villa	1-0
1911	Manchester United	Swindon Town	8-4
1912	Blackburn Rovers	Queen's Park Rangers	2-1
1913	Professionals	Amateurs	7-2
1920	West Bromwich Albion	Tottenham Hotspur	2-0
1921	Tottenham Hotspur	Burnley	2-0
1922	Huddersfield Town	Liverpool	1-0
1923	Professionals	Amateurs	2-0
1924	Professionals	Amateurs	3-1
1925	Amateurs	Professionals	6-1
1926	Amateurs	Professionals	6-3
1927	Cardiff City	Corinthians	2-1
1928	Everton	Blackburn Rovers	2-1

Year	Winner	Runner-up	Score
1929	Professionals	Amateurs	3-0
1930	Arsenal	Sheffield Wednesday	2-1
1931	Arsenal	West Bromwich Albion	1-0
1932	Everton	Newcastle United	5-3
1933	Arsenal	Everton	3-0
1934	Arsenal	Manchester City	4-0
1935	Sheffield Wednesday	Arsenal	1-0
1936	Sunderland	Arsenal	2-1
1937	Manchester City	Sunderland	2-0
1938	Arsenal	Preston North End	2-1
1948	Arsenal	Manchester United	4-3
1949	Portsmouth	Wolverhampton Wanderers	1-1*
1950	England World Cup XI	FA Canadian Tour Team	4-2
1951	Tottenham Hotspur	Newcastle United	2-1
1952	Manchester United	Newcastle United	4-2
1953	Arsenal	Blackpool	3-1
1954	Wolverhampton Wanderers	West Bromwich Albion	4-4*
1955	Chelsea	Newcastle United	3-0
1956	Manchester United	Manchester City	1-0
1957	Manchester United	Aston Villa	4-0
1958	Bolton Wanderers	Wolverhampton Wanderers	4-1
1959	Wolverhampton Wanderers	Nottingham Forest	3-1
1960	Burnley	Wolverhampton Wanderers	2-2*
1961	Tottenham Hotspur	FA XI	3-2
1962	Tottenham Hotspur	Ipswich Town	5-1
1963	Everton	Manchester United	4-0
1964	Liverpool	West Ham United	2-2*
1965	Manchester United	Liverpool	2-2*
1966	Liverpool	Everton	1-0
1967	Manchester United	Tottenham Hotspur	3-3*
1968	Manchester City	West Bromwich Albion	6-1
1969	Leeds United	Manchester City	2-1
1970	Everton	Chelsea	2-1
1971	Leicester City	Liverpool	1-0
1972	Manchester City	Aston Villa	1-0
1973	Burnley	Manchester City	1-0
1974	Liverpool	Leeds United	1-1**
1975	Derby County	West Ham United	2-0
1976	Liverpool	Southampton	1-0
1977	Liverpool	Manchester United	0-0*
1978	Nottingham Forest	Ipswich Town	5-0
1979	Liverpool	Arsenal	3-1
1980	Liverpool	West Ham United	1-0
1981	Aston Villa	Tottenham Hotspur	2-2*
1982	Liverpool	Tottenham Hotspur	1-0
1983	Manchester United	Liverpool	2-0
1984	Everton	Liverpool	1-0
1985	Everton	Manchester United	2-0
1986	Everton	Liverpool	1-1*
1987	Everton	Coventry City	1-0
1988	Liverpool	Wimbledon	2-1
1989	Liverpool	Arsenal	1-0
1990	Liverpool	Manchester United	1-1*

*trophy shared ** won on penalties

CHARITY SHIELD

Holding the Charity Shield is Liverpool manager Bill Shankly. This particular win for Liverpool came in 1974 when they beat Leeds United on penalties following a 1-1 drawn match. The game was noted, and marred, by the sending off of Bremner (Leeds) and Keegan (Liverpool) who took off their shirts as they left the pitch. This was interpreted by the FA as unnecessary petulance and the players were charged with bringing football into disrepute. In the 1970s, Leeds v Liverpool matches were never the friendliest, and the rather acrimonious match was a sign of the times.

CHARLES, John

1931 Born in Swansea

1947 Joins Leeds United as a 15-year-old

1949 Makes first-team debut

1950 At the age of 18 years 71 days he becomes the youngest player to win a Welsh cap

1956 Helps Leeds win promotion to the First Division

1957 Top scorer in First Division with 38 goals; transferred to Juventus for £65000

1962 Returns to Leeds; joins Roma for £70000

1963 Transferred to Cardiff City

1966 Ends League career

John Charles was supremely gifted, almost unfairly so. At 6 ft 2 in and nearly 14 stone he was a magnificent physical specimen, and unlike many men of his size his talent was also enormous. His touch was sensitive, his control precise, his finishing decisive; but most of all he was a master in the air.

Originally on Swansea Town's ground staff, Charles was signed by Leeds United as an amateur when he was 15. By 17 he was in the first team at centre-half and within a year he had won the first of 38 Welsh caps. In the 1952/3 season Leeds experimented with him at centre-forward where he scored 27 goals in 30 matches. The following season he was the League's top marksman with 42 goals, which is still a club record. In 1956 Charles helped Leeds to the Second Division Championship.

The following year Juventus broke the British transfer record with £65000 to lure Charles to Turin, where he enjoyed the five best seasons of his career. Playing alongside Boniperti (Italy) and Sivori (Argentina), he helped Juventus to three Italian League championships in the next four years in addition to 2 Italian Cups. In all he scored 93 goals in

JOHN CHARLES

John Charles lines up with team-mates Terry Medwin *(on his left)* **of Spurs and Colin Webster of Manchester United before a Wales match in the 1958 World Cup finals held in Sweden. Charles was then playing with Juventus. His stance in the picture does little to disguise the impression he gave on the field – a big man with an imposing presence. Oddly, it seems as if he was wearing brand-new boots for this game, presumably not fearful of blisters on the big day. Wales, during their only appearance in the finals, did well, drawing three matches, beating the Hungarians and losing only 1-0 to Brazil (eventual winners) to be eliminated.**

155 League games for Juventus, a staggering record in the ultra-defensive Italian League.

In 1962 he returned briefly to Leeds before going back to Italy with Roma. The old dash was gone, however, and he finished his League career with Cardiff alongside his brother Mel, also Welsh international.

Throughout his career Charles was never sent off or even cautioned. He had a lovely temperament so much so that the Italians christened him 'Il Buon Gigante', ('the gentle giant'). A giant he truly was, the greatest Welsh player of all time.

CHARLTON ATHLETIC

Founded 1905

Joined League 1921 (Div.3 S)

Honours Div. 3 (S) Champions 1929, 1935; FA Cup Winners 1947

Ground The Valley

Charlton Athletic may now be typecast as gutsy little survivors against all odds, but there was a time when they held their own among England's top clubs and were second only to Arsenal in the London pecking order. That was in the 1930s when the 'Valiants', having spent an inauspicious first decade in the League, suddenly assumed new stature.

Under the shrewd management of Jimmy Seed they rose from the Third to the First Division in successive seasons, and missed the Championship by only four points in 1936/37, their first campaign in the top flight. Thus established, even the Second World War did not shatter their momentum and they reached the FA Cup Finals of 1946 and 1947, losing first to Derby County and beating Burnley in the second. Throughout this era, and into the 1950s, the most notable playing personality was red-head Sam Bartram, often described as the finest 'keeper never to play for England.

In 1957, Seed having departed, Charlton were relegated, and it was to be 31 years before they climbed back. In between came a 15-year stay in the Second Division, which saw distinguished service from the likes of South African strikers Eddie Firmani (who also did a stint in the 'boss's chair') and Stuart Leary, followed by two short spells in Division Three. The 1980s brought fundamental change. With the big clubs taking an ever higher percentage of fans, Charlton struggled to make ends meet, and in 1985 they left the Valley, that vast concrete amphitheatre, to become tenants of Crystal Palace. The admirable Lennie Lawrence, manager since 1982, contrived success on a shoestring and took his side into the First Division, where he pulled off a series of eleventh-hour escapes before the 'Valiants' finally dropped in 1990. The following year saw a planned return to the Valley, but the need for economy remained urgent.

CHARLTON ATHLETIC

21 September 1985, and a sad day at The Valley, home of Charlton Athletic since 1920 (with one short break), when spectators were allowed to take home pieces of the pitch as souvenirs. The reason for this odd behaviour was the end of Charlton's occupation of the famous old ground and their move to Selhurst Park and a sharing scheme with south London neighbours Crystal Palace. The move was down to financial pressures. Ironically, the site was left undeveloped and the Valiants were able to prepare to return there in 1991. For the record, Charlton finished at the ground with a 2-0 win over Stoke City, a result that contributed to their winning promotion from the Second Division in 1985/86.

CHARLTON, Bobby

1937 Born in Ashington, Northumberland, a member of Milburn footballing clan.

1954 Signs for Manchester United

1956 Scores twice on debut, against Charlton Athletic

1957 Wins first club honour, a League Championship medal

1958 February – survives Munich air crash; April – scores against Scotland as he wins first of record 106 England caps; May – picks up second successive FA Cup runners-up medal

1963 Helps United beat Leicester City to become Wembley winners at last

1965 Shows brilliant form as 'Red Devils' take first of two League Championships in three years

1966 Plays major role in England's World Cup victory; English and European Footballer of the Year

1968 Skippers United to European Cup glory, scoring twice in final against Benfica

1973 April – bows out of Old Trafford after scoring 247 goals in 754 games; samples management with Preston North End

1974 Comes out of retirement to boost his side on the pitch

1975 Leaves Deepdale after disagreement with board over transfer policy

1983 Short spell as caretaker boss of Wigan, of which he was a director

1984 Joins Manchester United board, combining the work with his soccer schools for youngsters

Bobby Charlton possessed a sublime talent, and those who witnessed him at his peak were privileged indeed. One of sport's most graceful movers, he was blessed with a pulverising shot, a thrilling body-swerve and an ability to pass the ball over long distances with devastating accuracy. As one of

BOBBY CHARLTON

As the legend of Bobby Charlton grows with the telling – and nobody deserves a place in history more than Charlton – so certain aspects of this play and character are remembered ahead of others. Yes, he was a sweet striker of the ball, and yes, he was the perfect gentleman on and off the pitch. But he was also a fighter, a team player and a man who hated losing. This picture, in a Manchester United shirt towards the end of his career, is just as typical of him as the ones where his left leg is raised in the perfectly balanced shooting posture and in which his appearance is both calm and composed.

Manchester United's 'Busby Babes', he was an inside-forward who played with a carefree exuberance which was to vanish forever when he took on extra responsibility in the wake of the Munich disaster. Then, for a time, he became a left-winger and there are those who reckon that was his most effective position.

But most shrewd judges agree that Charlton realised his full potential only as a deep-lying schemer, a more demanding role in which he achieved his most spectacular successes with club and country. There were many majestic international performances as a record 49 England goals would suggest yet it was his breathtaking combination with fellow Old Trafford greats George Best and Denis Law which will linger longest in the memory.

A self-effacing man, he was an idol without the proverbial feet of clay and was loved the world over. He remains the British game's finest international ambassador.

CHARLTON, Jack

1935 Born in Ashington, Northumberland

1952 Turns professional with Leeds United his only club as a player

1956 Helps Leeds win promotion to Division 1

1957 Plays for Football League

1960 Charlton's efforts can't keep Leeds in top flight

1964 Displays dominant form as United top Division 2

1965 Disappointment of FA Cup Final defeat by Liverpool is offset by winning first of 35 England caps, against Scotland at Wembley

1966 Plays crucial part in England's World Cup triumph

1967 Footballer of the Year

1968 Helps Leeds win League Cup and European Fairs Cup

1969 Adds League Championship medal to his collection

1971 A second European Fairs Cup triumph

1972 Finally pockets an FA Cup winner's medal, two days short of 37th birthday

1973 Retires as player to become Middlesbrough manager

1974 Manager of the Year as Boro' win Division 2 title

1977 Takes over at Sheffield Wednesday

1980 Leads 'Owls' up to Division 2; later narrowly misses promotion to top flight

1984 Moves on to Newcastle United

1985 Shocks 'Magpies' by resigning on eve of new season following criticism over sale of Chris Waddle

1986 Appointed Republic of Ireland boss

1988 Charlton's side reach the European Championship Finals . . .

1990 . . . then top that as World quarter-finalists

Bobby Charlton was elected Footballer of the Year in 1966. He was succeeded 12 months later by his brother Jack. It was yet another outstanding

JACK CHARLTON English born – he played for England in the 1966 World Cup Final – Jack Charlton has probably received most adulation from fans in the Republic of Ireland. His achievements with a small pool of players are well chronicled, but the key to his success is harder to discover. Perhaps it was his refreshing, honest approach that won the trust of his team; he frequently prefers to go fishing to watching soccer . . . and says as much. He is pictured here with Liverpool's John Aldridge during the 1988 European Championships. Ironically Aldridge might be counted as one of Jack's failures, seemingly playing less well at international than club level.

achievement by two members of a remarkable family. And it was in the then relatively unfamiliar role of speech-making that two brothers underlined the contrast in temperament which is almost a denial of their kinship.

Bobby spoke well, but Jack's speech was more memorable. Bobby was warm and sincere; Jack was no less sincere, but he was different. Unlike his brother he has never paid much account to tact. Two years older, he remains independent and stubborn.

Tall and bonily hard, Jack Charlton made no pretence at being a graceful footballer, but no defender won the ball more consistently in the air or sent it further from the danger area. And there was plenty of skill concealed in his apparent clumsiness. He could cope with tight situations and his passing was often surprisingly accomplished. The turning point in Charlton's career came in 1963 when Leeds were in peril of being relegated to the Third Division. 'If you get your attitude right, there is no reason why you shouldn't play for England,' said Don Revie, the Leeds manager. Two years later Leeds were emerging as a major force and Charlton made his international debut.

When Jack and Bobby collapsed in each other's arms on the turf after England won the World Cup in 1966, the romance appeared to be complete. But all that Jack Charlton made of his playing career would be overshadowed by the remarkable success he achieved with the Republic of Ireland. After experiencing success with Middlesbrough and Sheffield Wednesday, then finding life more difficult with Newcastle, it looked as though Charlton had abandoned the game until his interest was sparked by an offer from Dublin. Within two years he had revitalised the Irish cause, before taking them, and himself, forward to greater glory than they had ever known before as player or manager.

CHELSEA

Founded 1905

Joined League 1905 (Div.2)

Honours Div.1 Champions 1955; Div 2 Champions 1984, 1989; FA Cup Winners 1970; League Cup Winners 1965; European Cup Winners' Cup 1971

Ground Stamford Bridge

For many years Chelsea were not taken entirely seriously; they were regarded with amused affection rather than awe or envy. There was no lack of ambition when they were formed by Gus Mears, specifically to play at the Stamford Bridge athletics stadium which he had recently acquired, but they soon gained a reputation for unpredictability. The glamour and, perhaps, some of the attitudes of the nearby West End of London became associated with the club. The team frequently boasted a galaxy of stars, but they combined effectively too rarely for any sustained success to be achieved.

A new era dawned when Ted Drake became manager in 1952. He replaced Chelsea's familiar symbol, the Pensioner, and built a hard-working journeyman side which won the League, albeit with a modest points total. He then placed his faith in 'Drake's Ducklings', the young players emerging from the club's prolific youth scheme, but too many of them failed to maintain their early progress and, when the goal-scoring genius of Jimmy Greaves was lost to Italy, relegation soon followed.

Tommy Docherty succeeded Drake in 1961 and the energetic team he fashioned from a new generation of home-produced talent won promotion at the first attempt. Chelsea became established as serious contenders for honours, but these stormy years yielded only one major trophy despite a number of near-misses and this exciting period ended in bitterness and recriminations. The thoughtful, measured approach of Dave Sexton, who took over in 1967, was rewarded by two cup

CHELSEA The old and the new at Chelsea. One of the problems experienced by top clubs is the ageing of one team and the blooding of a new; it never seems easy to make the transition. Chelsea's exciting side of the 1960s and 1970s faded away from being League Championship contenders around the years 1964-72 to a mostly Second Division outfit in the late 1970s and 1980s. Trying to bridge the gap were veteran John Hollins *(left)*, who returned to Stamford Bridge in 1983 at the age of 37, and 20-year-old Scottish winger Pat Nevin. In the season they played together, 1983/84, Chelsea won the Second Division Championship.

triumphs, but the club then became infected by complacency and by the time the signs of decline had been recognised, it was almost irreversible. Relegation coincided with a financial crisis which threatened Chelsea's very existence and they remained in the grip of a seemingly terminal malaise until the advent of a new owner, Ken Bates, in 1982. After a drop into the Third Division had been narrowly avoided, manager John Neal was given the means to recruit a side which restored the Blues' pride and reclaimed their place among English football's leading teams. Despite a brief return to Division 2 in 1988/89, the foundations of the club now appear to be sound, although a shadow does hang over the future of their traditional home.

CHESTER CITY

Founded 1884

Joined League 1931 (Div.3)

Honours None

Ground Moss Rose, Macclesfield

Chester have been 'small fry' throughout their Football League history, and with so much of their potential support being lost to the Merseyside giants, there is scant hope of impending advancement. Having sold their long-time home, Sealand Road, to developers in 1990, they embarked on a new era as guests of non-League Macclesfield, and their main claim to fame – offering Welsh centre-forwards Ron Davies and Ian Rush their professional baptisms – seems unlikely to be superseded in the immediate future.
After spending nearly three decades in Division 3 (N), the 'Cestrians' became founder members of Division 4 in 1958 and made several successful re-election applications before winning promotion in 1975. There followed seven years in the higher grade and four back in the basement before they rose again as runners-up in 1986.

Their most illustrious achievement was reaching the League Cup semi-final in 1975, when they lost 5-4 on aggregate to Aston Villa.

CHESTERFIELD

Founded 1866

Joined League 1899 (Div.2)

Honours Div.3 (N) Champions 1931, 1936; Div.4 Champions 1970, 1985

Ground Recreation Ground, Saltergate

Chesterfield, one of the oldest clubs in the Football League, have remained homely and small throughout their history, unable to emerge from the shadows of big-time competition at nearby Derby and Sheffield. Their first stint in the League ended with failure to secure re-election to the Second Division in 1909 and they had to wait until the Third (N) was formed in 1921 to gain re-entry.
This time they were in to stay and enjoyed some modest success, even tasting the excitement of a Second Division promotion battle in 1947. Eventually they finished fourth and failed to consolidate their standing, slipping back into the lower reaches.
Since then the 'Spireites' – whose tradition for discovering fine goalkeepers has produced England internationals Sam Hardy and Gordon Banks, among others – have divided their time between Divisions 3 and 4, with occasional silverware to reward their few loyal fans.

CHESTER REPORTS

In 1966, and again in 1982, Sir Norman Chester (1907-1986) was invited to chair committees investigating the state of British football. The eventual reports, published in 1968 and 1983, contain important recommendations, many of which were at first ignored but then eventually accepted by football's ruling bodies.
Sir Norman Chester – he was knighted in 1976 – was

a passionate football enthusiast from an unprivileged Manchester background. Son of a factory worker, he left school at 14, then took an external degree and embarked on a high-flying academic career. He became an expert on local government and public administration and was warden of Nuffield College, Oxford, when asked by Minister of Sport Dennis Howell to chair the 1966 enquiry. Two years later, after countless interviews, the 135-page report was published with 36 recommendations. They included: the establishment of a Football Levy Board to match that of horse-racing; a restructuring of the Football League into five divisions (two regional) of 100 clubs; the replacement of the retention-and-transfer system by fixed-term contracts with an option clause for both player and club; a new category of player to cover so-called 'amateurs' who receive limited payments; an overhaul of disciplinary committees; a fresh look at taxation; and a Director of Referees who could appoint top referees on a substantial retainer.
Chester's second study was commissioned by the Football League in 1982, when the grass-roots game was thriving but Football League clubs had a combined debt of around £37 million. Then a member of the Football Trust, Chester chaired a five-man committee which also included Jack Dunnett (Football League president), John Smith (Liverpool chairman), Cliff Lloyd (ex-PFA chairman) and Tony Boyce (Torquay United director). The final report, published in March 1983, again recommended a reduction of Division 1 clubs and regional lower divisions. The committee proposed a 20-club Division 1 (by the end of 1983/84) and four lower leagues, each of 12 clubs with a system of mini-series and play-offs. Other recommendations were to allow natural wastage of clubs to reduce the size of the Football League, to

permit home clubs to keep all receipts from League games, to allow the top non-League club automatic promotion, and to distribute a greater proportion of television money to the home club.

CLOUGH, Brian

1935 Born in Middlesbrough

1952 Turns professional with Middlesbrough

1959 October – first full England cap v Wales

1961 Signs for Sunderland

1962 Boxing Day – serious knee injury v Bury

1964 Plays for last time – injury forces him out

1965 Becomes manager of Hartlepool United, with Peter Taylor as assistant

1967 With Taylor, joins Derby County as manager

1972 Wins League Championship

1973 Clough and Taylor join Brighton

1974 Joins Leeds United – Taylor stays at Brighton; quits Leeds after 53 days

1975 January – becomes manager of Nottingham Forest

1978 Wins League Championship

1979 Wins European Cup, 1-0 v Malmo...

1980 ...and repeats the performance, 1-0 v SV Hamburg

1990 Wins Littlewoods (League) Cup Final, 1-0 v Oldham Athletic – Forest's fourth competition victory after five finals under Clough; Peter Taylor dies.

Clough played mostly in the Second Division, appearing in only three First Division matches for Sunderland. The injury that eventually ended his playing days was suffered

BRIAN CLOUGH
Brian Clough, with his right-hand man Peter Taylor appropriately positioned, on the bench during the 1979 European Cup Final in which their Nottingham Forest side beat Malmö 1-0 to secure the first of two successive victories in the competition. Clough often preferred casual wear to either the lounge suits or smart club tracksuits worn by other managers and coaches. While some accused him of posturing with such unconventional displays, few have found fault with Clough's desire to build good footballing sides.

after a hopeless chase for the ball on a slushy Roker Park. He scored 251 League goals in only 274 appearances and won several representative honours including two full England caps, playing centre-forward.

Clough is best known as a successful – and controversial – manager. His League Championship with Derby was a major surprise to the football world, as was his, and Peter Taylor's sudden departure from the club. Clough's Brighton sojourn was short-lived. He then joined Leeds United, at the time England's representatives in the European Cup. Poor results and disagreements with the players, among other reasons, saw Clough leave after only 53 days.

Nottingham Forest have enjoyed considerable success under Clough, with consistent League performances matched by regular Cup success. Clough's style has been built on bringing the best out of players who have sometimes not performed well for other managers. Outspoken and thriving on publicity, he is generally popular with the fans, although not always with administrators and directors. Reckoned by many to be the best manager England never

had, he was once offered the part-time managership of Wales. Out of football, but also in the public eye, he is active in politics and a champion of family life. His son, Nigel, plays for Nottingham Forest and has represented England.

CLYDE

Founded 1878

Joined League 1891 (Div.1)

Honours Scottish League Division 2 Champions 1905, 1952, 1957, 1962, 1973; Second Division Champions 1978, 1982; Scottish Cup Winners 1939, 1955, 1958

Ground Douglas Park

The Glasgow club's history is particularly distinguished by its three Scottish Cup victories, with the triumphs of 1955 and 1958 particularly renowned.

The first match of the Final against Celtic in 1955 was also the first Scottish Cup Final to be televised live. Clyde's stars of the era included internationals Tommy Ring and Harry Haddock. The club also performed notably in the late 1960s.

Sharing Partick Thistle's ground since 1986 has drained Clyde's vitality, and they were relegated to the Second Division in 1991. They hope to move to a new stadium in Cumbernauld in 1992 after a season in Hamilton.

CLYDEBANK

Founded 1965

Joined League 1966 (Div.2)

Honours Scottish League Second Division Champions 1976

Ground Kilbowie Park

Clydebank emerged from the failed attempt to move East Stirling to the town. They are a sprightly club both on and off the field. Clydebank possess an innovative streak and were pioneers in establishing a social club to generate revenue.

They employ a coach, not a manager. All important decisions are taken by the Steedman

family (Jack is president of the Scottish Football League) and a happy knack of finding gifted youngsters has usually kept the club buoyant in the First Division and, after transfer, solvent. The astoundingly talented Davie Cooper, later an internationalist with Rangers and Motherwell, was their most famous discovery. Clydebank were Scottish Cup semi-finalists in 1990.

COVENTRY CITY

Founded 1883

Joined League 1919 (Div.2)

Honours Div.2 Champions 1967; Div.3 (S) Champions 1936; Div.3 Champions 1964 FA Cup Winners 1987

Ground Highfield Road

Until the 1960s Coventry City hardly caught the eye. Then came a revolution which placed them among the most talked-about soccer phenomena of the decade and paved the way for a lengthy tenure in Division 1. Indeed, as the 1990s dawned, the Midlanders' top-flight longevity was exceeded by that of just three rivals, Arsenal, Everton and Liverpool.

After graduating from the Southern League, Coventry had made a faltering start in the senior competition, six seasons of Second Division travail ending with relegation in 1925. Under the guidance of Harry Storer and boosted by the marks-manship of Clarrie Bourton, they gained promotion in 1936 and retained their regained

COVENTRY CITY
Especially since Jimmy Hill's reign as Coventry City manager (1961-67), the club have placed great importance on a good relationship with their fans and the game at large. Their ambitions were well served by the popular partnership of George Curtis (left) and John Sillett who both coached and managed the team at various times. They are seen here flanking young Dave Bennett, a goal-scorer in City's memorable 1987 FA Cup Final victory over Tottenham Hotspur.

status until the early 1950s.

A drab period – enlivened by one victorious term in the newly created Fourth Division, and England caps for goalkeeper Reg Matthews – was ended emphatically by the arrival in 1961 of dynamic chairman Derrick Robbins and innovative manager Jimmy Hill. Together they transformed not only City's playing fortunes but also the club's entire approach to the business of selling football to the public. Given a new sky-blue strip with a nickname to match, Coventry came up with bright schemes – Sky Blue special trains, Sky Blue Radio, etc – which were often dismissed as gimmicks at the time but which were later copied by their competitors. The razzamatazz was matched by rapid progress on the field, with players such as 'keeper Bill Glazier, winger Ronnie Rees and, most influential of all, iron-man centre-half George Curtis – destined to become team boss and then managing director in the 1980s – being moulded into a side which, in 1967, claimed a place among the elite.

Since then, Coventry have waged more relegation battles than they would care to recall and, though they have finished as high as sixth, have more frequently been in the bottom half. Highfield Road has, however, seen some talented performers – notably midfielder Willie Carr and winger Tommy Hutchison in the 1970s, and forwards Cyrille Regis and David Speedie in the 1980s – and in 1987 extrovert manager John Sillett led the Sky Blues to their finest hour, FA Cup triumph over Tottenham. In 1990 former England star Terry Butcher took on the task of consolidating still further the club's top-flight tradition, initially in the role of player-manager.

COWDENBEATH

Founded 1881

Joined League 1905 (Div.2)

Honours Scottish Football League Division 2 Champions 1914, 1915, 1939

Ground Central Park

Cowdenbeath's last success in a national trophy went

unrecognised. They swashbuckled their way to the Division 2 title in 1939 with 120 goals, but in the reorganisation which followed the Second World War they were left in the lower Division.

The early 1930s had been good for the club and, as they held their own in Division 1, men like Jim Paterson and Alex Venters won Scotland caps. In general, though, spells in the top flight have been short.

Current Scotland defender Craig Levein received his first taste of senior football with Cowdenbeath before being sold to Hearts in 1983.

CREWE ALEXANDRA

Founded 1877

Joined League 1892 (Div.2)

Honours None

Ground Gresty Road

Crewe Alexandra may be a humble club – having spent all but four of their Football League seasons in the lowest available division – but no one can deny that they are born survivors. Since being formed by a group of railway workers in a pub, the 'Alex' have somehow managed to avoid the financial and footballing disasters which have befallen various of their contemporaries, and are now soldiering on into their second century.

One early and uncharacteristic highlight was an appearance in an FA Cup semi-final against Preston in 1888. Thus encouraged, Crewe became original members of Division 2, only to be outclassed and drop ignominiously out of the competition. Resurfacing in Division 3 (N) in 1921,

they henceforth usually managed to avoid the re-election zone but were naturals for Division 4 when it was created in 1958. Since then they have three times reached the Third Division until relegation in 1991.

CRUYFF, Johan

1947 Born in Amsterdam, Holland

1965 Senior debut for Ajax Amsterdam

1966 Debut for Holland v Hungary

1971 Voted European Footballer of the Year as Ajax win the European Cup...

1972 ...which they do again; top scorer in the competition (5 goals) and in the Dutch League (25 goals)

1973 Another European Cup victory; European Footballer of the year

again; joins ex-Ajax boss Rinus Michels at Barcelona for £922,300

1974 Captains his country in the World Cup Final and picks up another European Footballer of the Year award

1978 Announces retirement to concentrate on business

1979 Comes out of retirement to sign for Los Angeles Aztecs; receives NASL's Most Valuable Player award

1982 Returns to Ajax as player and then coach

1987 Guides his old team to Cup Winners' Cup victory

1989 Having taken his coaching skills to Barcelona, does the same for them

1991 Suffers mild heart attack; rest prescribed

A natural and consistent goal-scorer like Cruyff, blessed with breath-taking ball control, deadly acceleration and superb balance, would have flourished in any era. As it is, he was fortunate that his peak coincided with that of Dutch football, both at club and national team level, thus providing him with an international arena in which to display and perfect his talent. The success of Cruyff, and that of Ajax, Holland and indeed Feyenoord, are,

JOHAN CRUYFF
Johan Cruyff in a typically athletic stance in Holland's first-stage game against Argentina in the 1974 World Cup. He scored twice in the 4-0 victory as Holland won every match in their group, progressing ultimately to the Final where they lost to West Germany. Cruyff was the first Dutch player to be voted European Footballer of the Year. His association with Ajax Amsterdam, his first team, is well rooted. He was born near the ground and his mother worked as a cleaner there. He was recruited at the age of 10 and worked his way up through the youth system.

however, inextricably linked and the debt is a reciprocal one. He was surrounded by gifted players such as Neeskens, Krol and Rep, whose football intelligence was the key to the 'total football' practised in 1970s Holland – a tactical system so suited to Cruyff's versatility. His awareness of colleagues' positions, his vision and ability to hit accurate passes (much in evidence later in his career when he dropped deeper and wider) could unsettle even the best defences; to this must be added his prowess in front of goal (33 goals in 48 internationals, 215 League goals in Holland).

At times the questionable temperament of the tall, lean Dutchman threatened to undermine his ability, but he was able to command respect as a captain. His travels took him to North America, Spain and back to Holland where he played for old rivals Feyenoord Rotterdam before proving his talent in management.

CRYSTAL PALACE

Founded	1905
Joined League	1920 (Div.3)
Honours	Div.2 Champions 1979; Div.3 (S) Champions 1921
Ground	Selhurst Park

After a largely unremarkable history, Crystal Palace seem finally to be a club on the up. The surge which took them to the FA Cup Final in 1990 and then saw them consolidate with a fine First Division showing in the following campaign may have flattered to deceive; but somehow there is a solid look about the South Londoners these days. In Steve Coppell they have an intelligent, progressive manager, and with all the capital's bigger clubs being situated a comfortable distance from Selhurst Park there is undoubted potential for increased gates.

Palace made an auspicious start to their League life, topping the newly created Third Division in their first term. But they soon returned to the lowest level, there to remain until they won promotion from the Fourth Division in 1961 under the guidance of former Tottenham boss Arthur Rowe. The 1960s proved prosperous for the 'Eagles', as first Dick Graham and then Bert Head carried on Rowe's good work. In 1969 they tasted top-flight soccer for the first time, before plunging back to Division 3 with Malcolm Allison in the mid 1970s. Terry Venables effected a revival, taking the club back to the First Division, but most of the 1980s were spent in the Second before Coppell extricated them in 1989.

Star names have been few down the years, but players of note have included 1930s goal-poacher Peter Simpson, skilful centre-forward Johnny Byrne, who won an England cap as a Division 3 player in 1961, England left-back Kenny Sansom in the 1970s, and striker Ian Wright, a current leading light. Coppell is bold enough to back his judgement – witness his £1 million investment in 'unknown' Bristol Rovers

CRYSTAL PALACE The moment it nearly all came true for Crystal Palace, as substitute Ian Wright slides in to score his second goal of the 1990 FA Cup Final to put his side in front, 3-2. Unfortunately for Palace, opponents Manchester United fought back to 3-3, and won the replay 1-0, confirming the book-makers' view but dumbfounding a confident Wright who had told reporters, before the match, that he knew he was both going to score and to win a Cup winner's medal.

goalkeeper Nigel Martyn – and if he remains in office there may be bright times ahead for this less fashionable London outfit.

CULLIS, Stan

1915	Born Ellesmere Port, Cheshire
1934	Makes debut for Wolverhampton Wanderers
1938	Wins first of 12 England caps, v Scotland
1939	Losing FA Cup finalist, 1-4 v Portsmouth
1947	Appointed Wolves assistant manager
1948	Elevated to secretary-manager
1949	Leads Wolves to FA Cup win, 3-1 v Leicester City
1954	Wins Championship, Wolves' first...
1958	...again
1959	...and again
1960	Second FA Cup victory, 3-0 v Blackburn Rovers
1964	Leaves Wolves
1965	Appointed manager of Birmingham City
1970	Leaves Birmingham

Although he was relatively short – 5 ft 10 in – Stan Cullis was one of the finest centre-halves England have produced. An aggressive though stylish player with an ability to deliver piercing through balls, he won 12 caps but would have collected many more but for the Second World War.

It was as manager of Wolverhampton Wanderers, however, that he left his most indelible mark. A sergeant-major of a man, he was an autocrat whose confidence was absolute and whose criticism, it was suggested, could strip paint from 20 paces. He believed in the most direct route to goal, insisting that the ball should be hoisted into the opposition penalty area as swiftly as possible and kept there. Individual expression was frowned upon. 'Our forwards,' he said, 'are not encouraged to parade their ability in an ostentatious fashion.'

The tactics were condemned as 'kick and rush', although no-one could argue with their effectiveness. Wolves had their most prosperous times under Cullis, winning the First Division Championship three times in the 1950s, a record matched only by Matt Busby and Manchester United.

Cullis, like Busby, had the foresight to look beyond Britain's boundaries and it was he who brought Moscow Dynamo and Honved, two of Europe's best sides, to Molineux for famous floodlit matches in 1954.

STAN CULLIS There's something about the posed photograph that makes a player look so composed: clean kit, hair in place and the pitch often in peak condition (if the picture is for the pre-season publicity). Stan Cullis, however, tended to look like this most of the time. In the old Wolves kit, and at the old Molyneux Ground, this picture perfectly captures the man who gave so much to the club as player and manager.

After beating both, he claimed Wolves as the 'champions of the world'. It was a remark that threw down the gauntlet to the continent and would quickly lead to the creation of the European Cup.

CUP COMPETITIONS

Cliches abound at the mere mention of knock-out cup football. A 'one-off' with 'eleven men against eleven men' ensure that the 'magic of the cup' is what, after all, 'football is all about'. It probably is this natural sense of familiarity with cup football that makes it so popular. So popular, indeed, that numerous tournaments have been proposed and competed for over the years in a bid to kindle that so-called 'magic'.

In addition to thousands of local competitions that

exist up and down Britain, the professional game has not been slow in trying to introduce new, largely sponsored, tournaments to win a bit of interest and a bit of cash. In recent years the main intention seems to be to include teams who are otherwise disenfranchised by, for example, playing in the wrong division, being banned from Europe or generally not being good enough for the senior competitions.

The Watney Mann Invitation Cup (1970-73) was one of the first that is noted for its early use of penalties to decide finals. The Texaco Cup, followed by the Anglo-Scottish Cup were apparently well-intentioned attempts to bring English and Scottish teams into competition – but they faded away with poor gates and almost no national reporting.

The late eighties saw a handful of tournaments trying to bring the top English clubs, banned from Europe, into meaningful competition, and to give lesser clubs a contrived opportunity for a place at Wembley. But examples like the Screen Sport Super Cup for would-be European representatives (dead after one season) and the Leyland Daf Trophy (for Third and Fourth Division teams) never really captured the imagination.

CUP COMPETITIONS
Bobby Cram of Colchester United holds the Watney Cup aloft in 1971, following victory over West Bromwich Albion – 4-3 on penalties following a 4-4 draw. The modern plethora of domestic tournaments in addition to the big three of League, FA Cup and League Cup has been seen in some quarters as being to the detriment of football. However, who would want to deny smaller clubs, in particular, their moments of glory? Colchester, now out of the Football League, and Third Division WBA had theirs.

DALGLISH, Kenny

1951 Born in Glasgow

1970 Makes debut for Celtic

1971 Wins first Scottish cap, v Belgium at Aberdeen

1972 Plays leading role as Celtic win League and Cup double

1977 Joins Liverpool for a record £440,000, having helped the Scottish club lift a further seven major domestic trophies

1978 Scores only goal of European Cup Final against FC Bruges

1979 Footballer of the Year after performing brilliantly as Liverpool lift the first of five League Championships in six seasons

1981 Pockets the first of four consecutive League Cup winner's medals

1983 Footballer of the Year and players' Player of the Year

1984 Takes home his third European Cup winner's medal after 'Reds' beat Roma

1985 Succeeds Joe Fagan as Liverpool boss, continues as player

1986 Leads 'Reds' to League and FA Cup double and is named Manager of the Year; November — completes international career with 102nd cap, v Luxembourg at Hampden Park

1989 Liverpool win FA Cup in aftermath of Hillsborough disaster

1990 Third League title and Manager of the Year award in five campaigns in charge at Anfield; final senior appearance as player

1991 Stuns football world, and Liverpool in particular, by announcing 'retirement' with three months of season to go.

Throughout more than a century of British soccer, no man has assembled a catalogue of achievements to rival that of Kenny Dalglish. There may have been finer players – although not many – but none of them could point to

KENNY DALGLISH
Kenny Dalglish scoring the only goal of the 1978 European Cup Final, played at Wembley, when Liverpool beat Belgian side Bruges to retain the trophy. This goal was delicately chipped in over the advancing 'keeper from a difficult angle – it was also made to look quite simple. Darting runs, close skills and an ability to shield the ball were Dalglish's hallmarks as a player. As a manager he was better known, outside the club at least, for his steely exterior and curt comments.

a managerial record which remotely approaches the lustre of the single-minded Glaswegian's. The combination of two such honour-strewn careers puts Dalglish in a class of his own.

As a footballer he had shining natural talent, his game both aesthetically pleasing and exhilarating. After prodigious deeds with Celtic he headed for Anfield to fill the gap left by Kevin Keegan, and succeeded beyond even the Kop's wildest dreams. The goals flowed, and they were often spectacular, but they represented only the most superficial aspect of his value. His magnetic control, superb distribution and almost uncanny anticipation made him an all-rounder *par excellence*, though admittedly he did not always reproduce club form for his country.

As a manager Dalglish was very much his own man. After inheriting an excellent side, he proceeded to improve it with inspired excursions into the transfer market, and deserves monumental credit for enhancing the Liverpool tradition. A private, sometimes uncommunicative individual, he had the shrewdness, steel and flair to continue his phenomenal success into the next century had he not announced his retirement from football, citing stress as the major reason for his decision.

DARLINGTON

Founded 1883

Joined League 1921 (Div.3 N)

Honours Div.3 (N) Champions 1925; Div. 4 Champions 1991

Ground Feethams

It hardly seemed like a shot in the arm at the time, but Darlington's demotion from the Football League in 1989 might have been just what the 'Quakers' needed. As champions of the Vauxhall Conference, they returned from the wilderness at the first attempt and then lifted the Fourth Division crown in 1991.

It was, at any rate, nice to win something, even if it wasn't a senior competition, after a history of struggle in the shadow of their more illustrious north-eastern neighbours. Apart from two Second Division seasons in the 1920s, Darlington have spent all their time in the lower reaches, grappling with the economic difficulties which face all small clubs.

Highlights have been few, two of the brightest

being in the FA Cup. In 1911, while still amateurs, they reached the last 16, and repeated the feat in 1958 thanks to a 4-1 thrashing of Chelsea in a replay at Feethams. During the 1980s the club's most positive spell came during the managerial era of Cyril Knowles, who inspired their promotion in 1985.

DEAN, Dixie

1907 Born in Birkenhead

1924 Makes debut for Tranmere Rovers

1925 Moves to Everton for £3000

1926 Fractures skull in motorcycle accident; makes rapid recovery

1927 Scores twice for England on international debut v Wales

1928 Breaks League

scoring record with 60 goals in season as Everton win title

1932 Helps Everton to another Championship

1933 Scores at Wembley as Everton win FA Cup, 3-0 against Manchester City

1936 Passes Steve Bloomer's League record of 352 goals

1938 Joins Notts County

1939 Ends English career, having scored 379 goals in 437 games, and signs for Sligo Rovers

1940 Retires to keep a pub in Chester

1980 Dies at Goodison Park

William Ralph Dean - how he hated the nickname Dixie, preferring the more ordinary Bill - was a goal-scorer supreme whose memory will be revered, especially on Merseyside, as long as football is played.

He began his career as a teenage prodigy with Tranmere Rovers, but such was his talent that an early departure from Prenton Park was inevitable. He duly crossed the river to Goodison and rapidly established a well-nigh peerless reputation. Tall and immensely powerful, Dean was majestic in the air and became Everton's main attraction during one of their most successful periods. Dean's golden season was 1927/28, when he notched his record-breaking 60 goals, sealing the achievement - which is unlikely to be emulated - with a hat-trick in the final

DIXIE DEAN William Ralph Dean – Dixie – kicking in before a match. Much has been said about Dean's prowess as a player, but it's worth pointing out that he was also a great friend to football after his retirement – ever willing to speak at events, to give advice to youngsters and simply to shake hands with scores of admirers who wanted to say they had met the great Dixie Dean. And 'great' he was.

game against Arsenal.

The Everton star was also a lethal performer for England, scoring 18 times in a mere 16 games, and it's a mystery that he was not selected more often. On retirement he kept a pub in Chester, and later became a popular after-dinner speaker. It was somehow fitting that he should die at the home of his beloved Everton, shortly after watching a derby clash with Liverpool.

DERBY COUNTY

Founded 1884

Joined League 1888 (founder member)

Honours Div.1 Champions 1972, 1975; Div.2 Champions 1912, 1915, 1969, 1987; Div.3 (N) Champions 1957; FA Cup Winners 1946

Ground Baseball Ground

From the early days, Derby County's history has been dramatic. Although a founder member of the Football League, early achievements were in the FA Cup, with eight semi-finals in 13 seasons (1895-1909). The team reached three finals during this period but all were lost, including the record 6-0 defeat by Bury in 1903.

George Jobey, manager from 1925 to 1941, assembled internationals such as Sammy Crooks, Jack Barker, Tom Cooper, Jack Bowers, Hughie

Gallacher and 'Dally' Duncan, but second place (twice) was the best League position in the inter-war years. The momentum was broken by the Second World War and FA suspensions after the discovery of illegal payments.

On a wave of euphoria Derby County won the first post-war FA Cup Final, beating Charlton 4-1 after extra-time. The stars were inside-forwards Raich Carter and Peter Doherty, while centre-forward Jack Stamps scored two goals in the Final. Derby were one of the country's top teams in the late 1940s, paying record transfer fees for Billy Steel and Johnny Morris, but a slump in the

DERBY COUNTY League Champions for 1974/75, Derby County, parading the trophy at their Baseball Ground. Perhaps distance lends enchantment, but the Derby side of the period did seem to be an especially attractive one. In the photograph are *(left to right)* young Welsh international Rod Thomas, veteran 'keeper Colin Boulton, striker Roger Davies and stalwart campaigner Kevin Hector. Glimpsed between Boulton and Davies is a solid-looking Francis Lee, capped 27 times by England.

early 1950s saw them drop from Division 1 to Division 3 (N) in three seasons.

Derby returned to the First Division in 1969 under the management of Brian Clough and Peter Taylor with new signings including Roy McFarland, Dave Mackay, John McGovern, John O'Hare, Alan Hinton and Willie Carlin. Three more important signings - Colin Todd, Terry Hennessey and Archie Gemmill - finally brought the League Championship. Three years later, under

new manager Dave Mackay, there was a second Championship success. Colin Boulton, Ron Webster, David Nish, Peter Daniel and Henry Newton all made important contributions, and goals came from Bruce Rioch, Roger Davies, Francis Lee and, inevitably, Kevin Hector, who made a record 581 appearances (201 goals) for the club.

The club's low point came in the centenary season (1984), when relegation to Division 3 coincided with a winding-up petition from the Inland Revenue and seven High Court appearances. A rescue package, involving the Maxwell family headed by publisher Robert Maxwell, preceded success in the late 1980s, when manager Arthur Cox achieved two promotions and signed internationals such as Englishmen Peter Shilton and Mark Wright and Welshman Dean Saunders.

DERBY MATCHES

Such was the importance of one particular horse-race - the Derby Stakes at Epsom - that the name 'derby' came to be applied to any

sporting contest of equal note. A derby game is often one of the most important of the year, and games between teams from the same city (local derbies) are the most hotly contested of all. There is always extra tension, because rival supporters are likely to meet in the days surrounding the match.

The Glasgow games between Celtic and Rangers are legendary. The two teams have met in 23 major finals (10 Scottish League Cup and 13 Scottish FA Cup) and the honours are even in those games. An extra occasion was the 1909 Scottish Cup Final, when the trophy was withheld after two drawn games and crowd trouble. A 1905 League game was also abandoned, and more recently there was a riot after the 1980 Rangers-Celtic Scottish Cup Final. Extra tension emanates from the religious backcloth to these games, Celtic being associated with the Catholic faith and Rangers having been reluctant to sign Catholic players until the late 1980s.

Everton-Liverpool League games have been frequent since 1962, when

Liverpool returned to Division 1. In the late 1980s Liverpool passed Everton in number of wins, and big Cup games have definitely favoured Liverpool, who won all three post-war FA Cup semi-finals (but lost in 1906). The most controversial was in 1977, when Bryan Hamilton (Everton) appeared to have scored an Everton winner in the first match only to see it disallowed. Surprisingly, the first Everton-Liverpool League Cup meeting was as late as 1984, when a goalless Milk Cup Final ended with the crowd chanting 'Merseyside, Merseyside...' Liverpool won the replay 1-0. In the late 1980s they met in two FA Cup Finals; Liverpool won 3-1 in 1986 and 3-2 in 1989, and Ian Rush scored twice in each final.

Results in Manchester derbies (City v United) are tipped slightly in favour of United. There have been almost as many away wins as home wins. The Manchester clubs haven't emulated the Merseyside Wembley achievements, but they have met in the semi-final of both the FA Cup and the League Cup. City beat United in the

1926 FA Cup semi-final, and won a thrilling League Cup semi-final in 1970, a late goal by Mike Summerbee taking the final score to 4-3. United won the only Charity Shield meeting, in 1956. Perhaps the most dramatic game was the last of the 1973/74 season, when the only goal was scored by City's Denis Law, ironically an ex-United player. Although the crowd invaded the pitch and the game was abandoned, the 1-0 result stood and United were relegated to Division 2. Big goal-scorers In Manchester derby games include Joe Hayes and Francis Lee (10 each for City), Bobby Charlton (9 for United), Colin Bell (8 for City) and Brian Kidd (5 for United and 3 for City).

Another evenly balanced fixture is the north London derby between Arsenal and Tottenham Hotspur. The last League game of 1970/71, at White Hart Lane, ranks highly, a late goal by Arsenal's Ray Kennedy ensuring that the League Championship and FA Cup double was achieved.

The north-east has had its fair share of exciting derby matches, none more

DERBY MATCHES The Liverpool v Everton derby match has been dominated by the Reds (Liverpool) over the past two decades, especially when it mattered in cup finals and important League meetings. But at least when the Blues had Gary Lineker leading the attack there was hope. Here he is scoring past Liverpool 'keeper Bruce Grobbelaar, at Anfield, in Everton's 2-0 win early in 1986.

staggering than Sunderland's 9-1 win at Newcastle United in 1908 in which Sunderland scored eight second-half goals in less than 30 minutes. The 1989/90 season ended with Sunderland (sixth) winning a vital play-off game 2-0 at Newcastle (third) after the first leg was drawn. Although Sunderland lost to Swindon in the play-off final, they were promoted to Division 1 following Swindon's subsequent failure to be promoted for disciplinary reasons.

Aston Villa have slightly the better record in games against Birmingham City, and Sheffield United have the edge on Sheffield

Wednesday though there were 11 seasons without a League game before 1990/91. Derby matches between Bristol Rovers and Bristol City achieved new significance in 1989/90 when the clubs finished first and second in Division 3, but by that time Rovers had moved to Bath.

Local derbies don't come any more local than that at Selhurst Park in 1989. The opponents, Crystal Palace and Charlton Athletic, were sharing the same ground at the time. In 1987/88 the Football League included four Welsh clubs and all four were in Division 4, although Wrexham were some distance from the others. For Bradford City and Bradford Park Avenue the record is now complete, Park Avenue showing one more League win than City. And for Nottingham Forest and Notts County rivalry has been resurrected by County's promotion to Division 1 in 1991.

The first 38 Wembley FA Cup Finals failed to produce an all-London local derby, but the next 16 finals compensated with four such occasions. Tottenham Hotspur were involved as Cup-winners in

1967 (against Chelsea) and 1982 (against Queen's Park Rangers), and West Ham United beat Fulham (1975) and Arsenal (1980).

The concept of a local derby could be applied to the international arena. A Scotland fan's description of England as the 'auld enemy' highlights a fierce rivalry of neighbours which spills over into political history. A more obvious example of political rivalry was that of Germany when the Berlin Wall divided East from West, and the game between East Germany and West Germany in the 1974 World Cup finals was a unique occasion. Vital World Cup qualifying games between Holland and Belgium have added something extra to games between these bordering countries. In other areas of the world, rivalry has at times been so belligerent that countries have been deliberately kept apart in World Cup draws.

There are so many club rivalries outside the British Isles that it is impossible to begin to compile a comprehensive list. In the Italian League three pairs of old rivals now share grounds - AC Milan and Inter-Milan (Milan),

Juventus and Torino (Turin) and Roma and Lazio (Rome). In other countries also, inter-city rivalry has a national profile to compare with that of Scotland's Rangers and Celtic. Examples that spring to mind are FK Austria and Rapid Vienna in Austria, and Feyenoord and Ajax in Holland.

DISASTERS

The biggest soccer disaster in the world may have been the crush in the Lenin Stadium in Luzhniki Park, Moscow, on 20 October 1982, at the end of a UEFA Cup second-round·first-leg match between Spartak Moscow and Haarlem of Holland. Some post-*glasnost* accounts estimate that 340 people were killed, although the official Soviet figure put the number at 69. The exact number may be impossible to determine. When spectators streamed towards the exits in one part of the ground they found all but one door closed, and the situation was aggravated by a last-minute Spartak goal and the icy conditions.

Excluding the Moscow crush, the biggest soccer

disaster was that at Lima, Peru, on 24 May 1964, a few minutes before the end of a Peru-Argentina Olympic qualifying tie. The referee disallowed a Peruvian goal, a riot broke out, police stepped in with tear-gas and 301 were killed and 500 injured in a rush for the exits.

Britain's worst football disaster occurred at the Hillsborough Stadium, Sheffield, on 15 April 1989, when 95 people were killed and 170 injured. The tragedy happened at the start of the FA Cup semi-final between Liverpool and Nottingham Forest, when a gate was opened to admit Liverpool supporters into the overcrowded Leppings Lane enclosure at the smaller end of the ground and spectators at the front of the stand were crushed or suffocated. South Yorkshire police were heavily criticised in the resultant enquiry, but the decisions to stage the game at Hillsborough and to allocate the Leppings Lane end to Liverpool supporters were also considered culpable *(see Taylor Report)*.

Sixty-six people were killed and over 140 injured

at Ibrox Park, Glasgow, on 2 January 1971. The occasion was a Rangers-Celtic Scottish League derby, and Celtic appeared to have won the game with a goal two minutes from time. Then, as people began to leave, Colin Stein equalised for Rangers. Reactions to the roar of the crowd - some turned round to see what was happening - caused the fatal crush on Stairway 13. Eventually, the Safety of Sports Grounds Act (1975) was introduced as a result of the enquiry into the 1971 Ibrox disaster.

On the last day of the 1984/85 season, a stand burned down in five minutes at Bradford City's Valley Parade ground. Fifty-five people were killed and 210 injured, either by the fire or the crush to get out. The fire started after 40 minutes of the game between Bradford City and Lincoln City, when a crowd of 12,000 were present to celebrate Bradford City winning the Division 3 Championship. An enquiry by Mr Justice Popplewell investigated the Bradford City fire and a riot at Birmingham City's ground the same day (11 May 1985). Popplewell recommended numerous safety measures and membership cards for supporters. He found that the Bradford fire was caused by the accidental lighting of debris below the floorboards of the stand.

On 29 May 1985, less than three weeks after the Bradford fire, 38 people died and 454 were injured in a crush inside the Heysel Stadium, Brussels, Belgium. Forty minutes before the start of the European Cup Final between Juventus and Liverpool, fans of the English side broke down a flimsy fence that was holding them in their overcrowded section of the ground. They overpowered the Belgian police and charged at spectators in a supposedly neutral area. A wall collapsed and people were suffocated or crushed. All but seven of the dead were Italian. FIFA reacted by banning English clubs

from European competition indefinitely. The ban was lifted in 1990 for all English clubs except Liverpool. In 1989, 14 Liverpool fans were given prison sentences in a Belgian court for their part in the Heysel Stadium disaster.

DISASTERS One response to the 1989 Hillsborough tragedy, when supporters died through being crushed against protective fencing (i.e. protecting the field from invasion), was the removal of similar barriers from around other grounds. This is the scene at Tottenham's White Hart Lane three days after the Hillsborough events. Such were the appalling scenes at the Sheffield ground that Spurs acted before being instructed to.

On 14 May 1949 a plane carrying back the Torino club from a game in Lisbon crashed into a hillside at Superga, near Turin, Italy. Among the 28 dead were 17 players – including eight internationals – and the club's manager, trainer and coach. Torino's youth team completed the season, and opponents sportingly fielded youth teams too. Torino's youths won all four games to complete four successive Italian League Championships.

On February 1958 the aircraft bringing the Manchester United party home from a European Cup tie against Red Star (Belgrade) crashed on take-off at Munich Airport. Eight players – Geoff Bent, Roger Byrne, Eddie Colman, Duncan Edwards, Mark Jones, David Pegg, Tommy Taylor and Bill Whelan – died as a result of the crash. Eight journalists, including ex-England goalkeeper Frank Swift, and seven others were also killed. The 20 survivors included seriously injured manager Matt Busby and two players, Jackie Blanchflower and John Berry, who never played again. Two books deal specifically with the Munich disaster: *The Day a Team Died* written by Frank

Taylor, a journalist who survived the crash, and *The Team that Wouldn't Die* by John Roberts.

At least four other major air disasters have involved football teams: 1961 eight players from Green Cross (Chile) were killed on Las Lastimas mountain; in 1969 19 players and officials of The Strongest (Bolivia) were killed in the Andes; in 1979 Pakhtator Tashkent (Soviet Union) lost 17 in an internal flight; and on 9 December 1987 Alianza Lima (Peru) lost all 34 players, officials, wives and supporters on board.

Seventy-four people were killed in a disaster at the River Plate Stadium, Buenos Aires, Argentina, on 23 June 1968. The crowd stampeded for the exits after lighted newspaper torches were thrown by spectators.

Seventy-one spectators died in Katmandu in 1988, when a hailstorm caused crowd panic during a game between teams from Nepal and Bangladesh.

The scenes of the two worst British disasters, Hillsborough and Ibrox Park, figure in other tragic incidents earlier this century. At Hillsborough, on 4 February 1914, a Cup replay between Sheffield Wednesday and Wolves

was halted for 20 minutes after a retaining wall collapsed and 75 people were injured. The Wolves goalkeeper was unable to resume after fainting in the dressing room at the sight of the injured. And at Ibrox Park, on 5 April 1902, 26 were killed and 587 later compensated for injuries when part of the West Stand collapsed during a Scotland – England international.

DI STEFANO, Alfredo

1926 Born in Buenos Aires

1944 Makes debut for River Plate

1947 Joins Millionarios in Colombia

1953 Transferred to real madrid

1956 Wins European Cup 4-3 v Reims . . .

1957 . . . and again, 2-0 v Fiorentina; awarded first of 31 Spanish caps; European Footballer of the Year

1958 Completes European hat-trick, 3-2 v AC Milan

1959 Fourth European Cup, 2-0 v Reims; European Footballer of the Year

1960 Scores hat-trick as Real win fifth European Cup, 7-3 v Eintracht Frankfurt

1964 Free transfer to Español

1964 Retires; appointed manager of Elche

1968 Becomes technical manager of Boca Juniors

1969 Promoted to manager

1970 Returns to Spain as manager of Valencia

1971 Valencia win Spanish Championship

1982 Appointed manger of Real madrid

1983 Leaves

1990 Back again as manager of Real

When Sir Matt Busby was asked which player he would most like to have signed for Manchester United, his reply was instant: 'Alfredo Di Stefano'. Given that his career coincided with Pele's, it underlines Di Stefano's stature. He is arguably the best post-war player and possibly the greatest of all time.

Di Stefano, a deep-lying centre-forward, played with an intensity that Busby described as 'win at all

times'. Stocky and strong, his phenomenal stamina, cultivated by running in the streets of his native Buenos Aires, enabled him to play flat-out for 90 minutes – a quality that was beyond even the genius of Pelé. He had the body and the brain to allow the game to flow through him.

Strategy rather than individual virtuosity preoccupied him. Di Stefano rarely sought to beat someone – although it was well within his powers – but he held the ball, waiting, watching for the right moment to release it. Consequently his greatest partnerships were with Puskas and Gento, both brilliant runners off the ball, rather than with fellow tacticians such as Didi and Kopa, who both had spells at Real in Di Stefano's time.

The fact that the man brandishing the field marshal's baton was also one of Real's most potent weapons was a wonderful bonus. In 59 European club matches he scored 49 goals, including one in each of the first four European Cup Finals and a hat-trick in the fifth, against Eintracht Frankfurt at Hampden in 1960. In 11 seasons in the Spanish League he found the net 219 times, while he also scored on 26 occasions at international level for Argentina and Spain.

When, at the age of 38, Di Stefano was given a free transfer, only one player could fill the gap. Real offered Santos £350,000 for Pelé (at the time the British record was the £115,000 Busby paid for Denis Law) but it was declined. So, almost inevitably, did Real. Di Stefano's relationship with Real continued into the 1980s and 1990s as he had two spells of management with the club with which his name will always be linked.

ALFREDO DI STEFANO
October 1963 at Wembley, and Bobby Moore *(left)* tussles with Alfredo di Stefano in England's 2-1 victory against a FIFA XI. Since those days both of these men, in their different ways, have become ambassadors for the game. Bobby Moore plays in testimonials all over the world and Di Stefano, heavily identified with football in two continents – Europe and South America – is still involved in promoting soccer. The team with which he is most closely associated, Real Madrid, played no small part themselves in promoting the finer qualities of football when Di Stefano was regularly finding the net for them. These days the club, managed

since 1991 by Raddy Antic (formerly of Luton Town), look to Mexican Hugo Sanchez (with an average of more than 30 goals per season with the club) and Emilio Butragueno for fire-power.

DOCHERTY, Tommy

1928 Born in Glasgow

1948 Signs for Celtic

1949 Transfers to Preston North End (£4000)

1958 Joins Arsenal for £28,000

1961 Joins Chelsea (as player-coach, later manager)

1967 Goes to Rotherham United as manager

1968 Brief spell as manager of Queen's Park Rangers; appointed Aston Villa manager

1970 Becomes FC Oporto manager

1971 Hull City assistant manager; manages Scotland (only three defeats in 12 games)

1972 Takes over at Manchester United

1977 Manages FA Cup-winning team; sacked at Manchester United, takes over at Derby County

1979 Queen's Park Rangers manager again

1980 Sydney Olympic (Australia) manager

1981 Returns to become Preston North End manager

1982 South Melbourne (Australia) manager

1984 Wolves manager

1987 Altrincham manager

As a player Tommy Docherty won an FA Cup runners-up medal with Preston North End in 1954 and 25 Scotland caps (eight as captain). He managed FA Cup Final teams at Chelsea (1967) and Manchester United (1976 and 1977) after taking each club into the First Division. On the other hand, there were problems - relegation at Rotherham, the sack at Aston Villa during a relegation season, and further relegation at Manchester United.

Docherty represented a new wave of management: controversial, outspoken, quotable, impulsive and occasionally wayward. He was always 'news', whether he was sending home eight Chelsea players for discipline reasons, trading

TOMMY DOCHERTY
In his GM Vauxhall Conference sweater, Altrincham manager Tommy Docherty watches yet another game of football. No matter what his critics said – and they said quite a lot – nobody could doubt Docherty's devotion to the game of football. His experience helped a lot of players and a lot of teams, but he may be remembered for off-the-field performances as much as those on the park.

players by the handful and being probed by the police at Derby County, being sacked twice by Queen's Park Rangers, being cleared of perjury offences, or simply entertaining with comments like 'I've had more clubs than Jack Nicklaus.'

DONCASTER ROVERS

Founded 1879

Joined League 1901 (Div.2)

Honours Div.3 (N) Champions 1935, 1947, 1950; Div.4 Champions 1966, 1969

Ground Belle Vue

Despite languishing in the League's lower reaches throughout most of their history, Doncaster Rovers can point to one enterprising period. In the 1950s, under the guidance of former Northern Ireland forward Peter Doherty, Rovers won promotion to Division 2 and remained there for eight campaigns.

During that glorious decade they reached the fifth round of the FA Cup four times and unearthed two top-class players. Harry Gregg was sold to Manchester United for £23500, then a world record for a goalkeeper. Inside-forward Alick Jeffrey was not so fortunate; he seemed a certainty for stardom when injury wrecked his career.

Doncaster's earlier League experiences were more prosaic. Twice in their first four years they failed to win re-election, rejoining as members of Division 3 (N) in 1923. Occasional promotions followed by success was never sustained until the Doherty days. Subsequently the club moved regularly between Divisions 3 and 4, employing such managers as Lawrie McMenemy, Dave Mackay and Billy Bremner without ever looking likely to acquire the stature of their Yorkshire rivals in Leeds and Sheffield.

DUMBARTON

Founded 1872

Joined League 1890 (Division 1, founder member)

Honours Scottish Football League Division 1 Champions 1891 (shared with Rangers), 1892; Division 2 Champions 1911, 1972; Scottish Cup Winners 1883

Ground Boghead Park

For a spell in its early history, Dumbarton clubs dominated Scottish football. Vale of Leven and Renton no longer exist at senior level, but Dumbarton survive as a reminder of that era.

Although soon eclipsed by the big-city clubs, Dumbarton have proved durable. When their existence was threatened in the early 1950s, local support swelled. Recent internationalists Graeme Sharp and Murdo MacLeod began their careers at Boghead.

DUNDEE

Founded 1893

Joined League 1893 (Division 1)

Honours Scottish League Division 1 Champions, 1962; First Division Champions 1979; Division 2 Champions 1947; Scottish Cup Winners 1910; Scottish League Cup Winners 1951/52, 1952/53, 1973/74

Ground Dens Park

These days First Division Dundee give the impression of a club burdened by memories of more exalted status. The recollection of great achievements renders the current mediocrity even less palatable. Dundee have also seen themselves within the city by Dundee United.

Dundee won the Scottish Cup in 1910 after a Final which stretched to three matches, but were at their greatest in the years following the Second World War. Their audacious signing of Billy Steel from Derby, for £17500, was quickly rewarded when he helped them win the 1951/52 League Cup and retain it the following season.

Their finest ever side, including names like Alan Gilzean, Ian Ure and Alex Hamilton, took them to the Championship in 1962. Dundee then went on to reach the semi-finals of the European Cup but soon lost players such as Gilzean and, a little later, Charlie Cooke to richer clubs.

Victory in the 1973/74 League Cup could not reverse decline. The club have struggled to secure a place in the Premier Division and were relegated in 1990.

DUNDEE UNITED

Founded 1909 (as Dundee Hibernian, renamed Dundee United 1923)

Joined League 1910 (Div.2)

Honours Scottish League Championship, Premier Division, 1983; Division 2, 1925, 1929; Scottish League Cup, 1979/80, 1980/81

Ground Tannadice Park

Dundee United demonstrate the extraordinary effect one individual can have in football. Under Jim McLean they have progressed from being the second club in the city to being, at times, in the forefront of European football.

Some of the Continent's wealthiest clubs fell to them as they reached the

DUNDEE UNITED With Aberdeen doing well at the same time, Dundee United's four Scottish Cup Final appearances (all losing) and one League title in the 1980s seemed part of a shift of power away from the big Glasgow clubs. Paul Sturrock was one of The Terrors' top players at that time, winning 20 Scottish caps during the decade and regularly appearing on the scoresheet and as 'assist'. He was coach for Dundee United at the start of the 1990/91 season.

European Cup semi-finals in 1984 and the UEFA Cup final in 1987. McLean may be a difficult and demanding manager but his nurturing of young talent is unsurpassed.

Year after year knowledgeable footballers with sound technique emerge at Tannadice. Perhaps the finest examples have been David Narey and Maurice Malpas, both members of the side which won the League in 1983. The club has not always won the trophies it deserved. 1991 saw their

sixth defeat in a Scottish Cup final.

As with Aberdeen, the club's past can only be seen as a prelude to the 1980s.

DUNFERMLINE ATHLETIC

Founded 1885

Joined League 1912 (Div.2)

Honours Scottish League Championship, First Division, 1989; Second Division, 1986; Division 2, 1926; Scottish Cup, 1961, 1968

Ground East End Park

Dunfermline vied with Kilmarnock for the position of Scotland's most successful provincial club in the 1960s. The Scottish Cup final victories over Celtic and Hearts, the first achieved under the management of Jock Stein, may be the substance of their achievement but there were other glittering displays as well.

There was aptitude for Europe especially. Everton were beaten in the 1962/63

Fairs Cup and Dunfermline saw off West Brom en route to the Cup Winners' Cup semi-finals in 1968/69. In the early part of the decade Charlie Dickson was a regular scorer of vital goals. Much of the flair flowed from winger Alex Edwards who was in the side soon after his 16th birthday.

Dunfermline's slump in the 1970s and 1980s took them as low as the Second Division, but they are now re-establishing themselves in the top flight although rarely shining.

EAST FIFE

Founded 1903

Joined League 1921 (Division 2)

Honours Scottish League Division 2 Champions 1948; Scottish Cup winners 1938; League Cup Winners 1947/48, 1949/50, 1953/54

East Fife are the only Division 2 team ever to win the Scottish Cup. Their hastily assembled side (two of whom had been acquired on loan) triumphed over Kilmarnock in 1938.

Their Cup achievements after the Second World War were also extraordinary, with three triumphs in the League Cup. The half-back line of Philp, Findlay and Aitken were daunting. Centreforward Henry Morris scored three for Scotland in his 1949 debut against Northern Ireland but was never capped again.

EAST STIRLINGSHIRE

Founded 1881

Joined League 1900 (Div.2)

Honours Scottish League Division 2 Champions, 1932

Ground Firs Park

The subjects of Scottish football's most celebrated court case. In 1964, amid furious protest, the Steedman family moved East Stirling to Clydebank and amalgamated it with the Junior club there to form E.S.Clydebank.

The new club competed in Division 2 throughout 1964/65 season before the Court of Session ruled that a share transfer of the Steedmans was invalid. East Stirling recovered their autonomy and returned to Falkirk. Sadly, the townspeople have otherwise failed to take much interest in them.

EDWARDS, Duncan

1936 Born in Dudley Worcestershire

1948 As an 11-year-old, becomes regular member of Dudley Boys, average age 15

1952 Joins Manchester United as an amateur

1953 April - makes his Division 1 debut as a 16-year-old; October - turns professional with United on his 17th birthday

1955 At 18 years 183 days, he is the youngest player to win a full England cap - impressive debut in a 7-2 victory over Scotland at Wembley

1956 Wins first of two successive League Championship medals

1958 Dies in a German hospital two weeks after sustaining multiple injuries in the Munich air crash.

Bobby Charlton once said: 'If I had to play for my life, and could take one man with me, it would be Duncan Edwards.' It was an eloquent way of summing up the worth of the multi-talented young Midlander to Manchester United and England during his tragically short career.

Edwards was a soccer colossus, the sort of player who surfaces once in a lifetime. He had everything: exemplary ball control and passing skills, a titan's tackle, awesome aerial and shooting power, an ability to read the game that was mature beyond his years, and a level head to ensure that all these gifts were not squandered.

Throughout the mid 1950s Edwards was the principal symbol of all that was best about the 'Busby Babes,' as well as representing his country's brightest hope. There are those who reckon that had he not perished at Munich, he would have been England captain for a decade and that Bobby Moore would never have lifted the World Cup. Certainly, as a 21-year-old with 18 caps to his credit, he appeared to have boundless potential. Edwards played most of his club games at left-half but he was outstanding in practically any position, being a particularly lethal emergency centre-forward, and invested every aspect of his play with a spirit that was seemingly unquenchable. Even when disaster struck he did not give in easily, fighting a two-week battle for life in the face of insurmountable odds. His death left the football world aching for what might have been.

DUNCAN EDWARDS
Duncan Edwards, in his Manchester United shirt, was already a regular England international when this picture was taken during the 1956/57 season. He certainly shows the classic build for a footballer, and those who saw him play talk of strength, skill, vision, speed, stamina ... indeed, there seemed to be no shortcomings to his game.

ENGLAND

In the beginning, English football was a rough, unruly folk game played in the streets, rival villages defending their territory. Vestiges of these origins remain today in rituals such as the annual Shrove Tuesday game at Ashbourne, Derbyshire. In 1863 the formation of the Football Association and formalisation of the first set of standardised laws led to football as an institution, although disputes between the London-based Football Association and the Sheffield Association lingered (*see* Laws).

Writing in 1900 in *The Real Football*, journalist James Catton described the diffusion of the game to the working class, a spread helped by the half-day Saturday holiday: 'Time was when football was the innocent diversion of the upper and middle classes who had no other thought than to pay for their own amusement, buy their own boots and clothes, take their own railway tickets, discharge their own hotel bills and entertain the teams which visited them. But the game was taken up by the mechanics, the artisans, the clerks, and thousands of others who depended upon weekly wages.'

Scottish stone-masons, encouraged by football clubs to work in England in the 1870s, complained that the stone was harder than in the north. Their hands swelled, they needed to rest, and their clubs took to supporting them financially. Other clubs then argued that they were 'professional'. In January 1884 Preston chairman William Sudell admitted that his players were paid. Preston were expelled from the FA Cup competition, and the debate stepped up. Threatened with the withdrawal of 'professional' clubs into a new association, the FA agreed in July 1885 that 'it is expedient to legalise professionalism under stringent conditions.' Three years later the world's first professional league, the Football League, was

formed, and professional clubs grew from various origins - churches (like Liverpool), chapels (like Aston Villa), schools (like Tottenham Hotspur), railway workers (like Manchester United) and cricket clubs (like Derby County).

A network of other leagues developed. By the early 1900s there were half a million or more players in leagues affiliated to the Football Association in England and Wales. Football became an easy game to arrange. It fitted in with factory life and needed little outlay on equipment; it offered players an outlet for their masculinity and physical prowess; and it emphasised teamwork and the competitive pursuit of victory. These values were particularly sought after in the post-war years. Such was the interest after the First World War that the Football League was

extended to include Division 3 (S) in 1920 and Division 3 (N) in 1921. Similarly, there was a boom in the late 1940s when English football peaked in its popularity. In 1947/48 Newcastle United averaged 56,299 spectators for home League games and 33,912 away... and they were in the Second Division. The following season (1948/49) saw an aggregate attendance of 41, 271, 414 for Football League games - an all-time record.

Football's appeal was especially strong in the industrial regions of Lancashire, South Yorkshire, the Midlands and the North-east. In the 1930s Arsenal broke through the dominance of northern and Midlands clubs, and the economic decline of the north in the 1950s changed the geographical map of football. Southern towns like Luton, Oxford and

Peterborough grew in both industry and football prestige, whereas Preston, Blackburn, Bolton and Huddersfield lost their First Division places. Lancastrian interest became concentrated on the big four - Liverpool, Everton, Manchester United and Manchester City.

Smaller clubs in the north were affected by a number of other problems. The restructuring of Division 3 (N) and Division 3 (S) into national Divisions 3 and 4 increased travel expenditure. The removal of the maximum wage in 1961 increased the gap between wages of top and bottom clubs. And the legal ruling in 1963 that clubs could not restrain the trading of players made it more difficult to hold on to good players.

The amateur game continued to develop dramatically, aided by the

Football Association's recognition of Sunday football leagues in 1960. Religious groups had opposed Sunday games, and only in 1955 had the FA permitted clubs or players under their jurisdiction to take part in Sunday football. In 1973/74 a coal-mining strike and the imposition of a shorter working week restricted floodlit games, so the professional game was forced to confront the Sunday football issue. Four FA Cup ties were played on Sunday 6 January 1974. Two weeks later came the first Sunday Football League games.

In 1966 English football received a tremendous fillip from the World Cup win. Playing interest increased, and the steady post-war decline in Football League attendances was halted. In fact attendances increased during the two seasons after 1966.

FOOTBALL IN ENGLAND
One reason given for the slow progress of English football following the Second World War is its isolation. Trying to fuel interest in the international game, Wolverhampton Wanderers played a number of friendly matches against top overseas sides. Here Billy Wright leads out the Wolves against the famous Moscow Spartak in 1954. The player following Wright is William Shorthouse. The match, played under (then rare) floodlights, resulted in a 4-0 win for Wolves.

English football, however, underwent rapid change in the 1970s. Substitution rules affected players and managers, sponsorship interested directors, and television

ENGLAND

An action shot from an historic match – England v Hungary at Wembley in 1953. This game is reckoned to have forced changes on complacent administrators and coaches in England because of the scoreline, a 6-3 defeat of England, and because the English side were completely outshone in both individual and team skills. The score certainly caused some hurt pride. The photograph shows an agile Grosics cutting out the danger while Stan Mortensen looks for any pickings and Hungarians Boszik (left) and Buzansky look on.

and hooliganism made their impact on supporters. English clubs broke through European barriers and at times took an almost permanent hold on two major club trophies. The last four Inter-Cities Fairs Cup Finals (1968-1971) and three of the first five UEFA Cup Finals (1972-76) were won by English clubs. Then, seven out of eight European Cup wins between 1977 and 1984 went to England - four for Liverpool, two for Nottingham Forest and one for Aston Villa.

The European run literally ended in disaster. After the 1985 Heysel Stadium riot, English clubs were banned from Europe for an indefinite period,

which later transpired to be five years. The ban was not surprising. Hooliganism had become tagged as the 'English disease' after previous riots by Spurs fans in Holland (1974 and 1981), Leeds United fans in Paris (1975), West Ham fans in Spain (1980) and England fans in Luxembourg (1977) and Italy (1980), just to mention a few.

Despite the adverse publicity following disasters at Valley Parade, Heysel and Hillsborough, aggregate Football League attendances rose for the last four seasons of the 1980s. But at the end of the decade they were still less than half the record 1948/49 figure (and there had been an increase of 10 per cent in

the number of games). English football will probably never regain the popularity it had in the late 1940s, but the nation is always willing to react to World Cup success like that achieved by Bobby Robson's team at Italia '90. The professional game may be ailing economically, but the semi-professional game is healthy, and at the start of the 1990s more people are playing soccer in England than ever before.

ENGLAND, NATIONAL TEAM

The history of the England national team begins with the first-ever international, the goalless Scotland-England game in Glasgow

ENGLAND

That special day for English football fans: the World Cup Final, 30 July 1966. This photograph shows the England team before the first period of extra time. They had been denied a 2-1 victory. Manager Alf Ramsey is reported to have said: 'You've won it once; now go out and win it again.' Bobby Charlton, standing behind manager Ramsey (balding, in track suit), seems to be pondering what might have been. And is Geoff Hurst (hands on hips, to the right of trainer Shepherdson) possibly thinking about completing a hat-trick?

on 30 November 1872. Scotland dominated early fixtures but the appearance of Wales (1880) and Ireland (1882) sparked some easier games and the birth of the home international championship. Between 1890 and 1896 England had an invincible period of 20 unbeaten games, assisted by Scotland's rejection of international-class Scots playing professionally in England.

The 1908 tour of Austria, Hungary and Bohemia - four wins and 28 goals was the first continental excursion, but foreign fixtures were not regular until the 1920s. Predictable wins against nations like Belgium and France were often achieved with understrength teams, but a 4-3 defeat in Spain in 1929 was the first warning sign of things to come. The most famous inter-war internationals included the brutal 'Battle of Highbury' in 1934, when England, with seven Arsenal players, beat world champions Italy 3-2, and the 6-3 win in Germany in 1938 when the English team gave the Nazi salute. A surprise defeat in Switzerland a week later was blamed on the garlic!

During the 1940s England boasted a superb team. The wartime half-back-line of Britton, Cullis and Mercer linked with forwards like Matthews, Carter and Lawton to produce some in 1986.

ENGLAND Italia '90, and the moment when it looked as if 1966 might be possible all over again, as Gary Lineker steers the ball into the West German net for the equalising goal in the drawn (1-1) semi-final. Throughout the tournament England had been improving and had been scoring goals late in matches. As Lineker scored with Illgner (in goal) and Kohler watching, even the most pessimistic England fans must have believed that lady luck was smiling on them. Sadly defeat in the penalty shoot-out was in store.

scintillating wins against Scotland, including scorelines of 4-0, 8-0, 6-2, 6-2 and 6-1. Only one of the first 18 post-war internationals was lost, and the 4-0 win against Italy in Turin in 1948 was one of England's best results.

England, priding themselves on an unbeaten home record against continental opposition, were hit hard when the Republic of Ireland beat them 2-0 in 1949 and Hungary won 6-3 at Wembley in 1953. The return match in Hungary six months later, a 7-1 defeat, reinforced the view that changes were needed. When they came, England went 16 unbeaten games (1955-57) before being unsettled by the loss of three players in the Munich Disaster.

Early in 1963, Ipswich Town manager Alf (later Sir Alf) Ramsey took over from Walter Winterbottom as England manager. England lost the first two games under Ramsey but only four of the next 42, winning the 1966 World Cup in England. The win was achieved after games against Uruguay (0-0), Mexico (2-0), France (2-0), Argentina (1-0), Portugal (2-1) and West Germany (4-2 after extra time). The winning team in the final was: Banks, Cohen, Wilson, Stiles, Charlton (Jack), Moore, Ball, Hunt, Charlton (Bobby), Hurst and Peters. Two years later England achieved their best ever European Championship placing (third) but in 1970 West Germany turned a 2-0 quarter-final deficit into a 3-2 victory to stop England's attempt to retain the World Cup.

The 11-year Ramsey era was the most successful in England's history; his teams notched 69 wins in 113 internationals with only 17 defeats. It ended with failure to qualify for the 1974 World Cup Finals after a frustrating 1-1 draw with Poland. Since Ramsey, England have been managed by Joe Mercer, Don Revie, Ron Greenwood, Bobby Robson and Graham Taylor. In the 1980s

Greenwood and Robson consistently steered England into the World Cup finals, but only in 1990 did they make an impact, when their run ended in the semi-final with a penalty shoot-out against West Germany. The England team for that match was: Shilton, Parker, Butcher (sub: Steven), Wright, Walker, Pearce, Platt, Gascoigne, Waddle, Beardsley and Lineker.

EQUIPMENT

The knickerbocker-type shorts worn in football's early years soon developed into the baggier knee-length variety, commonly called 'knickers', which lasted until the mid-1950s. Briefer shorts, worn by mainland European and South American players, were brought to British attention through the World Cup and European club competitions. In recent years some players have taken to wearing tights or clinging cycle shorts under their team strip.

Shirts have had a multitude of styles, ranging from early tie-at-the-neck, long-sleeved shirts to V-collared short-sleeve versions. In the late 1970s sponsors recognised that they could use shirt fronts to advertise company names, and other design trimmings developed. Experiments with numbered shirts took place occasionally in the 1930s, most notably for the 1933 FA Cup Final when the shirts were numbered from 1 to 22 rather than two sets of 1 to 11. Numbering was not compulsory in England until 1939. In Scotland, Celtic strongly resisted shirt numbering and resorted to numbering shorts instead. In the very early days of football, players were identified by the colours of their caps and stockings. Don Revie's Leeds United team pioneered numbered tie-ups which they gave to the crowd as souvenirs at the end of the game.

Goalkeepers have often been to the fore as fashion pacesetters. When restrictions on shirt colours were lifted in the late 1970s

- Football League rules had previously limited goalkeepers to royal green, royal blue, scarlet and white - other designs appeared. Goalkeepers have also experimented more practically with different forms of padding, gloves and caps. Superstition was fuelled by Cardiff City's FA Cup-winning goal in 1927, Arsenal goalkeeper Lewis blaming his slippy new jersey after Ferguson's shot had squeezed the ball between his arms and body.

Shinpads were invented by Sam Widdowson (Nottingham Forest and England), who patented them in 1874; the early versions were worn outside the socks. Charlie Bambridge, a famous England winger in the 1880s, once fooled the Scots when wearing only one shinpad. Aware of Bambridge's publicised shin injury, the Scots hacked at the protected leg only to discover after the game that Bambridge had craftily worn the shinpad on his sound leg. Around 1890 began the custom of putting shinpads inside socks. In the 1960s and 1970s it was common for players such as George Best to play without shinpads, but modern players sensibly use them as standard safety equipment. Other kit accessories include headbands, worn by players such as England international Steve Foster.

The original boots were made of strong, unsupple leather. They had hard top-caps and ankle protection, and studs were knocked in with nails. Players dreaded breaking in a new pair. The invention of the screw-in

EQUIPMENT Elisha Scott, a 'keeper with Liverpool from 1914 to 1935, demonstrating that nothing is new under the sun with his knee guards and gloves. Although a goalkeeper's equipment has changed dramatically over the decades, the need to protect parts of the body and to get a grip of the ball are ever-present.

stud and use of rubber moulded sole boots revolutionised the options available to footballers. Certain players - Alan Ball (Everton) and Peter Taylor (Spurs) come to mind - wore white boots for a time in the 1970s.

The Laws of football state that the ball must be spherical with an outer casing of leather or other approved materials. At the start of the game the ball must not weigh more than 16 oz or less than 14 oz. The laced-up leather-case balls used by early footballers often collected water and mud, so they probably weighed more than 16 oz during a game; reliable plastic coatings are now generally used. Valve balls replaced laced balls in the 1950s, and white balls became the norm around 1970, with the patterned ball arriving in the late 1970s. When England played West Germany in the 1966 World Cup Final the ball was the traditional brown.

Goal equipment evolved rapidly. Crossbars became compulsory in 1882 (they had been used in some areas as early as 1875), and goal-nets were invented and patented by J A Brodie of Liverpool in 1890. Attention to the detail of equipment is important. In November 1989 Portsmouth officials were embarrassed when a Danish referee discovered that one Fratton Park crossbar was an inch too low when he made his check before a youth international.

EUROPE

Once the British, codified form of football was introduced to mainland Europe it didn't take long to become popular, associations being formed in Belgium, Holland, Denmark, Switzerland and Italy before the turn of the century. The seeds were already there: primitive free-for-all types of the game already existed - and Ancient Greece, too, had had its form, *episkyros*. The other great empire of the ancient world, that of Rome, had a version called

harpastum and there is evidence to suggest that this was introduced to occupied Britain, so possibly making the city of the 1990 World Cup Final the originator of the sport.

Although early British teams did tour Europe, the development of the game on the continent prospered in spite of, rather than because of, the established game and its officiating bodies in the United Kingdom; their tendency to remain aloof from the game overseas continued well into the twentieth century (attitudes towards the inauguration of first FIFA, and then the World Cup being examples). It was largely through the efforts of British individuals (business representatives working in Vienna, the son of an expatriate mill-owner in tsarist Russia, etc.) and the infectious nature of casual recreational matches, as played by British sailors in the Balkans, for example, that football took root in Europe. Early this century, Scottish coaches introduced a short-passing style to central European sides; and the British influence in Italy is evidenced by the English spelling of 'Milan' in two of that country's top teams' names (Inter and AC Milan).

But much is owed to Switzerland (home of FIFA and UEFA) and France, founders of so many tournaments and awards, for the organisation and development of inter-national competitive soccer within Europe and, indeed, worldwide. Ironically Swiss football has made little impact internationally, and for a long time the French did not have a great deal of success in the competitions they initiated. But, European Championship winners in 1984, propelled by Michel Platini's eight goals, France had looked an increasingly useful outside bet in the World Cup two years earlier. By the time they met an impressive West German side in an enthralling semi-final, the team had gelled; with the experienced Tresor forming the nucleus of a

springboard defence, Rocheteau providing the fire-power up front, and Platini, Genghini, Giresse and Tigana harmonising in midfield, France played some of the most beautiful football of that or any World Cup. However, it was not to be, and the national team has struggled to find form since then.

Their victorious opponents on that day, West Germany, are the most successful footballing nation in Europe. Some might say in the world, and they would have an impressive case: three World Cup victories and three times runners-up (a record) and two European Championships (a record). And they played their first international only in 1950, since when qualification alone for the World Cup has become increasingly difficult. They suffer the occasional inexplicable defeat at the hands of inferior opposition, but seem to have the knack of winning important matches, and at their best appear supremely confident with an air of almost arrogant invincibility.

The West German game is a combination of the direct, pragmatic approach favoured in Britain and the patient, skilful build-up typical of Europe. Most of their successes are identified with the names Beckenbauer and Schoen. Current coach Berti Vogts will probably have to manage without them, but he does now have East Germany's footballers to help him. A limited number of East German teams have been admitted to the Bundesliga, whose club sides have always been prominent in European competitions, Bayern Munich's three consecutive European Cup victories in the mid 1970s standing out. In truth the GDR's teams, while hard to break down, achieved little, and most of the new German squad will be from the West; in Matthaus they have a player as fearsome to goalkeepers as Gerd Muller was in the 1970s. Germany's first game as a unified nation in 48 years took place on 19 December

1990 in Stuttgart against Switzerland, with East German Andreas Thom (who plays in the Bundesliga) replacing Sammer, the only East German to start the game, and scoring in the 4-0 victory.

It is not only the German game which will be affected by the political changes in post-1989 Eastern Europe. If professional status is adopted by footballers in former communist states, their national teams might grow in strength; devolution within the Soviet Union and Yugoslavia could mean the emergence of 'new' nationalities; Albania, something of a football desert owing to political insularity, might become more involved in the international scene. East European teams have always been tough opposition but, Olympic football apart, have won few major honours, Czechoslovakia's 1976 European Championship title being a notable exception. The Soviet Union won the first tournament in 1960, but the strongest nations did not compete. Despite the occasional success of its club sides, the USSR, somewhat mysteriously, has often shown lack of self-belief in crucial games, and individual talents such as Chivadze and Blokhin have not been able to carry them.

For twenty or more years Poland have sporadically promised great things with their capacity for exciting football, typified by first Lato and, more recently, Boniek. Tomaszewski in goal and Zmuda in defence have also been outstanding. Unfortunately the national team has proved unable to mount a sustained assault in a major tournament.

Hungary's golden age, May 1950 to February 1956, was blemished by only one defeat out of 48 internationals; sadly that defeat, in 1954, was Hungary's second in a World Cup Final. The Soviet invasion of their homeland in 1956 broke up the legendary team which included Puskas, Kocsis

EUROPE Three flying Dutchmen in Vienna representing an Italian club: *(left to right)* Marco van Basten, Frank Rijkaard and Ruud Gullit in Milan's 1-0 win against Benfica in the 1990 European Cup Final. When top European players turn out for their country, they stand a good chance of lining up against club-mates. So easily and frequently do these footballers switch from one foreign club to another that, in many cases, the opposition holds no surprises for them. Rijkaard, however, who scored in this game, is unlikely to play for Holland again, if we are to take him at his word. It has been widely reported that he was upset by the undue influence exerted by his old friend Gullit in the 1990 World Cup. Gullit, captain in that tournament, had still not recovered his best form at that time. More recently, van Basten, 1989 European Footballer of the Year, has captained the national side from the centre-forward position. Gullit, European Footballer of the Year in 1987, came to Milan in 1987 from PSV Eindhoven. Rijkaard and van Basten both played for Ajax before moving abroad.

and Czibor – players whose equivalents have never surfaced in modern-day Hungary. That team's emphatic double defeat of England in 1953/54 exhibited skills and tactical sublety which revolutionised the British attitude to the game.

Yugoslavia in the 1960s, and Romania in the 1970s, began to shake off the sort of reputation currently enjoyed by Bulgaria – that of dull but worthy opponents – and have continued to impress with individual displays of skill (Jankovic, Jovanovic and, more recently, Stojkvic of Yugoslavia) and the success of their club sides Dynamo Zagreb (Yugoslavia) and Steaua Bucharest (Romania).

The Italians are often credited with being the tightest defenders in the world and the best practitioners of the sweeper system; their Milanese club sides of the 1960s were expert at defending slim leads in two-leg European ties. Italy has consistently produced world-class players and performances to match; of European national teams only West Germany has a better record. Their rigorous defence and patient build-up are complemented by imaginative and incisive work around the penalty area. Of the present team (who produced some of the 1990 World Cup's best soccer), the *libero* Baresi,

although so different in appearance to Scirea, could be mistaken for his eminent predecessor in his style, distribution and reading of the game; and Schillaci, in a different physical mould to Rossi, Riva and Rivera, is proving every bit as deadly a striker as those great names.

Italy's northern neighbours, Austria, whose domestic league loses so many players to wealthier foreign clubs, have a poor record which does not reflect the quality of football displayed by their exciting, combative teams.

The Scandinavian countries have had football leagues for almost as long as any nation in Europe, but until recently were handicapped in the international arena by their semi-professionalism. Since turning professional in 1978, Denmark have earned worldwide respect with their skilful and mobile brand of football; their best players, however, have always moved abroad – Jesper Olsen, Morten Olsen, Simonsen, Molby and Laudrup, for example. Sweden, too, have proved their worth through club successes in Europe and by qualifying for several World Cups. Norway, and Finland especially, remain the weaker countries but have had their moments; no opponents can afford to be dismissive of them.

Spanish clubs, Real Madrid and Barcelona in particular, had great success in the early years of the three main European competitions and the national team won the 1964 European Championship, their only title. Then, as now, the domestic game relied heavily on imported players, which might explain the disparity between club and national achievements. As the Spanish challenge faded, Portugal, in the shape of Benfica and Sporting Lisbon, carried the Iberian flag. Then, in the 1966 World Cup, Eusebio, the 'Black Panther', showed just why he was being compared to Pele. But Portuguese soccer has never recovered from the decline which so rapidly followed that time. Currently the Spanish League, which still sends successful representatives into European competitions, is characterised by massive transfer fees, managerial dramas and the impossibly high expectations of the press and public.

The rise of Dutch soccer, some fifteen years after the introduction of professionalism, was breathtaking. From apparently nowhere, a new soccer power and a new approach – total football – emerged to dominate the club soccer of the early 1970s, Ajax and Feyenoord taking the spoils. The national team, inspired by Johan Cruyff, were runners-up in the 1974 and 1978 World Cups – consolation for rather poor showings in the European Championships of that decade.

The story of Belgian football seems an imitation in miniature of the Dutch success. Anderlecht, with goal-scorer van der Elst, won the Cup Winners' Cup in 1976 and 1978, as the national side, organised around the midfield skills of van Moer, grew in stature and lost only by the odd goal to West Germany in the 1980 European Championship Final. Whereas Belgian football has more or less stayed on an even keel, with the emergence of new talents such as Ceuleman's and

Scifo, Dutch soccer seemed to lose its way in the early 1980s. But a new team was emerging including players of the calibre of Gullit and van Basten, and it swept to victory in the 1988 European Championship – only to disappoint in the World Cup two years later, partly a consequence of low morale engendered by managerial disputes. Holland's future is still uncertain, their problems being compounded by key-defender Rijkaard's decision in late 1990 to quit the national team.

It is commonly said that there are no real minnows left in football, particularly in Europe, and the Faroe Islands' defeat of Austria in September 1990 underlined the danger of complacency on the part of the major teams. Even so, sides such as Luxembourg, Turkey, Greece, Cyprus, Iceland and Malta can hope for little more than the occasional thwarting of a bigger team's ambitions; it is to Holland, Italy, France, Spain and England that we look for a long-term challenge to the German hegemony.

EUROPEAN CHAMPIONSHIPS

The European Nations Cup, as it was originally known, was devised at the instigation of the French Football Federation. Now heartily contested, it took some time to establish itself, only 17 countries competing for the first trophy, the stronger nations declining to participate. By 1968, with a new title, there were enough entries to warrant groups rather than a knock-out system.

EUROPEAN CUP

Europe's foremost club competition was first contested in 1955 in response to extravagant claims that Wolves were the world's best club after their defeat of star-studded Hungarian team Honved the preceding year. The first competition was by invitation but thereafter the league champions of each country were entitled to compete. It was an almost immediate success. The talented Real Madrid in their all-white strip lifted the first five trophies, but they had to wait until 1966 to win with an all-Spanish team. Italian domination in the early 1960s, felt by many to be a negative influence, was interrupted by the first British successes. In the next decade the emergence of Dutch football and Bayern Munich's heyday eventually made way for a remarkable run by English clubs which was terminated by the ban (lifted by 1991) resulting from the 1985 Heysel disaster.

EUROPEAN CHAMPIONSHIPS

Year	Winner	Runners-up	Score
1960	USSR	Yugoslavia	2-1*
1964	Spain	USSR	2-1
1968	Italy	Yugoslavia	1-1
	Italy	Yugoslavia	2-0*
1972	West Germany	USSR	3-0
1976	Czechoslovakia	West Germany	2-2**
1980	West Germany	Belgium	2-1
1984	France	Spain	2-0
1988	Holland	USSR	2-0

* after extra time
** after extra time and penalties.

EUROPEAN CUP

Year	Winners	Runners-up	Score
1956	Real Madrid	Reims	4-3
1957	Real Madrid	Fiorentina	2-0
1958	Real Madrid	AC Milan	3-2*
1959	Real Madrid	Reims	2-0
1960	Real Madrid	Eintracht Frankfurt	7-3
1961	Benfica	Barcelona	3-2
1962	Benfica	Real Madrid	5-3
1963	AC Milan	Benfica	2-1
1964	Internazionale	Real Madrid	3-1
1965	Internazionale	Benfica	1-0
1966	Real Madrid	Partizan Belgrade	2-1
1967	Celtic	Internazionale	2-1
1968	Manchester United	Benfica	4-1*
1969	AC Milan	Ajax	4-1
1970	Feyenoord	Celtic	2-1*
1971	Ajax	Panathinaikos	2-0
1972	Ajax	Internazionale	2-0
1973	Ajax	Juventus	1-0
1974	Bayern Munich	Atletico Madrid	1-1
	Bayern Munich	Atletico Madrid	4-0
1975	Bayern Munich	Leeds United	2-0
1976	Bayern Munich	St Etienne	1-0
1977	Liverpool	Moenchengladbach	3-1
1978	Liverpool	FC Brugge	1-0
1979	Nottingham Forest	Malmo	1-0
1980	Nottingham Forest	Hamburg	1-0
1981	Liverpool	Real Madrid	1-0
1982	Aston Villa	Bayern Munich	1-0
1983	Hamburg	Juventus	1-0
1984	Liverpool	Roma	1-1**
1985	Juventus	Liverpool	1-0
1986	Steaua Bucharest	Barcelona	0-0**
1987	Porto	Beyern Munich	2-1
1988	PSV Eindhoven	Benfica	0-0**
1989	AC Milan	Steaua Bucharest	4-0
1990	AC Milan	Benfica	1-0
1991	Red Star Belgrade	Marseille	0-0**

* after extra time
** after extra time and penalties

EUROPEAN CUP That glorious moment for Celtic and Scotland fans, as Steve Chalmers has just deflected a shot past Inter Milan's 'keeper Sarti for an 85th minute winner in the 1967 European Cup Final. Celtic won, deservedly, 2-1 against a very negative and tired-looking Italian side that had tried to hold on to an early lead achieved through a penalty. That day (and night) in Lisbon will go down in Scottish folklore; apart from the historical importance, it was seen, then, as a victory for the enthusiastic Scottish style over the dull continentals. Rumour has it that the team and supporters enjoyed a quiet drink afterwards too.

EUROPEAN CUP WINNERS' CUP

Since its inception in 1960/61, this trophy has inspired many European countries to establish domestic cup competitions so that their winners will be entitled to compete. The tournament boasts a wide range of winners from a large number of countries, some of them Eastern European. For football clubs it generates revenue as well as offering a chance of televised international success for teams which may not have done well in league competitions. The rounds are decided over home and away legs but the fact that the final is settled in one match makes it popular for television audiences. Anderlecht's thrilling performances helped to revive the popularity of the competition in the mid 1970s. No distinct pattern of domination emerges, but Barcelona enjoyed three victories in one decade. Glasgow Rangers have appeared in three finals and West Ham in two, winning one apiece. The ban on English clubs prevented Everton from defending their 1985 title. In 1991 Manchester United celebrated the return of English clubs to Europe by winning the trophy.

EUROPEAN FOOTBALLER OF THE YEAR

The Ballon d'Or is awarded on the basis of a poll among journalists. A footballer's chances of success depend upon outstanding performances in the televised European competitions, in particular the European Cup.

Three home nations were represented by the Manchester United triumvirate of the 1960s. Kevin Keegan remains the only British player to have picked up two awards and, like Michel Platini (unique in winning it three years running, he won it while playing for a foreign club.

EUROPEAN CUP WINNERS' CUP

Year	Winners	Runners-up	Score
1961	Fiorentina	Rangers	2-0 (1st leg)
	Fiorentina	Rangers	2-1 (2nd leg)
1962	Atletico Madrid	Fiorentina	1-1
	Atletico Madrid	Fiorentina	3-0
1963	Tottenham Hotspur	Atletico Madrid	5-1
1964	Sporting Lisbon	MTK Budapest	3-3*
	Sporting Lisbon	MTK Budapest	1-0
1965	West Ham United	Munich 1860	2-0
1966	Borussia Dortmund	Liverpool	2-1*
1967	Bayern Munich	Rangers	1-0*
1968	AC Milan	Hamburg	2-0
1969	Slovan Bratislava	Barcelona	3-2
1970	Manchester City	Gornik Zabrze	2-1
1971	Chelsea	Real Madrid	1-1*
	Chelsea	Real Madrid	2-1*
1972	Rangers	Moscow Dynamo	3-2
1973	AC Milan	Leeds United	1-0
1974	Magdeburg	AC Milan	2-0
1975	Dynamo Kiev	Ferencvaros	3-0
1976	Anderlecht	West Ham United	4-2
1977	Hamburg	Anderlecht	2-0
1978	Anderlecht	Austria/WAC	4-0
1979	Barcelona	Fortuna Dusseldorf	4-3*
1980	Valencia	Arsenal	0-0**
1981	Dynamo Tbilisi	Carl Zeiss Jena	2-1
1982	Barcelona	Standard Liege	2-1
1983	Aberdeen	Real Madrid	2-1*
1984	Juventus	Porto	2-1
1985	Everton	Rapid Vienna	3-1
1986	Dynamo Kiev	Atletico Madrid	3-0
1987	Ajax	Lokomotive Leipzig	1-0
1988	Mechelen	Ajax	1-0
1989	Barcelona	Sampdoria	2-0
1990	Sampdoria	Anderlecht	2-0*
1991	Manchester United	Barcelona	2-1

* after extra time   ** after extra time and penalties.

EUROPEAN FOOTBALLER OF THE YEAR Achievement in European competition is one of the requirements for success in the poll for European Footballer of the Year, and Marco van Basten of AC Milan and Holland certainly achieved that in 1989 (his second successive award) when he helped his side win the European Cup. In 1987, when playing for Ajax, van Basten had helped his team win the Cup Winners' Cup with this, the only goal of the game against Lokomotive Leipzig. There is often universal acclaim for the choice of European Footballer of the Year, contrasting sadly with the general attitude to football — broadly defensive and slightly cynical — that seemed to pervade the continental game at the dawn of the nineties. Perhaps the return of English clubs will spread some light!

EUROPEAN FOOTBALLER OF THE YEAR

Year	Winner	Club
1956	Stanley Matthews	Blackpool
1957	Alfredo di Stefano	Real Madrid
1958	Raymond Kopa	Real Madrid
1959	Alfredo di Stefano	Real Madrid
1960	Luis Suarez	Barcelona
1961	Omar Sivori	Juventus
1962	Josef Masopust	Dukla Prague
1963	Lev Yashin	Dynamo Moscow
1964	Denis Law	Manchester United
1965	Eusebio	Benfica
1966	Bobby Charlton	Manchester United
1967	Florian Albert	Ferencvaros
1968	George Best	Manchester United
1969	Gianni Rivera	AC Milan
1970	Gerd Muller	Bayern Munich
1971	Johan Cruyff	Ajax
1972	Franz Beckenbauer	Bayern Munich
1973	Johan Cruyff	Barcelona
1974	Johan Cruyff	Barcelona
1975	Oleg Blokhin	Dynamo Kiev
1976	Franz Beckenbauer	Bayern Munich
1977	Allan Simonsen	Borussia Moenchengladbach
1978	Kevin Keegan	SV Hamburg
1979	Kevin Keegan	SV Hamburg
1980	Karl-Heinz Rummenigge	Bayern Munich
1981	Karl-Heinz Rummenigge	Bayern Munich
1982	Paolo Rossi	Juventus
1983	Michel Platini	Juventus
1984	Michel Platini	Juventus
1985	Michel Platini	Juventus
1986	Igor Belanof	Dynamo Kiev
1987	Ruud Gullit	AC Milan
1988	Marco van Basten	AC Milan
1989	Marco van Basten	AC Milan
1990	Lothar Mattheus	Inter Milan

EUROPEAN SUPER CUP

Contested by the winners of the European Cup and the Cup Winners' Cup; interest in the latter tournament was rekindled by this competition's inauguration. The UEFA ban on English clubs prevented Everton from playing in 1985. Twice clubs have not been able to agree on dates – an indication of the trophy's status.

EUSEBIO, Ferreira Da Silva

1943 Born in Mozambique

1958 Taken on by local team Sporting Club of Laurenco Marques

1961 Transferred to Benfica for £7500; International debut for Portugal v Luxemburg

1962 In his first full season scored 2 goals in European Cup Final victory

EUROPEAN SUPER CUP

Year	Winners	Runners-up	Aggregate (two-leg) Score
1973	Ajax	Rangers	6-3
1974	Ajax	AC Milan	6-1
1975	Dynamo Kiev	Bayern Munich	3-0
1976	Anderlecht	Bayern Munich	5-3
1977	Liverpool	SV Hamburg	7-1
1978	Anderlecht	Liverpool	4-3
1979	Nottingham Forest	Barcelona	2-1
1980	Valencia	Nottingham Forest	2-2*
1981	No competition		
1982	Aston Villa	Barcelona	3-1
1983	Aberdeen	SV Hamburg	2-0
1984	Juventus	Liverpool	2-0**
1985	No competition		
1986	Steaua Bucharest	Dynamo Kiev	1-0**
1987	FC Porto	Ajax	2-0
1988	Mechelen	PSV Eindhoven	3-1
1989	AC Milan	Barcelona	2-1

* won on away goals
** played as one match

v Real Madrid

1965 European Footballer of the Year

1966 Top scorer in the World Cup for Portugal with 9 goals

1968 Winner of the Golden Boot award with 43 goals...

1973 ...and again with 40 goals

Twenty-four years before such displays merited front-page copy, Eusebio cried at the end of a World Cup semi-final. England, by the simple tactic of standing off the lithe striker, had negated to a certain extent the powerful acceleration and dribbling skills which had been used to such great effect against the committed tackling of earlier rounds. The World Cup medal which would so justly have crowned a memorable career was never to be his.

Strangely enough, this popular and most sportsmanlike athlete began his European career among some controversy. Sporting Lisbon, the founders of Laurenco Marques, his first club, felt they, among European teams, had first claim on the young talent, but Benfica had been tipped off. The dispute between the two Portuguese clubs took some months to settle, during which time Eusebio was obliged to lie low in an Algarve fishing village.

At Benfica, and for Portugal, his goal-scoring instincts found their perfect foil in the aerial strength of Torres. A knee injury in the 1970s effectively finished his first-class career, although he resurfaced in Mexico and the United States and in 1976 helped Toronto Metros-Croatia win the Soccer Bowl. The end of the decade saw him playing in the Portuguese Second division.

As a player he will be best remembered for having one of the most ferocious right-foot shots ever seen, but perhaps the most abiding memories for the British public are the emotion shown at Wembley in 1966 and, at

EUSEBIO 28 March 1973 and Eusebio, nearing the end of his career in top-class football, turns out for his country, by now a fading force, against Northern Ireland in a World Cup qualifying game. The result was a 1-1 draw, which wasn't enough to take either team to the finals. Northern Ireland were the home team but had to play at Coventry's ground because of the troubles. Eusebio won 77 international caps and, in the European Cup, scored a total of 46 goals. He was a vital ingredient in the success of Portuguese football at both club and national level in the 1960s; the following two decades, however, were the trough which so often follows a peak. In recent seasons, Benfica, Eusebio's old club, have re-emerged as a top side; whether the success bug will be caught by the national team remains to be seen.

the same venue two years later, his astounded congratulations to Stepney after the Manchester United 'keeper had saved one of Eusebio's best-ever shots to ensure European Cup victory for the English club.

EVERTON

Founded 1878

Joined League 1888
(founder member)

Honours Div.1
Champions 1891, 1915,
1928, 1932, 1939, 1963,
1970, 1985, 1987; Div.2
Champions 1931; FA Cup
Winners 1906, 1933,
1966, 1984; European
Cup Winners' Cup Winners
1985

Ground Goodison Park

When Will Cuff, the man
who founded Everton,
retired in 1946 he passed on
a guiding principle: that
only the classical and stylish
players should be signed.
With a few exceptions
Everton have been true to
this code, and the same
pride in the club's style can
still be sensed at Goodison.
As they say in the theatre,
Everton are a class act.

Founded as a church
team, St Domingo's, in
1878 they began in Stanley
Park and are still there.

**EVERTON Alan Ball, in
the (at the time) trendy
white boots, and
Howard Kendall take a
quick free kick for
Everton in the First
Division fixture against
Leeds United at Elland
Road in August 1970. In
the preceding season
Everton had been
champions and Leeds
runners-up in both
League and Cup. Both
teams fielded
impressive line-ups for
the game, and included
a number of future
managers. From the
Leeds team Terry
Cooper, Billy Bremner,
Jack Charlton, Eddie
Gray, Johnny Giles and
Allan Clarke all
managed League sides,
with Charlton and Giles
both having spells in
charge of the Republic of
Ireland. For Everton,
future managers
Kendall, Ball, Joe Royle
and Colin Harvey all
featured (although
Harvey was replaced by
Jimmy Husband on the
day). The result was 3-2;
Leeds were League
runners-up again,
heading for a hat-trick,
while Everton finished
14th.**

They voted to become
non-denominational in
1879 in a hotel hard by Ye
Ancient Everton Toffee
House; six years later the
club was recruiting
professionals, and became
a founder member of the
Football League.

Another three years and
Everton were champions, a
prelude to a row with their
landlord, leading to a move
on the other side of the
park, Anfield Road being
left for the beginning of
another club whose name

escapes most Evertonians.

By 1902 they were
wearing the famous royal
blue and were second in the
League. They won the FA
Cup at the third attempt in
1905. The First World War
halted what might have
been a glorious era, the
next landmark coming in
1925 when William Ralph
Dean (aged 19), a centre-
forward, was signed from
Tranmere Rovers for
£3000. Despite being
dropped Dixie scored 32
goals in 38 matches, and 21

the following season after
having his jaw and skull
fractured in a motor-cycle
accident; in 1927/8 history
was made as Dean's 60
League goals swept
Everton to their third
Championship.

An increasingly ragged
defence brought Everton
relegation, for the first
time, in 1930, but so swift
was the reconstruction that
the Second and First
Division Championships
were won in successive
seasons by the 'School of

Science' side. These were
great years at Goodison,
Joe Mercer joining Cliff
Britton to give the club
England's midfield. In 1935
Everton paid Burnley
£6500 for Tommy Lawton,
then aged 17, thus ensuring
the greatest succession in
football history, Dixie
Dean going to meet the boy
at Lime Street Station.
With the majestic Tommy
Jones emerging at
centre-half, Everton won a
fourth Championship in
1939, a season when

EXETER CITY

Founded 1904

Joined League 1920 (Div.3)

Honours Div.4 Champions 1990

Ground St James's Park

One of the League's habitual strugglers, Exeter City can always blame its lack of distinction in history on the accident of its weakness in geography. Devon was already regarded as a rugby stronghold when the club was founded; young local talent has proved hard to find and harder to develop, and this outpost of soccer civilisation, devoid of glamour and financial resources, has seemed an uninviting lure to established players. In the circumstances, mere survival has often been the club's most meaningful target, with the occasional attainment of a decent mediocrity the highest of its realistic aspirations.

Goalkeeper Dick Pym, who later found fame with Bolton Wanderers, and subsequent Arsenal wing ace Cliff Bastin were local products who starred in early League sides, but the first flirtations with success, in the early 1930s, were achieved with teams shrewdly developed from 'cast-offs' by wily manager Billy McDevitt. In 1931 City took Sunderland to a replay in the sixth round of the FA Cup (and attracted a still-record home gate of 20,984), and in 1933 an honourable second place in Division 3(S) was reached. Yet only three years later the club was bottom of the table and extinction was only narrowly averted.

Another excursion to the sixth round of the Cup (and defeat at Tottenham) in 1981 was the highlight of the post-war era until, after 70 years in the League, the first honour was won. Under dynamic manager Terry Cooper, City took the 1990 Division 4 title by a ten-point margin at the end of a campaign in which the team was undefeated at St James's Park. Injuries then dampened the fire that had been lit.

Everton players won 32 caps.

Everton struggled after the war and a second relegation followed in 1951. A scrambled return in 1954 was followed by John Carey's appointment as manager under John Moore's chairmanship. But it took Harry Catterick's arrival in 1961 with a team based upon a brilliant midfield trio of Alan Ball, Howard Kendall and Colin Harvey to slake a thirst for glory. The League in 1963, the FA Cup in 1966, a Cup Final in 1968 and the League again in 1970 ensued.

Catterick left, and neither Billy Bingham nor Gordon Lee could give Everton the consistency to win top honours.

In 1981 Everton turned to Howard Kendall, who transferred 13 players and signed 11 in his first season. In his second he signed Peter Reid, followed later by Trevor Steven and Andy Gray. From 18th in the League in January 1984, Everton went on to lose a League Cup Final replay to Liverpool but won the FA Cup. More recruiting (Gary Lineker) and 1984/85 was a resplendent and dramatic season: the Championship was won in style, as was the European Cup Winners' Cup, but in the FA Cup Final three days later, on a humid Saturday, Everton were limp. The following season was heart breaking - second to Liverpool in both League and Cup - but Kendall regained the title in 1987 before shaking the club by resigning to manage in Spain for two years.

Everton then had two seasons of comparative hardship under Colin Harvey, despite massive spending on new players. Kendall's return to management in late 1990 was as euphoric a moment as any in Everton's history. A future in Europe is anticipated, and quite possible!

FALKIRK

Founded 1876

Joined League 1902 (Div.2)

Honours Scottish League First Division Champions 1991; Division 2 Champions 1936, 1970, 1975; Scottish Cup Winners 1913, 1957

Ground Brockville Park

Falkirk's greatest moment had an unlikely setting. With relegation threatening in season 1956/57, Englishman Reggie Smith was appointed as manager. He not only kept them up but led Falkirk to victory in the Scottish Cup, a tournament they had also won in 1913.

Cultured talents such as interntionalists Alex Parker and John White came to prominence with the club in the 1950s but were soon to find more affluent employers.

Falkirk's ambitions have never been killed off. The club which took Syd Puddefoot away from West Ham for a mammoth £6000 in 1922 now has players such as former QPR striker Simon Stainrod on their books.

FANZINES

A phenomenon born in the 1980s, fanzines are the popular low-budget alternative programmes produced and sold by fans of football teams. They may focus their attention on certain aspects of their club (such as away travel, opposition to proposed ground moves, etc.) or just provide a fan's eye view of their team. Originally springing from similar magazines produced by followers of pop groups, they normally rely upon humour, criticism of the established football order and cheapness of production to get their audiences. Anarchic in approach, and forthright in opinion, they do represent the voice of a large section of football's support. They spring up, and die away, with healthy rapidity - some being worthy of note for their clever titles alone.

FIFA

The inaugural meeting of FIFA (Federation Internationale de Football Association) took place in Paris on 21 May 1904; present were representatives of the French, Swiss, Belgian, Spanish, Dutch and Swedish associations. England had shown little response to two years of French overtures and initiative, but such was the country's status that, on joining in 1906, the FA's treasurer D.B. Woolfall was elected president, replacing the original incumbent Robert Guerin.

The organisation, whose headquarters are in Zurich, aims to monitor and lay down guidelines for international competitions and proceedings and to promulgate new laws of the game and administrative rulings as need be. Bodies such as UEFA are answerable to it. It is during World Cups that FIFA receives more attention than at any other time, and some of its decisions are controversial: in 1982 penalty shoot-outs were introduced, and referees were instructed not to add on stoppage time; in 1990 the 'professional' foul merited a dismissal but problems of interpretation arose - and persisted when the edict was carried into domestic leagues. Referees were also instructed to penalise players for untidy dress, although some officials ostentatiously ignored the ruling. Many ideas being mooted for the 1994 competition are causing concern.

There have been several expulsions and withdrawals, the most noted of the latter being all four home countries in 1928 over the issue of broken-time payments.

Jules Rimet, one of the most famous past presidents (from 1921 to 1954), called soccer the jousting of modern times and saw FIFA as its protector. Sir Stanley Rous, equally popular, was president from 1961 to 1974 and strove in vain to keep football and politics apart. Membership increased in his time as he encouraged development of the game in Asia and Africa - a policy pursued by the present chief Joao Havelange. Membership in 1991 was 165 nations - one less than in 1990 because of Germany's momentous reunification.

FINNEY, Tom

1922 Born in Preston

1940 Signs for Preston North End as a part-timer

1941 Preston North End win wartime League North and Cup

1951 Wins Second Division Championship medal

1953 Preston miss the League Championship on goal average

1954 Losing FA Cup finalist against West Bromwich Albion; voted Footballer of the Year

1957 Footballer of the Year again

1958 Scores 26 goals in 34 League games at centre-forward; Preston are Championship runners-up again

1960 Retires to concentrate on his plumbing business

Despite the disruption of the Second World War, Tom Finney played 76 internationals for England and scored 30 goals. His versatility was such that he started 40 internationals on the right-wing, 33 at outside-left and three at centre-forward. On two occasions - against Wales in 1949 and Scotland in 1951 - Finney played brilliantly at inside-forward to compensate for a team-mate's injury. He played 433 League games and scored 187 goals. All were for Preston North End, his only Football League club. Yet his single European appearance was for Distillery in 1963, when George Eastham enticed him from retirement to help the Irish club draw 3-3 with Benfica in the European Cup.

Nicknamed the 'Preston Plumber', Tom Finney was probably the most complete all-round footballer of his era. More direct than Matthews, he tackled like a defender and his heading ability was that of the centre-forward he became later in his career. He was two-footed to such an extent that he could adapt to either wing. He was admired by fellow professionals and gained worldwide respect for his modest personality, remaining loyal to his home-town club in spite of other offers. For 14

FANZINES It's rather cruel, but one of the Brighton fanzines is called *And Smith Must Score!*, repeating the broadcast commentary on this moment in the 1983 FA Cup Final. Inside the last minute, Brighton have clawed their way back into the match against hot favourites Manchester United; it now stands at 2-2. There's a mix up, a loss of concentration and Smith, the Brighton player, must score. Unfortunately, he doesn't. A half-save by Gary Bailey in the United goal and a scrambled clearance ensure a replay which United win 4-0. Football is a funny old game.

TOM FINNEY With the Football Writers' Association Footballer of the Year trophy for 1954, Tom Finney proudly displays both his award and his Preston North End shirt. He was nearly always photographed in a white shirt, playing either for Preston or for England. He won the FWA trophy again in 1957.

post-war years his name was synonymous with Preston North End. When he retired the club soon lost First Division status. Later awarded the OBE and honoured by the PFA's merit award, Finney is also the subject of a noted biography - Paul Agnew's *Finney - A Football Legend*.

FOOTBALL ASSOCIATION

The Football Association was formed on 26 October 1863 when representatives of 11 clubs met at the Freemason's Tavern, London. As the game's first ever association, it formed a model for associations worldwide, and it is still the ruling body of English football. Its enormous range of responsibilities include England international matches, various FA challenge competitions, nationwide coaching and the overseeing of games at all levels. Its work is controlled by the FA Council, which includes representatives from the Football League and local county football associations.

The FA's earliest administrators, who were largely from a public-school background, first unified the various and conflicting local rules of the game, then introduced the FA Challenge Cup competition in 1871 to develop and popularise association football. It certainly did that. However, competition brought conflict between amateurs and professionals which has since dogged relationships between the FA and the Football League. In 1885 professionalism was legalised, but all clubs, professional or amateur, were still ultimately responsible to the Football Association.

Besides the FA Cup, the early 1870s also saw the first England-Scotland international, soon after Charles Alcock became FA Secretary. A Sunderland man who was educated at Harrow, Alcock held the secretary's post from 1870 to 1895, the last eight years as a full-time official on £200 per annum. Alcock was succeeded by Sir Frederick Wall (1895-1934), who handed over to Sir Stanley Rous (1934-1961).

The Football Association became a limited company in 1903, a move stimulated by the previous year's Ibrox disaster. The First World War meant difficult decisions for the FA - to

FOOTBALL ASSOCIATION Ted Croker, in his time as secretary of the Football Association (1973-89), pushed hard to win good financial deals for soccer in England. Perhaps this approach stemmed from his time as a successful businessman before taking up his FA post. His autobiography was titled *The First Voice You Will Hear Is . . .* (Collins, 1987), recalling the broadcast FA Cup draws over which he used to preside; he may eventually be better remembered for this rather than any economic astuteness.

maintain league football in 1914-15 and then curtail it the following season - but popularity increased in 1923 when the FA was linked with the new Wembley Stadium.

Under Rous's influence the FA reacted better to world developments, rejoining FIFA in 1946 and sending a team to the 1950 World Cup. Youth was given its chance, too, with the launch of the FA County Youth Challenge Cup (1944), the England Youth team (1947), FA Youth Cup (1952) and England under-23 team (1954). The immediate post-war period also brought closer links with the English Schools FA and the appointment of Walter Winterbottom as Director of Coaching. More recent FA initiatives include the FA Sunday Cup (1964), the FA Challenge Trophy (1969) and the FA Challenge Vase (1974).

Football's problems of the 1970s and 1980s required responses from the FA. More time has been spent on disciplinary matters, monitoring drug tests and seeking measures to combat hooliganism. The have been protracted negotiations for sponsorship money and television deals, while ongoing concerns include ticket allocation for big games, liaison with UEFA and FIFA and arranging and administrating representative games. In 1989 Ted Croker retired after 15 important years as FA secretary. His successor, Graham Kelly, was appointed chief executive after 10 years as Football League secretary.

It was another step towards minimising the inherent conflict between the Football Association and the Football League.

FA CUP

It seems hard to avoid using cliches when writing about the Football Association Challenge Cup, to give the FA Cup its proper title. However, phrases like 'the magic of the Cup' and 'the road to Wembley' are both singularly appropriate and universally understood to apply to this and no other competition.

The FA Cup, which is often claimed to be the oldest knock-out competition in the world despite the fact that the idea was based on a similar tournament held at Harrow School, was conceived in 1871 under the guidance of FA secretary Charles Alcock. The first Final was played in the following year. That competition was completed in just 13 matches, with such

FA CUP FA Cup winners in 1883, Blackburn Olympic may not be jigging around Wembley adorned with the scarves of their supporters, but they display every bit as much pride. They had quite a route to the final: 9-1 v Lower Darwen, 8-0 v Darwen Ramblers, 2-0 v Church, 4-0 v Druids, 4-0 v Old Carthusians and 2-1 v Old Etonians to win the Cup at the Kennington Oval. The Astley brothers can be seen either side of the goalkeeper, a T.J. Hacking, in the back row.

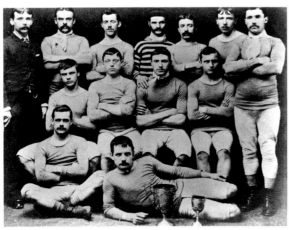

FA CUP

Year	Winners	Runners-up	Score
1872	Wanderers	Royal Engineers	1-0
1873	Wanderers	Oxford University	2-0
1874	Oxford University	Royal Engineers	2-0
1875	Royal Engineers	Old Etonians	1-1*
	Royal Engineers	Old Etonians	2-1
1876	Wanderers	Old Etonians	1-1
	Wanderers	Old Etonians	3-0
1877	Wanderers	Oxford University	2-0*
1878	Wanderers	Royal Engineers	3-1
1879	Old Etonians	Clapham Rovers	1-0
1880	Clapham Rovers	Oxford University	1-0
1881	Old Carthusians	Old Etonians	3-0
1882	Old Etonians	Blackburn Rovers	1-0
1883	Blackburn Rovers	Old Etonians	2-1*
1884	Blackburn Rovers	Queen's Park	2-1
1885	Blackburn Rovers	Queen's Park	2-0
1886	Blackburn Rovers	West Bromwich A	0-0
	Blackburn Rovers	West Bromwich A	2-0
1887	Aston Villa	West Bromwich A	2-0
1888	West Bromwich A	Preston North End	2-1
1889	Preston North End	Wolverhampton Wanderers	3-0
1890	Blackburn Rovers	Sheffield Wednesday	6-1
1891	Blackburn Rovers	Notts County	3-1
1892	West Bromwich A	Aston Villa	3-0
1893	Wolverhampton Wanderers	Everton	1-0
1894	Notts County	Bolton Wanderers	4-1
1895	Aston Villa	West Bromwich A	1-0
1896	Sheffield Wednesday	Wolverhampton Wanderers	2-1
1897	Aston Villa	Everton	3-2
1898	Nottingham Forest	Derby County	3-1
1899	Sheffield United	Derby County	4-1
1900	Bury	Southampton	4-0
1901	Tottenham Hotspur	Sheffield United	2-2
	Tottenham Hotspur	Sheffield United	3-1
1902	Sheffield United	Southampton	1-1
	Sheffield United	Southampton	2-1
1903	Bury	Derby County	6-0
1904	Manchester City	Bolton Wanderers	1-0
1905	Aston Villa	Newcastle United	2-0
1906	Everton	Newcastle United	1-0
1907	Sheffield Wednesday	Everton	2-1
1908	Wolverhampton Wanderers	Newcastle United	3-1
1909	Manchester United	Bristol City	1-0
1910	Newcastle United	Barnsley	1-1
	Newcastle United	Barnsley	2-0
1911	Bradford City	Newcastle United	1-0
	Bradford City	Newcastle United	0-0
1912	Barnsley	West Bromwich A	0-0
	Barnsley	West Bromwich A	1-0*
1913	Aston Villa	Sunderland	1-0
1914	Burnley	Liverpool	1-0
1915	Sheffield United	Chelsea	3-0
1920	Aston Villa	Huddersfield Town	1-0*
1921	Tottenham Hotspur	Wolverhampton Wanderers	1-0
1922	Huddersfield Town	Preston North End	1-0
1923	Bolton Wanderers	West Ham U	2-0
1924	Newcastle United	Aston Villa	2-0
1925	Sheffield United	Cardiff City	1-0
1926	Bolton Wanderers	Manchester City	1-0

Year	Winner	Runner-up	Score
1927	Cardiff City	Arsenal	1-0
1928	Blackburn Rovers	Huddersfield Town	3-1
1929	Bolton Wanderers	Portsmouth	2-0
1930	Arsenal	Huddersfield Town	2-0
1931	West Bromwich A	Birmingham City	2-1
1932	Newcastle United	Arsenal	2-1
1933	Everton	Manchester City	3-0
1934	Manchester City	Portsmouth	2-1
1935	Sheffield Wednesday	West Bromwich A	4-2
1936	Arsenal	Sheffield United	1-0
1937	Sunderland	Preston North End	3-1
1938	Preston North End	Huddersfield Town	1-0*
1939	Portsmouth	Wolverhampton Wanderers	4-1
1946	Derby County	Charlton Athletic	4-1*
1947	Charlton Athletic	Burnley	1-0*
1948	Manchester United	Blackpool	4-2
1949	Wolverhampton Wanderers	Leicester City	3-1
1950	Arsenal	Liverpool	2-0
1951	Newcastle United	Blackpool	2-0
1952	Newcastle United	Arsenal	1-0
1953	Blackpool	Bolton Wanderers	4-3
1954	West Bromwich A	Preston North End	3-2
1955	Newcastle United	Manchester City	3-1
1956	Manchester City	Birmingham City	3-1
1957	Aston Villa	Manchester United	2-1
1958	Bolton Wanderers	Manchester United	2-0
1959	Nottingham Forest	Luton Town	2-1
1960	Wolverhampton Wanderers	Blackburn Rovers	3-0
1961	Tottenham Hotspur	Leicester City	2-0
1962	Tottenham Hotspur	Burnley	3-1
1963	Manchester United	Leicester City	3-1
1964	West Ham United	Preston North End	3-2
1965	Liverpool	Leeds United	2-1*
1966	Everton	Sheffield Wednesday	3-2
1967	Tottenham Hotspur	Chelsea	2-1
1968	West Bromwich A	Everton	1-0*
1969	Manchester City	Leicester City	1-0
1970	Chelsea	Leeds United	2-2*
	Chelsea	Leeds United	2-1*
1971	Arsenal	Liverpool	2-1*
1972	Leeds United	Arsenal	1-0
1973	Sunderland	Leeds United	1-0
1974	Liverpool	Newcastle United	3-0
1975	West Ham United	Fulham	2-0
1976	Southampton	Manchester United	1-0
1977	Manchester United	Liverpool	2-1
1978	Ipswich Town	Arsenal	1-0
1979	Arsenal	Manchester United	3-2
1980	West Ham United	Arsenal	1-0
1981	Tottenham Hotspur	Manchester City	1-1*
	Tottenham Hotspur	Manchester City	3-2
1982	Tottenham Hotspur	Queen's Park Rangers	1-1*
	Tottenham Hotspur	Queen's Park Rangers	1-0
1983	Manchester United	Brighton & Hove Albion	2-2
	Manchester United	Brighton & Hove Albion	4-0*
1984	Everton	Watford	2-0
1985	Manchester United	Everton	1-0*
1986	Liverpool	Everton	3-1
1987	Coventry City	Tottenham Hotspur	3-2*
1988	Wimbledon	Liverpool	1-0
1989	Liverpool	Everton	3-2*
1990	Manchester United	Crystal Palace	3-3*
	Manchester United	Crystal Palace	1-0
1991	Tottenham Hotspur	Nottingham Forest	2-1*

*after extra time

highlights as Maidenhead's 2-0 victory over Great Marlow in the first round and Wanderers' 1-0 Final win over the Royal Engineers, in front of 2000 spectators at Kennington Oval, stealing what few headlines there were.

The wholly amateur tournament thrived with increasing numbers of entrants and continued southern success until the 1883 victory of Blackburn Olympic. Those early years of the Cup contained frequent oddities. In the first tournament, teams involved in drawn matches were allowed to progress to the next round; in the following year the Final was a challenge match, with teams playing in the rounds for a chance to challenge the holders. Blackburn Olympic's victory, (their neighbours Blackburn Rovers had been runners-up the preceding year), marked the start of a period of northern, and professional, domination. Although professionalism was to remain, the northern grip on the Cup was eventually broken by Southern League Tottenham Hotspur in 1901, who played their drawn Final in front of a crowd of 114,815 at Crystal Palace before their replay success against Sheffield United at Burnden Park, Bolton. The trophy that the Spurs won was not the familiar pot that is handed to today's winning captain. They won the second cup,

which was later presented to Lord Kinnaird (nine Final appearances) when he retired as FA President. The very first cup had been stolen in 1895 from a shop in Birmingham. The present trophy was first won by Bradford City in 1911 (their only Cup success).

Following that 1901 upset the north re-asserted their almost total control of the Cup, a run that continued well beyond the famous 1923 Final - the first to be played at Wembley and noted for its 126,000 spectators and the single police horse that gently guided the overflowing crowd off the playing surface. Wembley has staged every Final since that year with the exception of the 1970 Leeds United v Chelsea replay, played at

Old Trafford. Wembley finals are now part of the English national tradition, matches that attract a vast television audience both domestically and around the world. These Finals have included a number of memorable and emotional occasions, perhaps the most famous being the 1953 match in which Sir Stanley Matthews finally won his Cup winners' medal for Blackpool against Bolton Wanderers; the 1958 defeat of Manchester United's Munich survivors, this time by Bolton; and the 1973 shock defeat of Leeds United by Second Division Sunderland.

Of course, the Final is not the only match of importance. Every game contains its own significance for the 500-600 entrants who began battling it out in the late summer, some nine months before the tournament's eventual climax. It's the chance for non-League and smaller League sides to battle against the 'big boys' that appeals, and most seasons throw up a few shocks, a few moments of unexpected glory. The present rules exempt Third and Fourth Division sides until the first round proper, normally played in November, and First and Second Division teams until the magical third round, played in January.

As the record books show, the Cup is often the opportunity for a team not doing well in the League to grab some glory, and also a chance to qualify for a European competition. Aston Villa, who last won the Cup in 1957 join Manchester United (seven wins apiece) in chasing Tottenham Hotspur with their eight wins. Teams such as Newcastle United (six wins and four League Championships) figure prominently, in contrast to Liverpool (four wins and eighteen League successes). Perhaps it's the nature of the competition - a simple knock-out with no seeding, no penalty shoot-outs, no away-goal rules - that suits the style of some clubs better than others. Whatever it is, there is something about the Cup that marks it out as special for both fans and players. Even many modern professional players, financially hardened and media spoiled, consider their careers incomplete without a Cup winners' medal.

In recent years there has been increasing talk about lavish sponsorship for the tournament, although voices within the FA are loath to see their famous trophy linked to any other name save their own. There have also been grumbles and accusations about ticket allocations for the Final, the Football Association's big day; as the capacity of Wembley falls due to safety restrictions and the change to an all-seater stadium, so it appears that genuine fans lose out to the wealthier and more influential members of society. The Football Association has to be careful. Although the Cup may now seem inviolate, the ghosts of the Wanderers and the Royal Engineers will tell you that nothing remains the same.

FOOTBALL LEAGUE

The Football League is by far the most important of the 1500 or more leagues affiliated to the Football Association. The oldest in the world, it was formed by 12 northern and Midland clubs in 1988, three years after professionalism had been sanctioned reluctantly by the largely amateur and southern-dominated Football Association. The League's founder, William McGregor, a Scottish draper and Aston Villa committee man, was frustrated by the impromptu nature of Cup and friendly fixtures. He realised that pre-arranged home and away fixtures would boost gate receipts and thereby finance the fledgling professional game.

Although continually criticised for putting commerce before sport, the League has been an enduring success. It expanded to two divisions of 28 clubs in 1892 (after the absorption of the rival Alliance league), reaching 44 clubs by 1919. In 1920 it took over the Southern League's best clubs to form a Third Division, followed shortly by the best of the rest from the north and Midlands, bringing the total to 88 clubs by 1923.

By that time League players exclusively formed the English national team, while the last non-League club to have won the FA Cup was Tottenham Hotspur in 1901.

Four extra clubs joined in 1950, and in 1958 the Third Divisions North and South were replaced by nationally based Third and Fourth Divisions. By 1992 further expansion will raise the total to 94 clubs.

The League itself is an essentially democratic body whose main function is to organise the weekly fixtures and the Football League Cup (currently sponsored by Rumbelows), to oversee the financial and transfer arrangements of member clubs, and to distribute income accrued from outside sources such as sponsors, television companies and the football pools. The League's current sponsors are Barclay's Bank. League headquarters are in Lytham St Anne's, with a commercial office in London and a chief executive, Arther Sandford, based in Nottingham.

Policy decisions are taken by an eight-man elected management committee and by regular meetings of all clubs. Third and Fourth Division clubs, as associate members, are allowed only eight votes between them. Similarly, the distribution of funds is weighted heavily in favour of the First Division clubs.

For many years one of the most contentious issues concerning the League was its reluctance to elect new clubs in place of those which frequently finished at the foot of the Fourth Division. This so-called 'closed-shop' agreement ended in 1987, Scarborough becoming the first non-League club ever to win automatic promotion to the League as winners of the Vauxhall Conference (at the expense of Lincoln City). The

FOOTBALL LEAGUE
A print taken from the Football League minutes showing the results from the first ever season of competition. The final League positions are shown at the bottom of the chart. It was compiled by one R.H. Richards, who made one small error: Derby County's recorded 5-2 defeat of Notts County was, in fact, a 5-3 scoreline.

Position	The Football League 1888-1889 (Alphabetically Arranged)	WON	LOST	DRAWN	Goals For	Goals Against	Points	Position
7	Accrington	6	8	8	48	48	20	7
2	Aston Villa	12	5	5	61	43	29	2
4	B'burn Rovers	10	6	6	66	45	26	4
5	Bolton Wanderers	10	10	2	63	59	22	5
9	Burnley	7	12	3	42	62	17	9
10	Derby County	7	13	2	41	60	16	10
8	Everton	9	11	2	35	47	20	8
11	Notts County	5	15	2	39	73	12	11
1	Preston N.E.	18		4	74	15	40	1
12	Stoke	4	14	4	26	51	12	12
6	West Brom. Albion	10	10	2	40	46	22	6
3	Wolverhampton Wanderers	12	6	4	51	37	28	3
		110	110	44	586	586	264	

Results of 132 Matches. No. of Matches 22 Each

April 1889. R.H. Richards.

FOOTBALL LEAGUE
Founder of the Football League, William McGregor. He appeared to be universally popular in his native Midlands, where he died on 20 December 1911 at the age of 65. His involvement with football was total; at his funeral his daughter said he had 'the spirit of a schoolboy and the heart of a true, full-grown man'. Both parts of his character were instrumental in getting the Football League off the pages of committee meeting minutes and into reality.

Conference has thus become a de facto Fifth Division.

There have been other important rule changes in recent decades. The award of two points per win, agreed in 1888 and copied throughout the world, was modified to three points per win in 1981 in a marginally successful attempt to encourage attaching play.

To add interest at the end of the season, a controversial but profitable system of play-offs was introduced in 1987, involving clubs on the fringes of automatic promotion and relegation. Whereas before 1973 only two clubs were promoted and two relegated between the First and Second Divisions, the format has since been altered several times, for example to reduce the First

Division to 20 clubs by 1988, then, after a change of heart, to restore it to 22 clubs by 1992.

This financially motivated volte face angered the FA, which in 1991 announced its own plans for a Superleague, involving the top First Division clubs. The League, for its part, responded by threatening legal action.

Whatever the outcome of this power struggle – the latest of many – the pressure on League clubs to finance the implementation of the Taylor Report has put in question the entire framework of English football. As in 1888, money continues to be the dominant issue.

FOOTBALL LEAGUE CHAMPIONSHIP

The League itself consists of four divisions, but the 'Championship' refers to Division 1, often called the hardest league in the world on account of the quality of teams and the number of matches to be played.

Liverpool have been far and away the most successful side in the competition. By the end of the 1990s they had collected 18 wins, eight more than nearest rivals Arsenal. Interestingly, it appears to be a title that, if won once, can be won again. Of 23 clubs that have lifted the Championship, only five are once-only winners.

FOOTBALL LEAGUE CHAMPIONSHIP

Year	Winners	Runners-up
1888/89	Preston North End	Aston Villa
1889/90	Preston North End	Everton
1890/91	Everton	Preston North End
1891/92	Sunderland	Preston North End
1892/93	Sunderland	Preston North End
1893/94	Aston Villa	Sunderland
1894/95	Sunderland	Everton
1895/96	Aston Villa	Derby County
1896/97	Aston Villa	Sheffield United
1897/98	Sheffield United	Sunderland
1898/99	Aston Villa	Liverpool
1899/1900	Aston Villa	Sheffield United
1900/01	Liverpool	Sunderland
1901/02	Sunderland	Everton
1902/03	The Wednesday	Aston Villa
1903/04	The Wednesday	Manchester City
1904/05	Newcastle United	Everton
1905/06	Liverpool	Preston North End
1906/07	Newcastle United	Bristol City
1907/08	Manchester United	Aston Villa
1908/09	Newcastle United	Everton
1909/10	Aston Villa	Liverpool
1910/11	Manchester United	Aston Villa
1911/12	Blackburn Rovers	Everton
1912/13	Sunderland	Aston Villa
1913/14	Blackburn Rovers	Aston Villa
1914/15	Everton	Oldham Athletic
1915/19	No competition	
1919/20	West Bromwich Albion	Burnley
1920/21	Burnley	Manchester City
1921/22	Liverpool	Tottenham Hotspur
1922/23	Liverpool	Sunderland
1923/24	Huddersfield Town	Cardiff City
1924/25	Huddersfield Town	West Bromwich Albion
1925/26	Huddersfield Town	Arsenal
1926/27	Newcastle United	Huddersfield Town
1927/28	Everton	Huddersfield Town
1928/29	Sheffield Wednesday	Leicester City
1929/30	Sheffield Wednesday	Derby County
1930/31	Arsenal	Aston Villa
1931/32	Everton	Arsenal
1932/33	Arsenal	Aston Villa
1933/34	Arsenal	Huddersfield Town
1934/35	Arsenal	Sunderland
1935/36	Sunderland	Derby County
1936/37	Manchester City	Charlton Athletic
1937/38	Arsenal	Wolverhampton Wanderers
1938/39	Everton	Wolverhampton Wanderers
1939/46	No competition	
1946/47	Liverpool	Manchester United
1947/48	Arsenal	Manchester United
1948/49	Portsmouth	Manchester United
1949/50	Portsmouth	Wolverhampton Wanderers
1950/51	Tottenham Hotspur	Manchester United
1951/52	Manchester United	Tottenham Hotspur
1952/53	Arsenal	Preston North End
1953/54	Wolverhampton Wanderers	West Bromwich Albion
1954/55	Chelsea	Wolverhampton Wanderers
1955/56	Manchester United	Blackpool

1956/57	Manchester United	Tottenham Hotspur
1957/58	Wolverhampton Wanderers	Preston North End
1958/59	Wolverhampton Wanderers	Manchester United
1959/60	Burnley	Wolverhampton Wanderers
1960/61	Tottenham Hotspur	Sheffield Wednesday
1961/62	Ipswich Town	Burnley
1962/63	Everton	Tottenham Hotspur
1963/64	Liverpool	Manchester United
1964/65	Manchester United	Leeds United
1965/66	Liverpool	Leeds United
1966/67	Manchester United	Nottingham Forest
1967/68	Manchester City	Manchester United
1968/69	Leeds United	Liverpool
1969/70	Everton	Leeds United
1970/71	Arsenal	Leeds United
1971/72	Derby County	Leeds United
1972/73	Liverpool	Arsenal
1973/74	Leeds United	Liverpool
1974/75	Derby County	Liverpool
1975/76	Liverpool	Queen's Park Rangers
1976/77	Liverpool	Manchester City
1977/78	Nottingham Forest	Liverpool
1978/79	Liverpool	Nottingham Forest
1979/80	Liverpool	Manchester United
1980/81	Aston Villa	Ipswich Town
1981/82	Liverpool	Ipswich Town
1982/83	Liverpool	Watford
1983/84	Liverpool	Southampton
1984/85	Everton	Liverpool
1985/86	Liverpool	Everton
1986/87	Everton	Liverpool
1987/88	Liverpool	Manchester United
1988/89	Arsenal	Liverpool
1989/90	Liverpool	Aston Villa
1990/91	Arsenal	Liverpool

FOOTBALL LEAGUE CUP

This was first competed for in 1960/61, although the idea of a competition solely between teams within the Football League had been suggested as early as 1892. Initially it was not well supported, with many top clubs refusing to enter. The persistence of League officials Alan Hardaker and Joe Richards kept the tournament going until the mid 1960s. It was in 1967 that the final was first held at Wembley and in the same year that success in the final brought automatic qualification for the UEFA Cup (for First Division sides). Both moves, pushed through by Hardaker, were successful in encouraging greater interest and, very quickly, an entry from every League club.

With major sides competing, and Wembley full-houses and television exposure adding to the interest, the tournament became established. Several of the early Wembley finals were memorable affairs, particularly the successes of Third Division sides Swindon and Queen's Park Rangers over First Division opponents. Today the future of the tournament seems assured, although the name changes regularly with the sponsors. From 1982-86 it was the Milk Cup, then the Littlewoods (pools company) Cup, and in 1990 teams competed for the Rumbelows (household appliances) Cup. Time will tell who takes over the sponsorship of what sniffy Liverpudlians (when they declined to enter) once called the 'Mickey Mouse Cup'.

FOOTBALL TRUST

Formed in 1979, the Football Trust was initially funded entirely by Littlewoods, Vernons and Zetters from their spot-the-ball competitions. In 1990 the Trust was granted an additional budget from funds created by the reduction in football-pools tax announced in the Chancellor's budget.

The Trust has worked extensively to support and fund community initiatives in the professional and semi-professional game. It has also contributed to the improvement of stadium facilities and anti-hooliganism measures such as closed-circuit television. Among its work at grass-roots level is support for the Disabled Sports

FOOTBALL LEAGUE CHAMPIONSHIP The beauty of the League Championship, the experts say, is that it rewards endeavour over the whole season, not just in one or two matches. That, of course, is true, although the 1988/89 season ended in a 'cup final' with the two title contenders, Arsenal and Liverpool, playing each other in the last match of the season. Arsenal needed to win at least 2-0 at Anfield to secure the Championship, and did just that, grabbing the winner in the dying seconds of the match. A delighted squad display the traditional Championship trophy (held aloft) and the Barclay's League trophy presented by the sponsors.

FOOTBALL LEAGUE CUP

(Played with two-leg finals until 1966).

Year	Winners	Runners-up	Score
1961	Aston Villa	Rotherham United	0-2, 3-0*
1962	Norwich City	Rochdale	3-0, 1-0
1963	Birmingham City	Aston Villa	3-1, 0-0
1964	Leicester City	Stoke City	1-1, 3-2
1965	Chelsea	Leicester City	3-2, 0-0
1966	West Bromwich A	West Ham United	1-2, 4-1
1967	Queen's Park Rangers	West Bromwich A	3-2
1968	Leeds United	Arsenal	1-0
1969	Swindon Town	Arsenal	3-1*
1970	Manchester City	West Bromwich A	2-1*
1971	Tottenham Hotspur	Aston Villa	2-0
1972	Stoke City	Chelsea	2-1
1973	Tottenham Hotspur	Norwich City	1-0
1974	Wolverhampton Wanderers	Manchester City	2-1
1975	Aston Villa	Norwich City	1-0
1976	Manchester City	Newcastle United	2-1
1977	Aston Villa	Everton	0-0, 1-1*, 3-2*
1978	Nottingham Forest	Liverpool	0-0*, 1-0
1979	Nottingham Forest	Southampton	3-2
1980	Wolverhampton Wanderers	Nottingham Forest	1-0
1981	Liverpool	West Ham United	1-1*, 2-1
1982	Liverpool	Tottenham Hotspur	3-1*
1983	Liverpool	Manchester United	2-1*
1984	Liverpool	Everton	0-0*, 1-0
1985	Norwich City	Sunderland	1-0
1986	Oxford United	Queen's Park Rangers	3-0
1987	Arsenal	Liverpool	2-1
1988	Luton Town	Arsenal	3-2
1989	Nottingham Forest	Luton Town	3-1
1990	Nottingham Forest	Oldham Athletic	1-0
1991	Sheffield Wednesday	Manchester United	1-0

* after extra time

Foundation and the Sports Turf Research Institute. It has also funded research projects and in April 1987 helped establish the Sir Norman Chester Centre for Football Research at Leicester University.

In 1990 the Football Trust combined with the Football Grounds Improvement Trust to form 'The Football Trust 90', an important organisation with a budget of £30 million per annum to allocate to ground-safety projects, in particular the conversions to all seater-stadia. The Trust members are chosen to represent all the interested parties: the football associations and leagues of England and Scotland, local authorities, the Professional Footballers' Association, the police and the pools companies.

FOOTBALLER OF THE YEAR

It seems natural for there to be a trophy acknowledging the top player for a season - although perhaps not so understandable that there are two! In 1948 the Football Writers' Association began the FWA Footballer of the Year trophy for their choice of the season's top player from the Football League. This seemed fine, until 1974 when the Professional Footballers' Association set up their own awards for what they called the 'Players' Player of the Year'. The PFA also award young players and give special merit awards.

The two accolades sit uneasily together, although nobody minds picking up an award and in some years the same player picks up both. In 1983 Ian Rush (Liverpool) won the PFA Young Player award and in 1984 he picked up both senior awards.

Scotland has similar awards, again with trophies being presented by two bodies, the Scottish FWA and PFA. These are for players in the Scottish League and, unlike the English awards, have been won almost exclusively by players born in Scotland.

DAVID PLATT The 1990 winner of the Professional Fotballer's Association Player of the Year award. The Villa man is seen here, in England shirt, having just scored a last-ditch winner against Belgium in the World Cup of 1990. His all-round skills demonstrated in that tournament bought much acclaim.

FOOTBALL WRITERS' ASSOCIATION AWARDS

Year	Winner	Club
1948	Stanley Matthews	Blackpool
1949	Johnny Carey	Manchester United
1950	Joe Mercer	Arsenal
1951	Harry Johnston	Blackpool
1952	Billy Wright	Wolverhampton Wanderers
1953	Nat Lofthouse	Bolton Wanderers
1954	Tom Finney	Preston North End
1955	Don Revie	Manchester City
1956	Bert Trautmann	Manchester City
1957	Tom Finney	Preston North End
1958	Danny Blanchflower	Tottenham Hotspur
1959	Syd Owen	Luton Town
1960	Bill Slater	Wolverhampton Wanderers
1961	Danny Blanchflower	Tottenham Hotspur
1962	Jimmy Adamson	Burnley
1963	Stanley Matthews	Stoke City
1964	Bobby Moore	West Ham United
1965	Bobby Collins	Leeds United
1966	Bobby Charlton	Manchester United
1967	Jackie Charlton	Leeds United
1968	George Best	Manchester United
1969	Tony Book	Manchester City
	Dave Mackay	Derby County
1970	Billy Bremner	Leeds United
1971	Frank McLintock	Arsenal
1972	Gordon Banks	Stoke City
1973	Pat Jennings	Tottenham Hotspur
1974	Ian Callaghan	Liverpool
1975	Alan Mullery	Fulham
1976	Kevin Keegan	Liverpool
1977	Emlyn Hughes	Liverpool
1978	Kenny Burns	Nottingham Forest
1979	Kenny Dalglish	Liverpool
1980	Terry McDermott	Liverpool
1981	Frans Thissen	Ipswich Town
1982	Steve Perryman	Tottenham Hotspur
1983	Kenny Dalglish	Liverpool
1984	Ian Rush	Liverpool
1985	Neville Southall	Everton
1986	Gary Lineker	Everton
1987	Clive Allen	Tottenham Hotspur
1988	John Barnes	Liverpool
1989	Steve Nichol	Liverpool
1990	John Barnes	Liverpool

PROFESSIONAL FOOTBALLERS' ASSOCIATION AWARDS

Year	Winner	Club
1974	Norman Hunter	Leeds United
1975	Colin Todd	Derby County
1976	Pat Jennings	Tottenham Hotspur
1977	Andy Gray	Aston Villa
1978	Peter Shilton	Nottingham Forest
1979	Liam Brady	Arsenal
1980	Terry McDermott	Liverpool
1981	John Wark	Ipswich Town
1982	Kevin Keegan	Southampton
1983	Kenny Dalglish	Liverpool
1984	Ian Rush	Liverpool
1985	Peter Reid	Everton
1986	Gary Lineker	Everton
1987	Clive Allen	Tottenham Hotspur
1988	John Barnes	Liverpool
1989	Mark Hughes	Manchester United
1990	David Platt	Aston Villa

SCOTTISH FOOTBALL WRITERS' ASSOCIATION AWARDS

Year	Winner	Club
1965	Billy McNeill	Celtic
1966	John Greig	Rangers
1967	Ronnie Simpson	Celtic
1968	Gordon Wallace	Raith Rovers
1969	Bobby Murdoch	Celtic
1970	Pat Stanton	Hibernian
1971	Martin Buchan	Aberdeen
1972	Dave Smith	Rangers
1973	George Connelly	Celtic
1974	Scotland's World Cup Squad	
1975	Sandy Jardine	Rangers
1976	John Greig	Rangers
1977	Danny McGrain	Celtic
1978	Derek Johnstone	Rangers
1979	Andy Ritchie	Morton
1980	Gordon Strachan	Aberdeen
1981	Alan Rough	Partick Thistle
1982	Paul Sturrock	Dundee United
1983	Charlie Nicholas	Celtic
1984	Willie Miller	Aberdeen
1985	Hamish McAlpine	Dundee United
1986	Sandy Jardine	Hearts
1987	Brian McClair	Celtic
1988	Paul McStay	Celtic
1989	Richard Gough	Rangers
1990	Alex McLeish	Aberdeen

SCOTTISH PROFESSIONAL FOOTBALLERS' ASSOCIATION AWARDS

Year	Winner	Club
1978	Derek Johnstone	Rangers
1979	Paul Hegarty	Dundee United
1980	Davie Provan	Celtic
1981	Sandy Clark	Airdrieonians
1982	Mark McGhee	Aberdeen
1983	Charlie Nicholas	Celtic
1984	Willie Miller	Aberdeen
1985	Jim Duffy	Morton
1986	Richard Gough	Dundee
1987	Brian McClair	Celtic
1988	Paul McStay	Celtic
1989	Theo Snelders	Aberdeen
1990	Jim Bett	Aberdeen

FORFAR ATHLETIC

Founded 1885

Joined League 1921 (Division 2)

Honours Scottish League Second Division Champions 1984; Div.C Champions 1949

Ground Station Park

Forfar have found their greatest fame in alarming mighty Rangers. With seven minutes to go of the 1977/78 League Cup semi-final they led the Glasgow side 2-1 before losing in extra time. In 1982 Rangers required two matches to dispose of them in the semi-final of the Scottish Cup. Forfar narrowly failed to beat the Ibrox men in a 1985 League Cup tie finally decided by a penalty shoot-out.

Those stirring matches occurred in the finest period of the club's history. In 1984 Forfar won the Second Division with a record 63 points.

FULHAM

Founded 1879

Joined League 1907 (Div.2)

Honours Div.2 Champions 1949; Div.3 (S) Champions 1932

Ground Craven Cottage

Fulham have always been a homely club who have placed heavy accent on entertainment; their very name has been a password for eccentricity. In the cut-throat business that soccer has become, however, such an admirable trait has sometimes seemed out of place, and even the most loyal Craven Cottage fan might, at times, have been willing to forgo the endearing foibles – often exemplified by the antics of long-time chairman, the late Tommy Trinder – in favour of a little more success and financial stability.

It all started when two clergymen formed the club on behalf of their churchgoers and, after twice winning the Southern League, Fulham were elected to the senior competition. At first they held their own in Division 2, but a gradual decline culminated in relegation in 1928. Four years later, bolstered by 43-goal Frank Newton, they bounced back and then consolidated.

After the war they managed three terms in the top flight and, perversely, demotion in 1952 heralded a buoyant period. Though the rest of the 1950s were spent in the Second Division, Fulham served up some of the capital's most attractive football and deserved promotion when it arrived in 1959. Life proved difficult in the First Division, though, and the 'Cottagers' spent the 1960s fighting rearguard actions, until a sudden slide dumped them in Division 3 in 1969.

During those two eventful decades, Fulham's most influential player was gifted schemer Johnny Haynes, with other major contributions coming from centre-forward Bedford Jezzard (who also served as manager), defenders Jim Langley and England World Cup star George Cohen, wingers Graham Leggat and the extrovert 'Tosh' Chamberlain, goalkeeper Tony Macedo, wing-halves Bobby Robson and Alan Mullery and inside-forward Jimmy Hill.

Since then Fulham have divided their time between the Second and Third Divisions. The 1970s were enlivened by the 1975 FA Cup Final (lost to West Ham), the presence for three years of Bobby Moore, and cameo stints from George Best and Rodney Marsh.

The early 1980s, with former Cottage Malcolm Macdonald in charge, saw many bright displays, but the promise faded and in 1987 the club came perilously close to a merger with Queen's Park Rangers. That was averted by a group headed by the aforementioned Hill, but the future of Craven Cottage was still in the melting pot as the 1990s dawned.

FULHAM

Fulham, despite their reputation for not being really up to the hurly-burly of modern football, have produced good sides and good players. Bobby Robson, who played for the club between 1950 and 1955, was one who went on to greater things. Most of his time with the club was spent in the middle of Division 2. Robson later spent a brief spell as manager with the team in 1968; the club finished bottom of Division 1, five points adrift in 1967/68, and were bottom of Division 2 by a similar margin in the following year.

GALLACHER, Hughie

1903 Born in Bellshill, Scotland

1920 Joins his first professional club, Queen of the South

1921 Signs for Airdrieonians

1924 International debut against Northern Ireland

1925 Moves to Newcastle United for £6500

1927 Captains the 'Magpies' to the League Championship

1930 Joins Chelsea for £10000

1935 Makes a £3000 switch to Derby County

1936 Moves on to Notts County for £2000

1937 His price still dropping, he joins Grimsby Town for £1000

1938 Gateshead sign him for £500

1957 Commits suicide on a railway line

Many shrewd pundits have described Hughie Gallacher as the most complete centre-forward British soccer has known. Standing a mere 5 ft 5 in, Gallacher was a muscular bundle of skill, strength and energy who thrived at every level of the game, but whose private life was a sad and sorry mess.

After playing as a schoolboy alongside Alex James, he made such an impact in the Scottish League that there were protest demonstrations when his transfer to Newcastle was announced. Gallacher was an instant success on Tyneside, becoming a skipper who led by both example and scathing criticism of those less talented than himself.

He was equally effective on the international scene – netting 22 times in 19 outings for Scotland – and was one of the famous 'Wembley Wizards', who thrashed England 5-1 in 1928. Gallacher went on to give five years' sterling service to Chelsea before dropping down the scale with smaller clubs, although he never stopped

HUGHIE GALLACHER
In his Newcastle strip, Hughie Gallacher giving a 'photo opportunity' to the press at St James's Park at the height of his career. Perhaps a trace of his arrogance can be glimpsed in his face – but certainly not a hint of the tragedy that was, ultimately, to lie in wait for him.

scoring and ended with a record of 387 strikes in 541 English and Scottish League games.

A temperamental, arrogant individual who was addicted to high living, he was involved in frequent controversy and would have been a gossip-writer's dream today. He ended up a lonely man who took his own life by stepping in front of a train the day before he was to appear in accused of ill-treating his child.

GAMBLING

People have always placed bets on the outcome of football matches either privately, through bookmakers or on football pools. Odds are also quoted for football competitions such as the FA Cup and Football League. In the past, bookmakers have taken bets on possible goal-scorers, but there is often dispute over this. One example is Arsenal's equaliser in the 1971 FA Cup Final, thought to be scored by George Graham until close scrutiny over several days revealed that Graham had not touched Eddie Kelly's pass.

In the early 1920s a Birmingham bookmaker launched the first football coupon. The idea was developed by John Moores, Colin Askham and Bill Hughes, who formed the

Littlewoods Pools organisation in 1923. John Moores bought out his colleagues during a period of early difficulties and by 1929 Littlewoods were hiring 50 girls to check coupons. A rival organisation, Vernon's Pools, was formed in 1929, and the biggest prizes became associated with forecasting drawn games.

In 1949 pools companies included Australian matches for the first time. The winter prize money grew, passing £100,000 in 1950 and £300,000 nine years later. In 1959 Football League fixtures were confirmed as the League's copyright, and pools companies agreed to pay for reproducing them. Around the same time clubs became aware that they could raise money by small-scale commercial ventures such as lotteries and bingo tickets.

In January 1963 the pools companies inaugurated the 'pools panel', a group of experts who could agree the results of postponed matches, enabling the pools to continue through bad weather. In August 1969 the points scoring system on treble-chance was altered to discriminate between goalless draws (two points) and score draws (three points); it was becoming too easy to predict some teams drawing away from home. The potential winnings continued to rise. In April 1987 a 60-year-old woman won a then record £1,032,088 for a £1.20 stake, and later that year a Northants lorry driver won £1,339,358.

Almost every country has had a major bribery investigation, often associated with gambling. Sometimes the suspects are officials who have allegedly bribed opponents to ensure bonuses or trophies, but more regularly they are players attempting to win money on bets placed.

One of the most dramatic investigations in recent years was in Hungary in 1983, when 260 players and 14 referees were among those suspended and 75 people were convicted of conspiring to fix matches in lower leagues.

A Football League game between Manchester United and Liverpool on 2 April 1915 was the subject of a lengthy enquiry. Nine players were suspended from football for allegedly fixing the game, profiting from bets and defrauding bookmakers. One accused player later failed to win a libel action against the FA. Manchester United won the game 2-0.

In January 1965 ten British players (or ex-players) were sent to prison for conspiracy to defraud by fixing matches. Jimmy Gauld, a former player with Waterford, Charlton, Everton, Plymouth, Swindon, St Johnstone and Mansfield Town, was sentenced to four years' imprisonment with £5000 costs. He had been named the ringleader by the *Sunday People*, the newspaper exposing the scandal.

The FA tightened regulations on football-club personnel betting on matches. (A ban which had operated from 1892 had been lifted in 1957.) In January 1990 former Swindon Town chairman Brian Hillier and ex-manager Lou Macari were charged with betting on Newcastle to beat Swindon in an FA Cup tie. Hillier was suspended by the FA for three years, Macari censured and fined £1000, and Swindon Town fined £7500. The investigation into Swindon's books also revealed irregular payments which later cost the club promotion to Division 1.

GARRINCHA

1933 Born in Pau Grande, Brazil

1952 Joins Botafogo of Rio

1955 Gains first of 59 Brazilian caps

1958 Helps Brazil to World Cup win, 5-2 *v* Sweden

1962 Sent off in World Cup semi-final against Chile — hit by a bottle as he leaves the field; after a personal plea from the Brazilian president, Garrincha is allowed to play in the final. Brazil win 3-1 *v* Czechoslovakia

1964 Botafogo are Brazilian champions

1965 Another championship, this time shared with Santos; car crash puts World Cup place in jeopardy

1966 Plays in World Cup in England but is not fully fit (Brazil go out in first round); transferred to Corinthians of Sao Paolo

1967 Retires

1983 Dies of alcoholic poisoning

Garrincha's life began badly and ended tragically, but in between his skills blazed with a brightness few have matched. An outstanding player in one World Cup, the dominant force in another and a goal-scorer in a third, he

was an innocent, flawed genius, brilliant on the football field but hopelessly equipped to cope with life off it.

Born into poverty and half crippled by polio as a small child, Garrincha (his real name was Manoel Francisco dos Santos but he was known by his nickname, meaning 'Little Bird', from an early age) learned to run on his disfigured right leg and, miraculously, at his peak was capable of explosive

speed. Indeed, his twisted limb may even have been to his advantage, aiding his body-swerve. He was only 5 ft 7 in but could leap spectacularly, adding strong heading to his ability to shoot powerfully from outside the penalty area.

In 1958 Garrincha missed Brazil's first two World Cup matches in Sweden, but after a 0-0 draw with England his Botafogo team mates pleaded with manager Vicente Feola for the right-winger's

GARRINCHA Garrincha, poised in readiness, in the 1958 World Cup which was won by Brazil. It was in the 1962 tournament that he really shone, scoring twice against England in the quarter-final and twice against Chile in the semi-final. There are two main regional championships in Brazil and the little forward competed in both: in the Rio de Janeiro Championships with

Botafogo — one of the main teams, along with Fluminese and Flamingo; and in the Sao Paulo Championship with Corinthians after his transfer in 1966. That league has been dominated historically by Santos, Sao Paulo FC and lalmeiras. The national championship was established in 1967 to determine the best team in Brazil. There has been a wide range of winners.

inclusion. Garrincha's introduction, coupled with that of the 17-year-old Pele, turned a good side into a glorious one, the only team to win outside its own continent. Four years later his contribution was even more important. Injury forced Pele out of the tournament so Garrincha, by necessity, became the focal point of Brazilian attacks. He responded magnificently, tore England to pieces in the quarter-finals and did the same to Chile in the semis, and, in addition to providing the cutting edge for several goals, scored four himself.

Age and a car crash had taken their toll by 1966 and his one worthwhile contribution in England proved to be a devastating free-kick against Bulgaria at Goodison. For Garrincha and Brazil the rest of the tournament was an anti-climax, as indeed was the rest of his life. He died a burnt-out alcoholic, in 1983.

GIANT-KILLING

Giant-killing traditionally refers to a Cup-tie victory by a club of lower status. The most extreme form of English giant-killing, non-League clubs beating First Division clubs in the FA Cup, has occurred several times since the First World War: Sheffield Wednesday 0 Darlington 2 (first-round replay in 1919/20), Corinthians 1 Blackburn Rovers 0 (first-round in 1923/24), Colchester United 1 Huddersfield Town 0 (third round in 1947/48), Yeovil Town 2 Sunderland 1 (fourth round in 1948/49), Hereford United 2 Newcastle United 1 (third round replay in 1971/72), Burnley 0 Wimbledon 1 (third round in 1974/75), Birmingham City 1 Altrincham 2 (third round in 1985/86) and Sutton United 2 Coventry City 1 (third round in 1988/89).

Most of these non-League teams lost heavily in the next round – Sutton went down 8-0 to Norwich City and Yeovil lost by the same score to Manchester United in front of 81,565 spectators – but others continued to surprise. Colchester United beat Second Division Bradford Park Avenue to reach the fifth round, and Wimbledon drew 0-0 at First Division Leeds United in the fourth, helped by Dickie Guy's penalty save. They were defeated by a deflected goal in the replay.

But mention of Wimbledon illustrates the transient nature of some giant-killing. Wimbledon were in the Southern League and Burnley sixth in Division 1 when they met in 1974/75. Ten years later, when they were paired together again, Burnley were a poor Division 3 team and Wimbledon in the Second Division. There was no surprise about Wimbledon's 3-1 win.

In Scotland there is a long history of surprise results, from Celtic's 4-2 defeat by non-League Arthurlie in 1896/97 through to Inverness Caledonian's win against Airdrie (on penalty-kicks after a replay) in 1989/90. Non-League Armadale beat three Scottish League clubs – Clyde, Hibernian and Ayr United – to reach the quarter-final of the 1919/20 Scottish Cup competition. Elgin City also beat three League clubs – Albion Rovers, Forfar Athletic and Arbroath – in 1967/68. Other major Scottish Cup upsets include Fraserburgh 1 Dundee 0 (first round in 1956/57) and Berwick Rangers 1 Rangers 0 (first round in 1966/67). The latter was especially dramatic. As Keevins and McCarra write in *100 Cups*, 'There are Celtic supporters with a perverted sense of history who can tell you where they were standing when they heard Rangers had lost 1-0, and such was the barely credible result that even BBC television's afternoon sports programme refused to accept it as being true in the first place.'

Jock Wallace, manager of Berwick Rangers in 1967, later took over at Rangers. In 1980/81, however, Wallace was manager of First Division Leicester City when they

GIANTKILLING Every year the bigger clubs must wonder if it's their turn to become the headlines for the wrong reason – beaten in the FA Cup by a team from a lower division or, worst of all, by a team from outside the Football League. In 1990/91 it was the turn of West Bromwich Albion to lose, 4-2 at home, to Vauxhall League side Woking. The non-Leaguers' hero was Tim Buzaglo, who notched a hat-trick and was chaired off by disgruntled WBA fans. The next round saw Woking draw Everton; they chose to play their 'home' match at Goodison and went down 1-0 – richer and wiser.

drew at home to Fourth Division Exeter City and lost the replay. Exeter beat another First Division club, Newcastle United, in the fifth round before losing to Spurs in the sixth.

English League Cup winners include two Third Division clubs. In 1966/67 Queen's Park Rangers beat two First Division teams and two Second Division teams to win the trophy; in 1968/69 Swindon Town overcame three First Division teams – Coventry, Burnley and Arsenal – and Second Division leaders Derby County. Several Third Division clubs have reached the FA Cup semi-finals: Millwall (1936/37), Port Vale (1953/54), York City (1954/55), Norwich City (1958/59), Crystal Palace (1975/76) and Plymouth Argyle (1983/84).

In 1984/85, non-League Telford United beat four League teams – Preston, Lincoln, Bradford City and Darlington – before losing to First Division Everton in the fifth round. The preceding season Telford had beaten Rochdale, Northampton and Stockport to reach the fourth round. In 1979/80, the season Leicester City won the Second Division Championship, they were beaten 1-0 by non-League Harlow Town in a third round replay. In 1963/64 non-League Bedford Town won 3-1 in a third round game at Newcastle United, then a strong Second Division club.

On several occasions the football public has been

stunned by defeat of the top team in the land. Walsall, a mid-table Third Division (S) team, beat Arsenal, the team of the decade, in a third round FA Cup tie in 1933. Leeds United were also First Division leaders when they lost 3-2 at Fourth Division Colchester United in the fifth round of the 1970/71 FA Cup competition.

Giant-killing in the World Cup could apply to countries with relatively small populations overcoming large nations, or surprise victories for countries lacking a footballing tradition over established soccer nations. Examples in the World Cup finals include: Romania 1 Cuba 2 (1938), England 0 United States 1 (1950), Northern Ireland 2 Czechoslovakia 1 (1958), Italy 0 North Korea 1 (1966), Tunisia 3 Mexico 1 (1978), Spain 0 Northern Ireland 1 (1982) and Argentina 0 Cameroon 1 (1990). In their first ever European Championship qualifier, the Faroe Islands beat Austria 1-0 in 1990.

GILLINGHAM

Founded 1893

Joined League 1920 (Div.3, founder member)

Honours Div.4 Champions 1964

Ground Priestfield

Gillingham have failed dismally to make the most of geographical advantage. Until Maidstone United achieved League status, the 'Gills' existed in splendid isolation from other clubs yet have been perennially unable to attract the huge potential audience which exists in the Medway towns.

Their history has been modest indeed. As founder members of Division 3, Gillingham faced a constant struggle for survival and after successfully applying for re-election four times they were finally dropped in 1938. The club was liquidated, then re-formed, and entered the Southern League before being given a second chance in the senior competition in 1950.

They sank to the newly-created Fourth Division in 1958, winning their sole honour six seasons later and spending all but three of the next 25 years in the Third Division. In 1979 the Gills were within a point of rising to Division 2, but subsequently have slumped back to the basement.

GREAVES, Jimmy

1940 Born in East Ham, London

1957 Scores on League debut for Chelsea

1959 First England cap in Peru

1961 Hat-trick in 9-3 defeat of Scotland at Wembley; Joins AC Milan, having scored 124 goals in 157 League games for Chelsea, including 4 in his last match; Signs for Tottenham for record fee of £99,999 after four unhappy months in Italy

1963 Scores twice in Spurs' 5-1 win in European Cup Winners' Cup Final v Atletico Madrid; 4 goals for England v Northern Ireland

1965 Badly affected by an attack of hepatitis

1966 Unable to regain place in England's World Cup-winning line-up after missing quarter-final through injury

1967 Last appearance for England (44 goals in 57 games)

1970 After 321 League matches for Spurs (220 goals), moves to West Ham in part-exchange for Martin Peters

1971 Retires and disappears from public view

1980 Begins a new career in television, having struggled against alcoholism for several years

The bare statistics of Greaves's career are sufficient to demonstrate that he was the most remarkable goal-scorer of his generation, but they cannot convey his unique talent. His detractors pointed to his lack of workrate and dependence upon others to create openings for him, but failed to appreciate that his deadly finishing could transform a match.

Although he had the born predator's ability to anticipate a half-chance, Greaves's greatest gift was perhaps his pace, which he never fully recovered after his illness. However, it was the economy of effort and coolness with which his goals were taken which set him apart from his rivals.

JIMMY GREAVES
Shadowed by the large presence of Dundee's Ian Ure (he later played for Arsenal), Jimmy Greaves (then with Spurs) plays for England against Scotland in 1963 at the peak of his career. Scotland won 2-1; perhaps Greaves took solace in the hat-trick he had scored in the corresponding fixture two years earlier when England won 9-3. A regular name on the scoresheet, Greaves played out his career in the limelight and not always happily. It's good to see now that his natural humour and love of football have given him a special place in the affections of the nation as a television presenter and personality.

He was always willing to take his time and felt no need to attempt the spectacular when it was more effective to wrong-foot the keeper and push the ball home. His pair of clinical far-post volleys against Atletico in 1963 were typical.

Always a popular figure, his courageous fight-back in the face of a challenge sterner than any he faced on the pitch has won him a new generation of fans and even greater admiration than he earned through his playing exploits.

GREENWOOD, Ron

1921 Born in Burnley

1945 Joins Bradford Park Avenue from his first club, Chelsea

1949 Moves to Brentford, wins England 'B' cap

1952 Starts a second stint at Stamford Bridge

1955 Turns out enough times to win Championship medal with 'Pensioners', then joins Fulham to end playing days

1957 Enters management with non-League Eastbourne United, coaches England youth side

1958 Becomes assistant boss of Arsenal and England under-23 team coach

1961 Takes over at West Ham United

1964 'Hammers' lift first trophy of Greenwood era, beating Preston North End in FA Cup Final...

1965 ...and the second, overcoming TSV Munich to take the European Cup Winners' Cup

1974 John Lyall takes over West Ham's team affairs; Greenwood becomes general manager

1977 Leaves Upton Park to replace Don Revie as England boss

1980 England reach European Championship finals, but fail to impress

1982 Greenwood's team qualifies for World Cup finals in Spain, where they are eliminated in second phase; manager steps down in favour of Bobby Robson.

Greenwood was the deep-thinking tactician who managed England through what was – despite the presence of fine players such as Bryan Robson, Kevin Keegan, Trevor Brooking and Glenn Hoddle – a rather pedestrian era. He succeeded Revie in the face of strong public opinion that the job should have gone to Brian Clough – hardly the ideal circumstances in which to take on such an onerous task.

Greenwood had qualified as a coach while still an

RON GREENWOOD

A thoughtful and quiet person – perhaps those qualities alone should have automatically disqualified Ron Greenwood from the job of England manager. He held it, however, with moderate success, for five years. During his reign he had, like many managers before and since, only a few players of the highest quality. Kevin Keegan was one of them, seen here with his national boss in 1977, a year which saw England's failure to reach the World Cup finals of 1978 despite winning five of their six qualifying matches.

intelligent, skilful centre-half, and he went on to preach the gospel of constructive football – which produced some notable triumphs – at West Ham. When the England call came, there was little chance of securing a place in the 1978 World Cup finals, and Greenwood set his sights on subsequent tournaments. No one could reasonably accuse him of being a dismal failure, but neither could he be deemed an outstanding success.

GRIMSBY TOWN

Founded 1878

Joined League 1892 (Div.2)

Honours Div.2 Champions 1901, 1934; Div.3 (N) Champions 1926, 1956; Div.3 Champions 1980; Div.4 Champions 1972

Ground Blundell Park, Cleethorpes

Grimsby Town, who carry the name of the famous east coast fishing port but play their home games at nearby Cleethorpes, have known better days than recent lowly League placings might suggest. Indeed, during their prime in the 1930s, the 'Mariners' finished fifth in Division 1 and reached two FA Cup semi-finals. Those were the days of heroes such as English international Jackie Bestall, a gifted, ball-playing inside-forward, and free-scoring marksman Pat Glover, capped seven times by Wales.

Sadly for Grimsby, the Second World War devastated the careers of their best players and the club never recovered. They were relegated in 1948, since when they have yo-yoed between the three lower divisions. Their list of managers includes such notables as Bill Shankly, who failed to lift them out of the Third Division in the early 1950s, and Lawrie McMenemy, who converted a poor side into Fourth Division champions and the League's highest scorers in 1972. Eight years later George Kerr led Grimsby up to the Second Division, although recent terms have been spent reclaiming that position following a slump to the Fourth.

Such regular movement between divisions mirrors the club's early history, most of which was spent in the Second but also involved stints in the First and Third Divisions. Grimsby's low point came in 1910 when they failed to gain re-election, although they bounced back one season later.

GULLIT, Ruud

1962 Born in Amsterdam

1979 Joins Haarlem from minor league football

1981 September – international debut v Switzerland

1982 Moves to Feyenoord

1984 Wins league and cup medals with Feyenoord

1985 Leaves Feyenoord and joins PSV Eindhoven

1987 June – transferred to AC Milan for a record £6 million; European Footballer of the Year and World Footballer of the Year

RUUD GULLIT A more usual setting for dreadlocks perhaps, but Ruud Gullit's are more often seen flapping in pursuit of a ball. Politics and music are two of his interests outside sport and they are both captured in this shot. Gullit's name will always be associated with the Dutch team of the 1980s and early 1990s, just as Cruyff's is with the 1970s side. Who will it be for the last few years of this century? Tragically, one contender will never have a chance to state his case. Early in 1990/91, 23-year-old Tom Krommendijk of Twente Enschende was killed in a car crash. Tipped by many to be a great future hope, he had not yet won an international cap; but in 1987, playing for the under-21s, he scored twice in a friendly against the national side as the youngsters won 5-2.

1988 Highs and lows – captains club to championship title and country to European supremacy; in friendly game during summer sustains injury to right knee which is to dog him for next two years

1989 Knee injury seriously aggravated in European Cup semi-final v Real Madrid – key-hole surgery allows him to play in Final; despite not being really match-fit, scores twice v Steaua Bucharest to secure victory; further operations and lay-off necessary

1990 Recovers in time to win a second European Cup medal, v Benfica, to play in World Cup, and to help AC Milan to victory in the European Super Cup and the World

Club Championship

Rudi Dil Gullit played as a sweeper until, eventually, both club and country used him as an attacking midfield player; his versatility, his intelligent approach to the game and his awareness of colleagues and opponents are typically Dutch. He is an expert finder of space, often running away from the penalty area and picking up the ball to launch an attack from an unexpected angle.

Off the field Gullit, of Surinamese origin, is confident and articulate – Dutch footballers pride themselves on expressing opinions fearlessly, and in this he is no exception. Holland's troubles since 1988, due in no small part to his injury, have been compounded by managerial squabbles, and Gullit's views have been made plain – at times, it would seem, regardless of team morale.

The fortunes of AC Milan are bound up with those of Holland, since top striker van Basten turns out alongside the Dutch captain in both strips. (Gullit's childhood friend and AC Milan team-mate Rijkaard no longer wishes to play for the national team.) The club's recent run of form has inspired hopes that Dutch football's lean period is but a brief phenomenon.

Gullit, winner of a half-century of international caps, is a natural goal-scorer but is often happy to act as a provider, especially when striker van Basten is on song.

HALIFAX TOWN

Founded 1911

Joined League 1921 Div.3 (N)

Honours None

Ground The Shay

Poor, beleaguered Halifax Town face a constant, unequal struggle for survival. Existing in a rugby league stronghold, and being surrounded by a host of other soccer clubs – almost all of which are more wealthy, more glamorous, or both – they could hardly be less advantageously placed in the crucial battle for support.

It is small wonder, therefore, that their history has not been an illustrious one. Their first 42 years in the League were spent in the Third Division, before they were relegated in 1963. High points of this period were two campaigns in which they missed out narrowly on promotion to the Second: in 1935, when inspired by former Sheffield United and England winger Fred Tunstall; and in 1971, during the first of George Kirby's two managerial reigns. The 'Shaymen's' most notable FA Cup runs, both of which ended in the fifth round, came in 1933 and 1953.

Since 1976 Halifax have toiled in the basement, making a number of successful applications for re-election. The future, it does not take a genius to predict, will not be easy despite considerable financial input from the local council.

HAMILTON ACADEMICAL

Founded 1875

Joined League 1897 (Div.2)

Honours Scottish League First Division Champions 1986, 1988; Division 2 Champions 1904

Ground Douglas Park

The derivation of the name from a local school gives Hamilton Academical a whimsical air but, as with all clubs of their size, survival has been a matter of grit.

The club was at its most stable from 1906 to 1947, retaining Division 1 status throughout. In 1935, with high-scoring David Wilson as spearhead, they even repeated their feat of 1911 by reaching the Scottish Cup Final.

Despite twice winning promotion to the Premier Division in the 1980s, their greatest recent impact was achieved by beating Rangers at Ibrox in the 1988 Scottish Cup .

HARTLEPOOL UNITED

Founded 1908

Joined League 1921 (Div. 3 N)

Honours None

Ground Victoria Ground

For most clubs, Hartlepool United's record of 10 wins and 19 draws in 1968/69 would represent dismal failure. But for the humble north-easterners, those 39 points were of momentous significance. They earned United the highest placing – 22nd in Division 3 – of their Football League history, even though it did not prevent an immediate return to the Fourth Division.

Indeed, that campaign is the only one Hartlepool had spent outside the lowest available flight until 1991. Their story is one of frequent applications for re-election and constant struggle for survival in an economically depressed area.

There was brief hope of a brave new era when Brian Clough created new impetus before departing for Derby County in 1967. His successor, Angus McLean, capitalised by winning promotion the following year but could not sustain success. The 1980s saw a sequence of seven managers in six years and United's few die-hard fans, while praying for the miracle of revival, were not holding their breath.

HAYNES, Johnny

1934 Born in Edmonton

1952 Turns professional with Fulham

1954 Full England debut against Northern Ireland

1959 Inspires Fulham to promotion to the First Division

1960 Takes over as England captain

1961 Becomes Britain's first £100-a-week footballer after Fulham reject bid from AC Milan

1962 Seriously damages knee in Blackpool road accident; never plays for England again

1964 Tottenham offer £90,000 for Haynes after death of their own midfield general, John White

1968 Returns to Second Division with Fulham...

1969 ...who slide straight down to the Third

1970 Free transfer from Fulham; joins South African club Durban City

Haynes was one of the most skilful English inside-forwards of the post-war era, yet his enormous talent never won him a club honour. The dearth of medals is easily explained – he played out his entire Football League career with unfashionable Fulham, even though top clubs at home and abroad attempted to lure him away.

He first caught the public imagination with a sparkling display for England Schoolboys in a televised Wembley encounter with the Scots in 1950. But then the young

JOHNNY HAYNES It may now seem incredible, but the announcement that Johnny Haynes was to become the first £100 per week footballer in 1961 bought howls of protest from outraged sections of society. That he was to be paid relatively so much was evidence of his worth and of the need to pay high wages to prevent players like Haynes migrating to Italy. Haynes, not untypically of his day, was a gentleman footballer who loved the game he played and would probably have done it for considerably less than the famous annual salary of £5,200.

Arsenal fan who was born in the Tottenham Hotspur heartland, surprised everyone by opting for Craven Cottage and the Second Division. Haynes soon built a reputation as a schemer sublime; his speciality was silky, long-distance passes which sliced open defences, and his full international breakthrough was not long in coming. He won 56 caps, many of them as captain, and might have had more but for the car crash which at one time threatened his career.

Yet, despite his obvious gifts, Haynes was not beloved of the entire football world. He was a perfectionist who sometimes struck melodramatic poses when admonishing team-mates of inferior ability, and was a particular target for northern fans. Haynes, who will always be remembered as the man who broke the £100-a-week wage barrier, left English soccer after loyal service to homely Fulham but with one tantalising question left unanswered: to what heights might he have risen with a leading club?

HEART OF MIDLOTHIAN

Founded 1874

Joined League 1890 (Division 1, founder club)

Honours Scottish League Championship, Division 1, 1895, 1897, 1958, 1960; First Division, 1980; Scottish Cup, 1891, 1896, 1901, 1906, 1956; League Cup, 1954/55, 1958/59, 1959/60, 1962/63

Ground Tynecastle Park

Hearts are one of the few clubs perennially expected to mount a challenge to the Old Firm. The prestige was established from the early years with League Championships and Scottish Cups racked up before the turn of the century.

One of the great stars was Bobby Walker, a silky inside-forward who had won a club record of 29 caps, in an era when fewer internationals were played, by 1913. His namesake

Tommy Walker, a great midfielder in the trophyless 1930s, was to find success as a manager two decades later.

He presided over the glorious side of the 1950s. Its 'Terrible Trio' of Alfie Conn, Willie Bauld and Jimmy Wardhaugh are renowned but they were

HEARTS Colquhoun of Hearts, with the ball, and Weir of Hibernian during Hearts' 1-0 win in an 1989-90 Edinburgh derby match. Both sides have seemed possible threats to the Glasgow domination of Scottish football, but neither have had the resources to build on glimmers of success over the years since the war. The future does not hold out the prospect for any change in the situation, although the proposed (and rejected) merger between the two teams did raise the possibility of a united Edinburgh onslaught on the Glasgow empire. Skilled players with 'smaller' clubs pictured can expect to be sold to pay the bills.

also flanked by menacing wingers in Alex Young and Jimmy Crawford. Although Conn played less often, all five were fielded as Hearts won the League with a record 132 goals in 1958.

A 2-0 defeat at home to Kilmarnock cost Hearts the title in 1965 and their fortunes waned. Later, relegation was to bring the threat of extinction. They have recovered since the early 1980s and contribute men like Dave McPherson and John Robertson to the Scotland squad but the trophy-winning days have not yet returned.

HIBERNIAN

Founded 1875

Joined League 1893 (Division 2)

Honours Scottish League Championship, Division 1, 1903, 1948, 1951, 1952; First Division, 1981; Division 2, 1894, 1895, 1933; Scottish Cup, 1887, 1902; League Cup, 1972/73

Ground Easter Road

For Hibs, as for Tottenham Hotspur, the move to Public Limited Company

status has been a disaster. In 1990 their debts were approaching £6 million and they only narrowly defeated a takeover bid by Edinburgh rivals Hearts.

Hibs' plight is made all the more poignant by their illustrious history. Founded by Edinburgh's Irish immigrant community, Hibs soon had an impact on the national scene but their most vibrant era came in the early 1950s.

The 'Famous Five' forward line of Gordon Smith, Peter Johnstone, Lawrie Reilly, Eddie Turnbull and Willie Ormond contained all of football's arts and gave Hibs unequalled attacking resources.

In 1955/56 Hibs represented Scotland in the first European Cup and reached the semi-final stage. The decline which followed was halted only in the early seventies by the cultured side which included internationalists like John Brownlie, Pat Stanton, and Alex Cropley. It delighted purists but did not win the trophies it might have.

In 1991 Hibs are in parlous condition.

Although many distant corners of the world can supply evidence of a form of proto-football, it is with England that the origins, development and standardisation of the game are most strongly identified. The sport commonly assumed to be soccer's ancestor is Shrove Tuesday football, various forms of which existed throughout England; these skirmishes, with their attendant fatalities, often involved whole villages and had local rules. Some are still extant, notably in Ashbourne in Derbyshire which boasts the oldest recorded version, played annually in the thirteenth century, having been introduced by Roman soldiers a thousand years earlier. What links these games, and contemporary contests in Brittany and Italy, to modern soccer is not the use of the foot to propel the ball – indeed, the participants were as likely to pick up the ball – but the involvement of two teams struggling to gain territory and move the ball

HISTORY OF THE GAME

Two sides, north and south of the border, epitomise the amateur game: Queen's Park from Glasgow and the Corinthian Casuals from London. This match, reported in the *Illustrated Sporting and Dramatic News* in December 1898, has the two sides locked in gentlemanly combat. It was played at the Queen's Club, West Kensington, and resulted in a win for the raiders from up north. The illustration depicts Queen's Park's third goal. Perhaps the goalkeeper could have made a better effort – although nothing too unsporting!

to a specified goal (which in medieval times might have been a single identifiable landmark or an area hundreds of yards wide). The ball games of the Far East demonstrated more skilful use of the feet but were really akin to juggling. The game in England was an outlet for aggression.

Approval was not universal, especially as, in smaller-scale versions, it ceased to confine itself to the day before Lent. A proclamation by King Edward II in 1314 forbade, on pain of imprisonment, the playing of football in city streets. There were similar edicts from successive monarchs, notably Richard II (1389), who worried that his subjects were neglecting their archery practice on its account. Similar prohibitions testify to the game's early popularity in Scotland. (Periodically throughout this century the English judiciary have acted against people for playing football in the street – the arena in which so many great skills have been honed; the motor car now seems to have succeeded where magistrates failed.) In 1583 one commentator described football as characterised by 'murder, homicide and great effusion of blood'. In 1581, however, Richard Mulcaster, a prominent headmaster, could write: 'Football strengtheneth and brawneth the whole body–

… It is good to drive down the stone and gravel from the bladder and the kidneys.' (There is no evidence that the modern game has inherited any of these mysterious medical qualities.) Royal disapproval vanished in the seventeenth century when James I and Charles II were happy to spectate. As much as anything else, the diversity of reaction is evidence of the variety of games sharing the title 'football'.

Despite its popular origins, it is to the public schools that we owe the protracted birth of the modern game. A desire to form a common code for inter-school and inter-university matches led to the establishing of the Cambridge Rules in 1848 and these were gradually adopted by gentlemen's clubs in London and the Home Counties, with Sheffield, the first football club, eventually coming into line. Parallel to this, the predominantly working-class game elsewhere in the north sought standardisation. It is the gradual

KEEPS YOU IN TIP-TOP FORM

T. G. BROMILOW, the Famous International and Liverpool Footballer, writes :—"It is absolutely essential that a player should be in the best possible condition to keep time with the present football speed. Personally, I have found that Phosferine is responsible for my attaining this end, it being a great stimulant to the nerves, is highly revitalising, and after a particularly strenuous game, Phosferine positively prevents any of that feeling of nerve exhaustion which is usually the forerunner of a legion of nerve disorders, Influenza, etc. Weakness and exhaustion of any description can be successfully opposed by the employment of Phosferine, which can be absolutely relied upon to keep a player in tip-top form."

Parents find that Phosferine is peculiarly adapted to children of a pale, or weakly physique, and to those outgrowing their strength. Two drops, night and morning, tend to brace up the whole system, restore colour to the cheeks, firmness to the flesh, renew the appetite and encourage a vigorous and healthy growth, and at the same time fortify the body against attacks of illness. It is also invaluable to women beset with household worries and family cares.

PHOSFERINE

CURES AND PREVENTS
GENERAL EXHAUSTION

The Greatest of all Tonics for

Influenza	Nervous Debility	Mental Exhaustion	Faintness	Malaria
Indigestion	Neuralgia	Loss of Appetite	Brain Fag	Headache
Sleeplessness	Maternity Weakness	Nerve Shock	Anæmia	Lassitude
Exhaustion	Premature Decay	Neuritis	Sciatica	

Liquid and Tablets. The 3/- size contains nearly four times the 1/3 size.

HISTORY OF THE GAME

The popular appeal of soccer has not been lost on advertisers over the decades. This ad, run in newspapers in the 1920s, extols the virtues of Phosferine with the help of Liverpool and England player Tom Bromilow. He won only five caps, but was a media celebrity all the same.

rapprochement between the two types which formed the bedrock of association football. Equally crucial was the formation of the Rugby Union in 1871; disputes about the legitimacy of handling in open play were near an end now that two distinct games existed.

The last three decades of the nineteenth century saw the development of rules still in use today, the formation of the Football Association, the Football League, a Challenge Cup, and similar institutions in the other home countries, and the participation of familiar names: Aston Villa, Blackburn Rovers, Notts County, Sheffield Wednesday. Meanwhile British engineers, entrepreneurs and servicemen were introducing the codified game abroad, laying the foundations for international competition. The prestige of the game was enhanced by its inclusion in the 1908 Olympics, its viability confirmed by the growing stature of the World Cup.

In this century, modifications to the game itself have been minimal; the simplicity of the rules and the potential of free-flowing play have been football's strong points, admitting as they do, a plethora of styles. The context of the sport, however, the nature of its institutions and the status of its practitioners have all been transformed by a common agent – money. This has been particularly evident in the last decade in Britain and throughout the world, with takeover bids and high-profile sponsorship, the spiralling of transfer fees, and an increase in football-related corruption all bringing the game into the headlines and transforming the image of football.

There seems little resemblance between the tumbling Shrovetide mauls of the Middle Ages and the game played by knicker-bockered Corinthians at the turn of the century; and little similarity between either of those and a game played under floodlights by sportsmen whose club crests are dwarfed by sponsors' insignia, who are supervised by a card-brandishing official and watched by a fenced-in public standing beneath executive boxes and television gantries. The evolution is remarkable, but they are, in essence, the same creature, animated by the same spirit. Pessimists and traditionalists need to be reminded that more people play and watch football worldwide than ever before, that Saturday morning pick-up games still flourish, and that in the professional game, apprentices still clean boots.

HODDLE, Glenn

1957 Born in Hayes, Middlesex

1975 Turns professional with Tottenham Hotspur

1977 Experiences trauma of relegation in first full season

1978 Helps to ensure Spurs' immediate return to top flight

1979 Scores on England debut, v Bulgaria at Wembley

1981 Takes first major club honour, an FA Cup winner's medal, as Spurs beat Manchester City after replay

1982 Scores in Final and replay as Spurs retain trophy, v Queen's Park Rangers

1987 Bows out of White Hart Lane on a losing note as Spurs lose FA Cup Final to Coventry City; July – signs for Monaco in £750,000 deal

1988 Hits top form as Monaco take French Championship; June – wins 53rd and final England cap in European Championship defeat against USSR in Frankfurt

1989 Knee injury sidelines Hoddle for more than a year and threatens to end his career

1991 Becomes manager of Swindon Town

Few players have provoked such extremes of opinion as Glenn Hoddle. His supporters claim he was the most gifted Englishman of his generation and contend that his frequent omission from the national side was little short of sacrilege. Detractors moan about inconsistency and poor work rate, an argument which apparently found some favour with successive England managers, Ron Greenwood and Bobby Robson.

Certainly, none could doubt the natural ability of the tall, elegant play-maker, who was blessed with breathtaking vision and had a devastating knack of changing the angle of attack with sweeping long-distance passes. His touch on the ball, with both feet, was superb, he possessed a powerful shot which was particularly effective at free-kicks, and he was one of the most delicate chippers of a ball the game has seen.

However, those who expected to see him carrying out the average midfielder's share of defensive duties were invariably disappointed; but of course, there was nothing average about Hoddle. By the end of his Spurs days his overall involvement in matches had improved significantly, but sadly it was too late. By then, with so much of his prime gone, the football world was left to rue the fact that an exceptional talent had never been utilised to the full.

GLENN HODDLE The tall, slim Glenn Hoddle scoring with a diving header in England's 2-1 win over Scotland at Wembley, April 1986. This was during a spell as an England regular, when his omission from the team seemed unlikely, even unthinkable.

HOME INTERNATIONALS

The British home international tournament was a four-way competition involving England, Scotland, Wales and Ireland (Northern Ireland after 1921). It began in 1883/84 and continued until 1983/84, interrupted only by two wars and the refusal of England and Wales to play in Belfast in 1980/81, when the programme was not completed. Poor attendances and the increasing importance of competitions like the World Cup and the European Championships led to the tournament's demise, England and Scotland being the first to pull out. The tournament ended on a bizarre note. In 1983/84 all four countries won, drew and lost a game, so Northern Ireland won on goal difference (3-2) from Wales (3-3), England (2-2) and Scotland (3-4).

In 1968/69 the tournament was moved to the end of the season in an unsuccessful attempt to revive it. As the tournament placings usually relied solely on number of points – until goal difference was taken into account in the last few years – as many as 20 championships were shared. England had more outright wins (34) than Scotland (24) and Wales (7). Ireland won a clear title in 1913/14, and Northern Ireland won two of the last four. England gained more points than any other country (378), followed by Scotland (339), Wales (202) and Ireland/Northern Ireland (142).

Given the consistency of the home international tournament – each country played three games a season – it is a good way of comparing different generations of inter-nationals. Players with most home international tournament appearances are as follows: Pat Jennings (Northern Ireland) and Billy Meredith (Wales) 48, Billy Wright (England) 38, Danny Blanchflower (Northern Ireland) and Ivor Allchurch (Wales) 37, Jimmy McIlroy (Northern Ireland) 36, Bob Crompton (England) and Billy Bingham (Northern Ireland) 34, Bobby Charlton (England) and Fred Keenor (Wales) 32.

Top goal-scorers in the championship were Steve Bloomer (England) 28, Hughie Gallacher (Scotland) 21, Jimmy Greaves (England) 19 and Bobby Charlton (England) 16.

In 1985 the Rous Cup, named after legendary English administrator Sir Stanley Rous, was launched as a direct contest between Scotland and England, Scotland winning the first competition 1-0 at Hampden Park. England won the trophy at Wembley the following year. Then came three years of the Rous Cup as a triangular tournament involving a guest nation from South America. Brazil won in 1987, England in 1988 and 1989 when Colombia and Chile were the respective South American visitors.

When Scotland pulled out of the 1990 Rous Cup, the future of home internationals passed to the hands of those who make the draws for the World Cup and European Championships.

HOOLIGANISM

Hooliganism is not a recent phenomenon. Consider these four examples, taken from different decades of early soccer.

In 1885 Preston North End players were trapped on the field by 2000 'howling roughs' after beating Aston Villa 5-1. They were attacked with stones, sticks, umbrellas and spittle. One player (Ross) was laid out by a missile.

An 1899 semi-final replay between Sheffield United and Liverpool was abandoned at half-time. Repeated invasions of the Fallowfield pitch meant the first-half took 90 minutes to complete.

The 1909 Scottish Cup Final between Rangers and Celtic was drawn, as was the replay. Spectators were incensed when extra time was not played in the replay. They invaded the pitch, destroyed goalposts and goal-nets, set pay boxes on fire and fought with policemen. About 130 spectators received medical treatment on the ground.

At the end of the 1913 Ireland-Scotland international in Dublin, players fought for the match ball as a souvenir and a spectator was injured in the melee. An angry mob kept the Scottish team prisoners in their dressing room for about an hour as windows were smashed and property damaged.

From the late 1960s, however, hooliganism has grown to epidemic proportions throughout Europe. Examples of major British outbursts include the following.

In April 1971 about 20 Leeds United supporters invaded the Elland Road pitch shortly after a disputed goal had given West Bromwich a 2-0 lead in an important Division 1 game. A linesman was knocked out when hit by a missile. Leeds United were fined £750 and ordered to play four home matches on another ground.

In March 1974 spectators invaded the Newcastle pitch and halted a sixth-round FA Cup game with Nottingham Forest. The referee took the players off the pitch. Thirty-nine people were arrested, 23 taken to hospital and 103 others treated on the ground. Nottingham Forest, winning 3-1 at the time, eventually lost 4-3. The FA ordered a replay. Newcastle won 1-0 after a 0-0 draw.

In June 1977 Scotland beat England 2-1 at Wembley. After the game, hundreds of Scottish fans invaded the pitch and caused damage estimated at £150,000. As a consequence, fences were erected at Wembley.

A Division 2 game between Oldham Athletic and Sheffield Wednesday (September 1980) was stopped for 30 minutes when Sheffield Wednesday supporters greeted the sending-off of Terry Curran by invading the pitch. An FA disciplinary committee banned Wednesday supporters from four away games and closed terraces for four home games.

Disturbances at a sixth-round FA Cup tie at Luton on 13 March 1985 – Luton Town beat Millwall 1-0 – led to 33 arrests and £25,000 worth of damage. Having watched televised scenes, then Prime Minister Margaret Thatcher became personally involved in the problem, setting up a special task force. A £7500 fine for Millwall was later rescinded on appeal. Luton Town introduced a membership scheme which effectively banned away supporters from the start of the 1986/87 season.

All sorts of remedies have been tried: fences, segregation of fans, police escorts for fans, all-seater stadia, more sophisticated policing, closed-circuit cameras and more careful monitoring of player behaviour. The methods have succeeded in restraining hooliganism within grounds, but violence outside them has increased, often with the involvement of highly organised 'firms'.

The real causes of hooliganism are very complex. The most detailed research has been undertaken at Leicester University and its Sir Norman Chester Centre for Football Research. Eric Dunning, Patrick Murphy and John Williams have written on hooliganism in *Hooligans Abroad*, *The Roots of Football Hooliganism* and *Football on Trial*. Autobiographical accounts include Stephen Ward's *Steaming In* and Jay Allan's *Bloody Casuals*.

Hooliganism is not limited to spectators. In April 1988 two incidents involving players reached the courts. Terry Butcher (Rangers) was fined £250 and his colleague Chris Woods £500 after a

HUDDERSFIELD TOWN
Huddersfield Town's side of 1924/25 when they won the League title for the second time in their three-in-a-row spell. Apart from this achievement it is worth noting that they finished in third place in the season before their hat-trick and runners-up in both of the seasons following. Their first Championship was won on goal average from Cardiff City (60-33 bettering 61-34, just!), the third by five points from Arsenal. The team: *(back row, left to right)* **Herbert Chapman (manager), Steele, Goodall, Cawthorne, Taylor, Wadsworth, Chaplin (trainer); Williams, Brown, Wilson, Wilson, Cook, Smith, Watson.**

four-day trial had found them guilty of conducting themselves in a disorderly manner and committing breaches of the peace during a Rangers-Celtic game the preceding October. Chris Kamara, then with Swindon Town, was fined £1200 for grievous bodily harm on Jim Melrose, who was on loan from Leeds United to Shrewsbury Town. Melrose suffered a depressed fracture of the cheekbone after an end-of-game incident. The game of soccer suffered more indignity.

HUDDERSFIELD TOWN

Founded 1908

Joined League 1910 (Div.2)

Honours Div.1 Champions 1924, 1925, 1926; Div.2 Champions 1970; Div.4 Champions 1980; FA Cup Winners 1922

Ground Leeds Road

Huddersfield Town are haunted by a ghost that is unlikely to be laid; it is the spectre of the phenomenal triumphs enjoyed by the club in the 1920s, when three successive League Championships were added to an FA Cup victory. Those far-off glories - all but the final title achieved under the managership of Herbert Chapman - were astonishing in that they were attained within less than two decades of entering the Football League, and after weathering a severe cash crisis which almost saw them amalgamated with Leeds United.

They remained a major power until the late 1930s, when a decline set in. It was no surprise when they struggled after the war, and the 1950s saw the start of regular movement between the divisions. By the late 1970s they had plumbed the depths of the Fourth Division, rising again to the Second in 1983 only to slide down a grade five years later.

Notable managers have included Bill Shankly before his 1959 switch to Liverpool and, most successful in the modern era, Ian Greaves, who took Huddersfield back to the top flight, briefly in 1970.

One remarkable tradition has been a succession of fine full-backs, including Sam Wadsworth and Roy Goodall in the 1920s, Ron Staniforth and Ray Wilson in the 1950s, and Bob McNab and Derek Parkin in the 1960s, though the greatest player in their history was inside-forward Denis Law, sold for a record £55,000 in 1960.

Today Huddersfield battle on in the League's lower reaches, finding fans hard to lure away from more fashionable neighbours.

HULL CITY

Founded 1904

Joined League 1905 (Div.2)

Honours Div.3 (N) Champions 1933, 1949; Div.3 Champions 1966

Ground Boothferry Park

It is surprising that Hull City, an ambitious club with plenty of potential support in the Humberside area despite strong competition from the oval-ball code, have never enjoyed a spell in the First Division. In fact, they made their most spirited attempt to gain top-flight status just five years after entering the Football League, failing only on goal average. Since then most of their time has been spent alternating between the Second and Third Divisions, with one brief stint in the Fourth. Two of the 'Tigers' most potent sides were those of the late 1940s and early 1950s, which featured Raich Carter (as player-manager) and Don Revie, and Cliff Britton's attacking combination of the mid and late 1960s, which contained the prolific Chris Chilton and Ken Wagstaff, both of whom notched more than 200 goals for City.

Other personalities of note have included stalwart goalkeeper Billy Bly, who served for two decades until 1959, and Terry Neill who, in his first managerial job, offered hope of a First Division breakthrough in the early 1970s. The club's best FA Cup run ended in a semi-final replay defeat by eventual winners Arsenal in 1930.

IPSWICH TOWN

Founded 1878

Joined League 1938 (Div.3 S)

Honours Div.1 Champions 1962; Div.2 Champions 1961, 1968; Div.3 (S) Champions 1954, 1957; FA Cup Winners 1978; UEFA Cup Winners 1981

Ground Portman Road

Ipswich offer an inspiring example of a club whose stirring deeds have belied their small-town stature, thanks largely to two men, Sir Alf Ramsey and Bobby Robson, who both left Portman Road to manage England. Their eras brought unprecedented glory to East Anglia, which then had little reason to expect much from Ipswich. After all, the Town had spent the 60 years after their formation in minor competitions, and then a further decade-and-a-half in Division 3 (S). Even when they eventually clambered into the higher grade, it was for just one term.

Relegation in 1955 was the cue for Ramsey's entrance, and a startling transformation. Within two campaigns they were back in the Second Division, but more momentous triumphs were in store: the Division 2 title and the League Championship were lifted in successive seasons.

Ramsey's 'miracle' was based on a sound defence, a midfield engineered by frail-looking Jimmy Leadbetter, and a lethal double spearhead of Ray Crawford and Ted Phillips. Of course, success on a shoestring could not be maintained and, Ramsey having departed, the Town soon went down. They rose again in 1968, the year before Robson took over to lead them into their longest period of First Division membership. During his 13 campaigns they won two major cups, narrowly missed several titles and became established as a side to be respected, with many high-quality players such as defender Mick Mills and striker Paul Mariner. In 1986 Ipswich were relegated, but they are a well-run club with a proven record of doing well in an area which is hardly a soccer hotbed. It would be surprising if they remain strangers to the First Division for too long.

IPSWICH TOWN

In 1960/61 Ipswich Town won the Second Division Championship. In the following year, the side photographed here won the First Division Championship. Many reasons for their remarkable success have been put forward. One factor is the loyalty of the players and the consistency of selection of the team. The numbers in brackets after each player's name represent the League appearances made for Ipswich Town Football Club: (left to right, back row) **Baxter (409), Carberry (257), Bailey (315), Compton (111), Elsworthy (396); Stephenson (144), Moran (a mere 104), Crawford (320), Nelson (193), Phillips (269), Leadbetter (344); a total of 2862 appearances, and the club record holder, Mick Mills (seen below left, with veteran Liverpool player Tommy Smith), with 591 League appearances between 1965 and 1982, hadn't joined yet!**

JAMES, Alex

1901 Born in Mossend, Lanarkshire, Scotland

1922 Debut for Raith Rovers

1925 Signs for Preston North End at a fee of £3250

1926 Wins first Scottish cap in 3-0 win over Wales at Cardiff

1928 James is brilliant in the 'Wee Blue Devils' 5-1 slaughter of England at Wembley

1929 Moves to Arsenal for £8750

1930 Helps 'Gunners' win FA Cup with Wembley goal against Huddersfield Town

1931 Picks up the first of four Championship medals

1936 Skippers 'Gunners' to FA Cup victory against Sheffield United

1937 Retires to become journalist

1947 Returns to Highbury as a coach

1953 Dies of cancer

James, the inspiration of Arsenal's all-conquering side of the 1930s, is one of the few figures in soccer history who may reasonably be described as legendary. The little Scot, whose trademark of baggy shorts was a cartoonist's dream, was the most influential player of his era, a master tactician blessed with sublime ball skills.

A natural showman, he took time to settle after manager Herbert Chapman brought him south from Preston. But after subjugating some of his characteristic individuality to the team cause, he became the darling of the Highbury faithful. Though a captivating dribbler when the mood took him, James

ALEX JAMES Wearing his trademark — the long shorts — Alex James is pictured in his Arsenal kit; the shirt badge reads 1935/36, a season in which the Gunners won the FA Cup and finished sixth in Division 1. They scored 78 goals; champions Sunderland notched 109.

usually opted to let the ball do the work, and his immaculate distribution to the likes of Cliff Bastin, Joe Hulme and David Jack was the source of most Gunners goals.

Amazingly he played only eight games for his country, an absurd circumstance which was widely believed to be due to his 'Anglo' status. But James, who clashed publicly with Chapman on several occasions, was a supremely self-confident individual, a personality trait which may not have endeared him to the Scottish selectors.

JENNINGS, Pat

1945 Born in Newry, Northern Ireland

1963 Leaves Newry Town for Watford in £6000 deal

1964 Full international debut v Wales; June - joins Tottenham Hotspur for £27,000

1967 Jennings' first club honour as Spurs beat Chelsea to lift FA Cup

1971 Helps Spurs win first of two League Cups in three years

1972 UEFA Cup Final triumph over Wolves

1973 Footballer of the Year

1976 Players' player of the year and MBE

1977 Moves to Arsenal for £45,000

1979 Another FA Cup winners' medal as 'Gunners' beat Manchester United

1985 Returns to White Hart Lane as a first-team cover

1986 During Mexico World Cup he establishes then world record of 119 caps, then retires.

Jennings, a softly spoken, modest man, is widely rated as one of the most outstanding goalkeepers of all time. His was a larger-than-life presence between the posts, and he exuded an impression of

PAT JENNINGS
During the 1974/75 season Pat Jennings, seen clearing his lines, struggled in what was generally a poor Spurs side. They finished in 19th place in the First Division and fell out of the FA Cup in the third round.

PAT JENNINGS
Pat Jennings playing in his 119th appearance in goal for Northern Ireland, against Brazil in Guadalajara during the 1986 World Cup finals. Northern Ireland lost this particular match, 3-0, to go out of the tournament and Jennings finished his international career. Off the field he was recognised as a quiet and charming man – a credit to the game, as all who knew him would testify.

impregnability that calmed the most hesitant of defences. Tall, strong and athletic, and with a courageous style cultivated as a youthful Gaelic footballer, he also possessed well-nigh flawless technique.

The Ulsterman was blessed with a pair of huge hands which enabled him to field crosses with apparent ease, and sharp reflexes which made him a superb shot-stopper. Yet Jennings was perhaps at his best when faced with a solitary forward bearing down on

his goal, never committing himself until the last moment and often beguiling his opponent into a rash move. He was also adept at unorthodox saves with almost any part of his anatomy.

His career with Spurs, during which he played nearly 600 matches, was enough to ensure him a place in soccer folklore. But when the club, wrongly supposing him to be nearing retirement, committed the howler of allowing him to join Arsenal, he underlined his

greatness with a further 326 appearances. Few players will be remembered with more admiration and affection.

JONES, Cliff

1935 Born in Swansea, Wales

1950 Welsh schoolboy international

1952 Welsh youth international; signs as professional for Swansea Town

1955 Heads winning goal against England in his

second international for Wales

1958 Signs for Tottenham Hotspur for a record fee for a winger (£35,000); stars in Welsh World Cup success (quarter-finals); breaks leg in a pre-season training accident

1961 Plays in Spurs' double-winning team

1962 Helps Spurs to second successive Cup Final victory

1963 Plays in victorious European Cup Winners' Cup Final team

with the Football League for more than 50 years from 1918 when his father, Ivor, later a Welsh international, joined Swansea. A nephew of the great Bryn Jones, an outstanding inside-forward who became the most expensive player in the game when Arsenal signed him from Wolverhampton Wanderers in 1938, Cliff first came to prominence when Swansea defeated Manchester to win the Schools Shield.

By the time Cliff was sold to Tottenham Hotspur for £35,000 in February 1958, the Jones family thus setting another transfer record, he was established as an outstanding winger, skilful, brave and breathtakingly quick. But Cliff, in common with his uncle Bryn 20 years earlier, took a while to settle in London and it was not until after the lay-off enforced by a broken leg that Spurs saw the best of him.

Cliff, at his peak unquestionably world class, became one of the most popular figures in Tottenham's history, thrilling their supporters with his courage, pace and goal scoring feats. For a relatively small man, standing barely more than 5 ft 6 in, he scored an extraordinary number of goals with his head, coming in fearlessly at the far post like a centre-forward, requiring only a few steps to take off and climb above much taller men.

Cliff Jones, Dave Mackay, Danny Blanchflower and John White are the four players most obviously associated with the triumphs of 1961 when Spurs became the first team in modern times to achieve the 'double' of League Championship and FA Cup. Subsequent success in Europe further established Cliff Jones as one of the game's most thrilling attackers, as Atletico Madrid discovered in the European Cup Winners' Cup Final of 1963. No British club had won a European trophy until Spurs defeated the Spaniards 5-1 in Rotterdam, with their wingers, Jones and Dyson, outstanding.

Jones later moved on to Fulham and a spell in non-League football before retiring from the game to become a sports master in London.

CLIFF JONES From a footballing family, and showing the breeding of a thoroughbred in this picture, Cliff Jones was a brave and classy winger for Swansea, Spurs and Wales. The swept-back hair, perhaps giving a hint of the speed he possessed, was one of Jones's trademarks. His hard, low crosses were another.

1967 A third Cup Winner's medal for Spurs (as substitute)

1968 Joins Fulham on a free transfer

1969 Wins the last of his 59 Welsh caps

1970 Retires from League football, later playing for King's Lynn and Wealdstone

Cliff Jones came from a Merthyr Tydfil family with the unique record of having at least one of its members registered as a professional

KEVIN KEEGAN One of Kevin Keegan's greatest assets was his ability to lift the performance of those who played alongside him. This might not have been so noticeable when playing for Liverpool or England, but was obvious in his spells with Southampton and Newcastle United. In 1980/81 and 1981/82 Southampton finished sixth and seventh respectively in the First Division (admittedly they were not a poor side before Keegan's arrival), while Newcastle finished fifth and third (securing promotion) in Division 2 in the following two seasons, the two that Keegan spent as the Geordies' adopted messiah. This picture, in Southampton's colours, shows another of Keegan's attributes – his remarkable jumping and heading ability – as he gets to the high ball before Arsenal's Willie Young. Like many smaller men, he had spring heels.

KEEGAN, Kevin

1951 Born in Doncaster

1968 Turns professional with Scunthorpe United

1971 Moves to Anfield for £35,000

1972 England debut v Wales

1973 Keegan is key to Reds' League title and UEFA Cup success

1974 Stars, and scores twice, in Liverpool's 3-0 FA Cup Final victory over Newcastle United.

1976 Footballer of the Year; another Championship/UEFA Cup double

1977 Bids farewell to the Kop by inspiring Liverpool to their first European Cup triumph, against Borussia Moenchengladbach in Rome; June - joins SV Hamburg for £500,000, a record fee for a Briton

1978 First of two consecutive European Footballer of the Year awards

1980 Re-enters English football with Southampton

861982 Players' Player of the Year; July - wins 63rd and final cap in World Cup clash with Spain; August - moves to Newcastle United

1984 Retires after helping to secure promotion to Division 1

Kevin Keegan was arguably the most influential player of his era. Never blessed with the extravagant natural talent of George Best, whom he succeeded as the darling of the media, he possessed instead an overwhelming desire to succeed, and matchless application to his work. After being plucked from the obscurity of Scunthorpe - the deal was later described by Bill Shankly as 'robbery with violence' - Keegan could hardly have made a greater impact at Anfield. The irrepressible, dark-haired front-man became the vital additive the Liverpool boss needed to lift his rebuilt side.

Keegan was a darting imp, quick, brave and apparently inexhaustible. He had good ball control, a nimble brain and amazing power in the air for a small man. With the 'Reds' he formed a lethal duo with John Toshack, and became an integral part of the England side, which he captained for a spell. Indeed, many would contend that he was prematurely dropped by Bobby Robson.

After enduring unwarranted criticism for taking his skills to Europe, he returned home with spirited stints at Southampton and Newcastle, playing a dominant role in restoring the Magpies' First Division status. He then retired to Spain, having never given less than value for money.

KILMARNOCK

Founded 1869

Joined League 1895 (Div.2)

Honours Scottish League Division 1 Champions 1965; Division 2 Champions 1898, 1899; Scottish Cup Winners 1920, 1929

Ground Rugby Park

Scotland's second oldest club (after Queen's Park) took part in the first ever Scottish Cup tie on 18 October 1873 but waited until the 1960s for their greatest success. In 1965 they beat Hearts 2-0 at Tynecastle on the final day to win the Championship, edging the Edinburgh side out by 0.04 on goal average.

The 1960s side, often drawing on the guile of the precocious Tommy McLean, enjoyed remarkable results in Europe. In 1964 they defeated Eintracht Frankfurt in a Fairs Cup tie after being 4-0 down on aggregate early in the second leg. Sterling deeds had also seen Kilmarnock win the Scottish Cup in 1920 and 1929.

After a dismal spell the club is presently growing in strength once again.

KEVIN KEEGAN Since there is space for two pictures of Kevin Keegan, he has to be seen in the famous red shirts of Liverpool . . . the hero of the Kop.

LAW, Denis

1940 Born in Aberdeen

1957 Turns professional with Huddersfield Town

1958 Scores on full Scottish debut, v Wales at Cardiff

1960 Moves to Manchester City for a British record fee of £55,000

1961 Scores 6 in abandoned FA Cup tie against Luton Town, all expunged from records; gets City's only goal in 3-1 replay defeat; Torino take Law to Italy for £110,000

1962 Joins Manchester United for £115,000, another record

1963 May - scores United's first goal in FA Cup Final victory over Leicester City; October - scores for Rest of the World against England in FA Centenary match at Wembley

1964 European Footballer of the Year

1965 Wins first of two League Championship medals in three seasons

1968 Helps United reach European Cup Final, then misses match with injured knee

1973 Returns to Maine Road on free transfer

1974 April - backheels goal for City at Old Trafford which helps seal United's relegation; June - wins last of 55 caps against Zaire in World Cup finals, and retires, having scored 300 goals in 585 club games.

Law was one of the most blindingly brilliant performers of the modern era, an inside-forward whose array of talents was virtually complete. His goals were many and spectacular, his all-round skills exemplary and his bravery a byword. On top of all that, he exuded a cocky panache which endeared him to the fans, who dubbed him 'The King' during his Manchester United heyday. The upraised fist, the spiky blond hair, the impudent grin, they were trademarks of the man who perhaps outdid even fellow heroes George Best and

DENIS LAW
Characteristically (one hand raised, shirt cuffs pulled down) saluting another goal, this one for Manchester United against Crystal Palace in 1970, Denis Law was one of the 'triumvirate' that electrified United's attack in the late 1960s and early 1970s. Playing alongside Best and Charlton for United, or in a Scottish shirt, the slim and quicksilver inside-forward excited strong emotions. His skills delighted his own supporters; his apparent cockiness and confidence infuriated those of his opponents.

Bobby Charlton in earning the sheer affection of the Stretford End.

When he began his career at Huddersfield, he appeared so frail that it was difficult to believe he could survive in the professional game. But opponents soon discovered that the apparent weakling was rawhide tough and possessed of a fiery temperament which was often to land him in trouble with referees.

The acquisition of Law, on his return from an ill-fated sojourn in Italy, was unquestionably one of Matt Busby's master strokes. His later move to neighbours City was

notable for the goal which helped to relegate United and which Law acknowledged with a mixture of pride (in the goal) and sadness (at its impact). After quitting football Law became a commentator.

LAWS

A set of rules closely resembling today's laws was drawn up at Cambridge University around 1848. Compared with the FA rules published in December 1863, they permitted more handling and contained a more severe offside ruling.

The 1863 FA rules helped to standardise some of the various approaches to the game, but there were still significant differences between the London Association and the Sheffield Association, most notably over the throw-in and offside. Sheffield Association clubs kicked the ball in from touch in any direction and needed only one player goal-side in their offside rule. London Association clubs threw the ball in straight from touch and needed three players goal-side in their offside rule. These differences were resolved in 1877 – a free throw in any direction and the three-person offside law. The 1925 change in this law – two opponents nearer to the goal-line rather than three – was probably the most dramatic change this century.

Many early laws proved well thought-out, but several familiar features of modern football came in only after the 1877 agreement between the London and Sheffield associations. These include the two-handed throw-in (1882), the penalty kick (1890), linesmen replacing umpires (1891), full control to the referee (1894), the goalkeeper restricted to handling inside his penalty area rather than anywhere on the field (1912), the 10-yard distance (rather than 6 yards) between defenders and ball at free kicks (1913) and also at corner-kicks (1914), no offside from a throw-in (1920), a goal scored direct from a corner kick (1924), the current offside law (1925), a goalkeeper to remain stationary on the goal-line for a penalty kick (1929), defenders no longer allowed to tap the ball into a goalkeeper's hands at a goal kick (1936), an increase of an ounce in the weight of the ball (1937), and obstruction included in indirect free kick offences (1951).

The *Referees' Chart and Players' Guide to the Laws of Association Football* is the best source for understanding the Laws of the game and international board decisions. It is updated annually. At the time of writing there is talk of extending the size of the goal. This, it is thought, would lead to higher-scoring matches and greater crowd-pulling powers for the game. It is partly a result of the power of television and sponsors that this, and other similar suggestions, have been made.

LAWTON, Tommy

1919 Born in Bolton

1936 Makes League debut for Burnley; December – moves to Everton for £6500

1938 Scores on England debut, v Wales in Cardiff

1939 Plays major part in

winning League title

1945 Switches to Chelsea for £11,500

1947 Joins Notts County in first ever £20,000 deal

1948 Wins final England cap, against Denmark in Copenhagen

1952 Makes a £12,000 move to Brentford and soon becomes player-manager

1953 Signs for Arsenal

1955 Links up with non-League Kettering Town as player-boss

1957 Returns to Notts County as manager

1958 Lawton is sacked and takes over a pub

No serious student of the game would deny Tommy Lawton his place among the all-time greats. The tall, muscular centre-forward, of the sleek centre-parting and jutting nose, has often been described as the finest header of a ball who ever lived, but there was much more to his game then mere aerial power. Lawton was blessed with the skill and pace to run at defenders, a searing and accurate shot, and deft distribution which brought many goals for his forward partners. He also had charisma. When he was in his pomp, the name of Lawton on the teamsheet was guaranteed to boost the gate, no matter how mundane the fixture. Sadly, his career was blighted by the war. In 1939, aged 19, he had already won a place in the England side and had just helped his new club, Everton, lift the League

TOMMY LAWTON
A smiling, dapper Tommy Lawton photographed in his Arsenal shirt at the end of his career. Lawton played only 35 League matches for them following spells with Chelsea, Notts County and Brentford. He may be best remembered as an England player, his name fitting alongside those of Finney and Matthews among others, and for scoring 22 goals in 23 internationals.

title. The soccer world was at his feet, and although his final goal tally – 231 in 390 League games and 22 in 23 internationals – was impressive by any standards, it would surely have reached awesome proportions if the conflict had not robbed him of seven seasons.

One of football's wanderers, Lawton was always very much his own man and was involved in several well-publicised disputes with clubs. After promising work at Kettering, his managerial career foundered and he made an unsatisfactory exit from the game he had graced so magnificently for 20 years.

LEEDS UNITED

Founded 1919

Joined League 1920 (Div.2)

Honours Div.1 Champions 1969, 1974; Div.2 Champions 1924, 1964, 1990; FA Cup

Winners 1972; Football League Cup Winners 1968; European Fairs Cup Winners 1968, 1971

Ground Elland Road

Leeds United were formed to succeed Leeds City, who were expelled from the League and disbanded after a scandal over illegal payments. Their history was one of modest achievement – they had never fallen below Division 2 or finished higher than fifth in Division 1 – before Don Revie's appointment as player-manager in 1961.

The former England forward transformed Leeds into a club challenging consistently for major honours, at home and abroad. Using players who had graduated from the youth team, he built initially around Jack Charlton, a gangling centre-half who was to begin an England career at 28, and two small Scots, Bobby Collins and Billy Bremner, whose volatile temperaments accompanied great ability.

After several near misses, Leeds beat Arsenal in a dour League Cup Final in 1968. A year later, with ex-Manchester United player Johnny Giles by now

partnering Bremner in midfield, they took their first Championship by drawing at Liverpool, and went on to finish with what was then a First Division record of 67 points after losing only two of their 42 fixtures. Further honours followed as the side began

LEEDS UNITED At last, the FA Cup for Leeds United under Don Revie in the Centenary Final of 1972 following a dour 1-0 win over Arsenal. Billy Bremner is aloft with *(from left)* Mick Bates, Paul Reaney, Johnny Giles, Allan Clarke (the scorer), Jack Charlton (kneeling) and Peter Lorimer in attendance. Certainly not supporting his skipper was centre forward Mick Jones who collected his medal in some pain following a shoulder injury in the second half. It was Jones who had supplied the cross for Clarke's winning, diving header. The numbered garters were all part of the Leeds image of the period; most probably they would have been given to fans during the lap of honour.

to win over those who had labelled them dirty and defensive. In 1972 Leeds won the FA Cup, again defeating Arsenal, but failed to clinch the Championship and the double 48 hours later at Wolverhampton.

Revie's departure for the England manager's job, following Leeds' second league title, caused player unrest. Brian Clough took over but was dismissed barely seven weeks later. Leeds recovered to reach the 1975 European Cup Final against Bayern Munich in Paris, but lost against a backdrop of violence initiated by some of their followers.

The dual dilemma of diminishing success on the pitch and growing hooliganism off it dogged Leeds through the next decade and beyond. A succession of managers, among them three players from their 1965/75 heyday, were unable to arrest the decline. Financial difficulties, exacerbated by relegation in 1982, forced the sale three years later of Elland Road to the city council, who granted the club a 125-year lease.

In 1988 Leeds secured Howard Wilkinson from Sheffield Wednesday as manager. He dealt extensively in the transfer market, having spent £6 million and banked £3 million by the time Division 1 status was regained in 1990. Gordon Strachan, whose leadership and skill drew comparisons with Bremner, also finished top scorer in 1989/90, 16 goals leaving him the small matter of 26 behind John Charles's club-record tally in 1953/54.

With support running at levels not enjoyed since the Revie era, Leeds finished fourth on their return to the top flight despite playing under threat of expulsion from the FA, the result of incidents involving their fans at Bournemouth on the weekend promotion was achieved.

LEICESTER CITY

Founded 1884

Joined League 1894 (Div.2)

LEICESTER CITY Leicester City fans have enjoyed many special moments during their club's history, but few of major importance. There seems to be something preventing the club from reaching the very top. Here was a special moment, in May 1963, when centre-forward Keyworth scored against Manchester United in the FA Cup Final; Stringfellow, in the white shirt, is the Leicester player looking on. Sadly Leicester lost this Final 3-1 to Manchester United, their third of four losing Final appearances in a competition they have never won.

Honours Div.2 Champions 1925, 1937, 1954, 1957, 1971, 1980; League Cup Winners 1964

Ground Filbert Street

Leicester City are a frustrating club. They employ enterprising managers to build entertaining sides, only to see them fail, with agonising predictability, on the verge of major achievement.

The 'Foxes' have spent much of their history proving they are too good for the Second Division, only to fall out of the First with equal regularity. When they were relegated in 1987 it was their 16th journey between the top two flights, and not since 1908 have they spent more than a dozen successive campaigns at one level.

City first threatened to make a major impact in the late 1920s, when they twice came close to the League Championship and their stars included marksman Arthur Chandler and long-serving full-back Adam Black. But, typically, the impetus died and despite remarkable goal-scoring feats by Arthur Rowley in the 1950s it was not until Matt Gillies became manager at the decade's end that some stability was achieved. The thoughtful Scot constructed a fluent side in which 'keeper Gordon Banks and wing-half Frank McLintock were outstanding, but Leicester's near-miss syndrome was to continue. In 1961 they lost the FA Cup Final; two years later they squandered a promising First Division position and were beaten FA Cup finalists again. A solitary triumph in the infant League Cup was scant consolation.

The 1960s ended with City's fourth FA Cup Final defeat in 21 years, and another relegation. There followed splendid work by managers Frank O'Farrell and Jimmy Bloomfield, whose 1970s teams included the likes of Peter Shilton, Banks's brilliant replacement, and forwards Keith Weller and Frank Worthington.

Nothing was won,

however, and the ups and downs continued unabated during the 1980s, despite prolific contributions from strikers Gary Lineker and Alan Smith, both sold for fortunes. Leicester are one of many Midlands sides battling each other for support. If they are to succeed, consistency must be their primary aim.

LEYTON ORIENT

Founded 1881

Joined League 1905 (Div.2)

Honours Div.3 (S) Champions 1956; Div.3 Champions 1970

Ground Brisbane Road

Twice rescued from the brink of financial disaster,

Leyton Orient offer an inspiring example of what spirit and hard work can achieve for the least fashionable of clubs.

After election to the League, the east Londoners – at different times known as Clapton Orient and just plain Orient – were a very ordinary outfit and it was no surprise when they slumped into Division 3 (S) in 1929. Not long afterwards they faced economic oblivion but were saved by Arsenal, who temporarily made the O's their nursery club.

More than two decades of mediocrity ensued until Alec Stock became manager, transformed their fortunes and led them back to the higher grade. Johnny Carey carried on the good work and amazed the football world by gaining promotion to Division 1 in 1962. But Orient were not ready for such a quantum leap, and near calamity followed: they finished 10 points adrift at the bottom of the table and then plummeted back to the Third Division, a descent which culminated in a second cash crisis in 1967. After salvation had been achieved, assisted by a collection organised by fans, a succession of enterprising managers, including Dave Sexton and Jimmy Bloomfield, there were better times at Brisbane Road, and although the club has continued to commute among the bottom three divisions, off-the-field stability has been achieved.

Orient, supervised since 1982 by the under-rated Frank Clark, can look back on some stirring FA Cup exploits, of which their runs to the quarter-final in 1971 and the semi-final seven years later have been the most notable.

LIDDELL, Billy

1922 Born in Dunfermline, Scotland

1939 Signs for Liverpool

1946 August - League debut v Sheffield United at Bramall Lane; October - wins first of 28 Scottish caps, v Wales at Wrexham; Helps the Reds clinch the first post-war League Championship

1947 Plays for Great Britain against the Rest of Europe

1950 Takes home loser's medal as Arsenal beat Liverpool in FA Cup Final

1954 Despite the prodigious efforts of Liddell, the Reds are relegated to the Second Division

1955 Liddell and Stanley Matthews are the only two players retained for Great Britain's second clash with the Europeans

1961 Retires after scoring 229 goals in 537 games for Liverpool

Any contemporary observer would confirm that Billy Liddell was Liverpool's finest player in the post-war years before Bill Shankly led the club towards lasting glory. Yet there is no shortage of shrewd pundits who would go even further; they would say the Scottish winger-cum-centre-forward was the Reds' greatest talent of all time, and that is with due deference to Messrs Dalglish, Keegan, Barnes and company.

Liddell's hallmarks were exhilarating pace and power, allied to the most delicate skill. Sadly, he lost his early prime to the war, and then played in a poor side for much of his time at Anfield. Indeed, throughout the late 1950s he laboured nobly, though unavailingly, to lift them out of the Second Division.

Such application was typical of the man, who was beloved of the fans, not only as a fabulous entertainer but also as a chivalrous, down-to-earth personality. After retirement he became a youth worker, lay preacher and justice of the peace.

BILLY LIDDELL Leading out Liverpool in the 1957/58 season, Billy Liddell prepares for another match in the more than 500 he played for the Reds. A Scottish international, like many other famous Liverpool players, he missed out on the glory days at the club but will always be remembered for his devotion to football and to his adopted home town.

LINCOLN CITY

Founded 1883

Joined League 1892
(Div.2, founder member)

Honours Div.3 (N)
Champions 1932, 1948,
1952; Div.4 Champions
1976

Ground Sincil Bank

When Lincoln City dropped out of the League in 1987, it was no new experience for them. After being founder members of Division 2, the 'Imps' failed to gain re-election on three occasions before joining the newly-formed Division 3 (N) in 1921.

There followed a roller-coaster existence between Second and Third Divisions which ended unhappily with a slump to the basement in the 1960s. Having narrowly survived a financial crisis during that decade, Lincoln toiled in the League's lower reaches until they were demoted to the Vauxhall Conference. They bounced back into the Fourth Division at the first attempt and now face the task of rebuilding in an area not renowned for its soccer tradition.

Notable managers have included long-serving Bill Anderson, whose side in the 1950s was one of Lincoln's most impressive combinations, and current England boss Graham Taylor, a former Imp who occupied the Sincil Bank hot seat in the mid 1970s.

LINEKER, Gary

1960 Born in Leicester

1978 Turns professional with Leicester City

1980 Wins Second Division title medal

1981 Struggles for his place as Leicester are relegated

1983 Boosts promotion campaign with 26 goals

1984 Makes England debut as substitute for Tony Woodcock, v Scotland at Hampden

1985 Joins Everton for £800,000 plus a third of future profit

1986 Scoops two awards - football writers' and

players' Player of Year - after scoring 30 League goals; nets in FA Cup Final defeat by Liverpool; June - 6 strikes, including a hat-trick against Poland, make Lineker top scorer in Mexico World Cup; July - moves to Barcelona for £2.75 million

1989 Returns to Football League as Tottenham Hotspur pay £1.1 million

1990 Finishes first season at White Hart Lane with 26 goals; scores for England in World Cup semi-final against West Germany, his fourth goal of tournament; September - becomes Graham Taylor's first England captain

1991 Passes the 150-goal mark in just over 300 league games.

In 1991, with 45 international goals to his credit, Lineker looked on course to become England's most prolific scorer of all time. But even if the fleet-footed marksman fails to overtake Bobby Charlton's record of 49, he had already done enough to claim a place on his country's roll of honour.

Lineker made a startling impact at every level after building his reputation in a Leicester side of rather indifferent quality. With Everton he assumed world-class stature; in Spain he overcame illness and adapted his game to earn generous praise; at Tottenham he provided a much-needed cutting edge; and for England he has often been an inspiration.

Few defences are proof against his phenomenal acceleration, to which he

GARY LINEKER In a career untroubled by controversy, though not by injury and illness, Gary Lineker emerged from the 1980s as the captain of England and a model for the professional game. Seen here playing in the 1-1 draw against Brazil in a friendly in 1987, his skills of great acceleration and snapping up the half-chance seem ideal for the game wherever it is played. His running into space to act as a target player has also contributed to his reputation and value, particularly in Britain where a long-passing game is more popular than in the rest of

allies enviable composure and a lethal instinct for arriving in front of goal at precisely the right moment. He is not a forager, however, and relies almost exclusively on intelligent service from his midfield. Blessed with an equable temperament and clean-cut image, Lineker excels at public relations, and has proved a perfect choice as skipper of England.

LIVERPOOL

Founded 1892

Joined League 1893 (Div.2)

Honours Div.1 Champions 1901, 1906, 1922, 1923, 1947, 1964, 1966, 1973, 1976, 1977, 1979, 1980, 1982, 1983, 1984, 1986, 1988, 1990; Div.2 Champions 1894, 1896, 1905, 1962; FA Cup Winners 1965, 1974, 1986, 1989; European Cup Winners 1977, 1978, 1981, 1984; UEFA Cup Winners 1973, 1976

Ground Anfield

In a journal of record such as this, the obvious has to be stated: Liverpool, quite simply, are the most successful club in English soccer history. Their exalted status comes courtesy of a phenomenal record in the modern era, which began with the arrival of Bill Shankly as manager in 1959. Yet, believe it or not, there was life at Anfield before Shankly.

In fact, the first stirrings were as an offshoot of local rivals Everton in the 1890s. After early vacillations between First and Second Divisions, the 'Reds' made their initial significant mark on the football world, winning two League Championships in the first decade of the new century, aided on the second occasion by England goalkeeper Sam Hardy. There followed a relatively uneventful spell before another brace of titles, with new custodian Elisha Scott and long-serving full-back Ephraim Longworth making prominent contributions.

The 1930s brought something of a decline, but Championship triumph in the first season after the war and the emergence of brilliant Scottish forward

Billy Liddell boded well for the future. The 1950s, however, failed to live up to this promise and the unthinkable happened: Liverpool were relegated. Cue Shankly, and the revolution. The indomitable Scot swiftly revamped a nondescript side. To promising youngsters such as goal merchant Roger Hunt and

LIVERPOOL A dedicated 'Red', Emlyn Hughes seen in 1977 FA Cup Final action against Manchester United's Stuart Pearson. When his children were young Hughes would book himself into a hotel before home matches to ensure a good night's sleep.

winger Ian Callaghan he added the likes of colossal centre-half Ron Yeats and Ian St John, a pugnacious, skilful centre-forward, and it wasn't long before the Reds were back in the top flight. But promotion was only the beginning. Having strengthened the team further with England flankman Peter Thompson and granite-tough local boy Tommy Smith, Shankly was ready to take on the elite. His new Liverpool served notice of the dominance in store by lifting two titles, and for good measure putting the club's name on the FA Cup for the first time - all in the space of three years.

By the early 1970s he had remoulded his side and, with such men as inspirational forward Kevin Keegan, 'keeper Ray Clemence, midfielder cum defender Emlyn Hughes and goal-getter John Toshack now holding sway, the trophies continued to accumulate.

When Shankly surprised everyone by resigning in 1974, erstwhile back room boy Bob Paisley moved into his seat and, astonishingly, the rate of success increased. New talents to savour included those of the superbly gifted Kenny Dalglish, Graeme Souness, an imperious play-maker, winger Steve

LIVERPOOL With so many victories to celebrate and so many great players to feature, it's hard to do justice to Liverpool FC with one photo. This shows the big club prize – the European Cup, 1977 – and two players that typify the Liverpool way of doing things. Phil Neal (left) and Alan Hansen were both tough yet skilful, both capped by their countries (England and Scotland respectively) yet not tempted away from Anfield. Neal made over 450 League appearances for the Reds, a figure not to be beaten by Hansen who, with more than 400 appearances under his belt, was forced to retire due to injury problems.

Heighway and Alan Hansen, the coolest central defender since Bobby Moore. Europe was conquered and fresh standards of achievement were set. After Paisley retired in 1983, first Joe Fagan and then Dalglish - who led Liverpool to the league/FA Cup double in his first term in charge-took up the challenge, establishing a supremacy which weighed heavily on their rivals and scotching former disparaging claims that the Reds were dull and machine-like. The sheer style of goal king Ian Rush, England striker Peter Beardsley, the magnificent John Barnes et al produced flowing one-touch football which was often a joy to behold. The 1980s were marred by the Heysel and Hillsborough tragedies but, in playing terms, the Liverpool story was one of unconfined delight. Depressingly for the rest, it shows every sign of continuing into the 1990s and beyond, although the sudden departure of Dalglish as manager in 1991 might seem to open a window of hope for the competition.

LOFTHOUSE, Nat

1925 Born in Bolton

1939 Signs for Bolton Wanderers

1950 Scores twice on England debut, v Yugoslavia at Highbury

1952 Press dub Lofthouse the 'Lion of Vienna'

1953 Footballer of the Year; scores in every round of the FA Cup, including the 'Matthews Final' against Blackpool, which Bolton lose 4-3; September - scores 6 for Football League against Irish League

1956 Tops First Division goal chart

1958 Skippers Bolton to FA Cup triumph over Manchester United, scoring both goals, the second through a controversial barge on 'keeper Harry Gregg; England swansong, v Wales at Villa Park, having scored 30 times in 33 internationals

1960 Career ended by

NAT LOFTHOUSE
Nat Lofthouse playing in the 1958 FA Cup Final for Bolton Wanderers against Manchester United. He scored both goals and captained his team – but will be remembered for his barge on United 'keeper Harry Gregg that gave Bolton the second goal and the game.

injury; joins Burnden Park coaching staff

1968 Takes over as Bolton boss

1971 Steps down to become chief scout

1985 Short spell as caretaker manager

1986 Becomes Bolton president

Lofthouse was an archetypal battering-ram centre-forward who, during his prime in the 1950s, terrorised defences all over the world. He followed another native of Bolton, Tommy Lawton, into the England side, and although he never had the craft of his illustrious predecessor, the tank-like Lofthouse could not be faulted for aggression, commitment

and courage.

It was after a typically brave performance in his country's shirt that he was nicknamed the 'Lion of Vienna', his two-goal show setting up a memorable victory over Austria, then one of Europe's leading sides. Dynamic in the air, blessed with a vicious shot in either foot, and dedicated to chasing causes that were apparently lost, Lofthouse was a difficult man to play against, and there were times when he was accused of being over-physical in his approach.

A one-club man, he served Bolton royally as a player, netting 285 times in 503 games, and later as an administrator.

LOST CLUBS

Clubs have usually left the Football League after failing to gain re-election, but very occasionally they have resigned from the League, an obvious example being Accrington Stanley part ways through the 1961/62 season when financial problems dogged the Lancashire club. More recently, a club finishing 92nd has been auto-

matically relegated to the GM Vauxhall Conference.

The most stable period in Football League history was between 1938 and 1960, when only New Brighton were lost. The surprise elimination of Gateshead in 1960 came as a shock, especially as the north-eastern club had been relatively successful in the post-war period, had not faced re-election for 23 years and had not even finished bottom when Peterborough United replaced them. This demonstrates the unpopularity of geographically isolated clubs, many of which are under the most threat.

Clubs lost to the Football League are as follows (with League career in brackets): Aberdare Athletic (1921-27), Accrington Stanley (1888-93 and 1921-62), Ashington (1921-29), Barrow (1921-72), Bootle (1892-93), Bradford Park Avenue (1908-70), Burton United (1901-07), Colchester United (1950-90), Darwen (1891-99), Durham City (1921-28), Gainsborough Trinity (1896-1912), Gateshead (1919-60),

Glossop North End (1898-1915), Loughborough Town (1895-1900), Merthyr Tydfil (1920-30), Middlesbrough Ironopolis (1893-94), Nelson (1921-31), New Brighton (1898-1901 and 1923-51), Newport County (1921-31 and 1932-88), Northwich Victoria (1892-94), Southport (1921-78), Stalybridge Celtic (1921-23), Thames (1930-32) and Workington Town (1951-77). In addition, Burton Wanderers (1894-97) amalgamated with Burton Swifts (1892-1901) in 1901 to form Burton United, and there are current League clubs with a discontinuous record: Blackpool, Chesterfield, Crewe Alexandra, Darlington, Doncaster Rovers, Gillingham, Grimsby Town, Lincoln City (now in their fifth spell), Luton Town, Port Vale, Rotherham United, Stockport County, Stoke City, Walsall and Wigan Athletic.

The list of lost Scottish League clubs is affected considerably by altercations involving rival Central and Western

Leagues in the early 1920s. A deal was struck to incorporate the rival Leagues into the Scottish League, which was extended to three divisions. However, many of the new clubs were soon threatened by an exodus of players and poor attendances. Division 3 collapsed in its third season.

The list of lost clubs from

'LOST' CLUBS 'And remember, the whole ball must cross the line' was a favourite phrase of early radio and television commentator Kenneth Wolstenholme. In this incident the ball was cleared by Accrington Stanley player Ken Holliday as his 'keeper Tommy McQueen looks on. Lol Chappell is the Barnsley forward left hoping. Barnsley won the encounter 3-2 and at the end of the 1954-55 season. Barnsley and Accrington were first and second respectively in Division 3 (N). Fans at that game could not have known that Accrington would not escape later notoriety for having to drop out of the Fourth Division in 1962 for financial reasons. Their name has remained synonymous with football failure ever since.

the Scottish is as follows: Abercorn (1890-1915), Armadale (1921-32), Arthurlie (1901-15 and 1923-29), Bathgate (1921-29), Beith (1923-26), Bo'ness (1921-32), Broxburn United (1921-26), Cambuslang (1890-92), Clackmannan (1920-22 and 1923-26), the original Clydebank (1914-30), Cowlairs (1890-91 and 1893-95), Dumbarton Harp (1923-25), Dundee Wanderers (1894-95), Dykehead (1923-26), Edinburgh City (1928-49), Galston (1923-26), Helensburgh (1893), Johnstone (1912-15 and 1921-26), Kings Park (1921-39), Leith Athletic (1891-1915, 1924-26 and 1927-53), Linthouse (1895-1900), Lochgelly United (1914-15 and 1921-26), Mid-Annandale (1923-26), Nithsdale Wanderers (1923-26), Northern Club of Glasgow (1894-95), Peebles Rovers (1923-26), Port Glasgow Athletic (1893-1911), Renton (1890-98), Royal Albert (1923-26), St Bernards (1893-1915 and 1921-39), Solway Star (1923-26), Third Lanark (1890-1967), Thistle (1893-94) and Vale of Leven (1890-92, 1905-15 and 1921-26). In addition, Ayr and Ayr Parkhouse merged in 1910 to form Ayr United.

LUTON TOWN

Founded 1885

Joined League 1897 (Div.2)

Honours Div.2 Champions 1982; Div.3 (S) Champions 1937; Div.4 Champions 1968; League Cup Winners 1988

Ground Kenilworth Road

Luton Town are a plucky club whose three spells in Division 1 have been achieved despite lack of consistently heavy support, a plight due largely to their position on London's doorstep.

The 'Hatters' early experience of Football League life was traumatic. After only three seasons they failed to gain re-election to the Second Division, and it was two decades before they were re-admitted as founder members of the Third. There they remained until 1937, when - boosted by 55 goals from Joe Payne, who had netted 10 times in one match during the previous campaign - they were promoted. They then consolidated before manager Dally Duncan led them into the top flight in 1955. Players such as centre-half Syd Owen, wing-half Bob Morton, 'keeper Ron Baynham and goal-scorer Gordon Turner

LUTON TOWN In the 1980s, and into the '90s too, Luton Town's presence in the First Division always appeared to be temporary – although they gamely stuck in there and actually recorded some very good final placings. They were known mostly for their fights against relegation, their plastic pitch and their cup success. In 1988 they won the Football League Cup against Arsenal (3-2) and were losing semi-finalists in the FA Cup. Centre-half Steve Foster *(left)*, irregular 'keeper Andy Dibble and two-goal hero Brian Stein celebrate the League (then the Littlewoods) Cup win.

impressed on the grander stage, but despite the purchase of talented forwards such as Billy Bingham and Allan Brown, Luton were relegated after five years. The highlight of this period was reaching the FA Cup Final in 1959, when they were beaten by Nottingham Forest.

Then came utter depression, followed by

some solid rebuilding work. An alarming slide, all the way to the Fourth Division, was arrested when Brown returned to Kenilworth Road as manager. He took Luton back to the Third Division, Alec Stock led them to the Second, and Harry Haslam restored them to the First, though only for 1974/75. Seven more years in Division 2 were followed by promotion under David Pleat in 1982. Luton's first major trophy, the League Cup, arrived in the form of a dramatic late victory over Arsenal in 1988.

During these switchback years, star performers included forward Bruce Rioch (1960s), marksman Malcolm Macdonald (1969-71) and midfielder Ricky Hill (1970s and 1980s).

In recent years Luton have hit the headlines more through their controversial chairman, David Evans MP, who introduced a synthetic pitch in 1985 and followed that by a ban on away supporters, than for any great success on the field of play - although they are always a team that are capable of turning in surprise performances.

MCGRAIN, Danny

1950 Born in Glasgow

1967 Signs for Celtic

1970 Makes debut for Celtic at right-back

1972 Suffers fractured skull in clash of heads with Doug Somner (Falkirk)

1973 Wins first Scotland cap

1974 Is diagnosed diabetic after playing in 1974 World Cup finals

1977 Is voted Scottish Player of the Year; suffers mysterious ankle injury, which sidelines him for over a year

1978 Jock Stein appoints him Celtic club captain

1980 Captains Scotland for the first time

1987 Receives free transfer from Celtic

In his 20-year career at Celtic, Danny McGrain played in seven Scottish League Championship teams, the last four as an inspirational captain. He won 62 caps for Scotland, 10 as captain, and it could have been far more. When at his peak he suffered an ankle injury which kept him out of internationals for three years. He was sadly missed at the 1978 World Cup finals, when Ally MacLeod's team fared so capriciously without him.

Danny McGrain was one of Celtic's 'Quality Street Kids' of the late-1960s - Dalglish, Macari, Hay and Connelly were other

DANNY MCGRAIN
Another Championship for Celtic, this time by two points from Aberdeen and twelve points from Rangers who finished in third place, in 1982. Captain Danny McGrain is chaired aloft by team-mates. By 1982 McGrain was on the way to becoming Celtic's most capped player, a reward for his all-round ability, something that was not widely recognised south of the border, perhaps because he never played English League football.

examples - and a true example of courage. He overcame injury and illness to play more than 600 games for Celtic. They included seven Scottish Cup Finals (five won) and seven Scottish League Cup Finals (two won).

On the field he had virtually everything except perhaps the clinical finish of a striker. Tall and lean, he had speed, beautiful ball control, strength in the tackle and the ability to trick players in the Scottish tradition. He read the play superbly and was so competitive that he could take over a game if it was going badly, overlapping as a full-back or moving into a midfield creative role. He was perfect for the era of 'total football'.

MACKAY, Dave

1934 Born in Edinburgh

1952 Turns professional with Heart of Midlothian

1955 Pockets first senior medal as Hearts win League Cup

1956 Helps the 'Jammies' lift the Scottish Cup

1957 Wins first of 22 Scotland caps, v Spain in Madrid

1958 Hearts' title triumph completes his set of medals

1959 Celebrates a second League Cup victory, then heads south to join Tottenham Hotspur

1961 Plays mammoth part in Spurs' League and FA Cup double

1962 Brilliant again as Bill Nicholson's side retain FA Cup

1963 Suffers first of two broken legs within a year

1967 Captains Tottenham to Wembley victory over Chelsea to claim his third FA Cup winner's medal

1968 Moves to Derby County

1969 Leads the 'Rams' to Second Division title and is voted joint Footballer of the Year with Manchester City's Tony Book

DAVE MACKAY In his Derby County shirt and using that trusty but oft-broken left leg, Dave Mackay shows the concentration and determination that brought him succes as a player and manager. Some people will remember him best as a Spurs player; he contributed tenacity to the skilful side of the double era. For others he will always be identified as a Derby man, as both player (1968-70) and manager (1973-76). Perhaps he's a genuine 'two-club' man!

1971 Becomes player-manager of Swindon Town

1972 Takes over as Nottingham Forest boss

1973 Succeeds Brian Clough as Derby manager

1975 Mackay emulates his predecessor as 'Rams' lift League Championship

1977 Takes over at Walsall

1978 Starts successful coaching stint in Kuwait

1987 Returns to Britain and slips into hot seat at Doncaster

1988 Rovers are relegated to the Fourth Division

1989 Switches to St Andrews to guide fortunes of ailing Birmingham City

1991 Resigns from 'Blues' job

With only a few hours left before the 1959 transfer deadline, Bill Nicholson, the manager of Tottenham Hotspur, persuaded Hearts to part with Dave Mackay. It turned out to be his best ever signing and, incidentally, not the fluke some people imagined. The story goes that Nicholson went for Mackay after Arsenal won the race to sign Mel Charles from Swansea, but in truth he had long since made the combative and marvellously gifted Scot his prime target.

For a fee of £30,000 that then equalled the British record for a half-back,

Tottenham had a player who proved to be the most inspirational in their history. Possessing more skill than he was given credit for, a master of all the kicking skills and a shrewd tactician, Mackay did more than anyone to forge a great Spurs team.

Daring and dynamic, he recovered from a twice-broken leg and was admired throughout the game. 'He was the best I ever played with,' said Jimmy Greaves. 'If he was ever missing, the rest of us had to work twice as hard to make up for it.'

In December 1963 Mackay's left leg was broken in two places during

a European Cup Winners' Cup tie against Manchester United. A year later, when attempting a comeback in the reserves against Shrewsbury Town, the leg went again. Now he became a legend, recovering to captain Tottenham and take a third FA Cup winner's medal in 1967.

Next came a move to Derby County. 'Signing Dave Mackay was the best day's work of my life,' said Brian Clough, the Derby manager. Playing alongside Roy McFarland, then a promising young centre-half, Mackay found a new lease of life. He captained Derby to the Second Division title and shared

the Footballer of the Year award.

Later he emulated Clough's managerial success at Derby before continuing his career in the Middle East and back in Britain.

MAIDSTONE UNITED

Founded 1897

Joined League 1989 (Div.4)

Honours None

Ground Watling Street, Dartford

After entering Division 4 as Vauxhall Conference Champions, Maidstone United made a promising start to Football League

life, finishing fifth and earning a place in the promotion play-offs. Though beaten by Cambridge United, they gave a good account of themselves and strengthened the widespread belief that many teams in non-League soccer are superior to some of their counterparts in the senior competition. Having become established under the management of Keith Peacock, the 'Stones' must seek to consolidate. Main local rivals are Gillingham, although potential support is also lost to London clubs, and filling their ground - situated at Dartford, 21 miles from their home-town – will not be easy.

Before joining the Conference, United played in a succession of leagues, including the Corinthian, Athenian, Isthmian and Southern. Their most glorious FA Cup exploit has been reaching the third round in 1979, when they lost to Charlton Athletic after a replay.

MANCHESTER CITY

Founded 1887

Joined League 1892 (Div.2)

Honours Div.1 Champions 1937, 1968; Div.2 Champions 1899, 1903, 1910, 1928, 1947, 1966; FA Cup Winners 1904, 1934, 1956, 1969; League Cup Winners 1970, 1976; European Cup Winners' Cup Winners 1970

Ground Maine Road

Manchester City have a special place in football's affections. Few clubs can match their range of performances, from brilliant to banal, always able to surprise and always likely to disappoint.

They began as West Gorton, had five early homes, mostly in east Manchester and entered the Second Division in 1892 as Ardwick, playing on Hyde Road. They fielded their first indisputably great player, Billy Meredith, in 1894, four years later had reached the First Division, and by 1904 had won the FA Cup and finished second in the League. That success brought allegations of illegal payments and the FA was severe: a former chairman, the secretary, two directors and 17 players were suspended, the club and each individual being fined. This setback enabled old rivals Newton Heath, under their new name of Manchester United, to emerge as the city's premier club for the first time.

In 1923 City moved into their present ground at Maine Road, went down again in 1926 despite scoring 89 goals and reaching the Cup Final, and saved an even bigger disappointment for the last day of the 1926/27 season.

They were joint leaders with Portsmouth, goal average almost identical. City walloped Bradford at home, and Portsmouth were losing 1-0 to Preston, but promptly went on to score five second-half goals, pipping City for promotion by 0.002 of a goal.

Ironically, that near miss heralded a golden era: another 100-goal season brought City their fourth Second Division Championship which was followed by a Cup semi-final in 1932, a Cup Final victory in 1934 (that team, led by Matt Busby, is still regarded by some as the club's best) and their first League title in 1936/37. City were relegated, on goal average, before the war but returned in 1946/47, went down again in 1950, and rose again a year later to enter a period of stability and success under an innovative manager, Les McDowell, who turned Don Revie into a 'deep-lying centre-forward', Hungarian style, and paid a record fee for Denis Law.

City reached successive Cup Final's in 1955/56 and played their first Cup tie under lights in 1961, but after selling Law to Torino they were relegated again in 1962/63. This setback again proved to be a prelude to an astonishing spell that made the club's modern image. Joe Mercer was appointed manager in July 1965, bringing with him Malcolm Allison. Five magnificent seasons followed, culminating in winning the European Cup Winners' Cup in 1970.

After Mercer and Allison the team was still powerful, especially with enterprising new chairman Peter Swales leading the way. Allison's return as coach, then manager, initiated some big spending, but with little success.

Season 1980/81 was extraordinary even by Maine Road standards. Twelve League matches without a win brought Allison's sacking, John Bond taking over in October; the team reached the League Cup semi-final and the Centenary FA Cup

MANCHESTER CITY
The deep-lying, and deep-thinking, centre-forward of Manchester City, Don Revie *(left)*, seen during the 1956 FA Cup Final. The Birmingham player is Jeff Hall. City beat Birmingham City 3-1, supposedly using the 'Revie plan', having lost the preceding year's Final by the same score to Newcastle United. This was the second of four years in which Manchester clubs were in the Final (this was their only success), with United losing in the following two season. Inspired by Revie and a number of other gifted players, City were enjoying one of their best spells in League and Cup. Unfortunately it coincided with the rise of their neighbours' fortunes under Matt Busby, and only rarely since have City stolen the national headlines away from United.

Final, losing to Spurs in a memorable replay.

Trevor Francis became City's third £1 million player in 1981, but by 1983 the familiar spectre of relegation could be seen in Moss Side. City needed to draw with Luton in their last home game but lost by one scrambled goal in a melee, and that drop set another 'yo-yo' pattern for the decade, relegated again in 1988 as Billy McNeill, Jimmy Frizzell and Mel Machin tried to give a club, still struggling with the debts of the Allison era, some stability. Two managers in the 1990/91 season continued the tradition that life is never dull if you wear the scarf of light blue and white.

MANCHESTER UNITED

Founded 1878

Joined League 1892 (Div.1)

Honours Div.1 Champions 1908, 1911, 1952, 1956, 1957, 1965, 1967; Div.2 Champions 1936, 1975; FA Cup Winners 1909, 1948, 1963, 1977, 1983, 1985,

1990; European Cup Winners 1968; European Cup Winners' Cup Winners 1991

Ground Old Trafford

Arsenal might have more tradition, and Liverpool have certainly won more trophies but there is about Manchester United an indefinable aura of magic which still marks them out – even in times of travail both on and off the pitch – as the most glamorous club in English football.

Such a mantle was not always theirs. Early financial struggles saw them on the verge of extinction and it was not until the first decade of the twentieth century that success was achieved in major competitions, with their first star, winger Billy Meredith, playing a prominent part. There followed, between the wars, a distinctly mundane period during which United suffered three relegations to the Second Division, and although they made a swift return to the top rank after each demotion, there was little hint of the glories to come.

Then, into the ruins of an Old Trafford which had been gutted by Hitler's

MANCHESTER UNITED
Manchester United have a special place in British football, based largely upon the exploits of Sir Matt Busby and the teams he built. This is his second great side, photographed in 1968/69, proudly displaying the prize they wanted so badly: the European Cup. The players and managerial team line-up: *(back row, left to right)* **Foulkes, Aston, Rimmer, Stepney, Gowling, Herd; Sadler, Owen (office staff), Dunne, Brennan, Crerand, Best, Burns, Armstrong (scout), Crompton (trainer); Ryan, Stiles, Law, Busby, Charlton, Kidd, Fitzpatrick. It may be hard to believe now, but in 1969 these were nearly all household names; in Manchester they were living legends.**

bombs, strode Matt Busby. The new manager revitalised the club, assembling a brilliant attacking side under the inspirational captaincy of Irishman Johnny Carey. United won the FA Cup in 1948, with scintillating contributions from forwards Stan Pearson and Jack Rowley, and for five consecutive campaigns they narrowly missed the League Championship before finally lifting it – a triumph which, ironically, heralded the break-up of Busby's first great side.

In the early 1950s he introduced a crop of precocious hopefuls to the big time; the 'Busby Babes' were born. Among them were left-back and skipper Roger Byrne; centre-forward Tommy Taylor, one of the few who cost a fee; jaunty wing-half Eddie Colman; inside-forwards Dennis Viollet, Liam Whelan and Bobby Charlton; and, most colossal talent of them all, Duncan Edwards. They won two Championships and threatened to dominate English soccer for the foreseeable future. Then came the Munich air disaster of 1958, which claimed the lives of eight players and shocked the soccer world.

Busby himself was at death's door but, incredibly, he recovered and built a third magnificent team. This was the prime of Bobby Charlton, Denis Law and George Best, the glorious trinity whose combined talents simply took the breath away. More titles were won and in 1968 Busby experienced his crowning moment when United became the first English club to take the European Cup.

Thereafter, United have experienced mixed fortunes. Sir Matt, as he became, was never adequately replaced and, despite vast expenditure, none of those who succeeded him has come remotely close to emulating his achievements. Of those who have tried, Tommy Docherty in the mid 1970s and Ron Atkinson in the early 1980s looked the most

promising. Docherty took over a poor side, reconstructed it during a one-term sojourn in Division 2, and returned to the top flight with a refreshingly positive line-up in which defender Martin Buchan and winger Steve Coppell were outstanding. But after winning the FA Cup the Doc was sacked following personal controversy. Atkinson built an attractive team around England

captain Bryan Robson and won two FA Cups but, having failed to win the League, he too was shown the door.

The expensive team created by his successor, Alex Ferguson, was less easy on the eye, and with a background of boardroom unrest, United ended the 1980s in poor fettle. However, two cup triumphs at the dawn of the new decade gave birth to fresh hope that their vast

legion of fans might be granted, before too long, what they most dearly desired – an entertaining side capable of winning the Championship.

MANCHESTER UNITED
Lee Sharpe, the newest star in the Old Trafford firmament, outpaces a Barcelona defender during the 1991 European Cup Winners' Cup Final in Rotterdam. United's achievement in

lifting the trophy was a magnificent riposte to all those critics who had predicted that English clubs would be shown up on their return to Europe by the sophistication of continental opposition. In fact, for the first 75 minutes of the final, the Spanish 'aristocrats' were ineffectual, only coming alive after Mark Hughes has given the 'Red Devils' the lead.

MANSFIELD TOWN

Founded 1910

Joined League 1931 (Div.3 S)

Honours Div.3 Champions 1977; Div.4 Champions 1975

Ground Field Mill

Although Mansfield Town have led a largely tranquil League existence, there have been times when they have stirred themselves mightily in sudden-death competitions. In 1929, as a non-League outfit, they beat Wolves at Molineux to reach the FA Cup fourth round, and 40 years later made it to the quarter-finals at the expense of a West Ham United side boasting World Cup heroes Moore, Hurst and Peters.

Since then the 'Stags' have even experienced Wembley glory, winning the 1987 Freight Rover Trophy under the management of Ian Greaves, a wondrous achievement for a small club usually overshadowed by their Nottingham neighbours. Other leading figures have included pre-war goal-scorer Ted Harston, 1960s forwards Mike Stringfellow and Ken Wagstaff, and bosses Raich Carter and Billy Bingham, though none of them was able to inspire even bread-and-butter success.

Mansfield did, however, establish a tradition for consistency: for four decades after joining the League they were solid members of the Third division. Since 1960 there have been four spells in the Fourth and, in 1977/78, a single campaign in the Second, but their spiritual home has remained in between.

MARADONA, Diego

1960 Born in Argentina

1976 Makes League debut for Argentinos Juniors, short of his 16th birthday

1977 Wins first full international cap as substitute in crushing victory over Hungary

1978 National coach Cesar Menotti shatters Maradona by dropping him from the World Cup squad on the eve of the finals in his own country

1979 Captains Argentina to triumph in World Youth Cup

1981 Moves to the more fashionable Boca Juniors club

1982 June – disappoints in World Cup finals in Spain, and is sent off against Brazil for retaliation; July – joins Barcelona for £4.2 million

1984 Breaks world transfer record with £6.9 million switch to Napoli

1986 Leads Argentina to World Cup victory in Mexico

1987 Attains god-like status in Naples as he inspires his club to their first League Championship; they lift the Italian Cup for good measure

1990 Neapolitans take their second title; June – struggles with injury in World Cup Finals in Italy, yet still skippers his team to the Final

1991 Quits Napoli and is arrested in Argentina on drugs charge; future uncertain at every level

Maradona was the first man since Pele to be universally acclaimed as the premier footballer on the planet. On song and fully fit, he was practically unstoppable, equally devastating as a maker and taker of goals.

No one else in his era could control a ball so instantly, nor dribble past opponents with such utter certainty as the diminutive, muscular Argentinian, and his shooting had the venom and accuracy of a striking snake. At turns awesomely powerful and delicately precise, he was the complete player.

Sadly, where Pele was loved and respected, Diego was often reviled, and it is undeniable that an apparently arrogant attitude did little to endear himself to opponents or crowds. In England, any unpopularity is due largely to the infamous 'Hand of God' goal he scored against Bobby Robson's team in the 1986 World Cup. However, it was Maradona's second strike in the same game – the first was when he waltzed through the defence to beat Peter Shilton for the goal of the tournament – which bore most eloquent witness to his prodigious ability.

It should be remembered, too, that he lived with constant pressure to perform miracles while soaking up savage physical punishment, and it would be sad indeed if the memory of Maradona were unduly marred by bitterness or by criminal associations.

DIEGO MARADONA

Diego Maradona, pictured in his Argentinian national shirt and captain's armband, playing against Italy in the 1986 World Cup finals; the Italian is Salvatore Bagni. This group game ended 1-1, enabling both teams to qualify. Maradona went on to lift the cup following Argentina's 3-2 victory over West Germany. This will be remembered as Maradona's 'Hand of God' year when he pushed the ball into the net (claiming divine intervention) in the game against England. It was, however, also the World Cup in which his skills shone most brightly, and his stocky frame remained upright long enough for him to score and make some wonderful goals.

MATTHEWS, Sir Stanley

1915 Born at Hanley, in the heart of the Potteries

1932 Debut for Stoke City

1933 Helps win promotion from Division 2

1934 Celebrates England debut with goal against Wales at Cardiff

1947 Plays for Great Britain v the Rest of Europe, an honour repeated eight years later; joins Blackpool for £11,500

1948 Footballer of the Year

1953 The 'Matthews Final' in which he inspires Blackpool, 3-1 behind against Bolton with 20

minutes left, to a 4-3 victory

1957 Wins last of 54 caps, against Denmark in Copenhagen

1961 Returns to Stoke for nominal £2500 fee

1963 Matthews is voted Footballer of the Year after playing vital role in the 'Potters' climb to Division 1

1965 January – knighted for services to football; February – aged 50 years 5 days, plays final League game, against Fulham, thus becoming oldest player to appear in Division 1; starts three-year stint as general manager of Port Vale

1969 Short spell managing Hibernian of Malta

For 30 years the name of Stanley Matthews was a byword for soccer excellence. He was a supremely gifted yet self-effacing individualist, a symbol of all that was good about the British game, and although he won comparatively few club honours, his fame eclipsed that of all his contemporaries.

A lean outside-right, whose obsession with physical fitness contributed hugely to his staggering professional longevity, Matthews was a sublime dribbler and perhaps the most accurate crosser of a ball in living memory. His perfect balance and mesmeric skills would take him past the ablest of

STANLEY MATTHEWS
The 'wizard of dribble', Stanley Matthews, crossing the ball from the right-wing side on the Wembley pitch – as he'll always be remembered. In this match he was playing for England in their 3-1 win over Wales. Perfect poise, eye on the ball – the master at work.

full-backs, and his astonishing speed from a standing start would render recovery impossible.

His critics said his trickery slowed the game down, yet in doing so it invariably pulled defenders out of position, thus creating space for team-mates. Others

pointed to a modest goal tally of 71 in around 700 League games, a fatuous argument in view of his exploits as a provider. Amazingly, Matthews' international career was chequered, the selectors omitting him as often as they picked him. Had it been left to most fans, to whom he was an almost god-like figure, no England side would have taken the field without him.

MEADOWBANK THISTLE

Founded 1974

Joined League 1974 (Div.2)

Honours Scottish League Second Division Champions 1987

Ground Meadowbank Stadium

Formerly Ferranti Thistle, Meadowbank gained their senior place when League reconstruction created a vacancy. Lacking their own ground and playing matches at Edinburgh's principal athletics venue made it difficult for them to settle, and they were initially regarded by their opponents as a source of easy victories.

That changed in the 1980s, and they are now established in the First Division. Talent-spotting is a necessity, and Premier Division men such as Darren Jackson (Dundee United), Peter Godfrey (Falkirk) and John Inglis (St Johnstone) came to notice with them.

MERCER, Joe

1914 Born at Ellesmere Port

1931 Signs for Everton

1938 England debut in 7-0 thrashing of Northern Ireland in Manchester

1939 Plays stirring part in winning League title

1946 Moves to Arsenal for £7000

1948 Captains Gunners to Championship, a feat repeated five years later

1950 Leads Arsenal to FA Cup victory over Liverpool and is voted Footballer of the Year

1954 Broken leg ends playing career

1955 Becomes boss of Sheffield United

1958 Takes over at Aston Villa but can't avoid relegation

1960 Leads Villa to promotion, followed by League Cup triumph the following year

1964 Ill health forces temporary retirement

1965 Returns as manager of Manchester City, winning promotion two years later

1968 City win League Championship

1969 Mercer's men lift FA Cup

1970 Double triumph — League Cup and European Cup Winners' Cup

1972 Becomes general manager of Coventry City

1974 Stint as England's caretaker boss after Alf Ramsey departs

1990 Dies on Merseyside

Joe Mercer was a magnificent player, an inspiring manager, and a lovely man. As an attacking wing-half with Everton, he was one of the brightest pre-war talents in English football. It was fitting that he should have gone on to captain his country, though

JOE MERCER The perfect picture of smiling Joe Mercer. So many stories are told about the man, nearly all of them relating to his humour and his refusal to get too wound up about soccer. He also had a fund of jokes that he would trot out whenever prompted — but they're not repeatable on the printed page.

not that his tally of caps was limited to a mere five because of the war. In 1946, with his prime apparently behind him, Mercer switched to Highbury and underwent an amazing renaissance in a more defensive role. A spindly figure on bandy legs, he was a master of interception and distribution, a shrewd, cultured tactician with the ability to lift the spirits of the men around him.

This quality proved invaluable throughout his days as a manager, the most distinguished of which were spent in tandem with Malcolm Allison at Manchester City. He became one of the most popular personalities in the game; that famous lop-sided grin and self-deprecating wit will be sorely missed on a British soccer scene which is increasingly devoid of humour.

MIDDLESBROUGH

Founded 1876

Joined League 1899 (Div.2)

Honours Div.2 Champions 1927, 1929, 1974; Amateur Cup Winners 1895, 1898

Ground Ayresome Park

Middlesbrough have contributed richly to the English soccer scene throughout the twentieth century without having one major honour to show for their efforts. In local boy Wilf Mannion, who won 26 caps, they boasted one of the most extravagantly gifted inside-forwards league football has seen, although their traditional speciality has been prolific centre-forwards. There was England international Alf Common, subject of the first four-figure transfer fee when he arrived from Sunderland for £1000 in 1905; George Camsell, who notched 59 goals – still a Second Division record – in 1926/27; and Brian Clough, who struck 197 times in 213 outings in the late 1950s

before embarking on an ill-fated sojourn at Roker Park.

Yet somehow all that talent has never translated itself into trophies, with eight FA Cup quarter-finals and one League Cup semi-final ending in defeat. Such a lengthy period of poverty had hardly seemed likely when 'Boro won promotion to the First Division at the end of their third League campaign in 1902. They remained solidly in the top flight, finishing fourth in 1914, until the mid 1920s, when they made two brief visits to the Second Division. On either side of the war, inspired by Mannion, they were renowned for a flowing, attacking approach, but as Wilf waned, so did the team, and they were relegated in 1954.

Despite Clough's exploits, they failed to bounce back and in 1966 slid into Division 3. Stan Anderson led them straight up, but it was not until Jack Charlton brought his long-ball game to Ayresome in the 1970s that

'Boro returned to the First Division, this time for eight years. Since then there have been interludes in every flight except the Fourth, and under ex-manager Colin Todd they were looking for promotion from the Second. With lowly Darlington and Hartlepool the only local competition for support, there is no reason why the Teessiders should not break back into the big time.

MIDDLESBROUGH
Middlesbrough have had many well-known players but their best known and most capped (26 appearances for England) was inside-forward Wilf Mannion. Mannion played for the club in the golden years of English soccer immediately after the Second World War when Middlesbrough were attracting huge gates and exciting their supporters with an attacking style that was to promise much, but deliver nothing, in terms of major honours.

MILBURN, Jackie

1924 Born in Ashington, Northumberland

1946 Makes debut for Newcastle United

1949 Wins the first of 13 England caps, v Scotland

1951 Scores in every round of the FA Cup including both goals in the Final, won 2-0 v Blackpool

1952 Second FA Cup Winner's medal, 1-0 v Arsenal

1955 Scores after 45 seconds, fastest goal in Wembley FA Cup Final, for third winner's medal, 3-1 v Manchester City

1963 Retires after 354 League games for Newcastle (179 goals); appointed manager of Ipswich Town

1964 Leaves Ipswich and becomes a journalist with the News of the World

1988 Dies in Ashington

Jackie Milburn was the most revered of Newcastle heroes. A modest, unassuming man who suffered from an acute lack of confidence and was embarrassed by the adulation he received from his neighbours, he entered Geordie folklore as the player who led United to three FA Cup Final victories in the 1950s. To the end he was 'Wor Jackie'.

Blessed with extraordinary speed and arousing pace of shot, he began his career as an inside-forward, moved to the right-wing and then to centre-forward. Wherever he played he had a tearaway style, verve and dramatic power. Len Shackleton, an illustrious contemporary, said 'Jackie was one of the quickest players I have seen. Once he got going he was unstoppable. Whenever I think of Jackie I think of a greyhound going out of a trap.' His initials – J.E.T. – were wholly appropriate.

Milburn, member of a famous footballing family that also included Bobby and Jackie Charlton, succeeded Tommy Lawton as England's centre-forward, scoring 10

JACKIE MILBURN Jackie Milburn scoring the opening goal of the 1955 FA Cup Final against Manchester City, after 45 seconds. It was a blow from which City never recovered, eventually losing 3-1. Milburn was to end his League career two years later and many Newcastle fans will say that there's never been a player to match him since – although Keegan and MacDonald have their supporters. Newcastle enjoyed a number of successful seasons while Milburn was playing and attracted large crowds both at home and away. For many, just saying they have seen 'wor Jackie' was enough.

goals in 13 internationals. But statistics alone cannot do justice to the man and the effect he had on those around him. He was a player who changed the course of games, a symbol of success.

At his funeral tens of thousands lined the streets of Newcastle to pay their respects. The grief was as genuine as the man.

MILLWALL

Founded 1885

Joined League 1920 (Div.3)

Honours Div.2 Champions 1988; Div.3 (S) Champions 1928, 1938; Div.4 Champions 1962

Ground The Den

Until the late 1980s, when they reached Division 1 for the first time in their history, Millwall had shown little likelihood of developing into a major soccer power. Their playing achievements had been moderate, and a distressingly high percentage of their headlines had been concerned with misde-meanours by unruly supporters.

There has, however, always been a warmth about Millwall that grander clubs have failed to emulate. They have produced unlikely folk heroes – such as Harry Cripps, the wildly enthusiastic full-back who epitomised the spirit of the 'Lions' throughout the 1960s and early 1970s – and their tough dockland environment has helped to breed a solidarity which, at times, is fearsome. No matter what the standard of the side at any given time, it was a rare opponent who relished a visit to The Den.

By the time Millwall settled at Cold Blow Lane in 1910 they had already made a considerable impact by reaching two FA Cup semi-finals – those of 1900 and 1903 – as a Southern League outfit, and when they became founder members of the Third Division, hopes of rapid progress were high. They won the Division 3 (S) title twice before the Second World War, and beat three top-flight sides before losing to Sunderland in the 1937 FA Cup semi-final.

But faced with fierce competition for support from the capital's more glamorous clubs, Millwall were forced to accept relative mediocrity, albeit enlivened occasionally by promotion campaigns and relegation battles. Bosses such as Benny Fenton

(1966-74) and George Graham (1982-86), in his first managerial job, did sterling work but it was not until 1988, with John Docherty at the helm, that the 'Lions' finally reached the premier grade. Alas, after leading the table during their first term, they fell away and were relegated after just two seasons.

MILLWALL Two tall men clash as Republic of Ireland international Tony Cascarino (Millwall) gets to the ball ahead of number 5, George Reilly (West Bromwich Albion). Millwall have enjoyed a number of brief spells of success over the years, the most recent spearheaded by Cascarino's goal-scoring ability. This match was played at the start of the 1987/88 season when Millwall were to emerge as Division 2 champions. Note the sponsors, Lewisham council, recognising close ties between Millwall and the local community.

MONTROSE

Founded 1879

Joined League 1923 (Div.3)

Honours Scottish League Second Division Champions 1985

Ground Links Park

Montrose had been a club with an unobstrusive history until the Cup exploits of the 1970s and mid 1980s. In 1975/76 they defeated Hibs en route to the semi-final of the League Cup and that same season they appeared in the quarter-finals of the Scottish Cup, a stage they had also reached in 1973. Season 1986/87 brought a League Cup defeat of Hearts.

In 1991 they achieved promotion to the First Division for the second time in their history.

MOORE, Bobby

1941 Born in Barking

1958 Signs for West Ham United

1962 Makes England debut in Peru

1963 Becomes England's youngest captain

1964 Helps 'Hammers' beat Preston North End to win the FA Cup, and is voted Footballer of the Year

1965 Leads West Ham to glory against Munich 1860 in the European Cup Winners' Cup

1966 Lifts the World Cup after England beat West Germany

1970 Endures infamous Bogota incident in which he is accused of stealing a bracelet; then plays brilliantly in Mexico World Cup

1973 Wins 108th and final cap, against Italy at Wembley

1974 Joins Fulham for £20,000

1975 Leads 'Cottagers' to FA Cup Final defeat - against West Ham

1977 Retires from League football

1984 Following managerial spell at non-League Oxford City, Moore takes over as boss of Southend United

1986 Leaves Southend; goes on to work in tabloid journalism and promotions

Bobby Moore was the outstanding central defender in Britain - some would say the world - throughout the 1960s and early 1970s. Tall, calm and immensely skilful on the ball, he radiated an imperious authority at the heart of England's rearguard, and it surprised many that such an illustrious career should be spent with relatively unfashionable clubs. His greatest assets were an almost uncanny sense of anticipation and utter composure in the most hectic of circumstances, but they represented only part of his rich catalogue of gifts. Moore's immaculate distribution made him the springboard of countless attacks - his partnership with Geoff Hurst for both club and country was particularly productive - and his timing in the tackle

BOBBY MOORE Bobby Moore could not really be characterised as a man of action. He relied more on timing and anticipation to perform his defensive duties for West Ham United and England. He also appeared to be languid at times, not chasing back quickly to cover, and slow to make a tackle. No player, however, with so many apparent weaknesses could have such a successful career, amassing 108 England caps in the process. The fact is that Bobby Moore was not always what he seemed; close examination of his game demonstrates stamina and toughness, quick reactions and an aggressive streak ... when they were needed. Perhaps this photo of him towards the end of his West Ham career gives a hint of these qualities. At other times he was a trifle slow – although he might say composed!

was impeccable.

It's true that his aerial power did not always match up to his all-round performance, and certainly he lacked pace. But his superb reading of the game meant that such weaknesses were rarely exposed, and the way in which he rose above them is a further tribute to his greatness.

Though Moore often faced hostility - presumably born out of jealousy - from non-London crowds, it was invariably underpinned by respect. How fitting that a player of such consistent excellence should lead England to their finest footballing hour.

MORTON

Founded 1874

Joined League 1893 (Div.2)

Honours Scottish League First Division Champions 1978, 1984, 1987; Division 2 Champions 1950, 1964, 1967; Scottish Cup Winners 1922

Ground Cappielow Park

Scotland's first limited company football club (1896), Morton have had to be content with only one major trophy. They won the 1922 Scottish Cup, beating Rangers in the final with an irresistible free-kick goal by Jimmy Gourlay.

Celebrities have not been lacking. Jimmy Cowan was one of the few Scottish 'keepers to excel at Wembley (Scotland's 3-1 victory of 1949). Current manager Allan McGraw created a club record back in 1963/64 with 58 goals. In the 1960s a series of ingenious signings from Denmark, in which Morton participated, brought freshness to the Scottish scene. And as recently as 1979, Morton had in Andy Ritchie Scotland's Player of the Year.

MORTON, Alan

1893 Born in Partick, Glasgow

1913 Playing for Queen's Park

1920 Is capped for Scotland, v Wales and Northern Ireland; turns professional, signing for Rangers

1921 Helps to win Scottish League Championship (eight were to follow up to 1930/31)

1928 Helps Rangers to Scottish Cup victory...

1930 ...and again

1932 Last international appearance, v France in Paris

1933 Retires and becomes Rangers director

1971 Dies 15 December

Alan Lauder Morton of Rangers, the 'wee blue devil', was the first of Scottish football's superstars. In a career spanning more than 20 years, first as an amateur with Queen's Park, then as a professional with Rangers, he played for Scotland 31 times. It was a record set when international football meant little more than matches against England, Ireland and Wales, and it stood until George Young passed it after the Second World War.

Morton was an outside-left of dazzling skills. At 5 ft 4 in and seldom weighing more than 9 stone, he was small and slight but remarkably strong and resilient, and his dribbling talents, founded on exceptional balance, made him a master of all the defenders and defensive systems - and there were many - set to check him. One of the most potent weapons in his armoury was his ability to float hanging crosses just under the crossbar so that, quite literally, goalkeepers would often find themselves tumbling into the net with the ball.

He played 11 times against England, notably in the famous 'Wembley Wizards' team of 1928 which beat England 5-1. Only Alex Jackson, outside-right, was taller than 5 ft 6 in in a forward line that read Jackson, Jimmy Dunn, Hughie Gallacher, Alex James and Morton. Jackson's three goals were all scored from Morton crosses.

Alan Morton was a professional man, a

ALAN MORTON
Glasgow Rangers' Alan Morton (right) in a Scottish League line-up alongside J.B. McAlpine from Queen's Park. Morton scored in the 1924 fixture against the Football League at Ibrox, no doubt delighting the 63,000 Scots attending but failing to give his side a win; the game ended 1-1.

qualified mining engineer who was always a part-time professional; more than once he was at work on the Saturday morning of an international match. What is certain is that in the long and rich panoply of British football, Morton must stand in the first rank beside the likes of Stanley Matthews and Bobby Charlton. He is still considered Rangers' greatest player and, his portrait in oils hangs in the entrance hall of the club's Ibrox Stadium. When he retired in 1933 he was made a director, surely the first player to go directly from dressing room to board room. He had played a total of 742 competitive games, 247 for Queen's Park, 495 for Rangers, scoring 166 goals.

MOTHERWELL

Founded 1886

Joined League 1893 (Div.2)

Honours Scottish League Championship, Division 1, 1932; First Division, 1982, 1985; Division 2, 1954, 1969; Scottish Cup, 1952, 1991; League Cup 1950/51

Ground Fir Park

Lanarkshire, with its history of heavy industry, is a hotbed of football in Scotland and its largest club, Motherwell have reflected that vitality. Their glorious side at the beginning of the thirties had an irresistible left-wing partnership in George Stevenson and Bobby Ferrier. The pair almost overshadowed centre-forward Willie McFadyen despite his 52 League goals in 1931/32.

They won the League Championship that year but lost Scottish Cup finals in 1931 and 1933. There were further defeats before they collected the trophy in 1952. Despite a welter of young talent towards the end of the fifties, including Ian St John, success proved elusive. After financial crises in the early 1980s they have prospered under Tommy McLean's management and won the 1991 Scottish Cup in glorious style.

NEWCASTLE UNITED

Founded 1881

Joined League 1893 (Div.2)

Honours Div.1 Champions 1905, 1907, 1909, 1927, Div.2 Champions 1965; FA Cup Winners 1910, 1924, 1932, 1951, 1952, 1955; European Fairs Cup Winners 1969

Ground St James's Park

Newcastle United are a club of proud traditions whose persistent under-achievement in modern times has sorely tried the devotion of what is potentially the most fanatical following in England. If ever a Clough-like messiah emerges to lead the Tynesiders out of the doldrums, he will find a bedrock of support all the more fervent because of recent failure.

The 'Magpies' built their reputation on two richly productive eras, the first of which dawned soon after the turn of the century when they won three titles in five campaigns and reached five FA Cup Finals in a seven-year span. Unfortunately, careers of leading players were blighted by the First World War and subsequent triumphs were intermittent. Scottish marksman Hughie Gallacher skippered United to the 1927 League title, and five years later there was FA Cup glory thanks to a hotly disputed goal against Arsenal. The Magpies, however, were on the slide and were relegated in 1934.

They remained in the lower flight until 1948, when their return to the elite signalled the start of their second spell as a major power. With goal-merchant Jackie Milburn in the van, United won the FA Cup three times in the first half of the 1950s. 'Wor Jackie' was the undisputed idol of Tyneside, but he received splendid support from the likes of wing-half Joe Harvey and winger Bobby Mitchell. When that side – managed for most of the decade by Stan Seymour –

broke up, the club was to embark on a perennial struggle for consistency. Defender Jimmy Scoular and schemer George Eastham were outstanding in the late 1950s, but Newcastle were down again by 1961. Harvey returned as manager, secured promotion and – with notable help from wing-half Bobby Moncur and goal-scorers 'Pop' Robson and Wyn Davies – went on to win a European competition, after qualifying by finishing tenth in Division 1.

The 1970s brought a new folk hero in centre-forward Malcolm Macdonald. 'Supermac' prospered for five seasons before heading for Highbury, but the nearest the Magpies came to an honour was a pitiful FA Cup Final display against Liverpool in 1974. Another demotion followed in 1978 and it was left to Kevin Keegan, approaching the end of his career but with ability and charisma to spare, to

inspire a return to the top flight in the early 1980s.

New stars such as Chris Waddle, Peter Beardsley and Paul Gascoigne promised much but they were sold for huge fees and United were relegated yet again in 1989. It seemed so long since their famous anthem, 'Blaydon Races', had been sung with anything approaching conviction although the choir still exists.

NICHOLSON, Bill

1919 Born in Scarborough

1938 Signs for Tottenham Hotspur

1950 Helps Spurs win Division 2 title...

1951 ...and then the League Championship; May – scores with first kick in sole appearance for England v Portugal at Goodison Park

1955 Retires as player to become coach at White Hart Lane

1958 Coaches England during World Cup in Sweden; October – succeeds Jimmy Anderson as Spurs manager

1961 Leads them to League and FA Cup double

1962 Back to Wembley to beat Burnley in FA Cup Final

1963 Spurs become first team from Great Britain to win European trophy as they slam Atletico Madrid 5-1 in European Cup Winners' Cup

1967 Another FA Cup triumph, against Chelsea

1971 First of two League Cup victories in three years

1972 Spurs win UEFA Cup

1974 Defeat, at last, in a major final, against Feyenoord in the UEFA Cup; August – resigns after disastrous start to season

1975 Helps West Ham United prepare for European campaign

1976 Returns to White Hart Lane as managerial consultant

NEWCASTLE UNITED
Under the managership of George Martin, Newcastle won promotion to Division 1 following the 1947/48 season and finished fourth, fifth and fourth in successive campaigns. Martin, seen here on the far left, had been followed by Stan Seymour for the 1951 and 1952 FA Cup Final victories over Blackpool and Arsenal respectively, but the seeds had been sown for one of the two most fondly remembered periods of the club's history – the other being the early part of the century when they captured three League Championships between 1905 and 1909. The team in the picture is: (left to right, back row) Martin (manager), Houghton, Graham, Fairbrother, T. Smith, Batty, Edward Robledo, N. Smith (trainer); Sibley, George Robledo, Milburn, Brennan, Hannah, Mitchell. George Robledo was a Chilean international.

BILL NICHOLSON

Bill Nicholson in the year his Spurs side win the double of FA Cup and League Championship. That 1960/61 success was the first double since Aston Villa's of 1897. It seemed unrepeatable, but Arsenal and Liverpool have since emulated the feat. Nicholson's managerial success put him in a small band of managers who had previously won a Championship medal as a player with the same club; his was with Spurs in 1950/51. Other notable members of the same 'club' include Bob Paisley and Kenny Dalglish (Liverpool), George Graham (Arsenal) and Howard Kendall (Everton).

Nicholson was the architect of one of the finest club sides the world has ever seen. In the early 1960s his Spurs played exhilarating, flowing football, a devastating cocktail of subtlety and power, and were justly rewarded with an avalanche of honours.

That he should create such an entertaining team amazed many who had watched him as a sturdy, industrious yet unspectacular right-half in Arthur Rowe's push-and-rush combination of the early 1950s. Yet Nicholson's management approach was markedly more adventurous. He was always willing to back his judgement in the transfer market – as the likes of Dave Mackay, John White and Cliff Jones in the 1950s, and Jimmy Greaves, Alan Gilzean, Pat Jennings and company in the 1960s bore ample witness – but also had the priceless knack of blending them with more ordinary individuals. He was also the first man to bring the best out of Danny Blanchflower.

Not surprisingly, Nicholson's later sides could not match the standard of his first, yet were good enough to maintain his reputation as one of the British soccer's most successful and positive post-war bosses. Hailing from the 'old school' of managership, he conducted his departure from Spurs, his later job with West Ham and his return to White Hart Lane with both honesty and dignity.

NICKNAMES

The 1990 World Cup finals were a reminder that nicknames help familiarise players and clubs, and make things easier for newspaper headliners. The top goal-scorer in the tournament was Italy's Salvatore 'Toto' Schillaci, while England star Paul Gascoigne had such a popular nickname ('Gazza') that his agent took the precaution of registering it as a trademark.

Most players' nicknames are surname adaptations, but some are more inventive. Sometimes they are coined from a player's style of play. Ernest 'Nudger' Needham was a wing-half who excelled in nudging short passes for Sheffield United and England at the turn of the century; Charlie 'Cannonball' Fleming of East Fife, Sunderland and Scotland, had one of the most powerful shots of the 1950s; Ron 'Chopper' Harris was Chelsea's hard man of the 1960s and 1970s; Allan 'Sniffer' Clarke was renowned for sniffing out goal chances with Walsall,

Fulham, Leicester City, Leeds United, Barnsley and England; and Clarke's Leeds United team-mate Norman Hunter became Norman 'Bites Yer Leg' – a self-explanatory sobriquet.

Perhaps the most famous inter-war nickname was that of Ralph William Dean, the Tranmere Rovers, Everton and England centre-forward. He was known as 'Dixie' Dean from an early age, either because he had a dark, southern-type complexion, or, much more likely, as an adaptation of 'Digsie' (because he dug his fingers in other children's backs when tagging them in street games). Football tradition caught up with John Deans, a 1970s striker with Motherwell, Celtic and Scotland; he was also nicknamed 'Dixie'.

Other sources of nicknames are family names (Ray 'Butch' Wilkins in the 1970s and 1980s), physical appearance (Billy 'Fatty' Foulke in the 1890s and 1900s), television names (Ron 'Rowdy' Yeats in the 1960s and 1970s) and the player's origins (1930s Welsh international Eugene 'Taffy' O'Callaghan). A Murphy often became 'Spud' as an association with Irish potato growing, and Anglo-Scots have often become 'Jock' regardless of Christian name. Manchester City had two players called William Smith in the 1890s, so they nicknamed them after their birthplaces – 'Stockport' Smith and 'Buxton' Smith. Gateshead remedied a similar problem more prosaically in the 1950s with Ken Smith No. 1 and Ken Smith No. 2.

Club nicknames also have various origins. Club colours are an obvious source, as with Coventry City (the 'Sky Blues'), Swindon Town (The 'Robins') and many clubs called the 'Reds' and the 'Blues'. Sometimes an old industry lives on in a nickname, such as with Sheffield United ('The Blades') and Luton Town ('The Hatters'). Other clubs rely on their specific location for a nickname, for example Brighton (the 'Seagulls') and Blackpool (the 'Seasiders').

However, many traditional nicknames are in decline and clubs are more likely to be known by other derivatives. West Brom, for instance, are usually the 'Albion' rather than the 'Throstles' or the 'Baggies'. At other times, teams have been tagged with a topical nickname. Manchester United's young 1950s team were named the 'Busby Babes' after legendary United manager Matt Busby, while Tottenham Hotspur in the 1960s were 'Super Spurs'. Whatever the nickname, it seems to provide supporters with an extra sense of belonging to their club.

NORTH AMERICA

North America has never made much of an impact on the world of association football. But if FIFA gives in to mounting pressure from the United States Soccer Federation to modify the Laws in order to pander to American sports fans who are used to high-scoring contests and would not tolerate a two-hour game ending in a goalless draw, and if any of those changes become permanent, then, as hosts of the 1994 World Cup, the USA will have had an influence on the game greater than any country in the last hundred years – although not one likely to be welcomed by the average football fan.

The 15th World Cup is football's second chance to take off in North America. The success of soccer as a spectator sport in the 1984 Los Angeles Olympics, and the USA's appearance in the 1990 World Cup finals – their first since 1950 and their oft-cited 1-0 defeat of an England team boasting Finney, Mannion, Ramsey and Mortenson – give some cause for optimism.

The case for pessimism may seem stronger, however – a dearth of home-grown talent (due in part to 1970s pro teams finding loopholes in regulations restricting the number of foreign players),

lack of television coverage and dwindling attendances has been the picture since the early 1980s. Factors in the decline of the professional game are soccer's unsuitability for US television audiences, lack of support in the colleges – the hotbed of North American sport – and the consequent failure to attract new European names.

The first surge of public interest in soccer in the USA came after the 1966 World Cup Final was shown live on television, but there was already a solid base for the sport in America. The USFA had been recognised by FIFA for 53 years; the national team had been semi-finalists in the first World Cup (incidentally, the USA has entered for every tournament and on that basis alone must merit the chance to host one of them); the new wave of immigrants and the return of Europe-based troops after the Second World War had given the game a minor boost; and, for the five summers preceding England's victory, New York had hosted a tournament featuring top clubs from around the globe which attracted crowds of up to 15,000.

Two rival bodies began operating in 1967: the National Professional Soccer League, which drafted European players into new teams set up in major cities, and the United Soccer Association, which imported whole teams such as Shamrock Rovers, Cagliari, Wolves and Dundee United to represent cities. (The game, then as now, was a summer one.) Some cities were therefore expected to support two teams in a minority sport. Moreover, the frequent commercial breaks in television coverage did not help the native audience to understand the dynamics of the game. The North American Soccer League was formed as a compromise in 1968 but it was almost too late; attendance figures plummeted and CBS declined to televise the

1969 season. However, financial backing and the dedication of men such as ex-Wales forward Phil Woosnam just saved the League from foundering.

In 1975 the status of American soccer was enhanced at a stroke by the signing of 34-year-old Pele by New York Cosmos. The following season saw the arrival of, among others,

NORTH AMERICA

It is somewhat sad, but nevertheless fitting, that North American football should be illustrated by two English players in their twilight years. Quite simply, Canada and the USA have failed between them to produce a single player of truly world-class stature and the NASL, before it sank from view, turned into a lucrative retirement playground for European footballers. Not that there was ever anything geriatric or second-rate about the pair pictured here in the 1979 Soccer Bowl on the Astroturf of the Giants Stadium, New Jersey. Rodney Marsh (foreground), playing for Tampa Bay Rowdies, was a maverick striker with dazzling close control, an eye for goal, and a flair for the unexpected. Like his Huddersfield contemporary Frank Worthington, he was a natural entertainer who had to remain contented with local admiration. His unorthodox and individualistic approach, the competing claims of other strikers, and the fact that he played most of his career in the Second and Third Divisions, limited him to nine England caps. Alan Ball, by contrast, was a perpetual-motion machine, a great team man and a superb one-touch player. Seventy-two caps were his reward. In 1966, at the age of 21, he picked up a World Cup medal. He also received honours after this game as his team, Vancouver Whitecaps, won 2-1.

George Best (Los Angeles Aztecs), Rodney Marsh (Tampa Bay Rowdies), Giorgio Chinaglia (Cosmos) and Eusebio (Toronto Metros-Croatia). Others followed; many were second-rate or were top players past their peak, but the trick had worked. In 1977, when Beckenbauer joined Cosmos as Pele retired, the total NASL attendance figure was 3.5 million with an average of 13,000, and in 1980 there were 24 teams. Two years later, however, only 14 clubs contested the Championship and the NASL disbanded in 1985.

In addition to introducing US-style razzamatazz and peripheral entertainments, the NASL had made many significant changes to the Laws, including a 35-yard offside line (since abolished at FIFA's insistence) to compensate for the narrower pitches, sudden-death extra time followed by shoot-outs (5 seconds to dribble and score from 35 yards out), if necessary to ensure a victory, and points for goals. This, plus the preponderance of artificial pitches, has done little to prepare Americans for international competition. The enterprising and skilful attacking play and creditable goalkeeping of the 1990 US team were undermined by defensive naivety. The names of the players – Meola, Caligiuri, Ramos, Balboa, Vermes – suggest that interest is still greatest among the immigrant population. In 1978, 50 per cent of NASL players were British.

It was Scottish and French immigrants who, towards the end of the nineteenth century, introduced soccer to Canada, a country whose modern top teams, still drawn largely from immigrant groups, found themselves homeless with the demise of the NASL. Soccer's origins in the USA were more or less confined, predictably, to New England and paralleled developments in the home country. In the mid nineteenth century there was a popular form of Shrove Tuesday football (with sightings in the Appalachians this century) and various college versions, 11-a-side, 20-a-side and so on with both handling and non-handling codes. In 1875 Harvard and Yale based their game on rugby, and grid-iron was born; it could as easily have been soccer.

Canada qualified for the 1986 World Cup but today the Canadian Soccer League (formed in 1987) shares the same problems as US soccer in that top gates rarely exceed 5000. NASL's successor, the American Professional Soccer League, semi-professional in truth, is not really national and current plans to merge the Western and Eastern Divisions will almost certainly result in fewer clubs.

Ironically, at grass-roots level the game is healthy – equipment is cheap and, unlike American football, children can play without fear of injury. Similarly, rounders is popular in the UK – but nobody could make a living from that. It is as a spectator sport that soccer must grow in North America.

NORTHERN IRELAND

The first organised game played in Ireland was probably that in Belfast between Caledonian FC and Queen's Park (Scotland) on 24 October 1878. The Irish Football Association, formed on 18 November 1880, was plagued by disputes in its earlier years. In 1912 senior clubs were at loggerheads with the Irish FA and threatened to break off into a rival association. There was more acrimony in 1923 with the formation of the Republic's Football Association after the political partition of Ireland.

The Irish Cup, held since 1880, has one of the most interesting histories of national cup competitions. The Irish FA withheld medals in 1886, although Distillery successfully took the case to court, and on two other occasions the Final wasn't played. During

the problems of 1912, Linfield were simply awarded the trophy by default. And Shelbourne were similarly awarded the title in 1919/20, when the Irish FA postponed the Final. They had been influenced in their decision by a riotous semi-final replay during which a player was sent off, stones were thrown, a gunman opened fire and over 80 people were injured.

The Irish League was formed in 1890 with eight clubs, including current Irish League clubs Cliftonville, Distillery, Glentoran and Linfield. In its early years it was an all-Ireland League, but the two Dublin clubs (Shelbourne and Bohemians) left for good in 1920. Professionalism was accepted in 1894. The most successful team has been Linfield. One of their main rivals, Belfast Celtic, won the Irish League 14 times but resigned in 1949 following a crowd riot after a game against Linfield. The Belfast Celtic directors

vowed that their team would not perform in front of an Irish crowd again.

Clubs from Northern Ireland have achieved slightly more European success than those from the Republic. Linfield reached the last eight of the 1966/67 European Cup competition but lost 3-2 on aggregate to CSKA Sofia after comfortable wins against Aris Bonnevoie and Valerengen. Seven years later, Glentoran reached the European Cup Winners' Cup quarter-finals after wins against Chimia Ramnicu and Brann Bergen. Glentoran also came close to glory in 1967/68 when they drew 1-1 and 0-0 against Benfica. They went out on the away-goals rule and Benfica went on to meet Manchester United in that season's European Cup Final. On the other hand, Crusaders lost a 1973 European Cup game 11-0 to Dinamo Bucharest, going out 12-0 on aggregate.

From 1969 civil unrest

often led to careful choice of grounds. Sometimes Northern Irish teams played outside the country, and in 1972/73 there were no Northern Ireland European entries. Two days after the 1980 murder of Lord Mountbatten and three others, there were ugly scenes at the Dundalk v Linfield European Cup tie in the Republic. The second leg, Linfield's 'home' match, was played in Holland.

The 1980s were particularly dominated by Linfield. During manager Roy Coyle's spell of over 14 years he helped the club to more than 30 senior trophies, including 10 Irish League Championships (making 40 for the club overall). But while Linfield were dominating the League during the 1980s, Glentoran were achieving remarkable success in the Irish Cup – seven out of nine, including five in succession. In 1989/90 Portadown were surprise winners of the Irish League, for the first time.

NORTHERN IRELAND NATIONAL TEAM

Northern Ireland's two appearances in the World Cup finals have been very successful for such a small nation. In 1958 they drew with West Germany and twice beat Czechoslovakia (once in a play-off). A tired team lost 4-0 to France in the quarter-final. In 1982, under Billy Bingham's managership, a 1-0 victory over Spain and two draws enabled Northern Ireland to win Group 5. Hopes of reaching a semi-final however, were dashed by France, 4-1.

The 1958 team – famous for stars such as Danny Blanchflower, Billy Bingham, Jimmy McIlroy and Harry Gregg – shared the home international championship with England. They ended England's 18-match unbeaten run with a 3-2 win at Wembley, a result rivalled by Terry Neill's team in 1972 when Neill himself scored the only goal.

Shared home-championship success also came in 1955/56, 1958/59 and 1963/64, but the only outright wins came in 1979/80 and 1983/84 during the era of Gerry Armstrong, Sammy McIlroy, Billy Hamilton and Pat Jennings, veteran of 119 internationals. Northern Ireland have never qualified for the European Championship quarter-finals.

NORTHERN IRELAND A not unfamiliar sight for Northern Ireland, as international opponents grab another goal. In this case it was Spain's Emilio Butragueno who ran the ball past Pat Jennings, with Chris Nicholl looking on. The game was won by Spain 2-1, effectively to end Irish hopes of progress to the next round of the 1986 World Cup finals in Mexico. That they reached Mexico, however, was an achievement.

NORWICH CITY

Founded 1902

Joined League 1920
(Div. 3, founder member)

Honours Div. 2 Champions 1972, 1986; Div. 3 (S) Champions 1934; League Cup Winners 1962, 1985

Ground Carrow Road

As the 1990s commenced, Norwich City, for so long renowned merely as plucky Cup fighters, were well established in the First Division as regular purveyors of sweetly attractive football. Yet such are the economic realities in the soccer outpost of Norfolk that maintaining their position of eminence was likely to prove a daunting challenge, as the sale of seven top players since 1986 had already demonstrated. Not that the 'Canaries' are used to an easy life. On becoming founder members of Division 3, they struggled for a decade before earning promotion in the 1930s and enjoying a five-year stint in the higher grade.

In the 1950s Norwich emerged as one of the more enterprising teams in the Third Division, but despite pocketing much-needed cash when future England defender Maurice Norman was sold, they ran into financial difficulties in 1957. A public appeal brought salvation, and two years later the Canaries reached

NORWICH CITY A club with flair, but not noted for winning much. This summary is only partly true – but football fans will certainly associate it with Norwich City. Typical of the kind of player that seems to flourish at Carrow Road, and that fans of the Canaries love, was Mick Channon who joined City in 1982 towards the end of a successful career, most notably spent with South-ampton. Channon is seen here calling for the ball in Norwich's 1-0 1985 League (Milk) Cup victory over Sunderland.

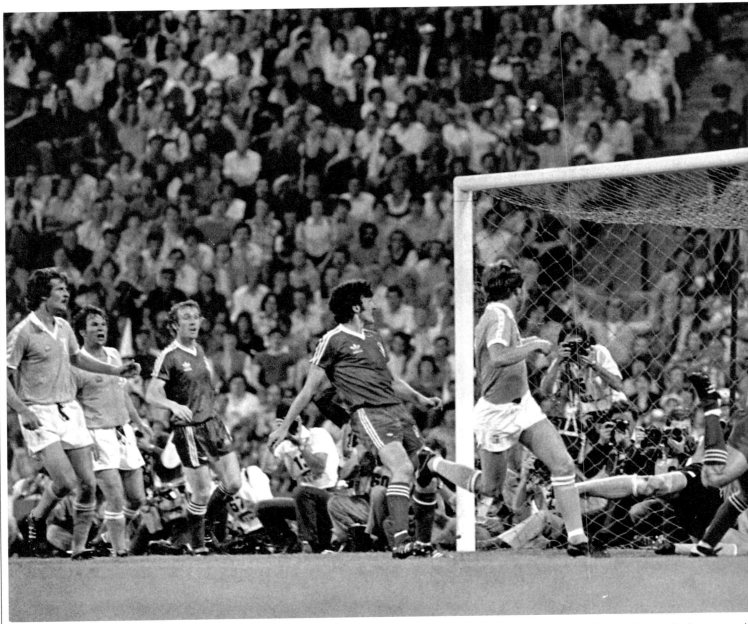

the FA Cup semi-final, disposing of Manchester United and Spurs on the way, with major contributions from forwards Terry Bly and Terry Allcock, and long-serving defender Ron Ashman.

Thus revitalised, Norwich went up in 1960 and consolidated their position. Highlights of the next decade included winning the League Cup, the buying and selling of star striker Ron Davies and, in 1967, an FA Cup victory at Old Trafford.

But it was in 1972, with Ron Saunders in charge, that the club really took off, reaching Division 1 for the first time. Since then they have been relegated three times, but on each occasion it was for one season only, and under the enlightened management of John Bond, Ken Brown – who presided over a second League Cup triumph – and Dave Stringer, they have continued to gain in stature.

Influential players of the modern era have included 'keepers Kevin Keelan and England's Chris Woods.

NOTTINGHAM FOREST

Founded 1865

Joined League 1892 (Div. 1)

Honours Div. 1 Champions 1978; Div. 2 Champions 1907, 1922; Div. 3 (S) Champions 1951; FA Cup Winners 1898, 1959; League Cup Winners 1978, 1979, 1989, 1990; European Cup Winners 1979, 1980

Ground City Ground

Over more than 100 years, Nottingham Forest had established a reputation as a club which invariably served up good football but usually lacked the ruthlessness needed to lift top prizes – and then along came Brian Clough. He transformed a team of also-rans into a combination which twice conquered Europe and became a lasting force on the domestic scene. Not that Forest were complete strangers to success. As stable members of Division 1, they won their first trophy, the FA Cup, towards the end of Queen Victoria's reign and continued to spend most of their time in the top flight until the mid 1920s.

Then came their dullest period. Forest remained in the Second Division for more than two decades, a period of vegetation which ended not with the long-hoped-for promotion but with an unprecedented slump into Division 3 (S).

It was then that the club showed both restraint and wisdom in standing by their manager, Billy Walker. He rebuilt the side, leading them back to the First Division in 1957 and winning the FA Cup two years later. His most outstanding player was centre-half Bobby McKinlay, who was to play more than 600 League games for Forest.

In 1967, with Johnny Carey at the helm, the club came close to the League and FA Cup double, finishing as runners-up and semi-finalists respectively. With fine players such as wing-half Terry Hennessey and forward Ian Moore, Forest were an attractive team, but a distressing decline was imminent. The ill-judged purchase of Jim Baxter, a once-great Scottish play-maker who was past his best, and a fire which destroyed the City Ground's main stand were followed by the unpopular sale of several stars, and Forest were relegated in 1972.

Enter Clough, three years later, and the transformation was under way. Working closely with assistant Peter Taylor, he dumbfounded the soccer world by securing

126

NOTTS COUNTY

Founded 1862

Joined League 1888 (founder member)

Honours Div. 2 Champions 1897, 1914, 1923; Div. 3 (S) Champions 1931, 1950; Div. 4 Champions 1971; FA Cup Winners 1894

Ground Meadow Lane

As the world's oldest surviving club, Notts County might be expected to boast an illustrious history. In fact, their achievements have been modest and their one major honour, the FA Cup, was won nearly a century ago.

After helping to launch the League, County never enjoyed the success of most co-founders, dropping out of the top flight twice before the First World War. They returned in 1914, thanks enormously to the form of goalkeeper Albert Iremonger, an eccentric giant who won another Division 2 title

medal in 1923 and still holds the club record of 564 League appearances.

Stability continued to prove beyond County's reach, and the late 1940s found them enduring their second sojourn in the Third Division. But in 1947 interest boomed with the unexpected purchase of England centre-forward Tommy Lawton, and promotion followed three years later. When the great man left, however, the good times went with him, and the end of the decade found the club in Division 4.

It was to be another 11 years before manager Jimmy Sirrel, who had three stints at Meadow Lane, began lifting them up the League, a renaissance capped by reaching the First Division in 1981. For a club with limited support and resources, survival at the top was always going to be hard, especially as influential schemer Don Masson was nearing the end of his career. But they

clung on for three terms before sinking back into the shadow cast by neighbouring Forest.

There followed a five-year spell in the Third Division before Neil Warnock led them to the First in 1991. He was clearly a young manager to watch.

NOTTS COUNTY Albert Iremonger, Notts County's record-breaking goalkeeper, collects the ball as a Burnley forward looks set to try a shoulder charge. Today we are used to seeing goalkeepers rolling out the ball before picking it up and kicking or throwing within four steps. Iremonger probably ran with the ball, bouncing it at about every third step before punting it as far as possible downfield. The attention of a challenging forward would simply have meant a quicker kick.

promotion, winning the League Championship and twice taking the European Cup, all in successive seasons. Key players during this heady interlude included winger John Robertson, 'keeper Peter Shilton, defenders Viv Anderson and Kenny Burns and forward Tony Woodcock. In the 1980s he built another excellent side in which his son Nigel, a skilful forward, and England international defenders Des Walker and Stuart Pearce featured prominently.

Despite their success, Forest are not accustomed to huge support. But while the Clough era lasts, they are likely to maintain their stature although, perhaps not to win the FA Cup.

NOTTINGHAM FOREST A moment of high drama as Trevor Francis's falling header goes into the net for the only goal of Nottingham Forest's 1979 European Cup Final victory over Malmö in Munich. The next nearest Forest player is the young Garry Birtles, whose form throughout the campaign was an inspiration. This, Forests' first European success, was largely unexpected although they had beaten holders Liverpool on the way. The goal, supplied by a cross from Robertson, is remembered for the tumble that Francis took on the discus circle just to the side of the goal. Both he and Forest survived.

OLDHAM ATHLETIC

Founded 1895

Joined League 1907 (Div. 2)

Honours Div. 2 Champions 1991; Div. 3 (N) Champions 1953; Div. 3 Champions 1974

Ground Boundary Park

The Coronation Street comedian who said 'Oldham Athletic – that's a contradiction in terms!' was forced to eat his words as Joe Royle, one of the most talented and loyal managers in the land, transformed the 'Latics' into a vibrant and entertaining side in the early 1990s.

In fact, although Oldham had experienced many a slough of despond down the years, they were not total strangers to success. After making an instant impact on Division 2, they were promoted and reached the FA Cup semi-final in 1913. Then, two years later, led by former Manchester United star centre-half Charlie Roberts, the Boundary Park club were runners-up in Division 1, missing the title by two points.

After the war, Oldham fell away badly, however, spending most of their time in the Third Division, until they were allocated to the newly created Fourth in 1958. Five years later, inspired by Scottish schemer Bobby Johnstone, they were promoted but could not consolidate and soon returned to the basement.

Relief was at hand in the form of Jimmy Frizzell, who became manager in 1970 and within four seasons took them to Division 2. Royle assumed control in 1982 and gradually constructed a team which, by the end of the decade, was making its mark. In 1989/90 the Latics narrowly missed elevation to the top flight, reached the Final of the League Cup and semi-final of the FA Cup. In the process of Cup wins over Arsenal, Everton, Aston Villa and Southampton, men like defender Earl Barrett, midfielder Mike Milligan

OLDHAM ATHLETIC On Oldham Athletic's plastic pitch are Andy Barlow, one of the heroes of a fantastic 1989/90 season, and *(in front of Barlow)* Leeds United's inspiring midfielder Gordon Strachan. Oldham's season promised much but ended without a trophy and, importantly, without promotion from Division 2. Their League Cup and FA Cup runs put Oldham back on the soccer map (they lost the Final and semi-final respectively) but probably cost them promotion as a fixture pile-up resulted. Oldham beat Leeds four times in the season in two legs of the League Cup and in two League matches; Leeds ended up as Division 2 champions, Oldham in eighth place.

and striker Andy Ritchie caught the imagination of the footballing public, their exhilarating skills doing more than enough to deflect jibes about Boundary Park's plastic surface.

Promotion followed in 1991 and Oldham, who have plenty of potential support despite their proximity to Manchester, were looking to the future with confidence – a future that will be played out on grass after 1990/91.

OLYMPIC GAMES

In the 1932 Los Angeles Olympics there was no football; the Depression and the prospect of a long sea journey kept many athletes away. Fifty-two years later, in the same city, 1,421,627 spectators paid to watch Olympic soccer, making it the best attended sport in the competition - a good omen,

it is hoped, for the 1994 World Cup, which will be hosted by the United States.

No such future for Olympic football could

have been foreseen in 1896 when the ancient Greek games were revived; and, in fact, soccer did not feature in the programme of that first modern

OLYMPIC GAMES

Year	Venue		Medallists
1896*	Athens	1	Denmark
		2	Greece
1900*	Paris	1	Great Britain
		2	France
1904*	St Louis	1	Canada
		2	USA
1908	London	1	Great Britain
		2	Denmark
		3	Holland
1912	Stockholm	1	Great Britain
		2	Denmark
		3	Holland
1920	Antwerp	1	Belgium
		2	Spain
		3	Holland
1924	Paris	1	Uruguay
		2	Switzerland
		3	Sweden
1928	Amsterdam	1	Uruguay
		2	Argentina
		3	Italy
1932	Los Angeles		no tournament
1936	Berlin	1	Italy
		2	Austria
		3	Norway
1948	London	1	Sweden
		2	Yugoslavia
		3	Denmark
1952	Helsinki	1	Hungary
		2	Yugoslavia
		3	Sweden
1956	Melbourne	1	USSR
		2	Yugoslavia
		3	Bulgaria
1960	Rome	1	Yugoslavia
		2	Denmark
		3	Hungary
1964	Tokyo	1	Hungary
		2	Czechoslovakia
		3	East Germany
1968	Mexico City	1	Hungary
		2	Bulgaria
		3	Japan
1972	Munich	1	Poland
		2	Hungary
		3	E Germany/USSR
1976	Montreal	1	East Germany
		2	Poland
		3	USSR
1980	Moscow	1	Czechoslovakia
		2	East Germany
		3	USSR
1984	Los Angeles	1	France
		2	Brazil
		3	Yugoslavia
1988	Seoul	1	USSR
		2	Brazil
		3	West Germany

* unofficial tournament

OLYMPICS The Great Britain team which won the 1908 Olympic football tournament at Shepherd's Bush were, in fact, all English: *(back row, left to right)* Barlow, Styles (FA official), Corbett, Bailey, Hawkes, Davis (FA official), Schumaker, Lewis (referee); Smith, Stapley, Woodward, Parnell, Hardman, Hunt; Berry, Chapman. They were presented with a certificate signed by Lord Desborough, president of the British Olympic Council. Note the basketball-style panelling on the ball, held by Woodward. Only six teams participated, all of them European (two of them from France!), and the sport enjoyed full Olympic status for the first time. Convincing wins against Sweden, Holland and Denmark (football victors in the 1906 Interim Games) ensured triumph for the home team. Four years later in Stockholm there were 11 entrants, still all European, and Great Britain beat Denmark in the final. It was to be their last ever gold in the sport. The FA's withdrawal from FIFA over the issue of broken-time payments, and their subsequent boycotting of the Games from 1928 until London's hosting of the 1948 tournament, did little to improve this statistic.

Olympics. There is something of a surprise, since among the Olympic principles outlined in 1894 is one stating that the sports should be international and modern - two qualities possessed by the increasingly popular team game. Moreover, the founder of the Games, the visionary Baron Pierre de Coubertin, while insisting on the modern-day relevance of the events, intended the competition to recreate the ethos of the original festivals, and it was to the English public-school sporting tradition - in particular their team games - that he looked for

inspiration; he had also been encouraged by the public response to exhibition matches he had organised. By 1921, however, he was opposing team sports because he believed they brought out the worst aspects of nationalism. But the revenue they raised formed a convincing counter-argument.

At times in Olympic history, it cannot be denied, football has rivalled boxing for demonstrations of all that is worst in sport. In the 1906 Athens Interim Games there came a hint of future disputes when Athens refused to play Thessaloniki because they had already defeated them earlier in the competition. In the 1920 final Czechoslovakia walked off in protest at certain refereeing decisions. Four years later in Uruguay, in the final, the host nation insisted the Dutch refereee be replaced because they anticipated bias. And the infamy of the 1936 Olympics was not limited to the political sphere: the German referee was manhandled in the violent Italy - USA encounter (a dismissed Italian, Piccini, incredibly, refused to leave the field and his team won 1-0); Peru's entire contingent withdrew when a re-match was ordered after a pitch invasion during their defeat of Austria; Colombia

withdrew in sympathy. And it was Peru's disallowed goal against Argentina in the 1964 preliminary round which sparked off riots resulting in 328 deaths. In 1968 there were brawls, and four players were sent off in the final as the crowd threw cushions onto the pitch.

Nevertheless, not least thanks to some excellent football, the event has gained in strength. Before 1912 not all the teams were truly national, some countries entering more than one team to make up numbers, and in the second and third Olympiads the sport had only exhibition status - a reflection of the uncertain start experienced by the Games themselves. In 1952, however, pre-Olympic knock-out rounds became necessary because so many countries had entered.

Boycotts, bans and withdrawals have not caused as much damage as the amateur/professional dispute threatens to. When the Uruguayan footballers of 1924 and 1928 won the 1930 World Cup for their country, it was not regarded as significant. Since the Second World War, however, Western amateurs have had to compete against full-time Eastern-bloc 'amateurs' with World Cup experience. Since 1952 only France, in 1984, have broken the East European monopoly. The 1964 Italian

team had to withdraw for fielding players from European Champions Internazionale, but in 1952 Puskas had helped Hungary win the gold. Political developments in Eastern Europe since 1989 and the recent precedent of allowing professional tennis players to compete in the Olympics may hasten the end of such anomalies.

OXFORD UNITED

Founded 1893

Joined League 1962 (Div. 4)

Honours Div. 2 Champions 1985; Div. 3 Champions 1968, 1984; League Cup Winners 1986

Ground Manor Ground

Oxford United have proved splendidly worthwhile members of the League since the withdrawal of Accrington Stanley gave them their big chance in the early 1960s. Despite never attracting a huge following from the university town, United fought their way through the divisions to enjoy a short sojourn in the First; campaigned doughtily, and at times with inspiration, in the FA Cup; and actually won the League Cup.

Much of the early credit must go to two men, manager Arthur Turner and wing-half and captain Ron Atkinson. Turner took over Headington United in 1959, demanded the change of name, and led them up

to the Second Division, being sacked for his pains in 1972. Atkinson played more than 600 games for the club, in and out of the League, departing just a year before his boss to start his own successful managerial career. Other stalwarts of that era included defenders John Shuker and Maurice Kyle, and striker Graham Atkinson, Ron's brother.

The mid 1970s and early 1980s saw Oxford slip back to the Third Division, but Jim Smith started a revival that took them to the First and Maurice Evans – getting the best from such men as midfielder Ray Houghton and striker John Aldridge – kept them there for three years. It was during United's stint in the top flight that they tasted Wembley triumph, crushing Queen's Park Rangers 3-0.

Prior to that, Oxford's most stirring exploit in a knockout competition had been in 1964, when they had beaten Division 1 pacesetters Blackburn Rovers to become Division Four's first quarter-finalist.

In the 1980s there was talk of a merger with Reading, but that plan was discarded and, after dropping into the Second Division and selling talented forward Dean Saunders, United experienced boardroom changes. The future seemed likely to be a challenging one.

PAISLEY, Bob

1919 Born in Hetton-le-Hole, County Durham

1939 Helps Bishop Auckland win FA Amateur Cup; signs for Liverpool

1947 Wins Championship medal with 'Reds'

1954 Retires as player to join Anfield coaching staff

1959 Becomes Bill Shankly's first lieutenant as the Scot moves into manager's chair.

1974 Succeeds Shankly as Liverpool boss

1976 Reds lift first trophies of Paisley era — League title and UEFA Cup

1977 Liverpool retain Championship and Paisley leads them to their first European Cup triumph; their second follows a year later

1979 Reds take first of four League titles in five seasons

1981 Liverpool win another European Cup and first of a hat-trick of League Cups

1983 Steps down as manager

1985 Becomes adviser to new manager Kenny Dalglish, eventually taking a place on the Anfield board.

Paisley is, quite simply, the most successful manager in the history of English soccer. Never charismatic like Shankly, controversial like Clough or revered like Busby, he outshone them all in the quest for honours.

Some have denigrated the achievements of the modest north-easterner, contending that Shankly had already done the hard work, but such claims do not tally with the facts. Admittedly Paisley, who played a more crucial role in his predecessor's triumphs than he is often credited with, inherited some top-class players, but many of his most glorious victories were won with a new side assembled by his own perspicacity in the transfer market. He it was who signed such magnificent performers as Kenny Dalglish, Graeme

BOB PAISLEY
In characteristic mood and garb, Bob Paisley bellows at the Liverpool team from the touchline. Paisley's 1974 takeover from the legendary Bill Shankly was something of a surprise, but his ascension to the throne was achieved with the minimum of fuss. Similarly, in 1983 when Paisley was succeeded by Joe Fagan, the transfer of power was made within the club and away from the glare of the media. Perhaps part of the success of Liverpool has been the saving of breath for where it's most needed — on the pitch.

Souness and Alan Hansen, and blended them into the Liverpool pattern.

Paisley, an effective wing-half in his playing days, was a meticulous planner, shrewd tactician and canny judge of a footballer's strengths and weaknesses. Never one to shout the odds, he always preferred to let the men on the pitch do his talking for him. They did so, for nine fabulous years, with the utmost eloquence.

PARTICK THISTLE

Founded 1876

Joined League 1893 (Div. 2)

Honours Scottish League First Division Champions 1976; Div. 2 Champions 1897, 1900, 1971; Scottish Cup Winners 1921; Scottish League Cup Winners 1971/72

Ground Firhill Park

Despite being based in Glasgow, Partick Thistle have survived the Old Firm and sometimes confounded them. In 1971 they gave Celtic a comprehensive 4-1 beating in the League Cup Final. Between the posts that day was a young Alan Rough, who was to go on to win 51 caps while with the club.

In 1921, guided by Jimmy McMenemy (then in the veteran stage after a career with Celtic), they defeated Rangers to win the Scottish Cup.

Recently Thistle have persevered with costly attempts to restore the club to the Premier Division status it lost in 1982. In the 1980s they did have the satisfaction of discovering striker Maurice Johnston, although he was soon sold to Watford.

PELE

1940 Edson Arantes do Nascimento (Pele), born in Tres Coracoes, Brazil; his father, 'Dondhino', is a lowly-paid professional footballer

1954 Starts to play for Bauru Athletic Club juniors in Sao Paulo; the coach, 1934 World Cup player Waldema de Brito, persuades him not to join senior team but to wait for Santos offer

1956 September — scores in his debut for Santos v Corinthians; finishes the season as club top scorer with 32 goals

1957 July — scores in first international v Argentina

1958 Still only 17 years old, scores twice in World Cup Final victory v Sweden, bringing his tournament total to 6 goals, despite missing first two games through injury

1959 Scores 126 first-class goals, many of them for the army (since he was doing national service

at the time), the rest for Santos

1969 November — converts penalty v Vasco da Gama to score 1000th first-class goal

1970 Mature display helps Brazil secure possession of Jules Rimet Trophy in perpetuity

1971 July — 111th and final game for Brazil, v Yugoslavia in Rio de Janeiro

1974 October — final game for Santos, v Ponte Preta

1975 June — comes out of retirement to sign $4.5 million contract for New York Cosmos

1976 Voted NASL Most Valuable Player

1977 Helps Cosmos to victory v Seattle in Soccer Bowl Final; retires, having scored 1283 first-class goals; October — plays one half for each of his old teams, Santos and Cosmos, in emotional testimonial

At times it seems as if half of the world's best players were nearly overlooked in their youth on account of being 'too slight'. The fact that this judgement was also made of Edson Arantes do Nascimento makes it incredible that coaches should ever again apply such a criterion.

Widely regarded as the greatest player in the world of his or any other era, Pele, as he was nicknamed, was also the most feted footballer ever. Initially somewhat shy, resentful even, of the attention his talent brought him, he quickly learned to deal with it and was soon to be hailed as football's first ambassador. A similar pragmatism was evident in his toleration of a different, less welcome sort of attention on the pitch; for much of his career he struggled with a knee injury sustained in a needle match when 16 years old, and he soon developed an instinct for self-preservation which became sharpened after the 1966 World Cup; even so, there was little to betray the fact that, as a youth, he had had to work hard to curb a natural temper.

Pele has acted in films, is a keen amateur musician, and studied part-time for a degree in physical education while playing for Santos in the 1970s; he has served as a conscript, and has known poverty and wealth (the first footballer truly to appreciate the commercial potential of fame, his name is a worldwide registered trademark and he is said to have been a millionaire by the age of 22). His experience-crammed life has created a rounded personality so that his current ambition, to be President of Brazil, seems anything but ridiculous. Meeting popes and heads of state is something he takes in his stride. Indeed, his power has, at times, proved to be greater than theirs; a two-day truce was called in the Biafra-Nigeria

PELE The most famous number 10 shirt in the world. When Pele left Santos, the shirt bearing that number was hung up, never to be used again. Who could fill it? The great man is seen here in October 1990 in an exhibition game to celebrate his 50th birthday – a timely appearance to remind everyone, as his political ambitions were taking shape, of the world-wide respect he had gained. Pele's life epitomises the dreams of every Rio urchin who ever kicked a bundle of rags in a back street. His mother, in the best rags-to-riches tradition, was dead set against him becoming a professional footballer. She had good reason: Pele's father barely scraped a living from the sport and economic pressure frequently forced him to play when he should have been resting an injury. Pele himself hasn't always been too clever with money, having lost two fortunes through taking bad advice. His second loss was the United States' gain, the offer from Cosmos being just what he needed to avoid financial ruin.

War so that both sides could see him play.

All great players seem to have that bit more time on the ball but Pele, despite his devastating speed, could appear positively languorous. His control was unsurpassed, the first touch absorbing all the impact of the ball; he could turn it with his chest. He would use his powerful physique to shield the ball, his balance and deft skills enabling him to take it right up to a defender, committing him to a futile tackle. Naturally right-footed, he developed his left foot to equal deadliness and scored 97 international goals. He was the most feared inside-forward of his day; of only average height, he had tungsten springs in his thighs and powerful neck muscles which combined with the immaculate timing that allowed him to 'hang' in the air, made him as dangerous with his head as with his feet. Whether passing or shooting, dribbling or running off the ball, time and again he did the unexpected. He was imaginative, quick-witted and courageous. Pele was effectively kicked into submission in the 1962 and 1966 World Cups, but in 1970, aged 29, at the peak of his powers and vastly experienced, he returned to play in every qualifying and final round, producing exquisite performances in a highly talented and expressive Brazilian team.

The only aspect of Pele's game which went largely unexamined was his defensive ability – a fact for which football fans are surely grateful. Most of his European counterparts enjoyed no such exemption, tackling-back being an integral part of defence-based strategies.

Pele's participation in a game was always a celebration of the sport, his joy and delight in his own skills being communicated to the spectator. This enthusiasm has since been translated into the commitment he makes to football clinics (often for children as poor as he once was) all over the world. His dedication to football (in addition to financial considerations) brought him out of retirement to put a spark into United States soccer – he is often credited with single-handedly creating the football boom in that country.

His son is currently on Santos's books as a 'keeper; if he shows only a tenth of his father's exuberance and sportsmanship he will do football no small service.

PETERBOROUGH UNITED

Founded 1934

Joined League 1960 (Div. 4)

Honours Div. 4 Champions 1961, 1974

Ground London Road

When Peterborough United finally achieved League membership, it was long overdue. They had made 20 previous applications, often impressed in the FA Cup, attracted large crowds and won the Midland League with monotonous regularity. Having gained admittance, to the exclusion of Gateshead, they showed their quality immediately, romping away with the Fourth Division title and scoring a record 134 goals (52 of them from Terry Bly) in the process.

Then, securely ensconced in the Third Division and with striker Derek Dougan as their leading light, they beat Arsenal on the way to the 1965 FA Cup quarter-finals. The following year they disposed of Newcastle and Burnley to reach the League Cup semi-finals, and their future seemed bright.

But disaster was to follow. In 1968 they were relegated as punishment for financial irregularities, and then faced a severe cash crisis. They have since recovered, manager Noel Cantwell leading them back to the Third Division in the 1970s, only to return to the basement for the ensuing decade before rising again in 1991.

With better support than most of their opponents, there always seems to be potential for the 'Posh' to better their lot.

PLATINI, Michel

1955 Born in Joeuf, France

1972 Joined Nancy – scored 98 league goals for them in 175 appearances

1976 March – international debut v Czechoslovakia; scores in 2-2 draw

1978 Scores v Nice in Cup Final victory

1979 Bought by St Etienne

1981 Scores 21 goals on way to picking up League Championship medal

1982 Having scored 58 goals for St Etienne in 107 League appearances, moves to Italian club Juventus for £1.2 million

1983 Top scorer (16 goals) for new club; European Footballer of the Year

1984 Cup Winners' Cup medal, Italian Championship medal (18 goals); captains France to victory in European Championships, scoring a record 8 goals – not surprisingly, is again voted Europe's top player...

1985 ...and again (3 successive awards – a record); scores penalty v Liverpool to win European Cup for Juventus in notorious Heysel Final

1987 Retires and takes over managership of French national team

MICHEL PLATINI
Michel Platini, in glamorous company and not looking at all out of place as he receives the 1984 Golden Shoe for scoring most goals in the European Championship, which was won by the French team he led. In his other hand is the European Footballer of the Year trophy – his second – which he also won that year. Since the 1960s, top soccer stars have enjoyed lifestyles which could not have been imagined by the journeymen footballers of previous eras. The distractions can bring problems, but they must be preferable to those which accompanied low wages and strict contracts.

Platini senior was coach at Nancy, Michel's first club, and the midfield player's dead-ball expertise was testimony to his own and his father's belief in the value of practice. Michel's natural gifts alone, however, would have guaranteed him recognition as a world-class player. Perhaps his greatest asset was his vision; time and again his laser-guided passes opened up Europe's best defences. Elegant in movement, industrious when need be, he was comfortable in possession and a sweet striker of the ball. His scoring record is impressive for a midfield player and he was a cool penalty-taker for both national and club sides. No country is harder to score in than Italy, and his 68 goals in 147 League appearances for Juventus represent a remarkable ratio.

Platini won 72 caps for France, many of them as captain, and scored 41 goals. He played for his country in three consecutive World Cups and was the linch-pin of the sophisticated midfield quartet which so nearly steered France to the Final in 1982.

As a player he was occasionally wont to show impatience with less-gifted colleagues who were unable to anticipate his through-passes or were slow to deliver the ball as he made one of his finely timed runs. His footballing intelligence has never been in doubt, and there are high hopes for his managerial career. A true cosmopolitan, he once had his own slot on Italian television in which he discoursed, in Italian, on the subject of current soccer tactics.

PLAY-OFFS

Play-offs in the Football League were used in the 1986/87 season as a way to readjust the make-up of the divisions and, expressly, to produce a First Division of 20 clubs. Some automatic promotion and relegation still took place, but play-off matches were played to finalise the construction of the League for the following season. At the

end of a round of home and away games, Swindon (third in Division 3) went to the Second Division (replacing Sunderland) and Aldershot (sixth in Division 4) went into the Third Division (replacing Bolton Wanderers).

Although the strain of these matches and the apparent unfairness of some of the promotions and relegations were pointed out by players, managers and fans, the general feeling was favourable. In particular the play-off system, coupled with three points for a win, meant that few League matches were played which did not affect either promotion or relegation, thus maintaining interest throughout the whole season. Although initially a short-term measure, play-offs have remained, in various formats, since. The 1989/90 season culminated in successfully staged play-off finals at Wembley which further cemented

support for the concept.

Play-offs are not new to the Football League. Called 'test matches' they were used in the early days of the League to determine promotion and relegation between the divisions. In the first season of Division Two (1892/93) Accrington (no relation to Accrington Stanley), Notts County and Newton Heath from the First played off against Small Heath, Sheffield United and Darwen from the Second for three Division 1 places. Newton Heath stayed up, to be joined by Sheffield United and Darwen.

PLYMOUTH ARGYLE

Founded 1886

Joined League 1920 (Div. 3)

Honours Div. 3 (S) Champions 1930, 1952; Div. 3 Champions 1959

Ground Home Park

Plymouth Argyle could hardly have a more apt nickname than the

'Pilgrims'. Isolated in deepest Devon, they are faced with regular marathon treks to the far corners of the country, which places a significant drain on both resources and energy. In such circumstances, and in view of the West Country's traditional lukewarm feeling for football, Argyle have done well to spend the majority of their campaigns in the Second Division, and to avoid the Fourth altogether.

Their earliest League efforts were encouraging, if extremely frustrating. For six consecutive seasons between 1922 and 1927 they were runners-up in Division 3 (S), with Sammy Black's goals and Welsh international Moses Russell's captaincy contributing largely to such astonishing consistency. They finally went up in 1930, and there followed 20 years in the Second Division before the 1950s brought two relegations and two promotions.

PLAY-OFFS Dave Regis celebrating his goal in the play-off final at Wembley that pushed Notts County into Division 1 at the expense of Brighton at the end of the 1990/91 season.

Wing-half Johnny Williams and marksman Wilf Carter were particularly influential in their Third Division title triumph of 1959, the last time an honour has landed at Home Park. Since then Plymouth have see-sawed between the Second and Third Divisions, with their most prominent character being flamboyant boss Malcolm Allison, who was in charge for a brief period in the mid 1960s. Other well-known Argyle figures have included Allison's protege, full-back Tony Book; striker Paul Mariner in the mid 1970s; and his successor in the number nine shirt, Tommy Tynan, in the 1980s.

Plymouth's best knock-out sequences have taken them to the FA Cup semi-finals in 1984, and the same stage of the League Cup in 1965 and 1974.

PORTSMOUTH

Founded 1898

Joined League 1920 (Div. 3 founder member)

Honours Div. 1 Champions 1949, 1950; Div. 3 (S) Champions 1924; Div. 3 Champions 1962, 1983; FA Cup Winners 1939

Ground Fratton Park

Since the war only four teams have won consecutive League Championships: Manchester United, Wolves, Liverpool and Portsmouth, a once powerful club who have languished out of the limelight - apart from one disastrous top-flight term in the late 1980s - for more than three decades.

After entering the League as original members of the Third Division, 'Pompey' ascended quickly and - thanks hugely to free-scoring Billy Haines - reached the First in 1927.

After surviving early struggles to avoid relegation, and recovering from the disappointment of FA Cup Final defeats in 1929 and 1934, they sold star centre-half Jimmy Allen and emerged as a major force.

Under the guidance of extrovert boss Jack Tinn, Portsmouth caused one of the biggest FA Cup upsets of the century by thrashing Wolves at Wembley in the last pre-war Final. After the conflict, with Bob Jackson now in charge, they entered their purple patch, chalking up their title double and remaining an accomplished team until well into the 1950s. The success was based on a splendid half-back line of Jimmy Scoular, Reg Flewin and long-serving English international Jimmy Dickinson, with wingers Peter Harris and Jack Froggatt also highly influential. The side broke up, however, and Pompey went down in 1959 to begin a lengthy mundane period spent mostly in Division 2, with low points including a financial crisis in the 1960s and a slide to the Fourth Division in the late 1970s.

The 1980s saw a gradual recovery under managers Frank Burrows and Bobby Campbell, and in 1987 Alan Ball took them into the top flight. Sadly they were not good enough, Ball was sacked, and Portsmouth entered the 1990s as solid, if rather uninspiring members of the Second Division.

PORTSMOUTH
The season is 1948/49 and Portsmouth win the Football League Championship. Proudly displaying the famous badge on their blue shirts are: (back row, left to right) Scoular, Rookes, Butler, Ferrier, Dickinson; Harris, Barlow, Reid, Phillips, Froggatt, Bowler. That year they were also FA Cup semi-finalists (losing 3-1 to Leicester City) before going on to retain the title the following season. They have not seen such times since down on the south coast.

PORT VALE

Founded 1876

Joined League 1892

Honours Div.3 (N) Champions 1930, 1954; Div. 4 Champions 1959

Ground Vale Park

Port Vale took their unusual name from the house in the northern end of the Potteries where a dozen men gathered to launch the club. Only occasionally have they emerged from the lower divisions and out of Stoke City's shadow. Indeed, Vale have played in a higher division than their neighbours in just three seasons.

The club added the prefix 'Burslem' in 1886, and were elected to the new Division 2 six years later. Financial problems forced them out in 1907, but the suspension of Leeds City for making illegal payments to players allowed the club (by now plain Port Vale again) to return in 1919. In 1931 a best ever position of fifth in Division 2 was achieved.

In 1943 they sold the Old Recreation Ground in Hanley - known locally as 'th'owd wreck' - and laid ambitious plans for their sixth home. Vale Park, in Burslem, was to be the 'Wembley of the North'. It opened in 1950, but the original 50,000 capacity was tested only twice by FA Cup ties.

In 1953/54 Vale won the Division 3 (N) title, conceding a mere 7 home goals and 21 overall in 46 games. They also reached the FA Cup semi-final in the same season, only for their former player Ronnie Allen to score West Bromwich's penalty winner.

Division 2 status was surrendered in 1957 and not regained until 1989. In between Vale became Division 4's first champions and rose from the bottom section a further three times. Sir Stanley Matthews briefly managed the club he supported as a boy, but in 1968 Vale were expelled from the League - ironically for making illegal payments.

They were re-elected soon afterwards, but only stalwart defender Roy Sproson remained from the heady days of the 1950s. He later managed Vale, though it was not until John Rudge took the post in 1983 that they began to threaten Stoke's ascendancy.

The 1991/92 campaign began with Vale in Division 2, one division above their local rivals. In the previous season they decided against moving to an all-purpose stadium proposed by Stoke-on-Trent council, and announced a multi-million pound scheme to modernise the crumbling Vale Park.

PRESTON NORTH END

Founded 1881

Joined League 1888 (founder member)

Honours Div. 1 Champions 1889, 1890; Div. 2 Champions 1904, 1913, 1951; Div. 3 Champions 1971; FA Cup Winners 1889, 1938

Ground Deepdale

Young fans may find it hard to believe, but Preston North End, a familiar sight in the lower reaches of the League throughout the 1980s, gave the world its first great football team. The 'Old Invincibles' as they were then known - how cruelly ironic that nickname seems now - lifted the inaugural Championship without losing a game, and in the same season took the FA Cup without conceding a goal.

Spearheaded by England marksman John Goodall, Preston - the first club to pay players openly - retained the title the following year and were runners-up in the next three terms before see-sawing between Divisions 1 and 2 for the first third of the twentieth century. Outstanding performers in this anti-climactic period were centre-half Joe McCall before the First World War, and schemer Alex James in the 1920s. By the mid 1930s greater consistency was found and, with Bill Shankly at

right-half, Preston won promotion in 1934 and the FA Cup four years later.

After the war they slipped into the Second Division but soon returned to the top flight to embark on an era which, although yielding no trophies, offered rich entertainment. Architect of the improvement was winger Tom Finney, one of the finest footballers ever known, with wing-half Tommy Docherty also making a telling contribution. In 1953 the Championship was missed on goal average, and the following campaign ended with a Wembley defeat by West Bromwich Albion, but, nothing daunted, North End remained a major force until 1961. Then, with Finney retired and the disappearance of the maximum wage striking a body blow to Deepdale finances, relegation signalled the start of an inexorable decline.

PRESTON NORTH END

Preston North End must look back to the end of the last century to find their most successful period in the game. The side photographed here were FA Cup winners in 1889, beating Wolverhampton Wanderers 3-0 at the Kennington Oval. The team: (back row, left to right) **Drummond, Howarth, Mr Hanbury MP, Mr Tomlinson MP, Russell, Holmes, Mr Sudell (Chairman), Graham, Mills-Roberts; Gordon, Ross, Goodhall, Dewhurst, Thomson. The scorers in the Final were Gordon, Goodhall and Thomson (sometimes spelt Thompson); Dewhurst had scored a goal in the preceding year's Final when North End lost 2-1 to West Bromwich Albion. Importantly, season 1889/90 was when Preston North End also won the first ever League Championship to complete the double. Their record over the first five years of the League's history was twice first and three times runners-up.**

Talented players such as winger Peter Thompson and wing-half Howard Kendall emerged but were sold through economic necessity, and the slide continued.

Preston did manage a further FA Cup Final appearance, their seventh - they unluckily lost to West Ham in 1964 - but little else went their way. In 1970 the club tasted Third Division fare for the first time. Subsequently there have been two spells in the Second, but also one in the Fourth, and with the Lancashire giants tightening their grip on floating support, supreme efforts will be needed to restore even a vestige of former glories. Indeed, during the 1990/91 campaign they had to accept that promotion from the Third Division would be a financial disaster as, under new League rules, they would have to take up their synthetic pitch - an asset to the club for the extra revenue it attracts.

PUSKAS, Ferenc

1926 Born in Budapest, Hungary

1943 Makes debut for Kispest (Budapest) at 16

1945 Makes international debut for Hungary

1948 Heads Hungarian League goal-scorers with 50 for Kispest

1949 Kispest becomes known as Honved, a Hungarian Army team

1952 Wins gold medal in Hungary's Olympic team

1953 Captains Hungary to 6-3 victory v England at Wembley

1954 Although injured, captains Hungary in World Cup Final

1956 Leaves Hungary during the People's Revolution

1957 Spends year in Austria but fails to get playing permit

1958 Joins Real Madrid

1960 Scores four goals in Real Madrid's fifth successive European Cup Final victory, 7-3 v Eintracht Frankfurt

1962 Scores another European Cup Final hat-trick

1964 Wins a second European Cup runner-up medal

1966 Retires as a player

1971 Coaches Panathinaikos of Greece to the European Cup Final

Ferenc Puskas scored 83 goals in 84 internationals for his home country before his Hungarian career was cut short by a popular uprising in October 1956. Two years later his career was revived in Spain. He made four international appearances for Spain, and scored 35 goals in 39 European Cup matches for Real Madrid. Puskas won one European Cup winner's medal and played in two other Finals. He won four Hungarian League Championships with Honved and five Spanish League Championships with Real. He was top scorer in the Hungarian League in four seasons, and in the Spanish League in four seasons.

Puskas made his impact on the British game at Wembley in 1953, in particular with the manner of the third Hungarian goal in a 6-3 victory. He changed direction by rolling back the ball with the sole of his foot before swivelling to hit a typical left-foot shot past Merrick. His left-foot power was legendary, but he also had deceptive acceleration combined with cunning anticipation. Unlike many stars, Puskas was stockily built and had obvious weaknesses - he was poor at heading, one-footed and not always at peak fitness - but his left foot more than compensated. His record ranks with the world's best, and only Pele has scored more international goals.

PUSKAS, FERENC Lining up at Wembley with the 'Magnificent Magyars' of 1953. Puskas, captain, is on the left. The rest of the side lines up: *(left to right)* Grosics, Lorant, Hidegkuti, Buzansky, Lantos, Zakarias, Czibor, Boszik, Budai and Kocsis. Puskas is acknowledged as having inspired the 6-3 victory; he also amazed many spectators and commentators with his ball artistry. How he moved his feet at all with such huge shinpads is a mystery; compare these with Dave Bennet's pads in the Coventry City photograph.

THE PYRAMID

The Pyramid gives shape and structure to non-League football. It is a system which links the various leagues outside the Football League, ensuring that clubs can progress through a hierarchy. Since 1986/87 the GM Vauxhall Conference (Alliance Premier League) champions have been granted automatic promotion to the Football League, providing they can satisfy League standards for ground and facilities.

Three leagues feed into the GM Vauxhall Conference – the Vauxhall League (Isthmian League), the HFS Loans League (Northern Premier League) and the Beazer Homes League (Southern League). Clubs in the premier divisions of these three leagues compete for promotion to the GM Vauxhall Conference. Below these premier divisions, the league network escalates. There are more divisions to the main feeder leagues, which in turn have leagues which officially feed into them. The result is an integrated structure which is bottom-heavy with grass roots leagues. This is the Pyramid.

The Alliance Premier League, formed in 1979, paved the way as the first national league outside the Football League. It later became known as the Gola League, later still the GM Vauxhall Conference. It is still the only national league in men's non-League football, but the opportunity for automatic promotion to the Football League means that in theory anyone can form a new club and reach Division 4 within a decade.

Colne Dynamoes were formed in 1963 by eleven schoolfriends, and 25 years later they won the FA Vase at Wembley. In 1989/90 their team of full-time professionals won the HFS Loans League by 26 points, but promotion to the GM Vauxhall Conference was hampered by negotiations over grounds. Chairman Graham White put the club into voluntary liquidation,

THE PYRAMID Gary Bull *(right)* and Paul Wilson of Barnet celebrate a Bull goal in his side's 4-0 win over Cheltenham Town in the GM Vauxhall Conference in 1989/90 season. Barnet were runners-up, delaying their promotion to the League by one season. For youngsters like Bull, who has played League soccer, a secure place in a high profile non-League team may represent a better prospect than life as a full-time professional with a struggling Third or Fourth Division team – although the editor (for whom Bull was once his postman while playing for Barnet) has not asked the player's opinion. Interestingly, playing for Barnet in this match was Andy Clarke who was transferred to Wimbledon for £300,000 in 1991. With soccer's changing fortunes, who will be higher by the end of the decade, Barnet or Wimbledon?

saying that his family had been under pressure – thus nipping in the bud a remarkable story of progress (nearly) to Football League status.

Each league outside the Football League has its own standards for football grounds and facilities, so clubs can prepare for the upward journey through the hierarchy. It is often argued that many non-league clubs are better run than those in the League. In addition, there is growing support for non-League football.

Aside from the FA Cup there are three major knock-out competitions for non-League clubs: the Bob Lord Challenge Trophy (named after the late Burnley chairman), the FA Challenge Vase (1975) and the FA Challenge Trophy (1970). The Bob Lord Challenge Trophy is for GM Vauxhall Conference teams. Top non-League teams are excluded from the Vase, but all non-League teams can compete in the FA Trophy.

QUEEN OF THE SOUTH

Founded 1919

Joined League 1923 (Div. 3)

Honours Scottish League Division 2 Champions 1951

Ground Palmerston Park

Geographically remote (in Dumfries) from other 22 clubs, Queen of the South have none the less made their presence felt. Their own rampaging Billy Houliston was centre-forward for Scotland in the 1949 Wembley victory against England, and 1920s attacker Hughie Gallacher was briefly with them before joining Airdrie.

They reached Division 1 in 1933 and were relegated from it only in 1950. Since those days life has grown considerably more difficult.

QUEEN'S PARK

Founded 1867

Joined League 1900

Honours Scottish League Division 2 Champions 1923, 1956; Second Division Champions 1981; Scottish Cup Winners 1974, 1875, 1876, 1880, 1881, 1882, 1884, 1886, 1890, 1893

Ground Hampden Park

Scotland's oldest club, Queen's Park take much of the credit for popularising the sport in that country. The game's development then left them stranded all the same. Professionalism was legalised in 1893 but they retained, as they still do, their amateur status.

Grandeur still attaches to the club whose early achievements included no less than ten Scottish Cups as well as appearances in the FA Cup Finals of 1884 and 1885. Charles Campbell won a record eight winner's medals in the Scottish Cup and other stars of the period included winger J B Weir.

Completion of Hampden Park (their third ground of that name) in 1903 gave Scotland a national stadium and Queen's Park a curious role – Scottish football's unofficial curators.

QUEEN'S PARK RANGERS

Founded 1885

Joined League 1920 (Div. 3)

Honours Div. 2 Champions 1983; Div. 3 (S) Champions 1948; Div. 3 Champions 1967; League Cup Winners 1967

Ground Loftus Road

As a football force to be reckoned with, Queen's Park Rangers are a thoroughly modern phenomenon. Throughout most of their first four-and-a-half decades of league life they created few ripples, often struggling financially and languishing in the Third Division apart from four post-war campaigns in the Second. In the mid 1950s they were particularly mundane, but the early 1960s, with enterprising manager Alec Stock at the helm and Brian Bedford banging in more than 170 goals in six seasons, brought new optimism.

The long-awaited impact on the national scene came, with a vengeance, in 1967 when Rangers not only won the Third Division title by 12 points, but also came from two goals down to beat West Bromwich Albion in the first League Cup Final played at Wembley. Star of the show and symbol of the West London club's rise to prominence was flamboyant goal-scorer Rodney Marsh, who netted 44 times during that glorious season. In the following term Rangers capitalised by earning top-flight status for the first time, but they were not ready for such dizzy heights and immediately returned to the Second Division.

But genuine progress was being made, and after Gordon Jago led them to promotion in 1973, Dave Sexton polished them into an accomplished side which finished only a point behind champions Liverpool in 1976. The new hero was midfielder Gerry Francis, who became England captain, and there were also crucial contributions from 'keeper Phil Parkes, veteran defender Frank McLintock, schemer Don Masson and mercurial forward Stan Bowles.

When Sexton left, however, the momentum died and Rangers spent four more years in the Second Division during which they made a plucky attempt to upset Spurs in the replayed 1982 Cup Final – before rising again, under Terry Venables, in 1983. Since then they have been solid members of Division 1, with outstanding players including 'keeper David Seaman, sold to Arsenal in 1990, and Paul Parker.

QUEEN'S PARK RANGERS In Terry Venables' time as a player at Queen's Park Rangers (1969-74) the club rose from the middle of the Second Division to a respectable position in the First. Indeed, by 1975/76 they were Championship runners-up. During that time they also began to challenge Chelsea as the style leaders in London, not for their play but for the clubs and events at which their players could be seen. Football, as a game in general, was moving closer to show business in those days and a young Venables was very much a part of the scene. Also popular around Venables' time, was Rodney Marsh (*above*). 'Rod-nee' was stylish, flamboyant, arrogant and, above all, an entertainer.

HOME TEAM
DRESSING ROOM

RAITH ROVERS

Founded 1883

Joined League 1902 (Div. 2)

Honours Scottish League Division 2 Champions 1908, 1910 (shared with Leith), 1938, 1949

Ground Stark's Park

Raith Rovers' greatest episodes have tended to end in disappointment. In 1913 they lost the Scottish Cup Final to Falkirk, and the League Cup Final of 1948/49 brought defeat by Rangers.

Yet watching the Kirkcaldy club has substantial compensations. Alex James, a brilliant play-maker for Arsenal, learned his trade with them in the 1920s. A Scotland great of the 1960s, Jim Baxter, also first caught the eye at Stark's Park. Of the stars who stayed, the half-back line of the 1950s, Andy Young, Willie McNaught and Andy Leigh, is particularly revered.

RAMSEY, Sir Alf

1920 Born in Dagenham

1944 Turns professional with Southampton

1948 England debut, v Switzerland at Highbury

1949 Moves to Tottenham Hotspur, with Welsh winger Ernie Jones going the other way

1950 Helps Spurs take Division 2 title...

1951 ...followed by the League Championship

1953 Wins last of 32 caps in Hungary's famous 6-3 Wembley annihilation of England

1955 Takes over as Ipswich boss

1957 East Anglians top Division 3 (S)

1961 Ipswich win Division 2 title

1962 Surprise success as Ipswich lift the Division 1 crown

1963 Ramsey succeeds Walter Winterbottom as England manager

1966 Leads England to World Cup victory

1967 Becomes Sir Alf

1970 Mexico World Cup campaign ends at quarter-final stage as England lose to West Germany after leading 2-0

1974 Ramsey is sacked after England fail to qualify for World Cup

1977 Brief spell as Birmingham City boss

ALF RAMSEY All England managers, sooner or later, seem to receive criticism from the fans and the press; it's just another part of the job. Sir Alf Ramsey was singled out as haughty and aloof but the loyalty of his players, and the evidence of numerous photographers like this one, tend to suggest a different truth. He did like to don a tracksuit, and he did find time for the fans. Pictured here at a 1971 training session, Ramsey is enjoying the antics of his squad (Bobby Moore facing the camera) prior to a European Championship match against Greece.

England WILL win the World Cup, Alf Ramsey announced repeatedly in the months leading up to the 1966 tournament. Few believed him, some even ridiculed him, but he it was who had the last laugh – and a knighthood to boot.

Ramsey, who enjoyed a productive playing career as a skilful right-back in Arthur Rowe's innovative 'push-and-run' Spurs team, made an inspired start in management. At Ipswich he achieved much with little, moulding a group of discards and previously underrated performers into a Championship side.

Next, faced with the ultimate challenge at international level, he adopted a 4-3-3 system in which wingers were redundant, suffered constant jibes for his so-called negativity, and proceeded to show the pundits that he was right and they were wrong.

Ever cautious and seemingly aloof, Ramsey never captured popular affection even after winning the World Cup – although he rejoiced in the esteem and loyalty of his players – and was blamed often for inflicting a 'dull'

approach on the whole of English football.

When England were eliminated in Mexico, Ramsey was again vilified for his tactics and few publicly mourned his eventual dismissal. His achievements, if not his demeanour, had merited a more sympathetic send off.

RANGERS

Founded 1873

Joined League 1890 (Div. 1, founder member)

Honours Scottish League Division 1 Champions 1891 (joint with Dumbarton), 1899, 1900, 1901, 1902, 1911, 1912, 1913, 1918, 1920, 1921, 1923, 1924, 1925, 1927, 1928, 1929, 1930, 1931, 1933, 1934, 1935, 1937, 1939, 1947, 1949, 1950, 1953, 1956, 1957, 1959, 1961, 1963, 1964, 1975; Scottish League Premier Division Champions 1976, 1978, 1987, 1989, 1990, 1991; Scottish Cup Winners 1894, 1897, 1898, 1903, 1928, 1930, 1932, 1934, 1935, 1936, 1948, 1949, 1950, 1953, 1960, 1962, 1963, 1964, 1966, 1973, 1976, 1978, 1979, 1981; Scottish League Cup Winners 1947, 1949, 1961, 1962, 1964, 1965, 1971, 1976, 1978, 1979, 1982, 1984, 1985, 1987, 1988, 1989; European Cup Winners' Cup Winners 1972

Ground Ibrox Stadium

Rangers Football Club is unique. It is unique because in the fabric of Scottish culture it is more, much more, than just a football club. It has dominated the Scottish game for a century, but more than that, the march of Scottish history has made it an institution which embodies the conservative, unionist, loyalist, Presbyterian ethic, in direct contrast to the other great Glasgow club, Celtic, which is identified with the Catholic religion and the Republic of Ireland. Other cities around the world – Milan, Turin, Madrid, Rio, Buenos Aires – have intense inter-club rivalries, but nowhere else are these based on religion.

The Rangers club was formed in Glasgow in 1872/73 by a group of youths from the Gareloch area of the west of Scotland. They first played on Fleshers' Haugh on Glasgow Green, the city's

great open space, then moved west to Burnbank and Kinning Park before settling on the present location at Ibrox in 1899. In those early days the game in Scotland was amateur, centred on Glasgow and the west. The fixtures were friendly with the exception of the Scottish Cup, which began in season 1873/74. Queen's Park, the dominant club of the time, won the first three competitions. Rangers were finalists in 1877 and 1879 but not until 1894 did they win, and their Scottish Cup record since has been uneven. From 1903 to 1928 they went 25 years without a win, and to date they have recorded 24 victories.

The Scottish League Championship was altogether another matter. Joint champions with Dumbarton in the very first year of the competition, 1890/91, Rangers to the end of season 1990/91 have been champions a record 41 times.

Great names sprinkle the Rangers story. There was an outstanding team at the turn of the century, famous for the full-back partnership of Nick Smith and Jock Drummond, and Alec Smith, the outside-left with the club for 21 years from 1894 to 1915. In 1898/99 Rangers won *all* of their 18 league matches, considered to be a world record. Before the First World War, Neilly Gibson, Jacky Robertson, Alec Bennett and R C Hamilton were famous Rangers names.

The 1920s and 1930s were decades which saw brilliant Rangers teams and players such as the great Alan Morton, considered by many to have been the greatest Rangers player of all, Andy Cunningham, Davie Meiklejohn, an inspiring captain, Bob McPhail, George Brown, Dougie Gray and Jerry Dawson. After the Second World War there came the famous 'Iron Curtain' defence of Brown; Young and Shaw; McColl, Woodburn and Cox,

backing exceptional forwards in Willie Waddell and Willie Thornton.

Since the passing of that team in the 1950s, outstanding Rangers players have included Eric Caldow, Ian McMillan, Jim Baxter, Willie Henderson, John Greig and Derek Johnston, but perhaps the greatest of all Rangers names has been that of Bill Struth, manager from 1920 to 1957. In his reign, Rangers won 18 Championships and 10 Scottish Cups. In European competition, Rangers were finalists in the Cup Winners' Cup in 1961 and 1967, and winners in 1972.

The club has known tragedy. At a Scotland *v* England match in 1902, 25 fans died when part of Ibrox's wooden terracing collapsed. From then on, earthen embankments became the norm. And on 2 January 1971, when 66 lives were lost on embankment exit steps at the New Year game against Celtic, that same Willie

Waddell, now the club manager, realised that the huge and old-fashioned Ibrox, which held 80,000 that day, was becoming obsolete. The rebuilding of a modern Ibrox eventually began in 1978 and was finished in 1981. On completion of additional work in 1990/91 it will have a capacity of 50,000, all seated, all under cover.

There have been critical dates for Rangers in the decade of the 1980s. In 1986 Graeme Souness was appointed manager of the club. Following a distinguished career with Scotland, Liverpool and Sampdoria, Souness began to bring an international flavour to Rangers by importing such exceptional English players as Terry Butcher, Chris Woods, Trevor Steven and Gary Stevens, paying huge transfer fees, and no doubt wages, to do it. Peter Huistra of Holland and Oleg Kuznetsow of the Soviet Union followed in 1990.

RANGERS As both Tottenham Hotspur and Manchester United will attest, success cannot be bought. However, Graeme Souness did use the chequebook quite heavily to bring together his early Scottish Championship-winning sides. Several of his top signings came from England. The players celebrating the 1988/89 Championship include six English-born players: *(back row, left to right)* Gough, Gray, Walters, Woods, Munro, Cooper, Brown; Sterland, Butcher, Robertson, Drinkell and Stevens. At that time, Woods, Butcher and Stevens were all England players. Changing rules about qualification for UEFA tournaments mean that British sides like Rangers will have to draw much more heavily on players born in the country of the club.

In 1988, a friend of Souness, David Murray, a Scottish businessman and entrepreneur, joined the manager in buying the equity of the club, and continued the Souness policy of making Rangers one of the outstanding clubs in the world. Their motivation was the prospect of first a British League, then a European League, funded by the financial muscle of cable and satellite television companies. Whether this level of determination continues after the shock departure in 1991 of Souness, off to manage Liverpool, remains to be seen.

RE-ELECTION

The original 1888 rule was that the bottom four Football League clubs would have to seek re-election at the end of each season. The number was reduced to three (in 1896) and two (in 1909).

When the Division 3 (N) was formed in 1921, the number was again extended to four – two from Division 3 (N) and two from Division 3 (S). From 1958 it was the bottom four in the newly-formed Fourth Division, until 1986/87, when the system of automatically relegating one club to non-League status was introduced.

Since the formation of the Third Division, the clubs facing re-election the most times are as follows: Hartlepool (14), Halifax Town (12), Barrow (12), Southport (11), Crewe Alexandra (10), Newport County (10) and Rochdale (10).

Re-election is determined by votes cast by League clubs and associate members. A variety of voting systems has been used over the years, but the collective weight of higher division clubs has always been greater than that of other interested parties. On

occasions, the re-election voting has resulted in a tie between two clubs. On second ballots, Stockport County defeated Doncaster Rovers in 1901, Torquay United defeated Aberdare in 1927, Chester defeated Nelson in 1931, Hereford United defeated Barrow in 1972 and Wigan Athletic defeated Southport in 1978. In 1950 Scunthorpe and Lindsey United defeated Wigan Athletic on a third ballot. But the closest voting came in 1908, when Tottenham Hotspur and Lincoln City tied on the first three ballots. The matter went to the League management committee, who voted five to three in favour of Tottenham.

New Brighton (1951), Bradford Park Avenue (1970), Barrow (1972), Workington (1977) and Southport (1978) have all lost Football League status on a post-war re-election vote.

Three clubs have

narrowly missed achieving League status: Mitchell St George's (by two votes in 1889), Yeovil Town (by three in 1976) and Altrincham (by one vote in 1980).

READING

Founded 1871

Joined League 1920
(Div. 3, founder member)

Honours Div. 3 (S) Champions 1926; Div. 3 Champions 1986; Div. 4 Champions 1979

Ground Elm Park

After half-a-century of League membership during which Reading experienced just one promotion from Division 3 and subsequent relegation, the 1970s and 1980s saw the 'Royals' transformed into soccer yo-yos. In two decades of frantic activity they made eight trips between divisions, with three spells in the Fourth and one, from 1984 to 1986 under the

guidance of Ian Branfoot, in the Second.

Yet the Third, of which Reading were founder members, would appear to be their natural habitat. After returning to it in 1931 following a five-year sojourn at the higher level, they remained there for 40 years despite many valiant attempts at betterment, notably under Ted Drake in the early 1950s.

READING Setting a record for Division 3, Reading won 13 League matches in succession in the 1985/86 season. Seen in the match in which the record was set is Reading's most famous player of recent times, prolific goal-scorer Trevor Senior. Reading won the Division 3 title that year; Newport finished 19th. Two years later Newport were bottom of Division 4 and out of the League.

Reading, whose greatest FA Cup achievement was defeating Manchester United and Portsmouth on the way to the 1927 semi-final, are disadvantaged in the quest for lasting progress by their proximity to London, whose major venues offer all-too-attractive alternatives to Elm Park. One avenue for possible advancement was closed when talks in the mid 1980s about a merger with Oxford United came to nothing.

REFEREES

In the 1990/91 season English football referees were under the microscope as at no other time. In an attempt to eradicate the 'professional foul', FIFA had directed 1990 World Cup referees to send off players committing such an offence, and the ruling was extended to national associations. Problems of interpretation soon arose, however, particularly with regard to such matters as intent, fouls in the penalty area, and handball. The result was inconsistency and confusion, with some baffling decisions.

This controversy highlights three crucial elements in modern refereeing which have broader implications: the role of television, the assimilation of law changes and new directives, and the referee's right to use his discretion.

The first is of increasing significance. The luxury of slow-motion replays allow studio pundits to analyse and criticise the instantaneous decisions of officials. In December 1990 the FA declared that, in exceptional circumstances, video evidence might be used in a player's prosecution or appeal. The lower reaches of football not having access to such resources, this runs counter to the unspoken principle of the uniformity of the Laws and their implementation, regardless of the level. Similar objections are voiced against the idea of replays on giant screens in the major stadiums, which would permit a referee to change a decision

REFEREES How times change. Neatly bow-tied and jacketed, referee J.T. Howcroft supervises the toss-up at the start of the match with Billy Flint (Notts County) and Frank Barson (Aston Villa), respective captains in this 1925 encounter. Both sides were in the First Division.

but might also undermine his authority. Another possible American import - microphone-linked referees explaining their decisions to the crowd - seems a logical extension of the red and yellow card system which was first introduced in the 1970 World Cup. Such striking additions to the referee's traditional equipment of stopwatch, wristwatch, coin, pencil, notebooks, whistles and cards may well become a reality in 1994 when the US World Cup will have to woo native television viewers.

Short-term problems of interpretation occur, typically, when new or modified laws are introduced. More lasting, and more irritating, are the varying interpretations throughout the world. British referees, for example, are generally considered too lenient in

REFEREES Referees came increasingly into the spotlight as newspapers took more interest in personalities than the play and as televised football became more common. One of the first refs to be widely recognised from televised matches was Clive Thomas, seen here wearing his FIFA badge in the 1976 season in which he took charge of the FA Cup Final. His style was typical of many modern referees — a fit man, keen to let the game flow and happy to strike up a rapport with players. He did, however, run into problems on a number of occasions, making, and sticking rigidly by, some controversial decisions.

permitting challenges from behind, whereas continental referees are seen as naive in matters of time-wasting and play-acting.

The 92 English League referees receive £100 per match, linesmen £50, with extra payment for Cup Finals and internationals; in 1888 referees got 10s 6d (52½p), and in 1896 linesmen got 5s (25p). Expenses were first allowed in 1946. There are frequent calls for full-time professional referees. In 1993/94 Italian referees will join their Brazilian counterparts with salaries starting from £48,000.

A good referee is unobtrusive, demonstrates a sense of humour and explains decisions if necessary. Using his discretion, he is guided by the spirit and feel of the game as much as by the letter of the law.

The referee's authority goes beyond the confines of the pitch and the time-span of the game. Players have been booked for comments made in the car park after a game, and in the changing room before a game. The referee can caution managers and trainers. He judges the suitability of the pitch, the equipment and the players' apparel. Surveys show managers, teachers and lecturers to be the main professional groups among League referees.

It can be a hazardous occupation, with such ignominies as assault, kidnapping, and death at the hands of enraged spectators not unknown. All this is a far cry from the nineteenth century when players appealed, in the manner of cricketers, to the umpire (each team supplied one) officiating in the relevant half of the pitch. In the 1871 FA Cup a neutral referee was used to make decisions when the umpires could not agree. Gradually the referee's powers increased until in 1891, disputes having become wearingly common, he controlled the game from the pitch and the umpires helped from the touchlines, thus establishing the system

used today. Three years later the referee made decisions without waiting for players' appeals. Today's linesman is a fully qualified referee, but usually specialises; problems arise, as in the 1990 World Cup, when officials not used to running the line take on that duty. The diagonal system of refereeing was introduced after the Second World War to halve the distance covered by linesmen.

In addition to earning their FA badge, League officials have to pass a fitness test. (It is estimated that referees cover, on average, 7 miles in a match.) They also, despite the belief of partisan spectators, undergo an eyesight test. The age limit is 47 but an extension can be granted. Referees may be subject to assessment at any time as they carry out their duties. There are regular seminars and meetings as governing bodies seek to improve the officiating of matches.

In 1974 Englishman Jack Taylor became the first referee to award a penalty in a World Cup Final - almost as soon as the game started. In the same half he had to award one to the other side, West Germany, who beat Holland 2-1. His contemporary Clive Thomas, George Courtney and Gordon Hill are other British referees with great FA Cup and international experience. A prominent name from the past is Major Francis Marindin who played in two FA Cup Finals, refereed eight and retired as FA President in 1890.

REPUBLIC OF IRELAND

Organised football in the southern part of Ireland began in 1883 when the Dublin Association club was formed. From the earliest days, however, Irish soccer clubs have had to compete for spectator interest with rugby, hurling and gaelic football.

Ireland's persistent fight for freedom from British rule led to the formation of the Republic of Ireland (Eire) in December 1921. The six northern counties

remained part of the United Kingdom (Northern Ireland). One consequence of this split was the formation of the Football Association of Ireland (FAI). This was recognised by FIFA in August 1923 but opposed by the British FAs, especially the Irish Football Association (Northern Ireland). A temporary change of name, to the 'Football Association of the Irish Free State', helped appease the Northern Irish for a while, but it remained an issue until after the Second World War.

The Football League of Ireland began in 1921/22, and that season St James's Gate won the League and Cup double. This has since been achieved by Shamrock Rovers (six times), Bohemians, Cork United, Cork Athletic, Dundalk and Derry City. Shamrock Rovers' record number of Cup wins includes six in succession in the 1960s. Cork United won five League titles out of six in the 1940s - the League of Ireland continued throughout the war - and Shamrock Rovers won four on the trot from 1983/84 to 1986/87, taking their record of League wins to 14. The League has usually contained a dozen teams, a separate shield competition extending the season.

In 1985 the League was extended to two divisions - the Premier Division and the First Division. This led to the fascinating rise of Derry City, a team from Northern Ireland with a Catholic following. Derry had played in the Irish League in 1964/65, but now re-formed to join the Republic's First Division

REPUBLIC OF IRELAND Lansdowne Road, Dublin, venue for the Republic of Ireland's home matches. Despite its open nature, with only two covered sides, it can be a very intimidating ground for opponents. There's great support for the home team and also a great deal of humour on the terraces – providing the Irish are winning.

REPUBLIC OF IRELAND
No single goal can change the footballing fortunes of a nation, but Ray Houghton's headed winner in the Republic of Ireland's 1-0 defeat of England at the European Championships of 1988 was still very important. It seemed to give the team the belief and confidence to go on to greater things – most noticeably in qualifying for, and doing so well in, the 1990 World Cup finals. After their performance in West Germany (1988) and Italy (1990) it will be many years before they start a game as underdogs again. In this picture Sansom watches, Adams points and Aldridge prepares to celebrate.

across the border. This meant that Derry played all their away games in another country. They won promotion at the second attempt and two years later won a remarkable treble: the League of Ireland Championship, the FA of Ireland Cup and the League Cup.

Since 1957/58 Irish teams have competed in the three major European club competitions but have never got beyond the second round. Finn Harps have the unenviable record of losing one game 12-0, to Derby County in 1976.

One of the features of Irish soccer is that promising young players are quickly whisked away to the mainland. Some of the most famous post-war players in the Football and Scottish Leagues grew up in the Republic, men such as John Carey, Charlie Hurley, Johnny Giles, Tony Dunne, Noel Cantwell, Gerry Daly, Don Givens, Pat Bonner, Liam Brady, David O'Leary, Frank Stapleton and Ronnie Whelan, but between them they played very few Irish League games. Others, such as Alan Kelly, Paddy Mulligan and Mick Martin, won their first caps for Irish clubs before being quickly signed by English clubs, in their cases Preston North End, Chelsea and Manchester United. Over the years, Manchester United have signed more players from the Republic than any other British club.

Irish soccer received a boost in 1971, when a rule change allowed countries to field non-native players in the Republic, men such as internationals, providing that such players had an Irish parent and their native country had not claimed them first. The rule was later extended to include other close relatives, and more than 40 non-nationals have been adopted into the Irish team, including stalwarts like Tony Grealish, Mark Lawrenson, Mick McCarthy, John Aldridge, Andy Townsend and Ray Houghton.

REPUBLIC OF IRELAND TEAM

An international team representing the Republic of Ireland played its first games at the 1924 Olympic Games and reached the quarter-finals. On 21 September 1949 the Republic became the first country outside the United Kingdom to defeat England on English soil, winning 2-0 at Goodison Park, Everton. The team included nine players from English clubs and two from Shamrock Rovers.

The Republic of Ireland entered the World Cup qualifying competition as early as 1934, failing to qualify for the finals on goal average. In 1966 they lost 1-0 to Spain in a qualifying play-off, and in 1982 failed on goal difference after taking three points from World Cup runners-up Holland and beating France (who finished fourth in the competition). Success finally came in 1990, when Englishman Jack Charlton successfully managed the team through the qualifying group to the quarter-final of Italia '90. In Italy they drew four games - beating Romania in an exciting penalty shoot-out - before losing 1-0 to the hosts.

The Republic reached the quarter-finals of the European Championship as early as 1964 (when the tournament was known as the European Nations' Cup), losing heavily to Spain over two legs. Although always capable of producing a good result such as the 2-1 win in Czechoslovakia in 1967 and a 3-0 home win against USSR in 1974, the

Republic did not qualify for the last eight until Charlton's team in 1988. They began the European finals with a 1-0 win over England and drew with both USSR and Holland. The late Dutch equaliser stopped the Republic from reaching the semi-finals on goal difference.

RIVELINO, Roberto

1946 Born in Sao Paulo, Brazil

1964 First appearance for Corinthians

1968 International debut for Brazil, v Mexico

1970 Scores 3 goals in World Cup finals, helping Brazil to win the trophy for third time

1975 Signed for Fluminense

1978 Signed £4 million contract with Saudi-Arabian team Al-Ahly

Even among the most colourful collection of Brazilian footballers - the 1970 team that won the Jules Rimet Trophy for ever - Rivelino stood out. A small, moustachioed figure, his buccaneering style and flamboyant gestures seemed to be the essence of Latin American football and he was popular with the spectators, who loved to watch his long-range pots at goal, readily forgiving his wilder efforts. The Brazil team of that era was one of the most fluid, their intricate passing and switching runs around the penalty area resembling, at times, nothing so much as the exhibition teamwork of basketball entertainers The Harlem Globetrotters. Such a framework suited the Corinthian, as he alternated between left-wing and left of midfield. He was a superb passer of the ball, but will be best remembered for his shooting. Even by Brazilian standards he was an exceptional striker of the ball, whether in open play or from a free kick. He could swerve, bend or dip the ball like no one else, negating the opposition's defensive wall, and such was the ferocity of his shots

ROBERTO RIVELINO
Rivelino *(right)* holds off another world-class player Franz Beckenbauer in a 1972 friendly between West Germany and Brazil. These two countries now rate as the most successful in the World Cup. The club for which Rivelino played during the greater part of his career, Corinthians, took their name from the famous English club of the same name whose all-conquering tour of Brazil in 1910 fired the imagination of the public. In 1926 Corinthians Paulista, to give the Brazilian team their full name, had their own tour – of Europe – and lost only one match. Corinthian, as in Corinthian spirit, is also

used to describe the ideal ethics of amateurism as displayed by the footballers of that English team at the beginning of the century. It would be interesting to discover how many of today's Brazilian Corinthians are aware of that meaning. Originally, of course, Corinthian meant 'coming from Corinth in ancient Greece', that corner of the world and historical era being models for the public schoolboys who formed those amateur teams. Not a bad journey for one little word: from Greece to England to Brazil. It's not only players who get transferred across continents.

it is hard to believe that, on starting his career, he had to go on a special diet to build up his strength. Referees and opponents might be more inclined to recall the extravagant rolling he would indulge in when fouled in order to cross the 18-yard line and persuade the official to award a penalty instead of a free-kick.

Rivelino came to wide notice in the 1970 World Cup tournament with three goals - a feat he was to repeat four years later. The 1978 tournament, however, was a disappointment both personally and nationally, and precipitated his move to the Middle East. He won 120 caps - more even than Pele - but whether all of those matches truly merited full international status is often the subject of debate.

ROBSON, Bobby

1933 Born in Sacriston, County Durham

1950 Gives up job as apprentice electrician to sign for Fulham

1951 Makes senior debut as inside-forward

1956 Joins West Bromwich Albion for £25,000

1957 Wins first of 20 England caps, scoring twice in 4-0 Wembley defeat of France

1958 Plays in World Cup finals in Sweden, losing place to Peter Broadbent after two games

1960 England comeback, at wing-half, against Spain in Madrid

1962 August - returns to Craven Cottage for £20,000

1967 Gives up playing to become manager of Vancouver Royals

1968 Back to Fulham as manager; gets sacked after nine months and goes on dole

1969 Becomes boss of Ipswich Town

1978 East Anglians beat Arsenal to win FA Cup

1981 Leads his club to UEFA Cup triumph and second place in League

1982 Another runners-up spot for Ipswich, then Robson succeeds Ron Greenwood as England manager

1984 England fail to qualify for European Championship finals

1986 Robson's men reach World Cup quarter-finals, then fall victim to Maradona and the 'Hand of God'.

1988 The team flop in the European Championships, losing all three matches

1990 England ride their luck into the last four of the World Cup; Robson resigns to take over the Dutch club PSV Eindhoven

Bobby Robson's eight-year reign as England manager ended on a higher note than had seemed remotely likely to anyone who had

BOBBY ROBSON

Perhaps it is unkind to depict Bobby Robson, whose 1990 World Cup team did so much for English football and a nation's humour, in such a downcast pose. But for much of his career in charge of the national side he did seem to be a man with the weight of the world on his shoulders. Perhaps nobody can blame him; one national newspaper ran a campaign to sack him, while others were scarcely less encouraging. Robson's hangdog expression here comes at the nadir of his career, with England having lost 3-1 to the USSR in the 1988 European Championships, completing a run of three straight defeats in the competition.

followed the team's fortunes in the run-up to the 1990 World Cup. An exit at the semi-final stage - and then only by means of a penalty shoot-out - represented riches indeed for a man who had been hounded mercilessly by the press for several years.

He was accused of inept selection, an excess of tactical caution and a general failure to knit a collection of talented individuals - the likes of John Barnes, Gary Lineker, Glenn Hoddle - into a winning team. The vilification, much of which was cruel, hysterical or both, caused deep hurt to a sensitive, decent man who probably should have stepped down after his side's disastrous showing in the 1988 European Championships. Their subsequent improvement in the latter stages of Italia '90

came only after the pressure was lifted by fortunate victories over Cameroon and Belgium.

As a player Robson had been at his best as his country's midfield foil for Johnny Haynes in the early 1960s, while his managerial peak was at Ipswich where, had he had the resources to assemble a bigger squad, he might have lifted several League Championships.

ROBSON, Bryan

1957 Born in Chester-le-Street, County Durham

1974 Turns professional with West Bromwich Albion

1976 Suffers first of three broken legs in one season

1980 Wins first England cap, v Republic of Ireland at Wembley

1981 Joins Manchester United for £1.5 million,

becoming Britain's most expensive player

1982 June - scores against France just 27 seconds into England's World cup campaign in Spain; succeeds Ray Wilkins as captain of club and country

1983 Lifts the FA Cup after netting twice in replayed final against Brighton

1985 May - another FA Cup triumph, this time against Everton; Autumn - skippers United to 10 straight League wins at start of season; then sustains injury and 10-point lead disappears

1986 Dislocates collar-bone and pulls out of Mexico World Cup

1990 May - becomes first captain to collect FA Cup for third time, as Crystal

Palace are beaten in replay; June - injuries force Robson out of second successive World Cup

When Manchester United manager Ron Atkinson wondered how much he should offer for the signature of Bryan Robson, no less a soccer sage than Bill Shankly had no doubt: 'Pay whatever you have to, just make sure you get him'. As usual, the shrewd Scot was offering gilt-edged advice. Atkinson took it, and Robson went on to become, in the reckoning of most observers, the dominant British midfielder of the 1980s. A dynamo in defence, attack and all points between, he became a motivator supreme for the 'Red Devils' and England. At its peak the Robson game had no discernible weakness; his tackling, passing, shooting

BRYAN ROBSON

Bryan Robson is known for his wholehearted approach to the game, fearlessly and tirelessly chasing down every ball. It is the level of his skill, however, that sets him aside from other lesser players who, nonetheless, show the same commitment to their game. Here he tangles with the Aberdeen player Neil Simpson during the 0-0 draw between Scotland and England at Hampden in 1987. It's the weekly struggle for points in extremely competitive leagues that keeps British players among the most feared in international matches. Although some international teams may be ahead in technique, and even guile, they know that the British players will not be outplayed through a purely physical approach.

and heading were exemplary, he was quick and strong, and he read the game immaculately.

His sole bane was injury, which disrupted some of United's most promising campaigns as well as depriving England of their most inspirational figure. Some claimed he was too brave, but to ask him to hold back would have been to deny his nature and nullify his special talent. As he approached the end of his playing career, Robson was spoken of as a future manager, perhaps even at Old Trafford, where some saw him doing for United what Kenny Dalglish did for Liverpool. That would be a tall order, even for Captain Marvel.

ROCHDALE

Founded 1907

Joined League 1921 (Div. 3 N)

Honours None

Ground Spotland

Despite their tradition of travail as one of Lancashire's football minnows, Rochdale can claim one distinction which is unlikely to be equalled:

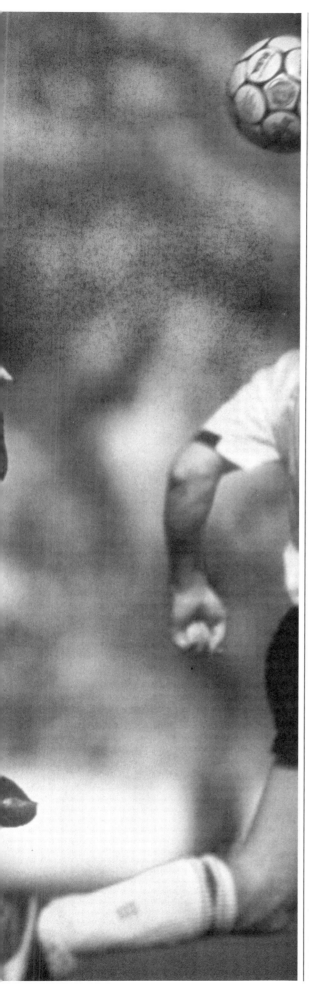

they are the only Fourth Division club to reach the final of a major competition. That was in 1962, when they contested the two-leg climax of the League Cup with Norwich City, losing 4-0 on aggregate. Admittedly, many top sides had not entered a competition which was still in its infancy, but it was nevertheless a remarkable achievement.

The Spotland club's League record, in contrast, has been wholly humble. After 38 years in Division 3 they were relegated in 1959, since when they have been promoted once, only to drop again. Their most promising period was in the mid 1920s, when three attempts to reach the Second Division ended in narrow failure.

In view of the local competition, Rochdale - managed for a spell in the 1950s by Harry Catterick who went on to success with Everton - have done well to survive for so long. Their finances were boosted in 1990 when they reached the last 16 of the FA Cup.

ROTHERHAM UNITED

Founded 1884

Joined League 1893 (Div. 2)

Honours Div. 3 (N) Champions 1951; Div. 3 Champions 1981; Div. 4 Champions 1989

Ground Millmoor

United, who took their current title when Rotherham Town and Rotherham County merged in 1925, have made a fair fist of surviving and, at times, prospering in the shadow of Sheffield.

Town spent three seasons in Division 2 but were not re-elected in 1896 and Rotherham's name did not appear in the League again until 1919, when County entered the same flight. After being relegated in 1923, the club was to spend nearly 30 years in the Third Division, despite spirited and narrowly unsuccessful efforts to gain promotion in the immediate post-war

years. They finally made it in 1951, a triumph which signalled the start of their finest era.

Under the management of former Millmoor stalwart Andy Smailes, and driven on by long-serving wing-half Danny Williams, United missed a Division 1 place on goal average in 1955. Though never coming so close again, they remained a solid member of the Second Division until 1968, and in 1961 reached the first final of the League Cup, losing on aggregate to Aston Villa.

Much commuting between divisions followed, with the Third being their usual berth. Notable former players include Dave Watson, who went on to become England's centre-half in the 1970s, and among big-name bosses have been Tommy Docherty and Emlyn Hughes.

ROUS, SIR Stanley

1896 Born in Norfolk

1934 Referees FA Cup Final between Manchester City and Portsmouth; succeeds Sir Frederick Wall as Football Association Secretary

1946 Plays prime role in promoting England's first national coaching scheme

1949 Receives knighthood in recognition of services to soccer

1962 Leaves FA post, becomes president of the International Federation of Football Associations

1974 Retires from FIFA

1986 Dies at the age of 91

Sir Stanley Rous stands unrivalled as the premier administrator - perhaps statesman would be a more apt description - in the history of world football. A tall, distinguished individual of immense personal presence, he was that rare being, an original thinker. Sir Stanley never progressed beyond village football as a player but he loved the game passionately, and his refereeing, which dovetailed neatly with his duties as a sportsmaster,

allowed him to keep in close touch with football at all levels.

One of his earliest innovations was the diagonal system of refereeing, a more efficient and logical way of doing the job than the traditional haphazard method, but it was later, in his roles of FA Secretary and FIFA president, that he exerted his greatest influence. Sir Stanley - along with his protege Walter Winterbottom, the first England team manager - was responsible for the introduction of organised coaching, which did much to change the face of the British game. He saw football on a global scale, encouraging the growth of European club competitions, urging the home countries to overcome their prejudices and enter the World Cup for the first time, and aiding the growth of the game in developing countries. How delighted he would have been to have witnessed the progress of Cameroon in 1990.

Sir Stanley Rous was a true visionary; how international soccer needs a figure of similar stature to guide the game into the new century.

ROWE, ARTHUR

1906 Born in Tottenham, London

1929 Turns professional with Spurs

1933 Plays major part in gaining promotion to First Division; December - wins sole England cap, against France at White Hart Lane

1935 Rowe's captaincy cannot avert relegation

1939 Cartilage operations end playing career; coaches in Hungary until outbreak of Second World War, then assumes control of British Army team

1945 Takes over at Chelmsford City, transforming them into one of the country's top non-League clubs

1949 Returns to White Hart Lane as manager

1950 Leads Spurs to Division 2 title...

1951 ...and then lifts the Championship for the first time in Tottenham's history

1955 Retires from the game due to ill health

1960 Makes comeback, as boss of Crystal Palace

1963 Steps down at Selhurst Park as Dick Graham moves in

1971 Takes control of Soccer Hall of Fame in London

Rowe was one of the major influences on British soccer in the post-war years. The clue to his success as an innovative manager with Tottenham Hotspur came in his playing days with the club; although a centre-half, he was never a mere stopper, employing a more constructive, thoughtful approach than most of his contemporaries.

When injury forced him to quit, Rowe took his expertise to Hungary, a nation which appreciated his reliance on skill. He was offered the job of managing the Magyars, but his ambitions in that direction were frustrated by the war.

ARTHUR ROWE
Picturing Arthur Rowe on the same page as Ian Rush serves to remind us that good passing has always been an important part of soccer. Rowe's sides outplayed opponents by virtue of this skill. Rush socres most of his goals by being on the end of intricate passing moves started by his Liverpool teammates.

Back at White Hart Lane, after a sojourn in the Southern League, he introduced his famous 'push and run' method, which involved quickfire 'wall passes' by all ten outfield players. Using the nucleus of the squad assembled by his predecessor Joe Hulme - his only expedition into the transfer market was to acquire the services of full-back Alf Ramsey - he brought unprecedented honours to the club. Some said he subsequently allowed his splendid side to grow old together, which is a matter for debate, but there is no doubting that Rowe - a man of intelligence and integrity, who worked himself into the ground - deserves his exalted place in the folklore of his beloved Spurs.

RUSH, Ian

1961 Born in St Asaph, Wales

1979 Turns professional with Chester

1980 April - signs for Liverpool in £300,000 deal; May - makes debut for Wales against Scotland at Hampden

1981 Picks up first of four consecutive League Cup winner's medals

1982 Helps the 'Reds' win

IAN RUSH Another goal celebrated by Ian Rush – but not just any goal. This one was his first, and Liverpool's second, in their 3-2 1989 FA Cup Final victory over Everton, delighting half a city and plunging the other half into gloom. Typically, it was scored after skilful shielding of the ball and a shot on the turn. Many of Rush's goals over the years have been scored from close in, without great power but perfectly timed and angled. Wherever he plays out the remainder of his career, Rush will always be remembered as a Liverpool player, particularly by Evertonians, against whom he makes a speciality of scoring.

first of four League titles in five years

1984 Takes part in European Cup Final victory over Roma

1986 Scores twice against Everton at Wembley as Liverpool secure the League FA Cup double

1987 Joins Juventus for £3.2 million

1988 Returns to Anfield at a slightly reduced fee

1989 Comes on as substitute to net twice as Liverpool beat Everton to win the FA Cup

1990 Returns to peak form as the Championship goes back to Anfield

Rush is a predator supreme. No one since the heyday of Jimmy Greaves and Denis Law has shown a more ruthless aptitude for finding the net. Throughout the 1980s - with the exception of one unhappy season in the Italian sun - he contributed an avalanche of goals to the Liverpool cause.

After taking a season to settle at Anfield, the lean, angular Welshman played a huge part in keeping his new club's trophy cabinet well stocked, at first forging a scintillating partnership with Kenny Dalglish, and later combining destructively with Peter Beardsley and John Barnes.

Rush's most obvious asset is speed, but he is also a delightfully crisp striker of the ball, boasts a finely-honed positional sense, and possesses more ball skills than he has been given credit for, although for a tall man he is not strong in the air.

On his return from Juventus, where he had suffered from a debilitating illness, he struggled for a time to find his form. When he succeeded, however, the Kop saw a more complete performer than ever before, a leader of the line who could shield the ball and create chances for colleagues, as well as adding to his own phenomenal tally, which by 1991 stood at more than 250 goals in fewer than 450 Liverpool outings.

ST JOHNSTONE

Founded 1884

Joined League 1911 (Div. 2)

Honours Scottish League Championship, First Division, 1983, 1990; Second Division, 1988; Division 2, 1924, 1960, 1963

Ground McDiarmid Park

Currently regarded as role models in Scottish football, St Johnstone have a new stadium (opened 1989) and a lively side.

Perth's population is only 50,000 but its club has often belied those limited resources. Under future Scotland manager Willie Ormond they were particularly unwelcome opposition, narrowly losing the League Cup final of 1969/70 and, in 1971, thrashing Hamburg 5-1 on aggregate in a UEFA Cup tie.

At one point in 1986 they were 38th and last in Scotland but manager Alex Totten has engineered a remarkable upsurge.

ST MIRREN

Founded 1877

Joined League 1890 (Div. 1 founder club)

Honours Scottish League Championship, First Division, 1977; Division 2, 1968; Scottish Cup, 1926, 1959, 1987

Ground Love Street

St Mirren's attainment of three Scottish Cups is a remarkable achievement. In 1926 they were to beat Celtic decisively in front of 100,000 at Hampden and the supporters hastened back to Paisley to watch footage of it all that same evening at the local cinema.

There was further work for cameras in 1959 when Aberdeen were beaten 3-1 in the Scottish Cup final. Their dynamic young manager Alex Ferguson succeeded in rousing the citizenry (often a problem for the club) in the late seventies with a precocious team. The impetus hasn't totally died away yet. One of Ferguson's proteges, Tony Fitzpatrick, later to manage the club, played in the 1987 final when St Mirren beat Dundee United to take their third Scottish Cup.

SALARIES

Professionalism was not recognised by the Football Association until 1885, but for almost ten years before this players had various financial arrangements with clubs.

From 1901 to 1961 clubs were bound to the Football League's maximum-wage rule. The weekly wage limit varied - £4 (1901), £5 (1910), £9 (1920), £8 (1922), £10 (1946), £12 (1947), £14 (1951), £15 (1953), £17 (1957) and £20 (1958) - but not all players could be paid the maximum, and the close-season maximum was a lower figure. In 1909 only one Barnsley player was paid the £4 maximum, two earned 70 shillings (£3.50) but the other first-teamers were paid between 50 shillings (£2.50) and £3 a week. The total wage bill for 23 players came to £57 10s (£57.50).

Richard Holt summarises the history of players' wages in *Sport and the British* (1989): 'Until very recently professional sportsmen have been regarded by directors as skilled workmen; footballers' incomes were not calculated in the same way as transfer fees according to market value but in relation to what other working-class men could expect to earn…. they were paid about double what a skilled man could expect for a fifty-hour week in return for working part-time at something they enjoyed.'

Clubs had the discretion to pay loyal players benefit money: a maximum of £750 for five years' and £1,000 for ten years' service in the post-war period. Top footballers always had the chance to supplement their earnings but the post-war advertising boom provided more opportunities, probably beginning with Denis Compton and the hair lotion called Brylcreem.

The late 1950s brought opportunities to earn higher salaries abroad, particularly in Italy. In England, pressure was put on the Football League to find ways of improving salaries. When the players threatened to strike - the proposed date was 21 January 1961 - the League agreed to a number of alterations, the most important of which was the removal of the maximum wage. This paved the way for salary rises and playing staff reductions. The Eastham case (1963) showed that clubs were in restraint of trade unless they permitted players a transfer, and even greater bargaining power for players came in April 1978, when the old retain-and-transfer system was replaced by freedom of contract.

In the year ending 31 May 1976, Manchester City had 13 employees earning 'emoluments' over £10,000. This was a top First Division club with eight internationals and 31 professionals. Seven years later the same club had 14 employees who earned over £20,000, including one in the £70,000 range. Stars' wages have continued to rise - in 1990 Derby County had 12 employees who earned over £50,000, including three £100,000 plus men - and today it is not unknown for a player to negotiate with the help of an accountant, a solicitor and an agent.

SANTOS, Nilton dos

1925 Born in Ilha do Governador, Brazil

1942 Joined Botafogo

1950 International debut v Uruguay

1958 Member of first Brazilian team to win World Cup

1962 Another World Cup medal - at the age of 37

When, in 1956, Santos was given the run-around by Stanley Matthews at Wembley in England's 4-2 victory, many felt that the left-back was getting too old for international soccer. Yet he kept his place in the victorious World Cup team two years later, demonstrating his attacking ability in the Final against Sweden, having scored against Austria in one of the earlier rounds. Such versatility was a hallmark of his style; strong on the ball, he and the other Santos, Djalma, his partner full-back, would augment the attack with their overlapping runs. The pair teamed up again in 1962 to help Brazil retain the trophy for another four years.

Santos was captain of Botafogo, the Rio de Janeiro club, and his disciplinary record was a good one; his dismissal in an ill-tempered match against Hungary in the 1954 World Cup must be counted as something of an aberration. The lengthy span of his service to the national team means that at various times he played alongside Ademir, Pinto and Julinho and the new generation of stars such as Amarildo and Pele.

SCHOEN, Helmut

1915 Born in Dresden

1932 Debut for Dresdner FC

1937 November – international debut v Sweden in which he scores twice

1940 Wins Cup medal for Dresdner FC

1941 Sweden are opponents again, this time in his last international appearance; Dresdner win the Cup again

1943 League Championship medal with Dresdner…

1944 …and again

1955 His playing days over, is appointed assistant national team manager under Sepp Herberger

1964 Becomes team manager on Herberger's retirement

1966 Takes West Germany to World Cup Final

1972 West Germany win European Championship

1974 World Cup victory

1976 West Germany lose European Championship to Czechoslovakia on penalty shoot-out

1978 Without Beckenbauer and Muller,

Schoen's inspiration dries up and West Germany do not get beyond first stage of World Cup finals; Schoen retires.

Schoen scored 17 goals in 16 appearances for Germany but, inevitably, his international career was interrupted by the war, and a knee injury brought his playing days as an inside-forward to a premature end. His background was, in fact, an academic one, and he became a foreign correspondent after the war, learning French and English. He first took up coaching at a regional level, in the Saar, before getting involved with the national squad.

Germany, and then West Germany, had been a significant force in international football since the 1930s, but their claim to supremacy in Europe began with Schoen's managership. Some of soccer's finest ever players came under the diffident manager's command; there was no lack of skill or application on the pitch and Schoen was able to develop a fluid system, trusting his players' maturity and footballing intelligence to steer them through games.

Franz Beckenbauer was to Schoen what Fritz Walter had been to Sepp Herberger, and it is unfortunate that they should have fallen out after the national team's debacle in the 1978 World Cup, in which the manager's inconsistency in team

HELMUT SCHOEN The mild-mannered West German team manager raises the new World Cup trophy in 1974, the highlight of his managerial career and a just reward for years spent in building a top-class team. You would have to look to another continent, South America, to find a manager, in the shape of Argentina's Cesar Menotti, with as long and successful a career as Helmut Schoen's. Menotti took over at Uruguayan club Penarol in 1990.

selection and tactics exposed his confusion. It is equally unfortunate that Schoen's retirement should be associated with defeat. He had brought together a splendid side to conquer Europe in 1972, and his 1974 World Cup-winning team, drawn largely from Bayern Munich, showed great character and resilience. Schoen had made changes throughout that tournament, like a mechanic tinkering with a Formula 1 engine; he unveiled a finely tuned machine when it mattered – in the Final.

SCHOOLBOY FOOTBALL

There are more children playing football regularly in Britain than there are adults. The growth and development of schools' football in England is linked largely with the English Schools' Football Association, acknowledged as the largest movement of its kind in the world. Similar programmes are provided by the Schools' Football Associations of Scotland, Wales and Northern Ireland.

Founded in 1904, the English Schools' FA has 468 member organisations, the 44 County Schools' Football Associations being subdivided into Area Associations. Some associations organise football for pupils of all ages (9-19), while others cater for either secondary-school pupils or pupils at primary and middle schools. All associations field representative teams, organise coaching and arrange league and cup competitions for schoolboys at different age levels. Nearly 14,000 schools are affiliated.

The English Schools' FA organises six national competitions. The oldest is the inter-association trophy for under-15s, which began in 1905. The most successful associations are Liverpool (12 wins), Sheffield (8), Manchester (7), Swansea (5), West Ham (4), Barnsley (3), Middlesbrough (3) and Sunderland (3). There are also national county

SCHOOLBOY FOOTBALL

Keeping his eye on the ball in prescribed fashion, a young Kenny Sansom of England chases Vogt of West Germany in a schoolboy international at Wembley in 1974. Sansom went on to win nearly 100 caps for the full international side as a full-back, winning his first as a Crystal Palace player five years after this match was played.

championships and individual schools' competitions at under-19 and under-16 levels, and, finally, the ESFA-Smith's Crisps 6-a-side Cup. This is the largest competition of its kind in the world. Almost 9000 primary schools enter, and the semi-finals and final are played at Wembley Stadium.

Internationals are played at under-15 and under-18 levels, and the four home countries compete for the Victory Shield. The two annual under-15 games played at Wembley attract crowds of up to 60,000. In 1959 Martin Peters (England) and Wolfgang Overath (West Germany) were Wembley opponents in a schoolboy international. Seven years later they met again in the same stadium in the World Cup Final.

Football authorities combine to promote festivals, coaching courses and award schemes, and every year 15 or 16 14-year-olds are selected to attend the Football Association School of Excellence at Lilleshall. Promising players can link with professional clubs as 'associate schoolboys' when they reach the age of 14. Many schoolboys also represent county FAs in youth competitions, in particular the FA County Youth Challenge Cup.

SCOTLAND

In the mid-1800s, chasing and kicking a football took over from caber-tossing as the major leisure interest of men in the Highlands. The 1860s Glasgow building boom spread this football interest to the Lowlands,

and on 9 July 1867 Queen's Park Football Club was formed. For the first two years it was almost impossible to find opponents, and the score of an 1869 game against Hamilton – Queen's Park won by four goals and nine touchdowns – shows that soccer was still evolving.

The first professional footballers were Scots. John Lang and Peter Andrews moved south from Glasgow to Sheffield in 1876 for the specific purpose of earning money. The Scottish FA, however, held out against legalising professionalism until 1893. As in England, though, players were paid for some years before professionalism was officially recognised.

Queen's Park dominated the early years of Scottish football, with 10 Scottish Cup wins in the first 20 seasons of the trophy (1873-93), but slipped away as a twentieth century competitive force by remaining loyal to the amateur ethic. Their touch of class has been maintained by their presence at Hampden Park, Scotland's major stadium, opened by Queen's Park in 1903.

The history of professional soccer in Scotland became dominated by the two big Glasgow clubs, Celtic and Rangers, nicknamed the 'Old Firm'. Rangers made their first appearance in a Scottish Cup Final in 1879 but failed to turn up for the replay with Vale of Leven after being incensed at a decision in the first game. Celtic were formed later (1887) and, more importantly, from a Catholic background. Religion became an omnipresent conflict between the Old Firm. In recent years, however, the fervently Protestant Rangers have departed from their policy of not signing Catholics, the most controversial acquisition being the ex-Celtic player Maurice Johnston for £1.5 million in July 1989.

Celtic had the edge in the period before the First World War, but Rangers won the Scottish League in 15 out of the 20 inter-war seasons. This was during the heyday of players such as Alan Morton, Davie Meiklejohn and Bob McPhail. In 1931 Celtic goalkeeper John Thomson was accidentally fatally injured when diving at the feet of a Rangers player during a game at Ibrox.

The dominance of Rangers continued after the Second World War when Jock Shaw captained a team known for 'iron curtain' defenders like George Young and Willie Woodburn. Rangers won the greater share of silverware in the first 20 post-war years. Then came Jock Stein's great Celtic team which took nine successive Scottish League Championships. In 1967 Celtic became the first British team to win the European Cup, beating Internazionale 2-1. The team that day was Simpson, Craig, Gemmell, Murdoch, McNeill, Clark, Johnstone, Wallace, Chalmers, Auld and Lennox. In the midst of Celtic's greatest consistent League success, Rangers also had to endure the tragedy of the 1971 Ibrox disaster, which took 66 lives.

There were occasional interruptions to the strangle-hold of Rangers and Celtic. Hibernian produced a great team in the immediate post-war period, winning the League three times with their 'Famous Five' forward line of Gordon Smith, Bobby Johnstone, Lawrie Reilly, Eddie Turnbull and Willie Ormond. East Fife won both the Scottish Cup (1938) and the League Cup (1947/48) as a Second Division team; Aberdeen, Hearts and Kilmarnock all came through to win the League in the late 1950s or early 1960s; and Partick Thistle surprisingly smacked four early goals past Celtic in the 1972 League Cup Final.

But the removal of the maximum wage in England encouraged more Scottish players to move south in the 1960s. Only Rangers and Celtic were able to hold on to star players, and then only some of them. Indeed, the history of the English Football League is also the history of Scottish footballers.

The 1980s brought another eastern challenge to the Old Firm. In that decade, Aberdeen won the League Championship three times, the Scottish Cup four times and the League Cup twice. Central defenders Alex McLeish and Willie Miller were particularly important to that success. In 1982/83 they emulated Rangers in 1971/72 by winning the European Cup Winners' Cup, beating Real Madrid 2-1 after extra time. In 1986/87 Dundee United became the first Scottish club to reach the UEFA Cup Final, losing 2-1 on aggregate to Gothenburg. But after Hearts had failed on goal difference to win the League in 1985/86, the next run of League champions had a familiar ring: Celtic, Rangers, Celtic, Rangers and Rangers. The traditional Scotland-England exodus was now reversed. Star Englishmen such as Terry Butcher, Trevor Steven and Chris Woods moved north of the border to Rangers.

Football is one of the few remaining ways that Scotland can show it is not consumed by its British political identity. Scottish football retains its legacy of passion, pride and skill, and yet, during the 1980s, Scottish supporters behaved far better than their English counterparts.

There is much more to Scottish football than Scottish League clubs and internationals. The Highland League has existed since 1893, and 'Junior' football has always been a rich source of talent for the English game. And if you ever wish to rediscover the roots of soccer, walk across Glasgow Green on a fine spring evening. You will see all kinds of football games, a reminder of where the world's first professional soccer players learned their trade.

SCOTLAND NATIONAL TEAM

After the world's first international match –

Scotland v England in 1872 – the early years belonged to Scotland, who lost only one of 31 internationals between 8 March 1873 and 17 March 1888. The decline in the early 1890s was largely self-inflicted since professional Anglo-Scots were outlawed by the Scottish FA.

The Scots dominated British internationals again in the 1920s, culminating in a superb exhibition by the 'Wembley Wizards' in 1928 when England were beaten 5-1. Captained by Jimmy McMullan, the team became a legend, in particular the forward-line of Jackson, Dunn, Gallacher, James and Morton. But Scottish stars were again lured to England, there were difficulties obtaining releases for internationals, and Scotland slumped in the 1930s.

In the immediate post-war period, Scotland, like England, were faced with improving sides from mainland Europe. Slow to react to World Cup opportunities – Scotland qualified in 1950 but did not attend the finals – no impact was made until the 1974 World Cup, when Scotland started an incredible run of playing through five successive World Cup qualifying tournaments. Managed by Willie Ormond, the 1974 team was one of Scotland's finest, boasting players of the calibre of Bremner, Law, McGrain, Hay, Dalglish and Lorimer. Although unbeaten, they failed to qualify for the second stage of the finals in West Germany.

There were also near misses in the World Cup finals in 1978 (when Ally

SCOTLAND The Scottish national team in 1897 looking stern and determined before their match with England: *(back row, left to right)* **Smith, Patrick, Mr Aitkin (trainer), Bell, Hyslop, Mr McDowall (SFA secretary), Allan, Wilson; Mr Crichton (SFA president), Cowan, Miller, Lambie, Doyle, Gibson, Mr McKenzie (SFA vice-president). Like all Scottish teams before and since, beating England seemed to be their most important ambition in football. It's easy to believe that this picture was taken after the event, as England won the encounter 4-0 at Sheffield. Of the Scottish players on view, four played their football in England.**

McLeod's team came unstuck against Peru and Iran), in 1982 (when Jock Stein's men went out on goal difference), in 1986 (when a team under the temporary charge of Alex Ferguson failed to beat 10-man Uruguay) and in 1990 (when Andy Roxburgh's team were eliminated by a late Brazilian goal).

Some memorable performances include post-war wins against England at Wembley in 1963 (2-1) and 1967 (3-2), and against Italy (1-0 in 1965), Holland (3-2 in 1978), Spain (3-1 in 1984) and Sweden (2-1 in 1990). Kenny Dalglish is the only player to have appeared in over 100 internationals, and Dalglish and Denis Law have scored most goals for their country (30 apiece).

SCOTTISH CUP

In 1873, 15 clubs subscribed towards the purchase of the Scottish Cup. The trophy and a set of medals cost £56 12s 11d. An 1885 game – Arbroath 36 Bon Accord 0 – remains a record. Celtic (29) and Rangers (24) have won the trophy the most times, but Aberdeen won four in five seasons in the 1980s. Bob McPhail (Airdrie and Rangers), Jimmy McMenemy (Celtic and Partick Thistle) and Billy McNeill (Celtic) all won seven Scottish Cup Winner's medals. Bobby Lennox (Celtic) won eight, but two were as a non-playing substitute. A history of the Scottish Cup, *100 Cups*, was written by Hugh Keevins and Kevin McCarra.

SCOTTISH CUP

Year	Winners	Runners-up	Score
1874	Queen's Park	Clydesdale	2-0
1875	Queen's Park	Renton	3-0
1876	Queen's Park	Third Lanark	2-0 after 1-1 draw
1877	Vale of Leven	Rangers	3-2 after 0-0 and 1-1 draw
1878	Vale of Leven	Third Lanark	1-0
1879	Vale of Leven	Rangers	1-1***
1880	Queen's Park	Thornlibank	3-0
1881	Queen's Park	Dumbarton	3-1
1882	Queen's Park	Dumbarton	4-1 after 2-2 draw
1883	Dumbarton	Vale of Leven	2-1 after 2-2 draw
1884	Queen's Park	Vale of Leven	****
1885	Renton	Vale of Leven	3-1 after 0-0 draw
1886	Queen's Park	Renton	3-1
1887	Hibernian	Dumbarton	2-1
1888	Renton	Cambuslang	6-1
1889	Third Lanark	Celtic	2-1
1890	Queen's Park	Vale of Leven	2-1 after 1-1 draw
1891	Hearts	Dumbarton	1-0
1892	Celtic	Queen's Park	5-1
1893	Queen's Park	Celtic	2-1
1894	Rangers	Celtic	3-1
1895	St Bernards	Renton	2-1
1896	Hearts	Hibernian	3-1
1897	Rangers	Dumbarton	5-1
1898	Rangers	Kilmarnock	2-0
1899	Celtic	Rangers	2-0
1900	Celtic	Queen's Park	4-3
1901	Hearts	Celtic	4-3
1902	Hibernian	Celtic	1-0
1903	Rangers	Hearts	2-0 after 1-1 and 0-0 draws
1904	Celtic	Rangers	3-2
1905	Third Lanark	Rangers	3-1 after 0-0 draw
1906	Hearts	Third Lanark	1-0
1907	Celtic	Hearts	3-0
1908	Celtic	St Mirren	5-1
1909	Cup witheld after riots;		Rangers v Celtic final
1910	Dundee	Clyde	2-1 after 2-2 and 0-0 draws
1911	Celtic	Hamilton Academical	2-0 after 0-0 draw
1912	Celtic	Clyde	2-0
1913	Falkirk	Raith Rovers	2-0
1914	Celtic	Hibernian	4-1 after 0-0 draw
1920	Kilmarnock	Albion Rovers	3-2
1921	Partick Thistle	Rangers	1-0
1922	Morton	Rangers	1-0
1923	Celtic	Hibernian	1-0
1924	Airdrieonians	Hibernian	2-0
1925	Celtic	Dundee	2-1
1926	St Mirren	Celtic	2-0
1927	Celtic	East Fife	3-1

1928	Rangers	Celtic	4-0
1929	Kilmarnock	Rangers	2-0
1930	Rangers	Partick Thistle	2-1 after 0-0 draw
1931	Celtic	Motherwell	4-2 after 2-2 draw
1932	Rangers	Kilmarnock	3-0 after 1-1 draw
1933	Celtic	Motherwell	1-0
1934	Rangers	St Mirren	5-0
1935	Rangers	Hamilton Academical	2-1
1936	Rangers	Third Lanark	1-0
1937	Celtic	Aberdeen	2-1
1938	East Fife	Kilmarnock	4-2 after 1-1 draw
1939	Clyde	Motherwell	4-0
1947	Aberdeen	Hibernian	2-1
1948	Rangers	Morton	1-0 after 1-1 draw
1949	Rangers	Clyde	4-1
1950	Rangers	East Fife	3-0
1951	Celtic	Motherwell	1-0
1952	Motherwell	Dundee	4-0
1953	Rangers	Aberdeen	1-0 after 1-1 draw
1954	Celtic	Aberdeen	2-1
1955	Clyde	Celtic	1-0 after 1-1 draw
1956	Hearts	Celtic	3-1
1957	Falkirk	Kilmarnock	2-1 after 1-1 draw
1958	Clyde	Hibernian	1-0
1959	St Mirren	Aberdeen	3-1
1960	Rangers	Kilmarnock	2-0
1961	Dunfermline Athletic	Celtic	2-0 after 0-0 draw
1962	Rangers	St Mirren	2-0
1963	Rangers	Celtic	3-0 after 1-1 draw
1964	Rangers	Dundee	3-1
1965	Celtic	Dunfermline Athletic	3-2
1966	Rangers	Celtic	1-0 after 0-0 draw
1967	Celtic	Aberdeen	2-0
1968	Dunfermline Athletic	Hearts	3-1
1969	Celtic	Rangers	4-0
1970	Aberdeen	Celtic	3-1
1971	Celtic	Rangers	2-1 after 1-1 draw
1972	Celtic	Hibernian	6-1
1973	Rangers	Celtic	3-2
1974	Celtic	Dundee United	3-0
1975	Celtic	Airdrieonians	3-1
1976	Rangers	Hearts	3-1
1977	Celtic	Rangers	1-0
1978	Rangers	Aberdeen	2-1
1979	Rangers	Hibernian	3-2 after 0-0 and 0-0 draws*
1980	Celtic	Rangers	1-0*
1981	Rangers	Dundee United	4-1 after 0-0 draw
1982	Aberdeen	Rangers	4-1*
1983	Aberdeen	Rangers	1-0*
1984	Aberdeen	Celtic	2-1*
1985	Celtic	Dundee United	2-1
1986	Aberdeen	Hearts	3-0
1987	St Mirren	Dundee United	1-0*
1988	Celtic	Dundee United	2-1
1989	Celtic	Rangers	1-0
1990	Aberdeen	Celtic	0-0**
1991	Motherwell	Dundee United	4-3*

* after extra time
** after extra time and penalties
*** Vale of Leven awarded Cup; Rangers missed replay
**** Queen's Park awarded cup; Vale of Leven did not appear

SCOTTISH FOOTBALL ASSOCIATION

The Scottish Football Association was formed at Dewar's Hotel, Glasgow, on 13 March 1873. Representatives of eight clubs were present at the meeting: Clydesdale, Dumbreck, Eastern, Granville, Queen's Park, Rovers, Third Lanark and Vale of Leven; Kilmarnock had also pledged support. The centenary was celebrated in 1973 with a Hampden Park game against England.

Scotland had no international team manager for much of the 1950s but the World Cup qualifying successes in the 1970s and 1980s owed much to administration and commercial sense. The Scottish FA also launched a Travel Club in the early 1980s.

SCOTTISH LEAGUE

The Scottish League was formed in 1890 with 11 founder members: Abercorn, Celtic, Cowlairs, Cambuslang, Dumbarton, Hearts, Rangers, St Mirren, Renton, Third Lanark and Vale of Leven. Unlike the English League, the clubs were still bound to amateur status. Renton were banned by the Scottish FA after only five League matches; their crime was playing against a club convicted of profes-sionalism.

Division 2 was formed in 1893 and re-formed in 1921 after a gap of seven years. Automatic promotion and relegation was also introduced in 1921. Division 3 was formed in 1923 but did not complete its third season, although a Third Division reappeared between 1946 and 1955.

In 1975 the modern-day structure was introduced – a 10-club Premier Division, Division 1 and Division 2. Premier Division clubs now play each other four times. Only 11 clubs have won the Scottish League, and only six of these have done so more than once: Rangers (40), Celtic (35), Aberdeen (4), Hearts (4), Hibernian (4) and Dumbarton (2).

SCOTTISH LEAGUE CHAMPIONSHIP

The Championship of the Scottish League from 1890/91 until 1974/75 was for the top team in the First Division. Since 1975/76 the title has been bestowed on the champions of the new Premier Division. Whatever the top division is called, the domination of Rangers and Celtic has been total. By 1991 Rangers had 40 wins (1 shared) and Celtic 35. Next nearest rivals are Aberdeen, Hearts and Hibernian on four titles apiece. There seems no end to the domination despite some periods of limited success from teams such as Aberdeen, Hearts and Dundee United in recent years.

SCOTTISH LEAGUE CHAMPIONSHIP

Year	Winners	Runners-up
1890/91	Dumbarton	Rangers
1891/92	Dumbarton	Celtic
1892/93	Celtic	Rangers
1893/94	Celtic	Hearts
1894/95	Hearts	Celtic
1895/96	Celtic	Rangers
1896/97	Hearts	Hibernian
1897/98	Celtic	Rangers
1898/99	Rangers	Hearts
1899/1900	Rangers	Celtic
1900/01	Rangers	Celtic
1901/02	Rangers	Celtic
1902/03	Hibernian	Dundee
1903/04	Third Lanark	Hearts
1904/05	Celtic	Rangers
1905/06	Celtic	Hearts

1906/07	Celtic	Dundee
1907/08	Celtic	Falkirk
1908/09	Celtic	Dundee
1909/10	Celtic	Falkirk
1910/11	Rangers	Aberdeen
1911/12	Rangers	Celtic
1912/13	Rangers	Celtic
1913/14	Celtic	Rangers
1914/15	Celtic	Hearts
1915/16	Celtic	Rangers
1916/17	Celtic	Morton
1917/18	Rangers	Celtic
1918/19	Celtic	Rangers
1919/20	Rangers	Celtic
1920/21	Rangers	Celtic
1921/22	Celtic	Rangers
1922/23	Rangers	Airdrieonians
1923/24	Rangers	Airdrieonians
1924/25	Rangers	Airdrieonians
1925/26	Celtic	Airdrieonians
1926/27	Rangers	Motherwell
1927/28	Rangers	Celtic
1928/29	Rangers	Celtic
1929/30	Rangers	Motherwell
1930/31	Rangers	Celtic
1931/32	Motherwell	Rangers
1932/33	Rangers	Motherwell
1933/34	Rangers	Motherwell
1934/35	Rangers	Celtic
1935/36	Celtic	Rangers
1936/37	Rangers	Aberdeen
1937/38	Celtic	Hearts
1938/39	Rangers	Celtic
1946/47	Rangers	Hibernian
1947/48	Hibernian	Rangers
1948/49	Rangers	Dundee
1949/50	Rangers	Hibernian
1950/51	Hibernian	Rangers
1951/52	Hibernian	Rangers
1952/53	Rangers	Hibernian
1953/54	Celtic	Hearts
1954/55	Aberdeen	Celtic
1955/56	Rangers	Aberdeen
1956/57	Rangers	Hearts
1957/58	Hearts	Rangers
1958/59	Rangers	Hearts
1959/60	Hearts	Kilmarnock
1960/61	Rangers	Kilmarnock
1961/62	Dundee	Rangers
1962/63	Rangers	Kilmarnock
1963/64	Rangers	Kilmarnock
1964/65	Kilmarnock	Hearts
1965/66	Celtic	Rangers
1966/67	Celtic	Rangers
1967/68	Celtic	Rangers
1968/69	Celtic	Rangers
1969/70	Celtic	Rangers
1970/71	Celtic	Aberdeen
1971/72	Celtic	Aberdeen
1972/73	Celtic	Rangers

1973/74	Celtic	Hibernian
1974/75	Rangers	Hibernian
1975/76	Rangers	Celtic
1976/77	Celtic	Rangers
1977/78	Rangers	Aberdeen
1978/79	Celtic	Rangers
1979/80	Aberdeen	Celtic
1980/81	Celtic	Aberdeen
1981/82	Celtic	Aberdeen
1982/83	Dundee United	Celtic
1983/84	Aberdeen	Celtic
1984/85	Aberdeen	Celtic
1985/86	Celtic	Hearts
1986/87	Rangers	Celtic
1987/88	Celtic	Hearts
1988/89	Rangers	Aberdeen
1989/90	Rangers	Aberdeen
1990/91	Rangers	Aberdeen

SCOTTISH CUP FINAL
Hamish French of Dundee United hurdles the challenge of Luc Nijholt in the 1991 Scottish Cup Final. These two sides fought out an exciting final with United losing at this stage of the competition for the sixth time since 1974. Motherwell last won the Cup in 1952. There are many Scottish sides snapping at the heels of the giants, but they normally lack the resources to put up anything more than a sporadic challenge.

SCOTTISH LEAGUE CUP

The Scottish League Cup, known as the Skol Cup after its sponsors from 1984, has had a chequered existence since its inception following the Second World War. It had been played with qualifying groups before a knock-out phase (in its early years) and as a knock-out only competition. The final has been played both before Christmas, as in 1990 with the final in October, and at the end of the season. The finals have been decided on corners (1942/43 and (1943/44) and on penalties (1987/88). Today the trophy is accepted as a valid part of the Scottish 'treble' and, like much else in Scottish football, it has a history dominated by Rangers and Celtic like much of Scottish soccer.

SCOTTISH LEAGUE CUP

Year	Winners	Runners-up	Score
1946/47	Rangers	Aberdeen	4-0
1947/48	East Fife	Falkirk	4-1
		after 0-0 draw	
1948/49	Rangers	Raith Rovers	2-0
1949/50	East Fife	Dunfermline Athletic	3-0
1950/51	Motherwell	Hibernian	3-0
1951/52	Dundee	Rangers	3-2
1952/53	Dundee	Kilmarnock	2-0
1953/54	East Fife	Partick Thistle	3-2
1954/55	Hearts	Motherwell	4-2
1955/56	Aberdeen	St Mirren	2-1
1956/57	Celtic	Partick Thistle	3-0
		after 0-0 draw	
1957/58	Celtic	Rangers	7-1
1958/59	Hearts	Partick Thistle	5-1
1959/60	Hearts	Third Lanark	2-1
1960/61	Rangers	Kilmarnock	2-0
1961/62	Rangers	Hearts	3-1
		after 1-1 draw	
1962/63	Hearts	Kilmarnock	1-0
1963/64	Rangers	Morton	5-0
1964/65	Rangers	Celtic	2-1
1965/66	Celtic	Rangers	2-1
1966/67	Celtic	Rangers	1-0
1967/68	Celtic	Dundee	5-3
1968/69	Celtic	Hibernian	6-2
1969/70	Celtic	St Johnstone	1-0
1970/71	Rangers	Celtic	1-0
1971/72	Partick Thistle	Celtic	4-1
1972/73	Hibernian	Celtic	2-1
1973/74	Dundee	Celtic	1-0
1974/75	Celtic	Hibernian	6-3
1975/76	Rangers	Celtic	1-0
1976/77	Aberdeen	Celtic	2-1*
1977/78	Rangers	Celtic	2-1*
1978/79	Rangers	Aberdeen	2-1
1979/80	Dundee United	Aberdeen	3-0
		after 0-0 draw	
1980/81	Dundee United	Dundee	3-0
1981/82	Rangers	Dundee United	2-1
1982/83	Celtic	Rangers	2-1
1983/84	Rangers	Celtic	3-2*
1984/85	Rangers	Dundee United	1-0
1985/86	Aberdeen	Hibernian	3-0
1986/87	Rangers	Celtic	2-1
1987/88	Rangers	Aberdeen	3-3**
1988/89	Rangers	Aberdeen	3-2
1989/90	Aberdeen	Rangers	2-1*
1990/91	Rangers	Celtic	2-1*

* won on penalties   * after extra time

SCUNTHORPE UNITED

Founded 1899

Joined League 1950 (Div. 3 N)

Honours Div. 3 (N) Champions 1958

Ground Glanford Park

It was never going to be easy for a club based in a small Humberside steel town to make headway in the Football League, but Scunthorpe United have made plucky efforts, with occasional success.

The 'Iron' as their fans lovingly know them, consolidated their new-found status throughout the early and mid 1950s, with long-serving full-back and penalty-king Jackie Brownsword outstandingly consistent, before rising to the Second Division and then, in 1962, failing by two places to reach the First. Sadly for United, they were then forced by economic pressures to sell free-scoring centre-forward Barrie Thomas, and a decline set in which saw them in the basement by the end of the decade. Since then they have remained in the lower reaches, and have been best known for producing 'keeper Ray Clemence and forward Kevin Keegan, who were both to find fame with Liverpool.

Towards the end of the 1980s they left the Old Showground and entered a new era at Glanford Park, one of very few modern grounds in the Football League. Any quest for honours, however, was likely to be sublimated to the struggle for survival which faces most small clubs.

SEELER, Uwe

1936 Born in Germany

1952 Debut for SV Hamburg

1954 International debut v England at Wembley

1958 Plays in the first of his four World Cups

1966 Captains national team in the World Cup and makes his only appearance in a World Cup Final – West Germany lose to hosts England

1968 Captains SV Hamburg to Final of Cup Winners' Cup

1970 Captains West Germany in his last World Cup

Over four consecutive World Cup finals series Uwe Seeler played 21 games, scoring in each competition. He made 72 international appearances in all, captaining the national team for many of those games, and yet never won a major honour with West Germany, thus proving that football is indeed a fickle master. There have been many footballers, less consistent, less reliable and less dedicated, who can boast a fine collection of silverware. Seeler's rewards with SV Hamburg, a club he represented for 20 years, were – a few

UWE SEELER The 1974 World Cup in West Germany and a picture to treasure for the young lad in the middle; he is strolling between two of the greatest goal-scorers of all time. On his right shoulder is the guiding hand of Pelé, who is carrying the Jules Rimet Trophy, the original World Cup, which had been won outright by Brazil four years earlier. The new trophy is being carried by Uwe Seeler; sadly, he was never to hold either Cup as a player. He must have watched the tournament with mixed emotions. His country were winners but his days as an international were over and he witnessed younger men, some of them playing in their first World Cup, achieve what he had been unable to in four attempts.

domestic triumphs apart – equally meagre; at times he might have wondered at his decision not to join Internazionale when they offered £60,000 for him in 1961.

But there never was a more steadfast player than this stocky, hard-working striker. Early in 1965 an Achilles tendon injury threatened to end his career; in September of that year, still not fully recovered or match-fit, he turned out to play against Sweden in a World Cup qualifying round. His loyalty and courage were never in question, and the second of these qualities, a vital ingredient for any close-range goal-scorer, combined with his great acrobatic ability to produce an exciting footballer who could score from almost any position.

By the 1970 World Cup he had dropped to more of a midfield role, another instinctive and chunky striker by the name of Gerd Muller having earned a team place, and manager Helmut Schoen greatly valued his captain's contributions to tactical discussions. Two years later, victory in the European Championship initiated a period of German supremacy, but for Uwe Seeler it was too late.

SHACKLETON, Len

1922 Born in Bradford, Yorkshire

1936 Plays for England Schoolboys

1938 Joins the Arsenal ground staff but is rejected within a year

1939 Spends a year working with London Paper Mills

1940 Working for GEC, signs as a part-time professional for Bradford Park Avenue

1946 League debut for Bradford; moves to Newcastle United for £13,000 (the third biggest fee at the time) and scores six on Newcastle debut (13-0 v Newport County)

1948 Signs for Sunderland for a British record £20,000; wins first

England cap

1954 Recalled to the England team

Len Shackleton did not win a major medal, and he played only five England games (plus one wartime international), but his non-conformist flair made him one of soccer's greatest entertainers. His type of individualism is now relegated to a bygone post-war era, surfacing only sporadically through the likes of Best, Marsh, Hoddle and Gascoigne.

An inside-forward, he could juggle the ball, deceive defenders and turn a game with an unorthodox move. In six wartime seasons he scored over 160 goals for Bradford Park Avenue. But he could also frustrate team-mates, and England selectors considered him too individualistic. Overlooked for five years, he was recalled for two England games in 1954, when he was 32 years old. Against West Germany – World Cup winners but under strength – he graced Wembley with a typical 'Shack' goal, tricking two defenders and coolly chipping the ball over the goalkeeper's head.

Shackleton was contemptuous of authority. His nickname, the 'Clown Prince of Soccer', was also the title of his autobiography. Chapter 9 entitled 'The average director's knowledge of football', consisted of one blank page. Len later became a sports journalist in the north-east.

SHANKLY, Bill

1913 Born in mining village of Glenbuck, Ayrshire

1927 Leaves school for job in local pit

1929 Signs for Carlisle United

1933 Joins Preston North End

1938 Wins first of 5 caps as Scotland beat England at Wembley; helps Preston win the FA Cup

1949 Quits playing to become Carlisle United boss

1951 Takes managerial reins of Grimsby Town

1953 Workington are his new employers

(1956 Accepts managership of Huddersfield Town

1959 The Shankly era dawns at Anfield

1962 Leads Liverpool to Second Division title

1964 Wins League Championship

1965 'Reds' lift FA Cup for first time in their history

1966 Another League Championship

1973 Wins double of Championship and UEFA Cup

1974 FA Cup triumph, and retirement

1981 Dies of heart attack

Shankly was the messiah-like figure who transformed Liverpool from a slumbering mass of unfulfilled potential into a soccer institution revered throughout the world. When he breezed into Anfield in 1959 his managerial credentials were not especially impressive, yet he exuded enthusiasm and a burning desire for success, and it was not long before the Reds were on the move.

He quickly assessed the merits of his inherited squad and found that many players were simply not up to the task of lifting the club out of Division 2, let alone winning the glittering prizes on which he had set his heart. Accordingly he discarded many, retained a few gems, and crossed the Scottish border to sign the

BILL SHANKLY
A photograph of Bill Shankly as he's best remembered. This picture of the great football character was taken as he lined up in a team photograph for Preston North End – the last club for whom he played before beginning his managerial career. Although young, the Shankly stare is there; you'd better not waste the ball or he'd never pass it to you again.

two men around whom he would build his first great side. Having secured centre-forward Ian St John and stopper Ron Yeats, Shankly embarked on the glory trail which brought a hat-trick of major trophies to Anfield in the mid 1960s.

Towards the end of the decade he began breaking up the side, going on to construct another in which Kevin Keegan was a vital constituent. Further triumphs followed, and it was a major surprise when he announced his retirement, a decision which, perhaps, he came to regret as he witnessed the subsequent runaway success of Bob Paisley.

But no one could take away from Shankly – as famous for his scything wit and utter devotion to the club as his actual achievements – the fact that it was he who had made it all possible. He will go down as one of the truly great soccer managers.

SHEFFIELD UNITED

Founded 1889

Joined League 1892 (Div. 2)

Honours Div. 1 Champions 1898; Div. 2 Champions 1953; Div. 4 Champions 1982; FA Cup Winners 1899, 1902, 1915, 1925

Ground Bramall Lane

Apart from one spell stretching from the reign of Queen Victoria to the mid 1930s, Sheffield United have never quite managed to settle in the First Division. There have been five other stints but none

longer than seven years, and for much of their history the 'Blades' have languished in the shadow of the more glamorous Sheffield Wednesday.

United owe their existence to Yorkshire Cricket Club, who introduced soccer to Bramall Lane to keep their players fit during the winter. Their first season ended with promotion to the top flight, and then began their golden era. In

SHEFFIELD UNITED The history of football in England is tightly bound up with the social development of the nation's northern industrial regions. Because football had a great working-class following, and later because of the north *versus* south rivalry, clubs from Yorkshire, Lancashire and the north-east have provided rallying points for support and sources of pride for local communities. Sheffield United's badge displays the date of their birth, the white rose of Yorkshire and the blades reflecting the city's past domination of the cutlery business – all emblems guaranteed to inspire the club's large following.

six years around the turn of the century, the Blades appeared in three FA Cup Finals (winning two), lifted one League Championship and twice finished as runners-up in the title race. Stars of the day included 22-stone goalkeeper William 'Fatty' Foulke and wing-half Ernest 'Nudger' Needham, so nicknamed for his tackling expertise.

Even after the decline of that vintage combination, United continued in relative prosperity. Twice more they won the FA Cup and by the 1920s could field a useful team which included Irish international inside-forward Billy Gillespie and marksman Harry Johnson. But the rot set in; United were relegated in 1934, and then they proceeded to switch regularly between the top two divisions until they slumped to the Third in 1979 and the Fourth two years later. Since then they have recovered to remind themselves what life was like among the elite, but have failed to create an impression of permanence at that exalted level.

Outstanding players down the years have been schemer Jimmy Hagan in the 1940s and 1950s, goalkeeper Alan Hodgkinson and unrelated defenders Joe and Graham Shaw (1950s and 1960s), forwards Mick Jones and Alan Birchenall (both sold to raise much-needed cash in the 1960s), and England play-maker Tony Currie, winger Alan Woodward and defender Len Badger (1960s and 1970s). Among influential managers have been Joe Mercer, John Harris and Dave Bassett.

SHEFFIELD WEDNESDAY

Founded 1867

Joined League 1892 (Div. 2)

Honours Div. 1 Champions 1903, 1904, 1929, 1930; Div. 2 Champions 1900, 1926, 1952, 1956, 1959; FA Cup Winners 1896, 1907, 1935; League Cup Winners 1991

Ground Hillsborough

Sheffield Wednesday are a

big-city club with a sumptuous stadium, yet somehow they have failed to fulfil their potential as one of the superpowers of British soccer.

The 'Owls' early years betrayed few hints of future frustrations as they garnered a succession of honours around the turn of the century. But all too soon their successful combination, in which goal-scorer Andy Wilson was prominent, lost momentum and Wednesday were demoted after the First World War. Recovery was swift, however, as manager Bob Brown assembled the greatest side in the Owls' history, which won four trophies and starred inside-forward Jimmy Seed, winger Ellis Rimmer and full-back Ernie

SHEFFIELD WEDNESDAY Derek Dooley in a Sheffield Wednesday team picture during his short playing career with the Yorkshire club. Scoring 62 goals in 61 League appearances between 1949 and 1952 ensured Dooley's fame. For Wednesday the period was one of mixed fortunes: they were Division 2 runners-up (winning promotion) in 1949/50, only to be relegated from Division 1 a year later. This was followed by the Division 2 Championship in 1951/52 before relegation in 1954/55 followed by an immediate Division 2 Championship. They have won the Second Division title on five occasions in all.

Blenkinsop.

Sadly, a rapid decline set in and Wednesday were relegated in 1937, not rising again until 1950. That promotion set off a merry-go-round of despair and elation, encompassing three further demotions, each followed by an immediate return to the top flight, by the end of the decade. The idol of Hillsborough in the early 1950s was Derek Dooley, who scored 63 goals in as many senior games before his leg was amputated following an injury. But despite the efforts of Dooley, and those of inside-forwards Jackie Sewell, Redfern Froggatt and Albert Quixall, consistency eluded Wednesday until the early 1960s.

Then, with Harry Catterick taking over from Eric Taylor as team boss – the latter continued as general manager and was largely responsible for ambitious ground improvements – the Owls showed signs of new stature. In 1961, with major contributions from 'keeper Ron Springett, centre-half Peter Swan and wing-half Tony Kay, they were title runners-up, and even after Catterick's departure they remained a solid force.

But then Hillsborough was rocked by a bribes scandal involving Swan, Kay and David Layne, and morale was damaged. Losing the 1966 FA Cup Final did nothing to help and Wednesday began to slide, plumbing the hitherto unknown depths of Division 3 by 1975. The managerial efforts of Jack Charlton and Howard Wilkinson eventually restored Wednesday to the First Division before yet another relegation interrupted their progress in 1990. Under the guidance of Ron Atkinson, however, they won the League Cup and promotion in 1991, only to lose their new messiah to Aston Villa. New manager Trevor Francis has inherited a firm foundation for future success.

SHILTON, Peter

1949 Born in Leicester, September 18

1965 Wins English Schools Trophy (Under-15) with Leicester Boys and first of four England schoolboy caps

1966 Joins Leicester City on apprentice terms

1967 First team chance as Gordon Banks leaves Leicester

1969 FA Cup final defeat, 1-0, by Manchester City

1971 Second Division championship and first full England cap

1974 Transferred to Stoke City

1977 Transferred to Nottingham Forest under Brian Clough

1978 Wins League Championship and Players' Player of the Year award

1979 First of two successive European Cup final victories

1982 Transferred to Southampton

1987 Transferred to Derby County

1990 Following mixed form in the World Cup finals

PETER SHILTON

Peter Shilton, who made several understudies wait in the wings while compiling his record of 125 England caps, shown training with the last in line of heirs apparent, Chris Woods, the man who seemed most likely to take over the job following 'Shilts' international retirement in 1990. Shilton made a virtue out of hard training, although it didn't do him a lot of good on this occasion as England were preparing for the 1988 European Championships in which they played three, lost three and conceded seven goals.

he retires from international football with a record 125 England caps

1991 Derby County relegated to Second Division

Everything written about the young Peter Shilton suggests that there was nothing else in his life except soccer.

His years at Leicester, marked by impressive displays and continual improvement, were contrasted with a few unhappy years at Stoke. It was under Brian Clough at Nottingham Forest that he came into his own, making the England position safe and finding himself regularly acclaimed 'the best goalkeeper in the world'.

Throughout this career he has been noted for his professional approach to the game, with a harsh training regime matched with great attention to both goalkeeping theory and practice. Never noted for spectacular saves, his reputation has been built on a good reading of the game, an excellent understanding of angles and exceptional reflexes. With both Southampton and Derby he frequently found himself starring in an average side. It was really when he pulled on the England jersey that the stage seemed appropriate for this remarkable player.

It is thought that he may move into management when he finally decides that he has played enough, an area where determination and dedication are no guarantees of success.

SHREWSBURY TOWN

Founded 1866

Joined League 1950 (Div. 3 N)

Honours Div. 3 Champions 1979

Ground Gay Meadow

For a provincial, small-town club, rather isolated in deepest Shropshire, Shrewsbury Town have given a good account of themselves since becoming members of the

SHREWSBURY TOWN
A minor legend, Arthur Rowley scored 434 goals (a Football League record) in 619 League games of which 152 were scored while at Shrewsbury, the club where he finished his playing career in 1964. For a team like Shrewsbury such entries in the record books are rare – but they have one of the loveliest grounds in the Football League, which supporters enjoy visiting – although not always in cup competitions, where they have achieved some notable giant-killing acts.

Football League. After struggling to adjust to life in the Third Division throughout most of the 1950s, they found

themselves in the newly-created Fourth at the end of the decade. Lifted by the lethal marksmanship of Arthur Rowley – who became the highest goal-scorer in League history during his six-year playing stint at Gay Meadow – Shrewsbury rose again to spend the next 15 years back in the Third Division. There followed a second one-term spell at the bottom level before, in 1979, the Town ascended to the unheard-of eminence of the Second Division, where they remained for 10 campaigns, eventually slipping back to the Third.

They have often excelled in knock-out competition, winning the Welsh Cup six times, reaching FA Cup quarter-finals in 1979 and 1982, and going one stage further in the 1961 League Cup.

SOUNESS, Graeme

1953 Born in Edinburgh

1968 Scotland schoolboy international

1968 Joins Tottenham Hotspur as an apprentice

1970 FA Youth Cup winner's medal for Spurs

1973 Signs for Middlesbrough for £30,000

1974 Second Division Championship medal with Middlesbrough

1975 Wins first Scotland international cap

1978 Moves to Liverpool for £352,000 (a record for two English clubs); lays on Dalglish's winning goal in European Cup Final

1984 Scores only goal of Milk Cup Final to defeat Everton; moves to

Sampdoria (Italy) for £650,000

1986 Joins Rangers as player-manager

1991 Returns to Anfield as Liverpool manager

A hard, skilful Scot, Graeme Souness had one of the most successful careers of the 1970s and 1980s. He started with Spurs and in the four-game FA Youth Cup Final of 1970 he scored two goals and was sent off. Then he made his mark with Jack Charlton's Middlesbrough team before joining Liverpool. In a little over six years at Anfield he won five League Championship medals, three European Cup winner's medals and played in Liverpool's four successive League Cup Final victories (1981 to 1984), although he was absent from the 1981 replay which brought the trophy to Anfield for the first time. Altogether he played 352 first-class games for Liverpool, scoring 56 goals. He played 54 games for Scotland, half of them as captain. His internationals included Scotland's famous World Cup defeat of Holland (in Argentina in 1978) and he scored a brilliant individual goal against the Soviet Union in Spain four years later.

Souness had perfect poise when in possession of the ball, controlling games by accurate passing and fearsome tackling. He also had a strong shot which could bring vital goals, such

GRAEME SOUNESS In typically agitated mood, Graeme Souness (right) shouts directions to his Rangers players during their 2-0 defeat in Cologne, in the 1988/89 UEFA Cup second round, first leg. They went on to lose the tie over the two legs. With Souness is assistant manager Walter Smith. Souness has produced a side capable of winning every domestic trophy, but did not succeed in Europe. No doubt Rangers fans are needled by the fact that Celtic remains the only Scottish name on the European Cup.

as the Milk Cup winner against Everton in 1984. But his aggression brought occasional trouble. He caused outrage when, in his autobiography *No Half Measures*, he admitted throwing a short right hook which broke Lica Movila's jaw during a European Cup game with Dinamo Bucharest.

When he returned to Scotland as Rangers' player-manager in 1986, it was in character that he was sent off in his first-ever Scottish League match. It was also typical that he

brought success to his new club: three League Championships in his first four seasons in charge, and three League Cup wins. Whether he will keep Liverpool supplied with silverware remains to be seen.

SOUTH AMERICA

Latin America followed hard on the heels of Europe in taking up football and establishing associations and competitions. The two continents have dominated the World Cup and the Olympic soccer

competition, exhibiting playing styles which have served as models throughout the rest of the world. South America is passionate about and dedicated to the game; at times the boundaries between enthusiasm, fanaticism and over-reaction become blurred, as do those between competitiveness and gamesmanship. Volatile or violent behaviour always seems a possibility when Latin Americans and football get together; but the brands of soccer on

display have enlivened and coloured the international scene and produced some of the world's greatest players.

The Brazilians, frequently described as the most natural footballing nation on earth, could easily have adopted basketball or baseball as their national sport. The first indigenous Brazilian club, the Mackenzie Athletic Association, found itself rebelling against faculty efforts to establish these North American sports as official games.

Although British sailors played matches among themselves in the coastal towns of Brazil, the introduction of soccer to the continent's largest country is credited to Charles Miller, born in Sao Paulo of English parentage. After a spell as an amateur with Southampton he returned to his native town in 1864 and began to organise matches. In 1902 the club Fluminese was founded in Rio de Janeiro; so it was that the two poles of Brazilian football were established, providing a rivalry which has not always been beneficial to the national team. The great World Cup teams of 1958-70 owed much to a fresh spirit of cooperation between the two geo-graphical centres which, despite the inauguration of a national championship in 1967, have maintained the regional competitions set up in the 1900s (an expedient system, given the size of Brazil).

Brazil's victory in the 1989 *Copa America* (South American Championship) was their first major trophy in 19 years. The decline of Brazilian football coincided with Pele's departure; the public still awaits new players to match his stature and that of Falcao, Tostao, Didi, Rivelino and Alberto. Experiments in the 1970s and 1980s with defence-based European tactics stifled the innate expressiveness of the players and the 1990 World Cup revealed a disappointing national team suffering from a footballing identity crisis, with natural flair and a systematic approach vying for the upper hand.

Argentina has the most convincing football pedigree in the continent, the first club, Buenos Aires FC, having been formed in 1865 by the British influx which also introduced polo and the railways. (About that time there were some 30,000 British nationals in the capital). Their Football Association was founded 30 years later and the game was given a boost by Italian immigrants after the First World War. The disgraceful exhibition by

SOUTH AMERICA The South American teams did not live up to expectations in Italia '90 and only occasionally did Brazil exhibit the flair which has made them every neutral spectator's favourite team. An outstanding individual did emerge, however, but from Argentina, not Brazil – Caniggia, seen here on the left getting to the ball before Brazil's Gomez, struck some wonderful goals and showed genuine interest in getting on with the business of playing world-class football. If only, some would say, the same could be written about his compatriots. The more cynical and negative aspects of South American football surfaced at times. Uruguay, not as physical as in previous tournaments, managed to reach the second round even though they conceded more goals than they scored. They then went out to Italy 2-0. Caniggia scored in the second-phase match from which this photo was taken when Maradona set him up after a rare exhibtion of the skills which had once had him acclaimed as the world's greatest player. That single goal put an end to Brazil's part in Italia '90. In addition to World Cup clashes such as this one, Brazil and Argentina frequently meet in the South American Championship and they play each other for the Rocca Cup. Also contested every two years are: Rio Branco Cup (Brazil v Uruguay); Bernardo O'Higgins Cup (Brazil v Chile); Oswaldo Cruz Cup (Brazil v Paraguay). And every year Argentina play Uruguay for the Thomas Lipton Cup.

the national team in the 1966 World Cup and their continued physical approach since have reinforced a poor image of Argentinian football which began with violent public demonstrations against the Argentinian FA prompted by World Cup failures in 1958 and 1962; the intimidating performances by their club sides in the World Club Championships of the 1960s and 1970s did little to dispel this reputation. It was not always thus; the elegance, artistry and sportsmanship of Argentinian football before the Second World war saw their players being sought by top European clubs. In the 1940s the centre-forward Adolfo Pedernera was as highly acclaimed as near-contemporary and Brazilian counterpart Artur Friedenreich.

The team of the late 1970s, inspired by Mario Kempes and Osvaldo Ardiles, stands out as worthy of future emulation. But the 1990 World Cup, with Maradona, arguably the preceding tournament's most exciting player, failing to find the net once, featured a lacklustre national side who many felt were fortunate to reach the Final.

The South American competitions have been dominated by teams from Argentina, Brazil and Uruguay - hosts (on the basis of their 1924 and 1928 Olympic football successes) and winners of the first World Cup in 1930. Uruguay is a relatively small country but it possesses a great footballing heart, typified by the successes of Penarol and Nacional in the South America Cup and the World Club Championship. After the late 1950s, however, the national team's game became imbued with cynicism and was characterised by temperamental outbursts and tackles whose legality no interpretation of the game's Laws could admit. The ultimate effect of this betrayal of the skill and spirit of early Uruguayan soccer was a dramatic slump in interest in the

domestic game after the 1986 World Cup. Victory in the following year's South American Championship, however, unveiled a new team and a fresh approach, and hopes for Uruguayan football have been revived.

In contrast to the three most successful nations in South America there stand Ecuador and Venezuela, countries which have made little footballing impact within the continent and virtually none outside it. Both set up their professional leagues late – 1957 – and in the case of Venezuela the game is second in popularity to baseball. The Brazilian international Jairzhino is the biggest name associated with Venezuelan football, signing as he did for top club Portuguesa Acarigua in 1977. Ecuador's best-known player, on the other hand, forged his career in Uruguay: Alberto Spencer played centre-forward for Penarol in the 1960s.

Chile's professional league dates from 1933 and its governing body from 1895, but its achievements are modest and the sport is rarely free from financial difficulties. It hosted the 1962 World Cup, widely regarded as the most disappointing post-war tournament, and took third place. Bolivia's record is equally undistinguished, its sole victory in the *Copa America* having been achieved at home, 3660 metres above sea level in 1963, and its few World Cup appearances having been largely colourless.

Peru and Paraguay, like Ecuador, have rarely been able to keep their best players, who have been easily tempted by the higher wages and bonuses offered by other South American clubs. This was particularly evident in the 1950s when football in both countries was going through a good phase. It was to be the same story twenty years later: Peru's goal-scoring forward Teofilo Cubillas was among those to leave for Europe after his country's creditable display in the 1970 World Cup, but he returned to his old club

Lima Alianza before demonstrating his long-range shooting in the 1978 competition. Paraguay's best player of recent times, Julio Cesar Romero, began the 1980s with New York Cosmos. In 1979 Paraguay had won the South American Championship and their top club Olimpia had won the South American Cup and the World Club Championship; but despite this high point in Paraguayan football, and his relative youth, the talented Romero chose to play in the NASL. Both countries have had intermittent success in the *Copa America* and have proved to be forces to reckon with in quite a few World Cups. It is tempting

to believe that a sounder economic background in both cases would provide serious rivals to the 'big three'.

Watching South American teams parading their skills in neat colourful kit, it is easy to forget that South America is still a continent beset with poverty and hampered by a tempestuous political tradition, and that it is in these difficult circumstances that soccer continues to thrive. Colombia's 1989/90 season neatly epitomises the paradox: the league competition was suspended because the game had become linked with the lucrative illegal cocaine trade and the laundering of drug money. In addition,

there were allegations of rigged results, and a referee was kidnapped. Meanwhile, Nacional Medellin became the first club from that country to win the South American Cup.

It was with a scandal that Colombian football first came to international attention: in 1950 a pirate league, operating without the approval of the Colombian FA or FIFA, poached top European and South American players without paying transfer fees. Di Stefano was the most famous name attracted by the higher wages, but the league soon disintegrated. Colombia's national side has become stronger in recent years but their performance in the

1990 World Cup didn't live up to expectations, their best player, Carlos Valderrama, failing to make his mark on the competition.

Most football associations in the continent have had their scandals and disruptions to deal with; but football survives as an intrinsic part of Latin American life and culture – and not just as an escape from poverty and the consequences of political instability. There is a strong middle-class following but it is a game appreciated by all sections of society, by both sexes and by all generations. It is impossible to imagine a future South America without soccer – or vice versa.

SOUTH AMERICAN CHAMPIONSHIP

South America's most important international competition has enjoyed a long but unsettled life. Falling attendances in the 1960s seemed to herald its demise but, after an eight-year hiatus, the competition was reorganised in 1979 to accommodate all of the 10 principal footballing nations; the league system was replaced by group tables and knock-out semi-finals and a final. The championship is now contested every four years; originally it was intended to be annual but after 1927 no regularity is discernible. There have always been gaps and – as if to

SOUTH AMERICA We don't have only old men's memories and scratchy photos like this to back up the stories of the delightful soccer played in South America in the first decade of this century. There is a good deal of film, shot mostly in Argentina, of training sessions and top-class games. Two things stand out from the footage. The first is the skilful control of the ball – remarkable when you consider the bulky, bulbous boots with inflexible toe-caps that were worn then, and the heavy laced ball. In building up an attack the player in possession would often stand still before deciding on his course of action, confident that he could dribble past any opponent who came near. The second thing which strikes the modern viewer is the bravery of the 'keepers who, at that time, could be shoulder-charged while catching the ball. They also had to dive at players' feet a good deal, as in this shot from the first ever World Cup Final in 1930, since many of the forwards liked to carry the ball as near to the goal as possible before shooting. Hector 'Manno' Castro of Uruguay is denied on this occasion by Argentina's Bottasso. Castro did find the net, though, in this game, and helped the home side to a 4-2 win and the first of their two World Cup victories.

compensate – extra-ordinary tournaments.

The infrequent appearance of Brazil's name in the roll of honour is striking; this is due in part to that country's absence from the tournament from 1923 to 1936 owing to disputes, but credit must also be given to the enduring strength of Argentinian and Uruguayan football.

Hosts, Chile were unable to participate in the 1991 Championship because of a FIFA ban.

SOUTH AMERICAN CHAMPIONSHIP

Year	Winners
1916	Uruguay
1917	Uruguay
1919	Brazil
1920	Uruguay
1921	Argentina
1922	Brazil
1923	Uruguay
1924	Uruguay
1925	Argentina
1926	Uruguay
1927	Argentina
1929	Argentina
1935*	Uruguay
1937	Argentina
1939	Peru
1941*	Argentina
1942	Uruguay
1945*	Argentina
1946*	Argentina
1947	Argentina
1949	Brazil
1953	Paraguay
1955	Argentina
1956*	Uruguay
1957	Argentina
1958	Argentina
1959*	Uruguay
1963	Bolivia
1967	Uruguay
1975	Peru
1979	Paraguay
1983	Uruguay
1987	Uruguay
1989*	Brazil

* extraordinary tournaments, cup not awarded

SOUTH AMERICAN CUP

The *Copa Libertadores*, first contested in 1960, was modelled on the European Cup. All rounds, including the final, are decided over two legs. As from 1966 two clubs from each of the ten main soccer nations have been invited to compete. The quality of the football has often been eclipsed by corruption, and violence on and off the field. Argentinian teams, Independiente and Estudiantes in particular, have had the greatest success in the competition.

SOUTH AMERICAN CUP

Year	Winners	Nation
1960	Penarol	Uruguay
1961	Penarol	Uruguay
1962	Santos	Brazil
1963	Santos	Brazil
1964	Independiente	Argentina
1965	Independiente	Argentina
1966	Penarol	Uruguay
1967	Racing Club	Argentina
1968	Estudiantes	Argentina
1969	Estudiantes	Argentina
1970	Estudiantes	Argentina
1971	Nacional	Uruguay
1972	Independiente	Argentina
1973	Independiente	Argentina
1974	Independiente	Argentina
1975	Independiente	Argentina
1976	Cruzeiro	Brazil
1977	Boca Juniors	Argentina
1978	Boca Juniors	Argentina
1979	Olimpia	Paraguay
1980	Nacional	Uruguay
1981	Flamengo	Brazil
1982	Penarol	Uruguay
1983	Gremio	Brazil
1984	Independiente	Argentina
1985	Argentinos Juniors	Argentina
1986	River Plate	Argentina
1987	Penarol	Uruguay
1988	Nacional	Uruguay
1989	Nacional	Uruguay
1990	Olimpia	Paraguay

SOUTHAMPTON

Founded 1885

Joined League 1920
(Div. 3, founder member)

Honours Div. 3 (S)
Champions 1922; Div. 3
Champions 1960; FA Cup
Winners 1976

Ground The Dell

After spending the bulk of their history as also-rans, Southampton have elbowed aside Portsmouth as the south coast's leading light and, against the odds for a provincial club, have emerged as a genuine force in British football.

Their early days, however, were not devoid of achievement. Formed as Southampton St Mary by a group of sporty church-goers – hence their enduring nickname of the 'Saints' – they were never cowed by the giants of the day and, while competing in the Southern League, reached the FA Cup Finals of 1900 and 1902. After entering the senior competition as founder members of Division 3, Southampton lost little time in gaining promotion as the Southern section's first champions, and remained in the Second until 1953.

Most of that sojourn was uneventful, but the immediate post-war years brought spirited bids to reach the top echelon, with the efforts of full-back Alf Ramsey and goal-scorer Charlie Wayman catching the eye. They never made it, instead dropping a level, and it was left to new manager Ted Bates – who was to remain at the helm until 1974 – to lead them back up in 1960, with the goals of Derek Reeves and George O'Brien playing a crucial part.

Boosted by the consistent excellence of winger Terry Paine, and the marksmanship of Martin Chivers, Ron Davies and Mick Channon, Bates built an impressively firm edifice and reached the First Division in 1966. There they remained for eight years before, with Lawrie McMenemy now in charge, they were relegated.

SOUTHAMPTON Many teams have a big day and then fade away again. Southampton's 'big day' came in 1976 when they beat Manchester United in the FA Cup Final, 1-0. After that victory, achieved as a Second Division side, they soon won promotion to the First and have been putting in consistently good performances ever since, rarely threatening to win the title but always dangerous and attractive to watch. Making sure that the momentum was not lost was shrewd and affable manager Lawrie McMenemy, seen here celebrating at the final whistle of the Saints' semi-final win against Third Division Crystal Palace (2-0).

The fall caused no lasting harm – indeed, it was while in the Second Division that the Saints earned their greatest triumph, the famous FA Cup victory over Manchester United – and when they were promoted again in 1978 they exuded stability. The following year they reached the League Cup Final and improved steadily until, in 1984, they were runners-up in the title race. McMenemy's policy was to bring top players to the Dell – the likes of Alan Ball, Kevin Keegan and Peter Shilton – and his boldness paid off. Chris Nicholl took over in 1985 and, with a small but recently improved ground and a talented squad, might have expected better than the sack – received in 1991.

SOUTHEND UNITED

Founded 1906

Joined League 1920 (Div. 3)

Honours Div. 4 Champions 1981

Ground Roots Hall

Southend United have never set the football world alight. They remained in Divisions 3 and 3(South) for 46 seasons, rarely threatening promotion, until they were relegated to Division 4 in 1966. After a few near misses they were returned to Division 3 in 1972 to begin a period as a 'yo-yo' club, achieving their fifth promotion from the lowest level in 1990 and following that with a move to Division 2 in 1991.

This step-up will at least mean exemption until the third round of the FA Cup – a tournament in which they have fared very badly.

Although a large catchment area appears to exist for the club, much of the potential support is easily lured away to London sides, many of which can be reached in little over an hour's travel time. In recent years, with only a solid bedrock of support attending matches, indecision about ground moves and improvements have cast a shadow over the team's modest successes. And while older fans fondly recall the likes of Scotsman 'Sandy' Anderson (a record 451 League appearances between 1950 and 1962) and Northern Ireland international Sammy McCrory (1955-59), the younger supporters are a little short of heroes of real substance although they do have Second Division football.

SPONSORSHIP

The era of sponsorship began in earnest in the 1970s. Pre-1970 sponsorship was often of the level shown in this quote from a 1969 Mansfield Town programme: 'The match ball for this game was kindly donated by Ind Coope (Northern Ltd).' Today everything is affected – even the FA Cup has been the subject of negotiations – and about 10 per cent of all sport's sponsorship money goes into football.

The longest-running major soccer sponsor was Bell's Whisky, who put their name to the 'Manager of the Month' awards between 1965 and 1988. The first match sponsor accepted by the Football League was Watney in 1970. The brewery financed a new knock-out tournament for the previous season's two top-scoring teams in each division; the competition lasted for four years. A similar competition, the Drybrough Cup, was organised in Scotland, where the four highest-scoring teams in the Scottish League's two divisions competed between 1971 and 1974.

A more complex competition was the Texaco Cup (1970/71 to 1973/74), sponsored by the oil company not long after its name change from Regent to Texaco. Sixteen teams represented four countries – England, Scotland, Northern Ireland and the Republic of Ireland – with a guaranteed Irish semi-finalist. Gillette and Ford sponsored early sportsmanship awards.

Tobacco companies, banned from television advertising, found a more inventive promotion method in sponsorship. Rothman's linked themselves with football's classic reference book, *Rothman's Football Yearbook,* first published in 1970, and then financed non-League football, beginning with the Isthmian League in 1973. (John Player and Benson & Hedges targeted cricket.) Later, however, the Football League excluded tobacco companies, breweries and South African companies from sponsoring its major competitions.

The first Football League sponsor was Canon in 1983. The electronics company was happy with its three-year deal. Company awareness grew considerably and the name was spread all over Europe by television. But the League's next deal, with *Today* newspaper in 1986/87, experienced problems, and the newspaper company gave way to Barclays Bank in 1987/88.

The League Cup has a longer sponsorship history than the Football League. The Dairy Council sponsored the Milk Cup from 1982 to 1986, Littlewoods took over the competition from 1986 to 1990 and then, in 1990, the Rumbelows League Cup

SPONSORSHIP One advantage of sponsoring soccer was well illustrated in 1990 when Paul Gascoigne, by virtue of some wonderful skills and a few televised tears displayed during the World Cup finals, became one of Britain's most photographed and written-about young men. Seen here playing for Tottenham Hotspur, he makes a good hoarding for Holsten (lager) and Hummel (sportswear). A club like Spurs, troubled by financial problems in 1990, could use Gazza's popularity as a bargaining chip in attracting sponsors.

came into existence. In Scotland, Skol first sponsored the Scottish League Cup in 1985, while the 1986 Scotland-Luxembourg game was the first British international to be sponsored.

A double-glazing firm craftily overcame the Rangers-Celtic problem by sponsoring both clubs in 1984. A club's sponsor is not always a profit-making organisation, as evidenced by deals between Millwall and Lewisham Borough Council (1987) and West Brom and Sandwell Council (1989). By 1990 there was an incredible range of sponsorship opportunities. It cost Wagsport only £15 to sponsor the gloves of Stafford Rangers goalkeeper Ryan Price, whereas Glasgow Rangers signed a deal valued around £6 million with McEwan's lager.

STADIA

Few aspects of football have been more controversial or newsworthy in recent years than the stadia in which the professional game is staged. The devastating fire at Bradford City's Valley Parade in May 1985, in which 56 people died, followed in April 1989 by the deaths of 95 Liverpool fans at Hillsborough, awoke everyone to the need for wholesale changes in the design, construction and

even location of Britain's ageing, outmoded football grounds.

When football first became a mass spectator sport in the late nineteenth century, most clubs rented fields or cricket grounds with rudimentary wooden stands and ropes around the pitch.

Everton and Celtic were among the first clubs to create purpose-built grounds, in 1892, and within a decade the three largest football grounds in the world were in Glasgow: Hampden Park, Ibrox Park and Celtic Park. A Scottish engineer, Archibald Leitch, carved a niche for himself in football history by designing the grounds and grandstands of several major clubs between 1900 and 1936, including those of Tottenham, Everton, Chelsea and Aston Villa. Many of his distinctive grandstands, such as those at Fulham, Sheffield Wednesday, Rangers and Dundee, are still in use today.

In Leitch's era the emphasis was on utilitarian structures providing seats on one side of the pitch with open terracing on the remaining three sides. Terrace covers were gradually added, as, in the 1950s, were floodlight pylons. The 1960s saw the introduction of executive boxes (first at Manchester United) and, sadly, anti-hooligan perimeter fences.

But football ground developments in Britain were always piecemeal - a stand here, a cover there - with few aesthetic considerations or hints of a master plan. By contrast, European and South American governments and civic authorities have, from the 1920s onwards, spent large sums building impressive stadia for their tenant clubs and local communities. Germany pioneered the concept of a stadium as part of a larger sports complex. Cantilevered roofing to facilitate a clear view of the pitch was developed in several countries during the 1930s but did not reach Britain until 1958 (at Scunthorpe United, surprisingly).

STADIA Vittorio Gregotti's distinctive corner towers at the Luigi Ferraris stadium in Genoa were completed for the 1990 World Cup finals. Few English grounds can match those of the Italians for sheer architectural style.

Change in Britain came about mainly as a result of disasters. The first Ibrox tragedy of 1902 signalled the end of high wooden terracing. Wembley Stadium's chaotic opening in 1923 forced the introduction of all-ticket matches and the division of terraces into manageable pens.

In 1946 the death of 33 spectators at Bolton warned of the dangers of poor control and overcrowding, but it took the second Ibrox disaster in 1971, when 66 died on a steep stairway, finally to alert the government to the need for legislation. The resulting Safety of Sports Grounds Act of 1975 began a system of inspection by local authorities which was to cost clubs a great deal in improvement work and to see once massive grounds drastically reduced in capacity.

The Bradford fire in 1985 increased the Safety Act's jurisdiction to Third and Fourth Division clubs, but its implementation was found tragically wanting by the Hillsborough disaster in 1989. As a result of this debacle, the government set up an enquiry under Lord Justice Taylor, who recommended in January 1990 that all Football League grounds be converted to all-seating - in the First and Second Divisions by 1994 and the rest by 1999. The shattering impact of this ruling on terrace regulars was hardly softened by parallel directives on all-seating from both UEFA and FIFA.

The Football League estimated that it would cost its clubs between £300 and £700 million to implement the Taylor Report. The government responded by re-allocating some £150 million of pools betting tax over a five-year period. But the shortfall still presents the clubs with a herculean task. Fans, meanwhile, worry that seats will be badly installed, will destroy the traditional atmosphere at matches, and will price the ordinary spectator out of football. But the Taylor Report has at least had the

STADIA
Leningrad's Kirov Stadium. Typically, many European stadia are owned by the municipality, hence the running track and a uniform, featureless design. Players and spectators with such stadia often voice a preference for the closed-in style found with most British and some continental football clubs.

desired effect of forcing British clubs to reassess completely their own grounds, many of which are hardly worth converting.

British stadia are not alone in facing huge repair bills. The largest venue in the world, the Maracana Stadium in Rio de Janeiro, had its capacity cut from 200,000 to 150,000 as a result of its crumbling infrastructure. The inadequacy of Belgium's Heysel Stadium was cruelly exposed in 1985 when Liverpool and Juventus fans rioted before the European Cup Final, resulting in 39 deaths.

Many of Germany's stadia were modernised in the 1970s but still have

large expanses of uncovered terracing which must be converted. Britain now boasts some of the most modern and atmospheric grounds in the world, such as Old Trafford and the newly revamped Ibrox Park. The difference is that whereas in Britain most stadia are privately owned, in Europe central and local governments play an active role in funding sports facilities. The Italians spent £600 million on modernising just 12 stadia for the 1990 World Cup, not a penny of which came from the tenant clubs.

To help pay for the modernisation of British grounds, future developments will

undoubtedly incorporate commercial and leisure facilities, such as shops, offices, social clubs and cinemas. In the absence of public grants, British clubs which can move will mainly follow the example of Scunthorpe, St Johnstone, Walsall, Yeovil and Wycombe Wanderers by selling their old inner-city grounds for commercial development and replacing them with smaller purpose-built stadia on green field sites holding around 10,000 spectators.

Although the use of synthetic pitches in Britain has proved unpopular in first-class football since its introduction at Queen's Park Rangers in 1981,

future developments abroad are likely to include retractable roofs, sections of moveable seating and even moving pitches - all of which are technically possible but, at present, unproven economically.

JOCK STEIN

1922 Born in Burnbank, Lanarkshire, Scotland

1942 Signs part-time for Albion Rovers while still a miner

1950 Joins Llanelli as full-time professional

1951 Signed by Celtic mainly to help with reserve and youth team coaching - and becomes first-team captain

1954 Celtic complete League and Cup double	**1977** Last of 10 Championships and 8 Scottish Cup victories with Celtic
1955 Injury – and Stein becomes reserve team coach	**1978** Becomes manager of Leeds United – to leave later in the same year to become Scotland team manager
1960 Appointed manager of Dunfermline Athletic	
1964 Appointed manager of Hibernian	**1979** Awarded the CBE
1965 Rejoins Celtic – as manager. They win Scottish Cup; also temporary Scotland manager for World Cup qualifying matches	**1985** Dies at the end of the match at Ninian Park, Cardiff, in which Scotland drew 1-1 with Wales to ensure qualification for the 1986 World Cup finals in Mexico.
1966 First of nine Scottish Championships in a row	
1967 Celtic become first British club to win European Cup	Never can the Scottish tag of the 'Big Man' have been more appropriately applied than in the case of John

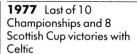

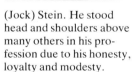

(Jock) Stein. He stood head and shoulders above many others in his profession due to his honesty, loyalty and modesty.

Stein's phenomenal success at Parkhead will probably always be remembered for the European Cup victory in Lisbon in 1967. That victory, achieved by attacking flair against the defensive Italian champions Internazionale, has a permanent place in Scottish soccer folklore.

Stein's eventual departure from the Glasgow club was both unexpected and sad; the board wanted him to move on to promotional work to make room for Billy McNeill to return as manager. Although Stein, characteristically, treated the affair with dignity, he was known to be hurt by the 'dismissal' and reluctantly moved south to manage Leeds United. He was with the Yorkshire club for only a few months when he was enticed back to Scotland to look after the national side.

His fatal heart attack, moments after a World Cup qualifier in 1978, occurred on just the kind of emotional and stirring night that Stein had provided for Scottish fans for so long.

JOCK STEIN Jock Stein, in his prime, with yet another trophy. This time it's the Scottish Cup for 1977 following a 1-0 win against Rangers. No wonder he's smiling. Although always determined in his approach to football, a modesty stemming from his family upbringing ensured he never glorified victory and never gloated over beaten opponents. His sudden death meant the loss of another strong influence for good in the game and a friend for many fans.

STENHOUSEMUIR

Founded 1884

Joined League 1921 (Div. 2)

Honours None

Ground Ochilview Park

Ochilview was the scene of the first senior match in Scotland under modern floodlighting (v Hibs, 7 November 1951), but Stenhousemuir have not always been seen as part of the future of the game. Proposed reconstruction in 1964 threatened to push them out of the League, but legal action followed and an out-of-court settlement secured their place.

The judiciary was also involved after a bookmaker attempted unsuccessfully to bribe goalkeeper Joe Shortt in 1925. It was one of the few attempts at match fixing ever uncovered in Scottish football.

Stenhousemuir's most distinguished discovery was Willie Ormond, a star winger of the 1950s with Hibs and later Scotland's manager.

STIRLING ALBION

Founded 1945

Joined League 1946 (Div. C)

Honours Scottish League Division 2 Champions 1953, 1958, 1961, 1965; Second Division Champions 1977, 1991

Ground Annfield Park

The club's early days reflected the makeshift nature of the post-war period. Their first stand, for example, rested on two lorries. By 1949, however, they had been promoted all the way to Division 1.

League success was difficult to sustain but Albion, in the 1970s and 1980s, consistently discovered good young players. They were also the first senior club in Scotland to play on artificial turf (laid in 1987) but have been compelled to return to grass by 1992. In season 1984/85 they had a 20-0 victory over Selkirk in the Scottish Cup, a record margin for the competition in the twentieth century.

STOCKPORT COUNTY

Founded 1883

Joined League 1900 (Div. 2)

Honours Div.3 (N) Champions 1922, 1937; Div. 4 Champions 1967

Ground Edgeley Park

Just down the road from Manchester is hardly the most viable location for a club of modest means but, in those daunting circumstances, Stockport County have been making a plucky fist of League life throughout the twentieth century.

Formed by members of the Congregational church, they occupied numerous grounds before settling at

STOCKPORT COUNTY In 1920/21 this Stockport County side won Division 3 (North), something of a landmark as it was the inaugural season of the division. Stockport may have started off favourites as they had been relegated from Division 2 the previous year. In securing their Championship and their return to the higher ranks, they beat off challenges from such sides as Stalybridge Celtic, Ashington, Durham City and Nelson. For the record, they line up: (middle row, left to right) Walmesley, Richardson, Hardy, Layton, Lachlan (manager), Reid; Crosthwaite, Heath, Gault, Steele, Jones, Waterall, O'Kane.

Edgeley Park two years after joining Division 2. In 1904 they failed to win re-election but regained their status the following season, then embarked on an up-and-down existence which saw them sink to the Third Division on three occasions. In 1959 they dropped to the Fourth, where they remained for three decades apart from three seasons at the end of the 1960s. During that enterprising but gimmicky period, in which dancing girls provided pre-match entertainment and the slogan 'Go Go County' was employed, hopes ran high.

But public support was not forthcoming, results declined and Stockport resumed their familiar role in the soccer hierarchy until promotion in 1991 brought relief.

Diversion through success in knock-out competitions came in 1935 and 1950, when they reached the last 16 of the FA Cup, and in 1972/73, when similar progress was made in the League Cup.

Understandably, star names have been few, although 'keeper Harry Hardy won an England cap in 1924 and former England defender Neil Franklin finished his playing days with County in the late 1950s. Former managers include Andy Beattie, Jimmy Meadows, Bert Trautmann and Mike Summerbee.

STOKE CITY

Founded 1863

Joined League 1888 (founder member)

Honours Div. 2 Champions 1933, 1963; Div. 3 (N) Champions 1927; League Cup Winners 1972

Ground Victoria Ground

Toil has featured more prominently than triumph in the story of Stoke City, yet the long years of striving have been enlightened by occasional

STOKE CITY Stoke City have something of a name for playing good football and not minding how old their players are . . . capitalising on the skills of individuals close to the ends of their careers. In this match at Queen's Park Rangers in 1974 a young Alan Hudson points the way to Jimmy Greenhoff and Geoff Salmons. All three were gifted footballers who spent probably their best playing days with Stoke. The Queen's Park Rangers player is John Beck, who went on successfully to manage Cambridge United. Stoke won the game 1-0 and finished fifth in Division 1 – heights to which they have yet to return.

high spots which have produced an intensity of emotion quite out of character with the normally down-to-earth 'Potters'.

Stoke's early League experiences were not auspicious. After propping up the table for two seasons they were not re-elected, and even after returning a year later they continued to struggle. Cash was short and in 1908, having been relegated, they went into liquidation.

The Potters regrouped after the First World War, spent the 1920s division-hopping, and finally, in the 1930s, built a side capable of making its mark. With a young winger named Stanley Matthews showing rich promise, Stoke ascended to the First Division, where they were to stay for 20 years. Managed by their former defender Bob McGrory, and with the future knight forming a potent combination with marksman Freddie Steele, they offered real hope for the future.

In the first season after the war – with accomplished centre-half Neil Franklin at his peak – Stoke missed the Championship by just two points. But then Matthews went to Blackpool, Franklin to Bogota, and in 1953 the Potters found themselves back in the Second Division.

Revival was heralded by the arrival of Tony Waddington as boss in 1960. He re-signed Matthews, recruited other veterans including forwards Jimmy McIlroy and Dennis Viollet, and achieved promotion in 1963. The town had never witnessed such scenes of celebration. Continuing to buy seasoned campaigners, Waddington consolidated Stoke's status, and 1972 brought the club's first major trophy, the League Cup, with telling contributions from the likes of schemer George Eastham, attacker Peter Dobing and 'keeper Gordon Banks. In the mid 1970s, inspired by front-man Jimmy Greenhoff and Peter Shilton in goal, they rode high in the table, but when

that side broke up, the club's fortunes faded. Two spells in the Second Division followed, and in 1990 came a slump to the Third.

Support in the Potteries has been traditionally luke-warm, perhaps because the five towns lack a focal point and the increase of easy motorway travel has lured many fans to plusher venues. The club faced a major task as the 1990s began.

STRANRAER

Founded 1870

Joined League 1949 (C Division)

Honours None

Ground Stair Park

Although created by the banding together of local clubs, Stranraer have rarely been secure. League membership was slow to arrive and, like Stenhousemuir, they have always resided in the lowest possible division.

As with Queen of the South, a distant location has created difficulties. While Queen of the South's players train in Glasgow, Stranraer's travel to Kilmarnock. Despite that,

however, attendances have been comparatively sound.

Stranraer's 1990 victory over Kilmarnock was the first Scottish Cup tie ever to be decided by penalty shoot-out.

SUNDERLAND

Founded 1879

Joined League 1890 (Div. 1)

Honours Div. 1 Champions 1892, 1893, 1895, 1902, 1913, 1936; Div. 2 Champions 1976; Div. 3 Champions 1988; FA Cup Winners 1937, 1973

Ground Roker Park

Sunderland, one of the first titans of British soccer, have had to settle for a more humble position in the game's hierarchy during recent decades. It has not been easy for such a proud club, whose expensive transfer policy has often proved ill-advised, and whose fervent fans demand success no matter that the facts of modern football life decree otherwise.

The Wearsiders got off to a magnificent start to their League tenure. They were champions within two years of entry, and went on to take the trophy three times

in four campaigns. As the century turned their dominance decreased, but with the brilliant Ted Doig between the posts and centre-forward Johnny Campbell scoring freely, they managed another title.

Even when the 'team of all the talents', as they were dubbed, broke up, it didn't herald an immediate decline. A new side was built, in which inside-forward Charlie Buchan was majestic, and in 1913 they narrowly missed the League-FA Cup double. The 1920s proved anti-climactic, but the 1930s saw the rise of what has proved, to date, to be Sunderland's last great team. The star was inside-forward Raich Carter, who was well supported by fellow attackers Patsy Gallacher and Bobby Gurney, a trio who contributed hugely towards bringing major prizes to Roker Park.

The war stopped their momentum, and, when life returned to normal the club attempted to buy glory. Costly arrivals included inside-forward Len Shackleton, striker Trevor Ford and winger Billy Bingham, yet their most

impressive performer was locally born wing-half Stan Anderson. The spending spree failed, and in 1958 Sunderland were relegated after a record 68 years in Division 1. Sterling efforts by centre-half Charlie Hurley and goal-machine Brian Clough helped to pave the way for promotion

SUNDERLAND The **Sunderland team of 1912/13 that came close to winning the League and Cup double. They secured the Championship, edging out Aston Villa by four points, but lost 1-0 in the FA Cup Final to the same rivals. Perhaps they were tiring of Cup football by the time they reached the Final, because it had taken them one replay to get past Burnley in the semi-final and two replays to overcome Newcastle United in the fourth round. The team:** *(back row, left to right)* **Milton, Cringan, Thomson, Butler, Gladwin, Low; Mordue, Buchan, Hall, Holley, Martin. The insets are Cuggy** *(left)* **and Richardson.**

six years later, but further questionable judgement – witness the purchase of gifted but wayward play-maker Jim Baxter – precipitated another demotion in 1970.

This time, with shrewd guidance by Bobby Stokoe, their stint in the Second Division was enlivened by a stirring FA Cup victory against Leeds United, featuring a heroic performance by 'keeper Jim Montgomery. But although Sunderland went up three years later, they could not consolidate, and were off on a roller-coaster tour of divisions which reached its lowest point in 1987/88, which was spent in the Third.

Since then the Rokerites have returned to the First Division – albeit in controversial circumstances involving the financial difficulties of Swindon Town – only to drop out after a single season. It was a sickening blow to the morale of an economically depressed area.

SUPPORTERS

Tony Mason, in *Association Football and English Society* (Harvester, 1980), concluded that throughout the late 1870s and 1880s football of a good standard could be watched for anything between threepence and sixpence. He says: 'There is no doubt that by 1915 the majority of spectators who went to watch professional football matches were working class in origin, occupation and life style. They paid 6d and stood on earth mounds or terracing, often made of cinders edged with wood. They might or might not be under cover.'

In the period after the First World War, more formal supporters' clubs first began, and the National Federation of Football Supporters' Clubs was formed in 1927. In the post-war period, when supporters first used cars to travel to more successful clubs, supporters' clubs helped keep some lower-league clubs solvent. Money was raised through social events and, once the Betting and Lotteries Act permitted, small-scale gambling activities. Later, football clubs took over their own commercial activities.

Supporters have always dressed for the match. In the early post-war days fans took rattles, rosettes and scarves. Of these, only the scarf has lasted. The tossing of toilet rolls was a disruption that began in the 1960s, and in the 1970s there was much talk of the hooligan's tools: boots to kick with, sharpened pennies to throw from the terraces, and so on. York police once held a press conference to parade a multitude of confiscated weapons. In the late 1980s, however, there was a new fad – inflatables. Manchester City fans brandished inflatable bananas, Grimsby Town supporters went for 'Harry the Haddock', and many others caught on.

Whereas some sport personalities, such as golfers and tennis-players, require quiet spectators, footballers thrive on a noisy environment. There have always been ritualised chants, such as the Pompey chimes at Portsmouth, and supporters have always adopted popular songs in the way West Ham supporters did with 'I'm Forever Blowing Bubbles' for the 1923 Wembley FA Cup Final. In the 1960s the South American chanting of team names ('Bra-sil, Bra-sil') was taking up by English supporters ('Liv-er-pool, Liv-er-pool'), and messages are now sent to the players through chants:- 'one nil, one nil', 'here we go, here we go', 'cham-pi-ons'.

SUPPORTERS In British football the Scots are considered to be the most loyal supporters of all. Stories of them selling up homes and leaving wives and families to attend matches in faraway places are legion – and not all of them apocryphal. The World Cup finals, for which Scotland regularly qualify, is the high point in the supporter's diary, with every effort made to attend; 'every effort' for the 1978 finals in Argentina included an attempt to hire a decommissioned submarine for the journey out! Unfortunately the trips too often end in disappointment, like the 1986 excursion to Mexico, with elimination at the first stage and a long journey home for the lads pictured here . . . but not by sub!

One outcome of the Taylor Report into the Hillsborough disaster was the recognition that supporters deserve a stronger say in the management of football clubs. Attempts in the 1950s and 1960s to co-opt supporters' club officials as directors sometimes ran into difficulties, and one Midlands director once complained that board meetings clashed with his night-shift at the pit. However, supporters had long-standing complaints about ticket allocation, ground facilities and the direction of the club. At Oxford United in April 1983 a game was delayed for 33 minutes when 1500 fans staged a sit-in on the pitch to protest at news of a possible merger with Reading. In 1990 Charlton Athletic fans, incensed at Greenwich Council's opposition to plans for a refurbished Valley Stadium, formed a political party to protest. The Valley Party scored a massive 14,838 votes in 60 council seats.

Supporters' complaints are usually about the team. 'I'm never going to watch them again,' says the true supporter before turning up at the next home game. For some supporters, winning is the only thing. Others perform best in adversity, sharpening their wit on a referee or manager. When Derby County had serious problems with results, creditors and hooliganism in 1984, supporters warned each other to be careful outside the ground: 'They'll try to push season tickets into your pockets'.

Not all supporters are partisan to one particular team. Some are more general in their support for football, travelling around the country to see grounds and games that interest them. The Ninety-Two Club, formed in 1978, is open to supporters who have attended a first-team competitive fixture at all of the current home grounds of the 92 Football League clubs (to be 93 in 1991/92). In 1989/90 there were 699 members.

The Football Supporters' Association, formed after

the 1985 Heysel disaster, also gained momentum very quickly. It now has a regional network, and details are available through its postal address: PO Box 11, Liverpool L2X 1XP.

The rapid growth of 'fanzines' during the 1980s has provided evidence of supporters' energy, humour and insight. In the past, supporters have been sadly neglected in football literature. One exception is *Saturday's Boys* (edited by Harry Lansdown and Alex Spillius), which captures the careers of supporters rather than those of players, managers, directors, referees or hooligans. Perhaps the 1990s will see a move away from 'the match' and towards 'the experience of supporters'. After all, supporters are football's biggest sponsors.

SWANSEA CITY

Founded 1912

Joined League 1920 (Div. 3)

Honours Div. 3 (S) Champions 1925, 1949

Ground Vetch Field

Twice in their history, Swansea have shown Division 1 potential. The first time, in the 1950s, it disappeared when a succession of richly talented youngsters were sold through economic necessity; on the second occasion, in the early 1980s, John Toshack actually led the 'Swans' into the top flight, whence they

SWANSEA Swansea City's surge up through the divisions was achieved with a blend of local players and those bought in by manager John Toshack — several from his old club, Liverpool. In this First Division duel, Swansea local lad, Alan Curtis, who had two spells at Vetch Field, challenges Liverpool's defender Phil Thompson. In the Swans' two years in the top flight they finished sixth and last; Liverpool were champions in both seasons.

disappeared after two campaigns to resume their struggles in the League's lower reaches. By the 1990s, with the eternal problems of poor attendances and the Welsh passion for rugby showing no signs of diminishing, there was little sign of a third opportunity.

Swansea were founder members of Division 3, from which they soon rose with a sprightly side which beat Arsenal to reach the 1926 FA Cup semi-finals. They could attain no more than Second Division mediocrity, however, and were relegated soon after the war despite the emergence of young centre-forward Trevor Ford. Manager Billy McCandlass took them up in 1949 and, though he sold wing-half Roy Paul, introduced youthful entertainers such as

schemer Ivor Allchurch, wingers Cliff Jones, Terry Medwin and Ivor's brother Len, and utility man Mel Charles. Each was transferred and, with a 1964 FA Cup semi-final appearance the only highlight, Swansea sunk eventually to the Fourth Division, where Toshack joined them in 1978.

Leaning heavily on his Liverpool connections and boosted by stalwart forward Robbie James, Toshack assembled a team which climbed all the way to the First Division and finished a creditable sixth in 1981/82. But he left, reality returned, and by 1986 they were back at the bottom level. Promotion followed two years later, but a return to Europe via the Welsh Cup seemed their most likely way of getting back into the big time and the headlines.

SWIFT, Frank

1913 Born in Blackpool

1931 Playing for Fleetwood in the Lancashire Combination — his brother keeping goal for Blackpool

1932 Signs professional forms for Manchester City in October

1933 First-team debut, on Christmas Day v Derby County

1934 Wins FA Cup winner's medal in 2-1 victory v Portsmouth

1937 League Championship success, by three points from Charlton Athletic

1938 Manchester City surprisingly relegated to Division 2

1945 Coaching in Norway for the Football Association

1946 First full international cap, v Northern Ireland in Belfast

1947 Plays for Great Britain in 6-1 victory over the Rest of Europe at Hampden; City win Division 2 Championship in first full post-war season

1950 Retires from playing

1951 Turns to coaching and journalism

1958 February — dies in Munich air disaster

Frank Swift, like some other famous goalkeepers, was known and respected as much for his personality as for the list of honours he achieved. Big 'Swifty' (6 feet tall, with enormous hands) was everybody's favourite; loved within the game for both his humour and modesty, he was admired by fans around the world for his agility and skill.

As he came from a family that already possessed one professional footballer, scouts were aware of the potential of the young Swift. He wasn't old enough to sign professional forms on leaving school and so took a job at Blackpool Gas Works, playing for them and Fleetwood before joining City. He soon won a first-team place, and in the following five eventful seasons he missed only one match.

The Second World War meant that his first (of 19) full England cap came as late as 1946, although he played in 17 wartime and 'victory' internationals. Swift thought it was a great honour to represent his country and was delighted

FRANK SWIFT
Displaying his jovial approach to life as well as his England 'keepers' sweater and cap, Frank Swift was probably doing his best to make the cameraman laugh as this shot was taken. Although he was able to complete his playing career, Swift died in the prime of life in 1958. There are times when football could do with another 'Big Swifty', just to remind us that, after all, it *is* just a game.

to become the first goalkeeper to captain England in 1948 – a 4-0 victory against Italy in Turin.

In his later playing years Swift was active in working for improved conditions and contracts for footballers, and also in coaching goalkeeping. Despite all this, he may go down in history as the player who fainted at the final whistle of an FA Cup Final – when reaching for his gloves after City's 1934 Wembley win.

Frank Swift died in the Munich air disaster; he had attended Manchester United's match in Belgrade as a newspaper reporter.

SWINDON TOWN

Founded 1881

Joined League 1920 (Div. 3)

Honours Div. 4 Champions 1986; League Cup Winners 1969

Ground County Ground

For a club who have spent more than 50 of their first 70 years of League life in Division 3, and who have never entered the top flight, Swindon Town have had a considerable impact on English soccer. They first made their mark just before the First World War when, as a Southern League outfit inspired by schemer Harold Fleming, they reached two FA Cup semi-finals. There followed a long, grey period, which ended in the early 1960s with the emergence of a bright young team under the guidance of manager Bert Head. Wingers Don Rogers and Mike Summerbee took the eye, but there was also a major contribution from full-back John Trollope – later to break the club's appearance record – as the 'Robins' won promotion.

But leading players departed and Swindon were relegated two years later, before bouncing back to enjoy their most successful campaign in 1968/69. With Rogers in the van, they overturned Arsenal to win the League Cup and also reached Division 2, with average gates of nearly 20,000.

Sadly they could not maintain progress and by 1982 were in the Fourth.

Lou Macari lifted them back to the Second, and his successor, Osvaldo Ardiles, transformed a workmanlike side into an attractive unit which won a place in the 1990 Division 1 play-offs. A Wembley triumph over Sunderland apparently earned promotion, but celebrations were halted when the League ruled that Swindon must stay down as punishment for financial irregularities during the Macari years. Ardiles was replaced by Glenn Hoddle, and in a growing town with limited local competition for support, there seemed a fair chance that – despite the club's heavy debts – he might succeed before too long as player and manager.

SWINDON TOWN Happy days for Swindon Town as manager Ossie Ardiles and ever-present midfielder Alan McLoughlin celebrate victory in the 1989/90 Division 2 play-off final against Sunderland. McLoughlin scored (or was it a Gary Bennett own goal?) the only goal of the match, watched by 72,873 at Wembley. Due to breaches of League rules, however, Swindon were relegated to Division 3, a ruling later changed to allow the club to stay in Division 2. Sunderland, who finished sixth in Division 2 and didn't win the play-offs, found themselves in the First Division for the 1990/91 season.

SYSTEMS OF PLAY

'Of late dribbling has given way to a more effective, if less scientific, kind of play,' wrote FA secretary Charles Alcock in 1876. He was mourning how the dribbling and 'backing-up' approach had been replaced by the 'passing-on' game, 'first introduced in any degree of perfection by the Northerners in the early matches between London and Sheffield.'

Whereas teams in the dribbling era consisted almost entirely of forwards, the passing game gradually brought a better balance. The classic 2-3-5 system – two full-backs, three half-backs and five forwards – became commonplace in the mid-1880s. But the full-backs were positioned more centrally – to watch three forwards down the middle – the centre-half went up and down the field in the manner of a central midfield player, and the two wing-halves played wider and marked wingers.

A major change was sparked by the 1925 offside law. Fullbacks such as Morley and Montgomery (Notts County) and Hudspeth and McCracken (Newcastle United) had used the old law by putting players offside rather than waiting for them to stray into an offside position. But when only two defenders were required behind the ball to keep players onside, the centre-half was needed in a more defensive role – as a 'stopper' centre-half. Full-backs moved wider to watch wingers, and wing-halves took on a more vital role in midfield. This new system was the W-M formation, so-called because defenders lined up on the points of a W, attackers on the points of an M.

After the 'stopper' centre-half came the deep-lying centre-forward. Hungary excelled against England at Wembley in 1953 with an elusive centre-forward called Nandor Hidegkuti. Don Revie helped Manchester City to Wembley in 1955 and 1956 with a similar plan, confusing centre-halves who relied on close marking a centre-forward.

Former footballers argued that many such tactics had been tried in other eras without being given fancy names like 'the Revie plan', 'overlapping full-backs' and 'near-post centres'. However, these and other moves became commonplace in the 1960s, complete with grand and scientific names. Similarly, the tactic of employing a defensive wing-half alongside the centre-half – as adopted by Joe Mercer at Arsenal in the late 1940s – became very popular in the 1960s. Based on the 1958 Brazilian system, a deep-lying forward and attacking wing-half worked as link men between attack and defence in a formation known as 4-2-4. But the 4-2-4 system needed two attacking wingers. When Alf Ramsey found himself without wingers of the calibre of Matthews or Finney, he shifted to 4-3-3 formation for England's 1966 World Cup win. Other managers resorted to 4-4-2, 5-3-2 – all kinds of shapes.

The zonal marking system was an alternative to man-to-man marking, and an additional option was the *libero*, a player given the freedom to hang behind other defenders and use his vision of the whole pitch to 'sweep' up dangerous situations. People became more system conscious. Managers later talked of a team's 'shape'.

The variety of systems was made more confusing for spectators by tricks with players' numbers. Dick Graham was one manager who kept the public guessing, as summarised with inimitable humour by Eric Foster in a scouting report of a 1967/68 game between Oxford United and Orient: 'The Orientals were running true to form. Number 2 was at inside-left, number 8 was at left-back, number 4 at outside-left. For one exciting moment it looked as though the goalkeeper was going to stay between the posts, but, typically he was nowhere to be seen when Oxford's goals went in.'

Yet Graham was prescient. A system of interchangeable players, later known as 'total football', was perfected in the early 1970s by teams such as Ajax, Holland and West Germany. The Dutch were attackers and defenders, free from constraints, as long as they did not sacrifice the overall system. Men such as Johan Cruyff and Wim van Hanegem had no obvious position. A *libero* like Ruud Krol was often seen in midfield or attack.

British football became more European in the 1970s, clubs such as Liverpool and Nottingham Forest dominating the European Cup, but in the 1980s some teams returned to the direct strategy of long passes and old-fashioned wing play. Game analysis showed that most goals came from moves of fewer than four passes. The quicker the ball was played into the penalty area, the more defensive chaos, some coaches argued. This direct approach helped Watford's rise to the First Division, manager Graham Taylor blending two strong central attackers (Luther Blissett and Ross Jenkins) with two fast, penetrative wingers (Nigel Callaghan and John Barnes). The long ball (Taylor prefers to call it the 'long-pass') game thrilled some pundits, while others moaned that they needed the roof taken off the stand to see their team's best passes. Wimbledon also reached the First Division with this system.

Other successful teams between 1966 and 1986 are analysed in *The Winning Formula*, a book and series of five video tapes produced by Charles Hughes, the FA Director of Coaching. Coaches, however, stress that individual skills – ball control, passing, defending, shooting – are more important than a system of play. Liverpool's team success has much to do with individual responsibilities: working hard at not losing the ball, not wasting a pass and supporting team-mates. And any system should suit the strengths of individual players. In the final analysis, systems of play may not be as important as a team's ability to turn set-plays into goals or, indeed, a goalkeeper's ability to save them.

SYSTEMS OF PLAY
Some fashions come and go in styles of play, but the idea of packing a defence to protect the goal will probably go on forever. Here, in a fourth-round FA Cup match in 1953 at Villa Park, the home side (Aston Villa) employ their 'stonewall' defence to thwart Brentford, whose centre-forward (number 9), Tommy Lawton, would find several defenders between him and the goal were he to get the ball in the first place. The result, not surprisingly, 0-0! Villa won the replay 2-1.

TAYLOR REPORT

Lord Justice Taylor chaired a two-month enquiry into the disaster which claimed the lives of 95 people at Hillsborough, Sheffield, on 15 April 1989. The enquiry, which heard evidence from over 170 witnesses, provided the most searching look at football in modern times. The judge produced a 71-page interim report on 4 August 1989, to permit some changes before the 1989/90 season, and the final report was released at the end of January the following year. The report ruled that the main cause of the disaster had been a failure of police control. However, Lord Justice Taylor was also critical of football club management for its failure to improve spectator conditions and safety.

The interim report contained 43 recommendations, and the final report a further 33. The most dramatic was that all English First and Second Division clubs should have all-seater stadia by August 1994, and that Scottish Premier League and other Football League clubs should follow suit by August 1999. The judge recommended that certain activities should be deemed criminal offences, namely the throwing of missiles at sports grounds, ticket touting, the chanting of racial or obscene abuse and running on to the pitch without reasonable excuse. Taylor's recommendations included methods for better police communications, electronic 'tagging' to detect convicted hooligans at grounds, and ways of improving first-aid and medical facilities (although he stressed that there was no criticism of the response by ambulance and fire services at Hillsborough). One specific recommendation was for one trained first-aider per thousand spectators.

Many of Taylor's recommendations concerned very specific safety issues. He suggested reductions in terrace capacities and improved systems for filling grounds and monitoring the progress of crowds. One recommendation was that spikes be removed from fences, which should be no higher than 2.2 metres. Emergency gates should be patrolled to allow swift opening. There were a number of specific points made about crush barriers, gangways, escape routes from terraces, stewarding, crowd partitioning and safety certificates, and the judge felt a need to spell out the duties of football clubs. Overall, the report highlighted the poor state of football grounds and management.

The Conservative government suffered a setback from the Taylor Report in that the judge recommended that the proposed computerised identity card scheme should be rejected. Taylor believed that the scheme would increase chances of congestion and disorder outside grounds. He also recommended that all sports grounds, including those for cricket and rugby, should be subject to the Football Licensing Authority, set up under the new Football Spectators Bill.

TELEVISION

Television coverage of football has gradually increased, but not without conflict between television companies and football authorities. Careful negotiations have often been needed to resolve issues of finance, the distribution of money among clubs, shirt advertising, overseas rights, live television and compensation for loss of attendance.

Part of the 1937 FA Cup Final – Sunderland v Preston North End – was shown on television, then after the war it became common for the FA Cup Final to be broadcast live. Internationals and other Cup games were occasionally edited for BBC's *Sports Special* programme, which began in September 1955. ITV was the first channel to televise a Football League game – a Division 1 clash between Blackpool and Bolton Wanderers on 10 September 1960.

A major breakthrough came in August 1964 when BBC2 launched a 45-minute programme showing highlights of a top League game. The programme, *Match of the Day,* was so successful that it was moved to BBC1 to reach a bigger audience.

The late 1960s brought experiments with closed-circuit television. On Wednesday 7 October 1965 Coventry City erected four screens on their own ground so supporters could watch a Division 2 match taking place in Cardiff. The game was watched by 12,639 in Cardiff and 10,295 in Coventry. Far more watched the 1967 Everton-Liverpool fifth-round Cup tie: 64,851 live at Goodison Park and 40,149 in front of screens at Anfield. The power of television was apparent by the end of the 1960s. Instant joy was brought into millions of British homes when big events were televised live, such as the 1966 World Cup Final, Celtic's 1967 European Cup Final victory and Manchester United's 1968 European Cup Final win. But television also brought controversy. The Celtic-Racing brawl in Montevideo, in which six players were sent off, brought outraged reactions. And in 1971 referee Ray Tinkler was subjected to a nationwide trial when he allowed a Jeff Astle goal for West Brom against Leeds United when Astle's team-mate Colin Suggett was in an offside position.

Negotiations for television deals were often difficult. As sponsorship came into football, so television contracts became even more important. There were fears that 'American' problems – one referee complained he had to blow for stoppages to allow advertisements to be shown – would be replicated in Britain, but the most common debate

surrounded whether television was good for the game. Would the revenue compensate for lower attendances and controversial publicity? In the late 1970s the Football League struck a special exclusive deal with ITV, nicknamed 'Snatch of the Day,' but it was later set aside by the Office of Fair Trading.

In 1983, for the first time, games were played on Sunday especially for the benefit of live television. The first was Tottenham Hotspur against Nottingham Forest on Sunday 2 October, and the audience was 5 million. A month later a man

murdered his girlfriend because she turned off the television when a football match was being shown.

Predictably, there was one season when talks between the Football League and television companies broke down completely. There was no television coverage during the first half of 1985/86. Agreement was finally reached in December.

With satellite and cable television, networks grew even bigger. It was estimated that over half the human race watched at least one game during the 1990 World Cup finals. In Britain, Screen Sport took advantage of new

TELEVISION The techniques for televising soccer have developed considerably over the years, although cameras behind goals are nothing new. This remotely controlled camera was positioned high above the goal during the 1990 FA Cup Final at Wembley and used particularly in action-replay analysis of goalmouth incidents.

technology to devote a channel exclusively to sport. Meanwhile, BBC1 and ITV continue their successful programmes *Match of the Day* and *The Match*, supplementing

them with Saturday lunchtime previews, *Football Focus* and *Saint and Greavsie* respectively.

TORQUAY UNITED

Founded 1898

Joined League 1927 (Div. 3 S)

Honours None

Ground Plainmoor

Torquay United's mark on soccer history has not, so far, been a notable one, as might be expected of a club based in a tourist resort on the south coast of Devon. Professional soccer has never figured highly among local entertainment options, and with almost every away game bringing steep travel bills, it would appear that, for United, becoming a major soccer force presents a well-nigh insurmountable task.

Early omens were not good. For more than 30 years after applying for re-election at the end of their first League campaign, Torquay remained members of the lowest available flight. Then, during the 1960s, they twice won promotion to the Third Division before returning both times to the basement.

Their most exciting spell came in the mid 1960s when, with Frank O'Farrell in charge, they rose to the Third Division and twice came close to reaching the Second. United's best-known players down the years have tended to be goal-scorers, with Sam Collins in the 1950s and Robin Stubbs in the 1960s springing to mind.

TOTTENHAM HOTSPUR

Founded 1882

Joined League 1908 (Div. 2)

Honours Div. 1 Champions 1951, 1961; Div. 2 Champions 1920, 1950; FA Cup Winners 1901, 1921, 1961, 1962, 1967, 1981, 1982, 1991; League Cup Winners 1971, 1973; European Cup Winners' Cup Winners 1963; UEFA Cup Winners 1972, 1984

Ground White Hart Lane

Even though their recent achievements have hardly matched their illustrious past, Spurs remain one of the glamour clubs of world soccer. Always ready, until recently, to compete for the most expensive players in the transfer market, and renowned for attractive football, they take the eye and dominate the back pages in a way that makes them the southern counterpart of Manchester United.

Yet Tottenham were comparatively late starters on the glory trail. In fact, when they won their first major trophy, the FA Cup, just after the turn of the century, they were in the Southern League, and a further seven campaigns passed before they were elected to the senior competition. Once in, they were promoted at the end of their opening campaign but then struggled in the top grade and were relegated in 1915. After the war Spurs were a more buoyant force, with the likes of wing-half and skipper Arthur Grimsdell, inside-forward Jimmy Seed and left-winger Jimmy Dimmock in their prime, and success in both Division 2 and the FA Cup soon came. There followed a lengthy period of mediocrity during which they twice slid back to the Second Division, and it was not until the late 1940s that Tottenham's star began to rise again.

The man responsible was Arthur Rowe, a former White Hart Lane player whose famous 'push-and-run' style not only achieved the longed-for promotion but also lifted the League Championship in the following term. Rowe's most influential players were goalkeeper Ted Ditchburn, full-backs Alf Ramsey and Ron Burgess, and inside-left Eddie Baily.

The mid 1950s saw the arrival of brilliantly constructive right-half Danny Blanchflower, bustling centre-forward Bobby Smith and wing speedster Cliff Jones, but it was not until Bill Nicholson, who played under Rowe, took over as manager in 1958 that the most famous side in Tottenham's history was assembled. In came ultra-combative left-half Dave Mackay, schemer John White and 'keeper Bill Brown, all from Scotland, and within two-and-a-half years Spurs had become the first club this century to win the League and FA Cup double. They were a wonderful side, skilful, adventurous yet with a core of steel, and, with ace goal-scorer Jimmy Greaves added, went on to further achievements, notably becoming the first British team to win a European trophy.

The inevitable break-up came and Tottenham, while winning cups on a fairly regular basis, have never since been such a League force, although there has been no shortage of stars to thrill the fans. Among the most dazzling have been subtle striker Alan Gilzean and inspirational 'keeper Pat Jennings in the post-double era, England forwards Martin Chivers and Martin Peters in the early 1970s and Argentinians Ossie Ardiles and Ricky Villa,

TOTTENHAM HOTSPUR
Few teams can have had such a well-known line-up as the Tottenham Hotspur 'double' side in the early 1960s. In photograph order (with positions in brackets), they were: (back row, left to right) Henry (FB), Norman (CH), Brown (G), Smith (CF), Baker (FB); Jones (W), White (IF), Blanchflower (HB), Allen (IF), Dyson (W), Mackay (HB). The balance of the team was often used as a model for other sides; the tall Maurice Norman dominated the air, while gritty, ball-winning half-back Dave Mackay complemented the passing abilities of Danny Blanchflower. Up front, the bruising and bustling Bobby Smith often won the ball for the quicksilver John White, both being supplied by fast wingers Dyson and Jones.

who arrived in 1978. Ardiles was still captivating White Hart Lane towards the end of the following decade, his creative talents complementing those of his visionary midfield colleague Glenn Hoddle, often to spectacular effect. By the dawn of the 1990s, with former Spur Terry Venables in charge, it was England striker Gary Lineker and media plaything Paul Gascoigne who held the stage. Entertainment value was high, but financial problems following the club's flotation on the Stock Exchange cast uncertainty over the future.

TRANMERE ROVERS

Founded 1885

Joined League 1921 (Div. 3 N)

Honours Div. 3 (N) Champions 1938

Ground Prenton Park

If the Mersey Tunnel had never been built, life would have been easier for Tranmere Rovers. Yet, despite the regular exodus of Wirral football fans to sample the more exalted delights on offer across the river at Anfield and Goodison, the Birkenhead club has striven valiantly to record more than seven decades of League existence.

All but one campaign – 1938/39, when Rovers proved incapable of meeting the standard demanded in Division 2 – have been spent in the lower reaches, and they have been periodically troubled by cash crises. But there have been compensations. Tranmere it was who unearthed two of England's greatest pre-war centre-forwards – Bill 'Dixie' Dean and Tom 'Pongo' Waring – and in the 1960s they gave a start to centre-half Roy McFarland, who also became an international star.

In 1987 Tranmere came perilously close to dropping into the Vauxhall Conference but since then, improving rapidly during manager John King's second spell at Prenton Park, they have won

TRANMERE ROVERS
A book claiming to be an encyclopedia of football must include reference to the breed of one-club players that have existed, and still exist, in football. Harold Bell made a club record 595 (including 401 consecutive) League appearances for Tranmere Rovers between 1946 and 1959. He came from Tranmere Rovers junior sides and was born in nearby Liverpool.

promotion to the Third Division and lifted the Leyland Daf Cup at Wembley. Indeed, in 1991 they capped the lot to reach the Second Division after winning the play-off final, and optimism for the future seemed well justified.

TRANSFERS

When a player changes clubs, his new club pays compensation to the old.

Transfer fees have risen steadily through the century, until a dramatic rise in the late 1970s sent them out of control. Since 1980 fees have been decided by a Football League tribunal if clubs cannot agree or a player thinks a fee put on his transfer is prohibiting him getting another club.

A transfer deadline – the second Thursday in March each season – was introduced in 1911 to prevent clubs engaged in relegation and promotion issues from strengthening their teams after that date. Football League permission is needed for a player to play a League game if signed in the last few weeks of a season. This is usually granted only for games not affecting the top or bottom places.

As transfer fees are private and confidential matters, and as deals sometimes take in more than one player, transfer fees quoted in the press are not always reliable. However, certain symbolic transfer barriers are often associated with certain players. Alf Common (£1000 from Sunderland to Middlesbrough in 1905); Syd Puddefoot (£5000 from West Ham United to Falkirk in 1922) and David Jack (£10,890 from Bolton Wanderers to Arsenal in 1928) all broke significant thresholds.

Tony Hateley's move from Aston Villa to Chelsea in 1966 was the first £100,000 transfer. Dennis Tueart's transfer from Sunderland to Manchester City in 1974 broke the £250,000 barrier. And four years later Gordon McQueen was the subject of the first £500,000 fee, Manchester United paying Leeds United.

In 1979 Trevor Francis became the first £1,000,000 British player when he moved from Birmingham City to Nottingham Forest.

This transfer sparked a rush of seven-figure deals, the most dramatic being those of Steve Daley (Wolverhampton Wanderers to Manchester City for £1,437,500), Andy Gray (Aston Villa to Wolverhampton Wanderers for £1,469,000) and Bryan Robson (West Bromwich Albion to Manchester United for £1,500,000).

Tony Cottee's transfer from West Ham United to Everton in 1988 broke the £2,000,000 barrier, and he was soon followed by Paul Gascoigne (Newcastle United to Tottenham Hotspur). In 1989 Manchester United paid £2,300,000 to Middlesbrough for the transfer of Gary Pallister.

Allan Clarke and Alan Ball go down in transfer history by twice figuring in British record deals. In the late 1960s Clarke moved from Fulham to Leicester City for £150,000 and then

to Leeds United for £165,000. Ball went from Blackpool to Everton for £110,000 in 1966 and on to Arsenal for £220,000 five years later.

Two earlier transfers are important for their legal implications. In March 1912 the judge ruled in favour of Aston Villa in the test case of Lawrence J Kingaby *v* Aston Villa. Kingaby claimed that another club had offered him employment but the transfer fee fixed by Aston Villa was stopping him taking it up. The judge felt the club was justified. In 1963 George Eastham (Newcastle United), however, successfully brought a case against his club to show that the system of retaining a player after expiration of contract was not binding in law.

Denis Law's transfer from Huddersfield Town to Manchester City in 1960 - the first over £50,000 - was soon followed by two more big transfers involving the same player. Law went from Manchester City to Torino for £100,000 in 1961 and from Torino to Manchester United for £115,000 in 1962. Both were records for transfers involving a British club.

In 1982 Diego Maradona was transferred from Argentinos Juniors to Barcelona (Spain) for £4,800,000. Two years later he moved to Napoli for £6,900,000. Both were world records. Tottenham Hotspur received £4,500,000 from Marseille for the transfer of Chris Waddle in July 1989, and then, in May 1990, Juventus paid £7,700,000 for Roberto Baggio of Fiorentina, a new world record.

TRANSFERS Some brilliant footballing skills may not have been enough on their own to encourage Juventus to pay a reputed (world record) £7,700,000 to Fiorentina for Roberto Baggio. His film-star looks and crowd-pulling ways will help to pay for the man who will have a lot to live up to as the world's most expensive footballer in 1991.

UEFA

UEFA (Union European de Football Associations) is the controlling body of national associations in Europe and the organiser and authority for the European club and national competitions. Based on the South American model, it was formed under the auspices of FIFA, to which it remains responsible, in Basel, Switzerland on 15 June 1954. The headquarters were established in Berne. The first president was Ebbe Schwartz of Denmark, and the current one is another Scandinavian, Lennart Johansson of Sweden. The organisation's first coup was to get a deal with Eurovision which made the new European Cup competition feasible.

Two recent UEFA decisions have had a great impact on British soccer. The first was the banning of English clubs from European competitions after the 1985 Heysel disaster; this resulted in many English players going to Scotland in order to qualify for football in Europe. In 1990 the ban was lifted from all clubs except Liverpool, who will be readmitted in 1991/92 to play in the UEFA Cup. The second was the limiting of clubs to three foreign players in European ties. England, Wales, Scotland, Northern Ireland and the Republic of Ireland are to be considered separate nations since they put out individual national teams. This ruling will severely limit the power of most British clubs.

UEFA CUP

This competition started life as the International Inter-City Industrial Fairs Cup, a tournament set up by UEFA in its inaugural year and designed to coincide with trade fairs held in major European cities which were invited to enter teams. In practice the competition was as unwieldy as its name; in the first five years only two tournaments were completed - not a situation guaranteed to maintain public interest. Club sides

UEFA CUP The rather splendid UEFA Cup trophy being kissed by John Wark *(left)* and Paul Mariner following Ipswich Town's two-leg victory over AZ 67 Alkmaar in the 1980/81 tournament. They won in Ipswich 3-0 but lost 4-2 in Holland. Mariner, an England international, and Wark, capped by Scotland, both scored, as did Ipswich's Dutch star Frans Thijssen who got two against his countrymen.

as well as *ad hoc* city teams such as London and Frankfurt entered.

By 1960/61 the competition began to take on a more familiar shape; club sides competed in the course of one season, each round, final included, being contested over two legs - still the case today. By 1964 there were enough entrants to warrant byes. Like all aspects of the competition, the admission criteria have fluctuated, but essentially it is open to also-rans in domestic league competitions, thus giving less glamorous clubs a chance

of glory. After a series of bewildering modificaitons to its name, it was rechristened the UEFA Cup in 1971/72.

The spread of winning nationalities is wide. Spanish clubs dominated the tournament's early years and English clubs won every year from 1967/68 to 1972/73 - a feat they should strike to emulate now they have been readmitted to European competitions.

UEFA CUP The Fairs Cup became the UEFA Cup in 1972 following successive years of English victories (Leeds United twice, Newcastle United and Arsenal). The name change made no difference as, in the first competition, both finalists were English. After a 2-1 win at Wolves a 1-1 draw was sufficient to see Spurs to victory in the two-leg match. In the picture from the second leg, England internationals Martin Peters *(left)* and Martin Chivers for Spurs pull away from a fellow England cap, Mike Bailey of Wolves.

WALES

The foundations of Welsh soccer were in North Wales. The epicentre was an unlikely place – a tiny border mining village called Chirk. T E Thomas, a Chirk schoolmaster and Welsh FA administrator, is credited with introducing 49 future Welsh internationals to the game. Even so, early Welsh administrators did not find it easy to put together a team to travel long distances. In 1878 the Scottish FA secretary had to journey south to help round up Welsh players for the 9-0 Scottish win in Glasgow.

One Chirk coal-miner was Billy Meredith, one of the most famous Welsh footballers. Meredith played for 30 years in England. He captained Manchester City to the FA Cup Final in 1904, helped Manchester United to their 1909 FA Cup win and played in the 1924 semi-final for Manchester City when aged nearly 50. He first played for Wales in March 1895, and his last international, 25 years later, brought a famous 2-1 win against England at Highbury, a victory which welcomed one of the greatest eras in Welsh football. By 1921 there were six Welsh clubs playing in the Football League: Cardiff City, Swansea Town, Wrexham, Newport County, Merthyr Tydfil and Aberdare Athletic.

In 1921/22 Cardiff City finished fourth in Division 1 at the first attempt. Two seasons later they missed the Championship by one goal, finishing behind Huddersfield Town on goal average. (Had today's goal difference system been operating, Cardiff would have been champions.) In 1927 there was the compensation of the FA Cup.

Seven years after winning the FA Cup, Cardiff City were seeking re-election to Division 3 (S). They were successful, unlike Aberdare (1927) and Merthyr Tydfil (1930). The era had ended, although Swansea Town continued as a steady Second Division team.

Between 1939 and 1955 Swansea won four of eleven English Schools Trophy competitions. The supply of excellent young players promised well for the Welsh international team, but Welsh clubs failed to win honours. When First Division football finally came to Swansea it was part of one of the most incredible rise-and-fall stories of soccer. Swansea City went from 22nd in Division 4 in 1974/75 to 6th in Division 1 in 1981/82. Five seasons later they finished 12th in Division 4.

Since 1961 a Welsh club has qualified for the European Cup-Winners' Cup by means of the Welsh Cup. In 1962/63 the Welsh representatives were Bangor City, who took Napoli to a play-off in the first round. The following year Borough United progressed to the second round by beating Sliema Wanderers (Malta). There were more memorable performances from Cardiff City. In 1967/68 Cardiff beat Shamrock Rovers, NAC Breda (Holland) and Torpedo Moscow to reach the semi-final. They drew 1-1 away to HSV Hamburg but lost the return 3-2 at home. Cardiff also suffered two odd-goal defeats at the quarter-final stage – to Real Zaragoza in 1964/65 and Real Madrid in 1970/71. Wrexham (1975/76) and Newport County (1980/81) have also reached the quarter-final of the European Cup Winners' Cup, the latter being unfortunate to go out 3-2 on aggregate to Carl Zeiss Jena. In 1987/88 Merthyr Tydfil faired very well against Italian Cup winners Atalanta, winning 2-1 at home but losing 2-0 away.

WALES TEAM

In the inter-war years, Wales won the British international championship outright on six occasions. Fred Keenor, captain for much of the 1920s, provided the springboard for this success. Other inter-war stars were Bob John, Bryn Jones, Stanley Davies and Len Davies.

After sharing the British international championship in 1951/52, Wales qualified for the 1958 World Cup finals in Sweden with a team managed by Jimmy Murphy and including some of the most famous players in Welsh history: goalkeeper Jack Kelsey, the Charles brothers (Mel and John), Ivor Allchurch and Cliff Jones. Three drawn group games led to a play-off against Hungary, which Wales won 2-1. In the quarter-final Wales, without the injured John Charles, lost 1-0 to Brazil, 18-year-old Pele scoring the goal.

The Welsh have not qualified for the World Cup finals since, but have often come close. They were kept out of the 1978 and 1986 World Cup finals by late penalties in vital qualifying games against Scotland. In 1982 they failed, on goal difference, to pip Czechoslovakia.

Their best European Championship performance came in the 1976 tournament, when Wales won a qualifying group which contained Austria, Hungary and Luxembourg. In the two-leg quarter-final against Yugoslavia, Wales lost 2-0 in Zagreb and drew 1-1 in Cardiff. Frustrations continued with near qualification in 1984, a year in which Yugoslavia won a tight group that included an amazing 4-4 draw in Titograd. In 1988, when defeats in Denmark and Czechoslovakia ended hopes, the team also came close to qualification. Some of the 1980s stars, such as Neville Southall, Ian Rush, Mark Hughes, Kevin Ratcliffe and Peter Nicholas, have deserved appearances on a grander stage.

WALSALL

Founded	1888
Joined League	1892 (Div. 2)
Honours	Div. 4 Champions 1960
Ground	Bescot Stadium

Situated on the doorstep of Birmingham, not far from Wolverhampton, and with the M6 – an avenue to numerous First Division venues – nearby, little Walsall are hardly well placed to make an impact on the football world.

Yet, in their time, the club who twice failed to gain League re-election in their early years and made four successive applications in the 1950s have experienced their moments of heady triumph. Among them have been a sensational FA Cup defeat of Arsenal at their mightiest, in 1933, and progress to the League Cup semi-finals, again at the Gunners' expense, in 1984.

After re-entering the League's Third Division in 1920, they remained in the lower levels until the early 1960s, when they reached the Second, thanks largely to the goals of Colin Taylor and Tony Richards. They lasted just two terms, however, then fell to the Fourth by 1979, before rising again to the Second a decade later and plummeting back to the basement through successive relegations.

Noteworthy talents whose transfer fees have helped the 'Saddlers' survive include 1930s 'keeper Bert Williams and, in the 1960s, Phil Parkes, another custodian, and England striker Allan Clarke.

As the 1980s closed, Walsall left their long-time home at Fellows Park for a purpose-built stadium, and – despite their disadvantages – are not short of ambition.

FOOTBALL DURING THE WARS

The Football League programme continued through the 1914/15 season, although there was much opposition. Thereafter it was suspended for the remainder of the First World War, although makeshift leagues were introduced. League fixtures were immediately suspended on the outbreak of the Second World War, three games into the 1939/40 season. The FA Cup was also abandoned, leading to Portsmouth's bizarre record of holding the trophy for seven years (1939-46).

The blanket ban on sport

in September 1939 was lifted within a few days. Football resumed with regional friendlies, and soon these were converted into regional leagues. However, players' contracts were suspended for the duration of the war. They were paid a match fee – 30 shillings in England (£2 from 1943) and £2 in Scotland – but their availability was unpredictable. Clubs often relied on guest players from other sides. There are many tales of teams being cobbled together at the last minute.

Clubs maintained a good standard if they had war-workers (e.g. coal-miners) or members of the armed forces stationed nearby. Aldershot were helped by an army base which housed international footballers. Portsmouth

Watford's years under the spotlight were masterminded by three men who, either before or since those heady days, have enjoyed fame beyond Vicarage Road. For Elton John *(centre, wearing hat),* being chairman of his favourite club meant a chance to indulge in his passion for soccer and to spend some of the vast wealth he had accumulated as a top international pop star. For Bertie Mee *(on his left),* having had ten years as manager of Arsenal, a period that included their 1971 double, joining the Watford administration was probably a good way to stay involved in football without managerial hassle. And for Graham Taylor *(on John's right),* the time as manager of a team on the rise stood him in good stead for future promotions to Aston Villa and England. In short, they were a talented trio who seemed motivated entirely by their enthusiasm for the game.

had the legacy of a good team and were potentially well served by the navy. As an example of an unpredictable game, consider Portsmouth against Clapton Orient in the London League in February 1942. Clapton arrived without a goalkeeper, Pompey were at their best, and the final score was 16-1. Andy Black scored eight.

League champions in the First World War were Manchester City, Liverpool, Stoke and Everton in the Lancashire section, Nottingham Forest, Leeds City, Leeds City and Nottingham Forest in the Midlands section, and Chelsea, West Ham United, Chelsea and Brentford in the London Combination.

After the fragmented system of the interrupted 1939/40 season, the League programme was divided into North and South. Beginning with 1940/41, the northern winners were Preston North End, Blackpool, Blackpool, Blackpool, Huddersfield Town and Sheffield United. The southern winners were Crystal Palace, Leicester City, Arsenal, Tottenham Hotspur, Tottenham Hotspur and Birmingham. In three seasons the north had a second Championship, won by Liverpool (1942/43), Bath (1943/44) and Derby County 1944/45).

League War Cup winners were West Ham United (1939/40), Preston North End (1940/41), Wolverhampton Wanderers (1941/42), Blackpool (North), Arsenal (South) and Swansea (West) in 1942/43,

Aston Villa (North), Charlton Athletic (South) and Bath (West) in 1943/44 and Bolton Wanderers (North), Chelsea (South) and Bath (West) in 1944/45. Arsenal's 7-1 victory over Charlton Athletic in 1943 was a record score for a Wembley cup final.

In addition to the club fixtures, wartime football saw regular representative matches. Towards the end of the Second World War, England dominated the domestic scene in a way rarely seen in peacetime internationals. They could call on players such as Frank Swift, George Hardwick, Joe Mercer, Stanley Matthews, Raich Carter, Tommy Lawton and Jimmy Hagan. In a two-year period, Scotland were beaten 4-0, 8-0, 6-2, 3-2, 6-2, 3-2 and 6-1.

WATFORD

Founded 1891

Joined League 1920 (Div. 3)

Honours Div. 3 Champions 1969; Div. 4 Champions 1978

Ground Vicarage Road

It all happened for Watford in the 1980s. League Championship runners-up in 1983 and FA Cup finalists the following year, they sold striker Luther Blisset to AC Milan for £1 million; nurtured the talents of two international stars-to-be, John Barnes and Mo Johnston; were managed by Graham Taylor, who was destined to become England boss; and, as if that were not enough, they were chaired by one of the world's most famous pop stars,

Elton John.

Such personalities and events seemed far removed from the bulk of the 'Hornets' history, which was uneventful to put it mildly. After becoming founder members of the Third Division, Watford remained in that grade for 38 years, occasionally flirting with betterment but always falling short. When they finally departed in 1958, it was to join the newly-created Fourth Division, from which they rose after two years, largely due to Cliff Holton.

The 1960s proved a more enterprising decade – thanks largely to managers Bill McGarry and Ken Furphy – with two splendid players, 'keeper Pat Jennings and schemer Tony Currie, being discovered and sold, and promotion twice being missed only on the season's final day. In 1970 Liverpool were defeated on the way to the

FA Cup semi-finals, and with a solid following established despite the proximity of London, the future looked bright. But Furphy left and by 1975 the Hertfordshire club were in the Fourth Division.

Fortunately, the illustrious rescue party was at hand, and the Hornets rose rapidly to spend six seasons in the top flight. Since then Taylor has departed, Elton John is no longer as closely involved, and Watford's fortunes have declined. In the absence of another football-crazy millionaire, new manager Steve Perryman faces a challenging task in saving Vicarage Road from a return to obscurity.

WELSH CUP

From its outset in 1877, the Welsh Cup has been open to all clubs in Wales and clubs in bordering English counties. Wrexham beat Druids 1-0 in the first final. Unfortunately, neither Cup nor medals were ready when the game was played, but when it did arrive the 100-guinea Welsh Cup proved a spectacular trophy worth competing for.

Between 1886 and 1894 Chirk appeared in the final six times and won the Cup five times. Billy Meredith played in two of these finals, and later became the first Welsh player to win Welsh Cup and FA Cup winners' medals. A team from South Wales did not reach a final until 1903 (Aberaman lost 8-0 to Wrexham); the first southern success came from Cardiff City in 1911.

South Wales dominated the inter-war Welsh Cup. In 1927 Cardiff City won a remarkable treble: FA Cup, Welsh Cup and Charity Shield. In 1929 there was a surprise winner – Connah's Quay – while in 1934 Bristol City beat Tranmere Rovers in an all-English final. The post-war period brought new names on the Cup: Lovells Athletic (1948), Merthyr Tydfil (1949), Rhyl (1952), Flint Town United (1954), Barry Town (1955), Bangor City (1962) and Borough United (1963).

The qualification for Europe gave the competition an added interest from 1961, but it also brought out the best from Football League clubs. Cardiff City won 10 out of 13 between 1964 and 1976. English clubs have continued to compete for the Welsh Cup but are not eligible for the European Cup Winners' Cup as a result of winning it. When Hereford United won in 1990, for instance, runners-up Wrexham qualified for Europe.

WEST BROMWICH ALBION

Founded 1879

Joined League 1888 (founder member)

Honours Div. 1 Champions 1920; Div. 2 Champions 1902, 1911; FA Cup Winners 1888, 1892, 1931, 1954, 1968; League Cup Winners 1966

Ground The Hawthorns

A history that takes in 13 major finals has built for West Bromwich Albion a Cup tradition that few can match. Yet there is frustration among supporters that the exhilarating football which has been the hallmark of many Hawthorns combinations has been marred by inconsistency, a serious handicap in their quest for League honours. The pattern was established early on. After losing the FA Cup Finals of 1886 and

WEST BROMWICH ALBION A picture to treasure for West Bromwich Albion fans as Ronnie Allen scores from the penalty spot to help his side to a 3-2 victory over Preston North End in the 1954 FA Cup Final. The team finished as runners-up in the First Division that season, but have had only modest successes since. The picture shows changing times – imagine a penalty kick today where players do not attempt to encroach as the kick is taken and where the goalkeeper stays on his line, not moving until the ball is kicked.

1887, Albion claimed their first trophy in the following campaign, with winger Billy Bassett – destined to be club chairman until 1937 – in irresistible form. But they struggled in the League, being twice relegated to Division 2 during the early 1900s.

However, under the leadership of Fred Everiss – a secretary-manager from 1902 to 1948 – they improved after the First World War and took what remains their only Championship, a fitting climax to the career of majestic defender Jesse Pennington. There followed a runners-up slot in 1925, then Albion slumped and spent four years in the Second Division before Billy Richardson's marks-manship helped to clinch promotion and the FA Cup in 1931.

Mediocrity reigned subsequently, and the 'Throstles' – the 'Baggies' to locals – started the post-war era back in the lower flight. They rose again and in 1953/54, with Vic Buckingham in charge, enjoyed a brilliant season, beating Preston at Wembley and narrowly missing the title. Stars included goal merchants Ronnie Allen and Johnny Nicholls, and wing-half Ray Barlow.

Bolstered by youngsters such as full-back Don Howe and wing-half Bobby Robson, Albion promised much and remained a solid First Division force until the early 1970s, but the only silverware they had to show for it was another FA Cup, courtesy of a Jeff Astle goal in 1968, and the League Cup two years earlier.

Come 1973 and, despite the efforts of long-serving forward Tony Brown, the Throstles were demoted. Johnny Giles led them back up, then Ron Atkinson created an entertaining team, with midfielder Bryan Robson and striker Cyrille Regis taking the eye. But stars departed, impetus faltered and Albion were relegated in 1986, since when performances declined so drastically that they slumped to the Third Division, for the first time in their history, in 1991. Albion have a fine ground and, if a good side is built, better days should be in store.

WEST HAM UNITED

Founded 1895

Joined League 1919 (Div. 2)

Honours Div. 2 Champions 1958, 1981; FA Cup Winners 1964, 1975, 1980; European Cup Winners' Cup Winners 1965

Ground Upton Park

WEST HAM UNITED
West Ham United's 1964 FA Cup Final success (3-2 v Preston) being celebrated by John 'Budgie' Byrne, with the hammer, and Ken Brown. Byrne, a stylish and skilful goal-scorer, played all his professional football for London clubs and won 11 full England caps; Brown made 386 League appearances for the Hammers, and played once for England before successfully managing Norwich City from 1980–87. This Cup victory for West Ham typifies their trophy achievement – often playing very well for short periods but never threatening to win the Division 1 Championship.

West Ham United have long been surrounded by a romantic aura. They are known as a friendly club who endeavour to serve up skilful, entertaining football even when a more down-to-earth approach might better serve their needs. In fact, such an image – exemplified by their whimsical anthem 'I'm Forever Blowing Bubbles' – is less appropriate in modern times, and a new pragmatism has become evident.

The 'Hammers' started life as Thames Ironworks – they are still known as the 'Iron' to many supporters – but were rejoicing under their current title when they made their League debut, getting off to a brisk start by winning promotion to Division 1 in 1923. In the same year they reached the first Wembley FA Cup Final, tasting defeat at a venue which was later to be the scene of their greatest triumphs. But despite the prolific plundering of centre-forward Vic Watson, they went down in 1932 to commence an uneventful quarter of a century in the Second Division, the first stage of which was adorned by the talents of England inside-forward Len Goulden.

By the 1950s the side contained original thinkers such as Malcolm Allison, Dave Sexton, Frank O'Farrell, Noel Cantwell and John Bond, all destined for managerial success, and it was a stimulating combination that Ted Fenton led back to the First Division in 1958. Three years later Ron Greenwood took over as boss and the Hammers embarked on their most successful era.

With stars such as wing-half and captain Bobby Moore, midfielder Martin Peters and striker Geoff Hurst, all to become England World Cup heroes in 1966, supplemented by the subtle contribution of deep-lying forward Johnny Byrne, West Ham covered themselves in Cup glory, but failed to find consistency in the League. By the end of the decade Greenwood was spending heavily on the likes of defender Billy Bonds, though the most notable newcomer, schemer Trevor Brooking, emerged from the Upton Park youth set-up.

As John Lyall succeeded Greenwood in 1974, a similar pattern was maintained, with two further FA Cup victories and an appearance in the 1976 European Cup Winners' Cup Final being balanced against brief spells in the Second division at the end of both the 1970s and the 1980s. Now in the wake of Lou Macari's short but tempestuous reign as manager, and with Bonds – who served long and nobly as a player – in charge, the newly promoted Hammers seem well prepared for the 1990s. They are blessed with a loyal bedrock of support – a minority of which tends towards over-enthusiasm – and a tradition for stability which has seen only seven bosses in 90 years. Such clubs deserve to succeed.

WIGAN ATHLETIC

Founded 1932

Joined League 1978 (Div. 4)

Honours None

Ground Springfield Park

When Wigan Borough folded and resigned from the League in 1931, it seemed there was little future for soccer in such a traditional stronghold of rugby. Yet within a few months Wigan Athletic were born. Although it took them 46 years to reach the league.

'Latics' quickly began making up for lost time after entering Division 4. Within four seasons they had risen to the Third, and came close to a Second Division place in both 1986 and 1987. Twice in the 1980s they reached the FA Cup fourth round, and once the last 16 of the League Cup, though their crowning moment was Freight Rover Trophy triumph at Wembley in 1985.

For a club sandwiched between the giants of Manchester and Merseyside, and faced with heavy competition for support from a clutch of other Lancashire sides, not to mention their famous Rugby League neighbours, Wigan have done well and appear to have the resolve to continue achieving modest success.

WIMBLEDON

Founded 1889

Joined League 1977 (Div. 4)

Honours Div. 4 Champions 1983; FA Cup Winners 1988

Ground Plough Lane

The phenomenal rise of Wimbledon since their election to the Football League represented an achievement of fairy-tale proportions, although the mantle of a simpering Cinderella sat ill on the feisty little outfit. In fact, since arriving in Division 1 in 1986, the Dons' uncomplicated long-ball style and combative outlook have earned them a reputation more in keeping with the ugly sisters, although as the 1990s dawned they hinted at entering a more attractive phase. Under new manager Ray Harford, Wimbledon were playing bright, successful football and the soccer world wondered what further miracles might emanate from Plough Lane.

Before joining Division 4 at the expense of Workington Town, the Dons were best known for their FA Cup exploits, the most famous of which came in 1975 when Dickie Guy

WIMBLEDON Against the odds (small crowds, lack of footballing tradition and few established star players) Wimbledon consolidated their Division 1 status in the late 1980s and early 1990s. One of their major strengths, to which they unashamedly played, was the height, speed and tenacity of John Fashanu. Few weeks seemed to pass without 'Fash the Bash' appearing on the Dons' scoresheet, a fact he recognised when agreeing a new deal with the club through which he received bonus payments for goals scored. In this picture he is trying to outpace Sunderland's Gary Bennett at the start of the 1990/91 season – who would have thought, a few years ago, that such a match would have started with Wimbledon as favourites to win? (It ended 2-2.)

saved a Peter Lorimer penalty and Leeds United were taken to a fourth-round replay. Within two years they were in the Third Division, but twice returned to the basement before embarking on their amazing ascent. In 1986 they reached Division 1, finished sixth in their first top-flight term, and then stunned the establishment by winning the FA Cup – against Liverpool, of all clubs – in their second. Leading players have included forward Alan Cork, who has been a constant factor throughout the fantastic journey, midfield hard-nut Vinnie Jones, 'keeper Dave Beasant and striker John Fashanu. But Wimbledon owe most to the managers who have guided them to the heights on gates more appropriate to the Fourth Division, such men as Allen Batsford, Dario Gradi, Dave Bassett and Bobby Gould.

As dozens of clubs with infinitely more glorious traditions struggled to survive, the facts of soccer life proclaimed that the Plough Lane bubble must burst. Yet, as Harford's enlightened policy took shape, the Dons were looking ever more buoyant.

WINTERBOTTOM, Walter

1913 Born in Lancashire

1934 Leaves amateur football to join Manchester United

1936 Makes senior debut as wing-half

1937 Spinal injury ends League career after 25 matches; recovers to guest for Chelsea and lead representative sides during the war

1946 Becomes England's first manager and FA director of coaching

1950 Presides over debacle in Brazil as England are dumped out of their first World Cup, losing to the unfancied United States

1954 Leads his men to World Cup quarter-finals in Switzerland, where they fall to Uruguay

1958 England flop in Sweden World Cup

1962 Another quarter-final of soccer's premier tournament; this time England are beaten, in Chile, by Brazil

1963 Winterbottom steps down to join Central Council of Physical Education; Alf Ramsey takes over England job

1978 Receives knighthood for services to sport

Walter Winterbottom is the one England manager who cannot be judged by his results. Though his record over 27 years, which includes four World Cup failures, is modest in the extreme, he was handicapped by the presence of a selection committee which often saddled him with baffling and unnecessary team changes.

In fact the one-time teacher, who initiated England's under-23 and youth team, arguably had his greatest influence in his role as FA director of

WALTER WINTERBOTTOM

Under Winterbottom's managership the England side was often picked by a selection committee – so perhaps he should not be held too responsible for the infamous and awful 1-0 defeat by the United States during the 1950 World Cup Finals in Brazil. Just to look on the bright side, here is the England team that lined up for the previous match in that tournament, on 25 June in Rio, before a 2-0 win over Chile. They are *(back row, left to right)* **Aston, Mannion, Ramsey, Laurie Wright, Billy Wright, Williams; Mullen, Bentley, Dickinson, Mortensen, Finney. Perhaps Billy Wright's dreamy look, and Mortensen's 'can't bear to look' are pointers to what lay in store.**

coaching. As such he offered organised instruction to various levels of the game for the first time, and though he was occasionally vilified for introducing too much theory, he can take much credit for advocating the importance of ball skills.

It had been widely expected that when Winterbottom relinquished the managership of his country, he would replace his mentor, Sir Stanley Rous, as FA Secretary. But the job went to Denis Follows, and the RAF's wartime head of physical education was left to serve sport in other capacities. He later became a member of the Sports Council.

WOLVERHAMPTON WANDERERS

Founded 1877

Joined League 1888 (founder member)

Honours Div. 1 Champions 1954, 1958, 1959; Div. 2 Champions 1932, 1977; Div. 3 (N) Champions 1924; Div. 3 Champions 1989; Div. 4 Champions 1988; FA Cup Winners 1893, 1908, 1949, 1960; League Cup Winners 1974, 1980

Ground Molineux

The mighty Wolves; the very name thunders from the pages of English football history, evoking memories of proud achievements and stirring deeds. Yet, in truth, the club's greatness relates largely to just one era, in which the inspired leadership of one man created a tradition that none of his successors have come remotely close to equalling. Yet Wolves did exist – enjoying some success – before Stan Cullis took over as manager in 1948. Indeed, they finished third in the Football League's inaugural season and won the FA Cup five years later, but as the

twentieth century got under way, mediocrity beckoned. The Midlanders slumped into the Second Division and, although another Cup triumph soon followed, they were to plumb the depths of the Third before resuming their place among the elite in the early 1930s.

With Major Frank Buckley in charge, Wolves again challenged for honours, and were surprisingly slammed by Portsmouth in the 1939 FA Cup Final. The war destroyed the team's impetus and Buckley, having unearthed many youngsters who were to become top names, left the club. It was the cue for Cullis, himself a Buckley discovery, to lead Wolves to unprecedented glory.

The new boss believed firmly in the effectiveness of the long-ball game played with pace and power, and on these principles he built a formidable team. His stars

included half-back Billy Wright, who was to play 105 times for England, 'keeper Bert Williams, goal-scorers Roy Swinbourne and Dennis Westcott, wingers

WOLVERHAMPTON WANDERERS The Wolverhampton Wanderers side with the League Championship trophy won in the 1957/58 campaign. Wolves were to win the title again in the following season, missing a hat-trick by one point from Burnley in 1959/60. The team: *(left to right, back row)* **Clamp, Murray, Harris, Finlayson, Slater, Flowers, Stuart; Mason, Deeley, Wright, Cullis (manager), Broadbent, Booth, Mullen. Stan Cullis showed his true ability as a manager by replacing several of this side but still keeping the Wolves at the top.**

Johnny Hancocks and Jimmy Mullen, schemer Peter Broadbent, and defenders Ron Flowers and Bill Shorthouse. As well as stringing together an enviable sequence of domestic trophies, Wolves played a major part in blazing English soccer's trail to Europe. During the 1950s they took on top continental opposition in what were ostensibly friendlies but which were played with fiercely competitive spirit.

When new tactics overtook the Cullis method, Wolves' fortunes declined. In 1964 Cullis was sacked amid loud controversy. Over the next 20 years Wolves twice won the League Cup, and in 1972 they reached the final of the UEFA Cup where they lost to Spurs, but they also experienced three demotions to the Second Division. Top players of this period included strikers Derek Dougan, John Richards and Andy Gray, wing-half Mike Bailey, and full-back Derek Parkin.

The 1980s brought a disastrous slide to the Fourth Division which almost ended in financial oblivion, but since then – inspired by England striker

Steve Bull and ably led by manager Graham Turner – they have climbed back to the Second. Given a successful team, the support can surely be found for a return to eminence.

WOMEN'S FOOTBALL

In the 1890s Nettie Honeyball, secretary of British Ladies, pioneered women's soccer in England. A typical

WOMEN'S FOOTBALL
Two of the most successful women's teams have been Friends of Fulham and Doncaster Belles who contested the 1990 Women's FA Cup Final. Brenda Sempare of Fulham and Jackie Sherrard of Doncaster chase the ball in the match, won 1-0 by the Yorkshire team. Perhaps a reflection of the game's current standing is that the 1990/91 edition of the important *Rothman's Football Yearbook* devotes one quarter of a page out of 992 pages to women's football. But this may change with a national league and increased TV coverage.

example was the North-South game at Crouch End Athletic Ground in 1895. The *Manchester Guardian* reported 'The ladies of the 'North' team wore red blouses with white yolks, and full black knickerbockers fastened below the knee, black stockings, red beretta caps, brown leather boots and leg-pads.' The North won that game 7-0. A similar initiative took place in Scotland in the same decade – a travelling team under the management of Lady Florence Dixie.

On 25 August 1902 the FA Council issued instructions to its affiliated associations not to permit matches against 'lady teams'. It was not until the First World War that women's football boomed. Dick-Kerr's Ladies (Preston) was formed in 1917 to raise money for a military hospital. After the war Dick-Kerr's toured the country playing to large crowds, including one of the 53,000 at Goodison Park, but in December 1921 the FA stopped women's football at Football League club grounds. Dick-Kerr's continued throughout the inter-war period, however, raising an estimated £70,000 for charities.

Local women's football continued after the Second World War, but other European countries offered more opportunities. In the 1960s a few British players went to Italy as professionals, a pattern which was repeated in the 1980s when Scottish international Margaret Wilson had two years with Bari and several England players joined other Italian clubs.

England's 1966 World Cup success attracted more women to the game. In December 1969 the FA recognised women's football, and the Women's Football Association was soon formed (officially recognised by the FA in November 1971). The Women's FA Cup was launched in 1971, and the first official international in Britain was played at Greenock on 18 November 1972. England beat

Scotland 3-2.

In 1971 England had 44 women's clubs, but by the end of the decade there were five times that number. The WFA was affiliated to the FA in May 1984, the year which also saw the completion of the first ever UEFA international competition. England lost 4-3 on penalties to Sweden in the Final.

Interest was raised by television coverage in the late 1980s, but women's football in Britain is still far behind other countries in terms of registered players.

WORLD CLUB CHAMPIONSHIP

The World Club Championship, started with the intention of finding the best club side in the world, is an annual competition between the winners of the European Cup and the winners of the South American Champions Cup (Copa Libertadores). Inaugurated in 1960 as a two-legged competition, at a time when jet travel began to make such events possible, the first winners were Real Madrid. Santos (1962 and 1963) and Internazionale (1964 and 1965) have won the trophy in successive seasons.

Culture clashes were frequent in the 1960s. Santos and AC Milan each had a player dismissed in the 1963 play-off, which was won by a penalty kick. Another play-off decider, between Racing (Argentina) and Celtic in 1967, had six players sent off. The Manchester United – Estudiantes (Argentina) confrontation in 1968 brought another three dismissals, including United's Stiles and Best, before Estudiantes won 2-1 on aggregate. The 1969 and 1970 World Club Championships, also featuring Estudiantes, were again no place for faint hearts.

Consequently, European Cup winners often spurned opportunities to compete in the 1970s. Only Ajax (1972) and Bayern Munich (1976) took part. Among the absentees were Liverpool (twice) and Nottingham Forest. The

WORLD CLUB CHAMPIONSHIP
Percudani of Independiente and Ronnie Whelan of Liverpool during the 1984 World Club Cup Final played in Tokyo. The Argentinian side won the match 1-0 and took home a lot of money as a result. Perhaps it is European sour grapes that accounts for the general lack of interest in the tournament. Celtic, Manchester United, Liverpool, Nottingham Forest and Aston Villa are the home nations losers – will a British team ever win it? One day, no doubt!

European Cup runners-up usually deputised, but there were no matches in 1975 and 1978. The World Club Championship received a boost in 1980, when the format was changed to a single match, played in Tokyo. Nottingham Forest did compete this time, losing 1-0 to Nacional (Uruguay), who, like Penarol (Uruguay) have the most World Club Championship wins (three). Overall, South American clubs have been more successful in a tournament that has been

WORLD CLUB CHAMPIONSHIP

(European team in italics)

Year	Winner	Runners-up	Scores
1960	*Real Madrid*	Penarol	0-0, 5-1
1961	Penarol	*Benfica*	0-1, 2-1, 5-0
1962	Santos	*Benfica*	3-2, 5-2
1963	Santos	*AC Milan*	2-4, 4-2, 1-0
1964	*Internazionale*	Independiente	0-1, 2-0, 1-0
1965	*Internazionale*	Independiente	3-0, 0-0
1966	Penarol	*Real Madrid*	2-0, 2-0
1967	Racing Club	*Celtic*	0-1, 2-1, 1-0
1968	Estudiantes	*Manchester United*	1-0, 1-1
1969	*AC Milan*	Estudiantes	3-0, 1-2
1970	*Feyenoord*	Estudiantes	2-2, 1-0
1971	Nacional (Uruguay)	*Panathinaikos*	1-1, 1-2
1972	*Ajax*	Independiente	1-1, 3-0
1973	Independiente	*Juventus*	1-0
1974	*Atletico Madrid*	Independiente	0-1, 2-0
1976	*Bayern Munich*	Cruzeiro	2-0, 0-0
1977	Boca Juniors	*Borussia Moenchengladbach*	2-2, 3-0
1979	Olimpia	*Malmo*	1-0, 2-1
1980	Nacional (Uruguay)	*Nottingham Forest*	1-0
1981	Flamengo	*Liverpool*	3-0
1982	Penarol	*Aston Villa*	2-0
1983	Gremio	*SV Hamburg*	2-1
1984	Independiente	*Liverpool*	1-0
1985	*Juventus*	Argentinos Juniors	2-2*
1986	River Plate	*Steaua Bucharest*	1-0
1987	*Porto*	Penarol	2-1
1988	Nacional (Paraguay)	*PSV Eindhoven*	2-2*
1989	*AC Milan*	Nacional (Columbia)	1-0
1990	*AC Milan*	Olimpia	3-0

* match decided on penalties

THE WORLD CUP

The first World Cup competition was staged, amid some controversy, in 1930 in Uruguay, then the reigning Olympic champion nation. It was instigated by FIFA under the auspices of the president, Jules Rimet, after whom the trophy was initially named. England, Scotland, Wales and Northern Ireland were not eligible, having withdrawn from FIFA in 1928, and indeed it was to be another twenty years before England, who had played such a large part in introducing football to the world, made their first appearance in the tournament. Thirteen countries, predominantly from the Americas, took part in the competition,

notable for poor matches, bad behaviour and unseemly squabbling. Perhaps it is the lack of success by European sides, having to play the match (or matches) in the middle of a domestic season, that has led to its less than enthusiastic reception in this part of the world; there's certainly no such reticence about the competition in South America.

WORLD CUP Sweden 1958: Brazil became the first and only team so far to win the World Cup outside their own continent. Pictured with the trophy are: (back row, left to right) Feola (coach), D. Santos, Zito, Bellini, N. Santos, Orlando, Gilmar; Garrincha, Didi, Pelé, Vava, Zagalo, Brito. Eight members of this squad played in the team which won the Final in Chile four years later.

and the host nation took the first title, beating Argentina 4-2 in the Final.

Italy was the venue for the tournament in 1934, and once again the host nation triumphed. Mussolini attended the Final, against Czechoslovakia, and the Italian team gave the fascist salute before the match, which they won 2-1. Maintaining their supremacy in the following tournament, held in France in 1938, Italy beat Hungary 4-2 in the Final, and the subsequent intervention of the Second World War saw that they held on to the trophy for 12 years.

England made their World Cup debut in the next competition, staged in Brazil in 1950, where their hitherto acknowledged mastery of the game was brought to an ignominious end as a side which included Alf Ramsey were beaten by rank outsiders the USA. They could not do enough in their other games to keep them in the tournament, and it was not until sixteen years later that England established any sort of presence in the competition. The Final of 1950 was a fine match between Uruguay and Brazil, but this time the host nation couldn't quite make it, and the trophy returned to Montevideo.

In 1954 Hungary, the 'Marvellous Magyars', were the team to beat, and they started out as firm favourites with a side including the remarkable striking quartet of Toth, Kocsis, Puskas and Czibor, and the all-time great 'keeper Grosics. They stormed through to the Final, but, facing a strong West German line-up, they allowed over-confidence and German exploitation of their tactical weaknesses to steal their early two-goal lead, and they lost 3-2.

In the 1958 competition in Sweden, all four British nations qualified for the finals. Northern Ireland were the least rated of the four, but under the guidance of Danny Blanchflower they succumbed only in the quarter-finals to France. Wales also progressed to a quarter-final against Brazil, but the combination of Pele, Garrincha and Didi was too powerful for them, and they went down 1-0. The supposedly stronger teams of England and Scotland were both eliminated in the first round, perhaps still suffering from the reverberations of the Munich air disaster. The Final was contested by Sweden and the elegant Brazilians, and was the first competition in which the

latter staked their claim to footballing supremacy by beating the host nation 5-2.

Czechoslovakia emerged as strong European contenders in Chile in 1962, and were beaten only in the Final by Brazil, who thus took their second successive title and confirmed their reputation as world champions. England, the only British nation to qualify, were also put out of the tournament by the Brazilians, in the quarter-finals, having narrowly scraped through the first round.

While the legality of England's third goal of the 1966 Final at Wembley, scored by Geoff Hurst in extra time, will always be debated, the West Germans' second goal just before full-time was also dubious because of an alleged hand-ball by Schnellinger, so that the final scoreline of 4-2 to England might seem a fair reflection of the game. Alf Ramsey's commitment to building a team which would win the World Cup had finally come to fruition. However, his concentration on physical stamina, his use of ball-players (such as Nobby Stiles, who successfully restricted the remarkable Eusebio of Portugal in the semi-final), and his scorn for public relations also left a negative imprint, perhaps leading to the more cynical and less stylish football of subsequent competitions.

The 1970 tournament in Mexico saw the rise of the strongest post-war Italian team, which reached the Final against supremos Brazil, who took a third title. In recognition of this achievement, the Jules Rimet Trophy departed with the Brazilian team to a permanent home in Rio de Janeiro. This tournament also witnessed perhaps England's most unfortunate exit from the competition, in their quarter-final against West Germany. Peter Bonetti, finding himself in goal at two hours' notice and unable to settle, made two errors which saw England's two-goal lead disappear. Muller wrapped it up for the Germans in extra time.

For the 1974 tournament in West Germany a new trophy was supplied by FIFA (despite Brazil's offering to provide the replacement), which has since been known as the 'FIFA World Cup Trophy'. Scotland were the only British side to qualify, but they found themselves in a tough group with Brazil and Yugoslavia and narrowly failed to progress beyond the first round. The Dutch were the most exciting side to watch in this competition, playing inventive and intelligent football. A world-class line-up including the masterful Johan Cruyff, Neeskens, Rep and Krol appeared set to beat West Germany in the Final, but over-confidence seemed to play its part, and while the Dutch players toyed with the ball, Helmut Schoen's Germans gritted their teeth and put themselves 2-1 ahead, a position from which Holland never recovered.

After managerial problems, England, under Ron Greenwood, failed to qualify for the 1978 finals in Argentina. Scotland, on the other hand, were on a wave of misplaced patriotic fervour under the managership of the inex-perienced Ally MacLeod. They did qualify but came home after the first round, having suffered defeat by Peru (for which match Gemmill, Souness, Macari and Derek Johnstone were available but not selected) and an embarrassing draw with Iran. The Final in 1978, between Holland and Argentina, was strongly criticised for the standard of its refereeing, and there were hints at collusion between South American sides to produce the goal differences necessary for qualification; it now seems likely that Peru were in fact bought off by an unpopular Argentinian regime desperate to improve their standing. However, Cesar Menotti's Argentinians included players of the calibre of Ardiles and Passarella, with Fillol in goal, and they took the title 3-1 with a less cynical display than they had shown for some time.

England, Scotland and Northern Ireland all qualified for the 1982 finals in Spain, and it was the Irish, under Billy Bingham, who provided the most inspired British interest. Their brave challenge took them through to the second round, when the French, and in particular the relentless attacking of Michel Platini, showed their superiority and put out the Irish 4-1. Scotland, under Jock Stein, battled hard in what was again a tough group, but could not find enough to get past the first round, while England, unable to score against Spain, just missed getting through to the semis. Diego Maradona made his first appearance in these finals and performed brilliantly, but he could not single-handedly take his country to a credible defence of their title. The Final, between Italy (who had failed to beat Cameroon in the group matches) and West Germany, saw poor refereeing against a plethora of fouls. The first half was dull, but action improved in the second with goals from Rossi, Tardelli and Altobelli for Italy and one late one from Breitner for West Germany, Italy thereby equalling Brazil's tally of three titles.

The 1986 tournament took place in Mexico – the first time a nation had hosted the competition for a second time. Once again, England, Scotland and Northern Ireland all qualified, but only England progressed beyond the second round, after a sparkling match against Poland in which Gary Lineker scored a hat-trick. Argentina proved too much for them in the quarter-finals, however, putting them out of the competition 2-1. The most exciting match of the tournament was probably that between the USSR and Belgium, which the latter won 4-3 after extra time, with Ceulemanns and Scifo displaying some inspiring play. The Final, between Argentina and Franz Beckenbauer's West Germans, provided five

goals for the watching millions, two for Germany from Rummenigge and Voller, and three – the last in the 84th minute – for Argentina, thus securing the Argentinians' second title.

Of the 24 nations competing in the 1990 World Cup, Brazil began as many people's favourites, although England, under Bobby Robson (in his last few weeks as manager before being replaced by Graham Taylor), had at last come back into contention as possible winners. The draw was managed so that all early England matches would be played on the island of Sardinia, with the aim of containing any supporter violence. Happily this did not materialise, the England squad in fact winning the Fair Play award of the tournament. England progressed to the semi-finals, their best performance since 1966, thanks to some skilful contributions from players such as Lineker, Platt, Wright, Walker and emerging star Paul Gascoigne. Their semi against West Germany was probably the finest match of the competition, lost only on a penalty shoot-out after extra time.

Scotland also qualified in 1990 but once again left their best performance until too late, and made an early trip home. The Republic of Ireland, under the managership of Jack Charlton, qualified for the first time and fared better, with some determined if sometimes over-defensive play, but were eventually ousted by Italy 1-0 in the quarter-finals. Italy, who took third place in the tournament, saw the rise of a new goal-scoring talent in the relatively unknown Salvatore Schillaci, who was top scorer of the finals. Holland, expected to do well, were disappointing, but Cameroon astonished the footballing world by reaching the quarter-finals – the first African nation to do so – thanks to some prolific goal-scoring by 38-year-old substitute Roger Milla.

The Final, once again

between Argentina and West Germany, was a shambles in which the football took a poor second place to the histrionics. Refereeing was confused and arbitrary and cynical fouling was rife, particularly from the Argentinian side. The scenes culminated in arguments with the referee and two Argentinians being sent off, Monzon becoming the first ever player to be shown the red card in a World Cup Final. After the match a tearful Maradona refused to shake hands with the president of FIFA. West Germany won the title 1-0 after Brehme scored from a penalty, but

international football was the overall loser.

Despite such undignified proceedings, however, the World Cup finals continue to be the showpiece of football for millions of fans world-wide. Unlike the Olympic Games, the tournaments have rarely been subject to political manipulation or boycottings – it would be a very brave or a very foolish leader indeed who would deny his country the chance to participate in this most celebrated competition. The vastly improved improved performances of African and Asian nations in recent tournaments is an indication of the ever-

WORLD CUP

Year	Winners	Runners-up	Score
1930	Uruguay	Argentina	4-2
1934	Italy	Czechoslovakia	2-1*
1938	Italy	Hungary	4-2
1950	Uruguay	Brazil	2-1**
1954	West Germany	Hungary	3-2
1958	Brazil	Sweden	5-2
1962	Brazil	Czechoslovakia	3-1
1966	England	West Germany	4-2*
1970	Brazil	Italy	4-1
1974	West Germany	Netherlands	2-1
1978	Argentina	Netherlands	3-1*
1982	Italy	West Germany	3-1
1986	Argentina	West Germany	3-2
1990	West Germany	Argentina	1-0

* after extra time
**played on league basis; score of 'deciding' match

WORLD CUP

Wembley 1966, and England's hopes take a knock, albeit a temporary one, as West Germany *(white shirts)* score in the last seconds of the Final in a move developed from a free kick. This made the score 2-2 and extra time had to be played before England could score twice more to win. On the far right, number 6, Weber *(partially hidden)*, starts to pick himself off the ground after squeezing the ball past number 3, Ray Wilson, and 'keeper Gordon Banks. West German goal ace Uwe Seeler (number 9) looks on as England captain Bobby Moore (number 6) appeals for an earlier suspected handball. No other English players dispute the goal at this point and the referee ignored later protests. It will be another English-speaking nation hosting the 1994 World Cup, and trepidation is mixed in with the usual keen anticipation since there is much talk of modifying the game to captivate the US audience who, popular belief has it, appreciate only high-scoring sports. Proposals which have horrified most members of the football world, fans, players, and coaches alike, include wider goals and 10-man teams. In October 1990 seven goals were scored in an experimental game played by top-flight players in France. The targets were wider by 43 centimetres (17 inches) and higher by 16 centimetres (6½inches) and it is reckoned that at least two of the goals would not have been scored if standard goals had been used. Most of these ideas are associated with FIFA president, Brazilian Joao Havelange.

increasing popularity of the game throughout the world – it seems that there are no longer any 'minnows' who can be written off before a ball is kicked.

The choice of the United States as the venue for the 1994 tournament promises to provide perhaps the most flamboyant ever backdrop for the finals, and it is certain that patriotism will, as usual, reach fever pitch. The depth of feeling aroused by the competition has in fact been the subject of psychiatric research, which indicates that in the weeks leading up to the finals there is a marked increase in reported cases of mental disorders, while during the tournament itself there is a sharp downturn in such cases.

WORLD YOUTH CUP

The World Youth Championship was launched by FIFA in 1977 as a competition for under-18s held every two years. Past winners have been the Soviet Union (1977 in Tunisia), Argentina (1979 in Japan), West Germany (1981 in Australia), Brazil (1983 in Mexico), Brazil (1985 in the Soviet Union), Yugoslavia (1987 in Chile) and Portugal (1989 in Saudi Arabia). The 1991 competition – in Portugal in June – has an under-19 age limit.

In 1985 FIFA inaugurated an under-16 World Cup, and the first finals were held in China. The hosts and Australia were among the surprise quarter-finalists. West Germany's Mercel Witsczek scored hat-tricks in the quarter-final and semi-final, but his country lost the final 2-0 to Nigeria. The second under-16 World Cup, in 1987, took place in Canada. Again the 16 teams produced surprise quarter-finalists – Australia, South Korea and Ivory Coast among them – but the Cup went to the Soviet Union after a penalty shoot-out against Nigeria. The 1989 finals, held in Scotland, saw the host nation progress to the final. Opponents Saudi Arabia, 2-0 down in the first half, fought back to draw 2-2 after extra time; Saudi won the penalty shoot-out 5-4 to take the trophy. In 1991 the first FIFA under-17 World Championship was scheduled for Ecuador in August, superseding the under-16 competition.

These tournaments run alongside the longer-established UEFA Youth Tournament, won initially by England in 1948 and most recently by Czechoslovakia in 1990 at under-16 level, and the UEFA under-18 trophy last contested in 1990.

WREXHAM

Founded 1873

Joined League 1921 (Div. 3 N)

Honours Div. 3 Champions 1978

Ground Racecourse Ground

Wrexham, the oldest surviving club in Wales, have broken out of their lower-division strait-jacket but once. That was in 1978 when young manager Arfon Griffiths, who as a skilful midfielder played more than 600 games for the 'Robins', led them into the Second Division. There they struggled for four campaigns before relegation restored them to more familiar surroundings.

The only other League triumphs in Wrexham's history were two promotions from the Fourth Division, the vast

WREXHAM Geoff Davies, one of a number of Liverpudlians to make the short journey across the border into Wales. Of the Welsh clubs in the Football League, Wrexham have made fewest headlines – but still nobody relishes the trip to play them

majority of their seasons having been spent at the bottom level, although knock-out exploits – in 1978 they reached the quarter-finals of both League and FA Cups – brought some relief.

Despite some enterprising cash-raising schemes, Wrexham have faced a continuing economic struggle, with many North Wales fans being attracted to Manchester and Liverpool. Occasional European forays, courtesy of Welsh Cup victories, a trophy they have won on 21 occasions, have helped keep interest alive, but as the 1990s dawned there were signs that the unequal struggle was becoming ever more difficult.

WRIGHT, BILLY

1924 Born in Ironbridge, Shropshire

1941 Turns professional with Wolverhampton Wanderers

1942 Recovers from serious ankle injury

1946 Makes full international debut, against Northern Ireland in Belfast

1947 Takes over club captaincy

1949 Collects the FA Cup after Wolves defeat Leicester City

1950 Skippers England through the first of three World Cups

1952 Footballer of the Year

1954 Leads Wolves to League title

1958 Holds aloft the Championship trophy

1959 Caps his Molineux achievements with a third title medal; May – makes 105th and last appearance for England, against the United States in Los Angeles and then retires

1960 Becomes manager of England youth and under-23 teams

1962 Takes job as Arsenal boss

1966 Sacked by the Gunners; goes on to work in television, with huge success

Wright, the leading English defender of the 1940s and 1950s, enjoyed a golden playing career which might have been scripted for a comic-strip hero. He won the game's top club honours, captained his country 90 times, and was the first player to win a century of international caps. Wright's image of perfection was heightened by his blond, clean-cut looks, a modest personality, and his marriage to pop singer Joy Beverley, an event greeted ecstatically by the nation.

Yet, despite the euphoria, he was not a footballer of great natural talent, his distribution being distinctly average and his ball skills unremarkable. He more than made up for it, however, with a fierce tackle, an instinctive ability to read the game, exceptional power in the air for a stocky man, and an inspiring knack of leading by example. The early part of his career was spent as a defensive right-half, but many believe he was more effective at centre-half, the role to which he was converted during the 1954 World Cup Finals.

Sadly, Wright's management days were less than glorious. At Highbury – where he initiated a youth policy which bore fruit under his successor, Bertie Mee – he was judged as being 'too nice' for such a ruthless profession. His subsequent decision to forsake football for television proved to be eminently wise.

BILLY WRIGHT
Billy Wright must have been photographed on hundreds of occasions leading out teams; he was a natural general. In this case it's a special occasion as he leads out England for his 100th cap, at Wembley against Scotland in a match Wright's team won 1-0. The player behind Wright is Ronnie Clayton (Blackburn Rovers); the Scottish 'keeper is Bill Brown (then with Dundee, later with Spurs).

YASHIN, Lev

1929 Born in Moscow

1953 Makes debut for Moscow Dynamo

1954 Wins first of 78 caps, 3-2 v Sweden

1955 Wins Soviet League Championship medal

1956 Olympic gold medallist

1957 Second Soviet Championship

1958 World Cup quarter-finalist

1959 Soviet Championship

1960 Wins European Championship medal, 2-1 v Yugoslavia

1962 World Cup quarter-finalist

1963 Soviet Championship; European Footballer of the Year

1964 European Championship runner-up, 1-2 v Spain

1966 World Cup fourth place

1967 Retires

1991 Dies, and is mourned around the world

The Soviet Union's initial distaste for international competition meant that Yashin's arrival at the World Cup was delayed until Sweden in 1958, when he was 29. But what an impact he made. The black-clad figure guarding the Russian goal seemed almost impregnable. Thirty years on, when sports journalists voted him into their all-time team, only Pele was a more indisputable choice.

LEV YASHIN A Russian press photograph of Lev Yashin taken in 1968 during a training session for Moscow Dynamo. Not wearing black, but showing the good looks that made him popular beyond the football field, Yashin became one of the great international statesmen for the game, frequently called upon to represent his country and continually in demand for exhibition matches and testimonial games.

Yashin played for only one club throughout his career but when, in 1953, he found it difficult to emerge from the reserves, he was tempted to turn his back even on his beloved Moscow Dynamo. He was proficient at basketball and volleyball, but it was ice hockey that was the rival attraction and it was fortunate for football that Yashin succeeded his country's other truly great goalkeeper, 'Tiger' Khomich, at club level in time. A year later, in September 1954, he embarked on an international career that extended to 78 caps and earned him international renown, not only for his

saves, which bordered on the miraculous, but also for his sportsmanship.

After his World Cup performance in Sweden it came as a shock when Yashin proved vulnerable four years later in Chile. Against Colombia he let in a goal straight from a corner, while the host country beat him twice from long range in the quarter-finals. L'Equipe noted that the match 'marked the end of the greatest modern goalkeeper, if not of all time.' Completely wrong. A year later Yashin had a magnificent match for the Rest of the World against England at Wembley, and in 1966 he was still in the Soviet goal when they reached the semi-finals in the World Cup, their best performance in that competition.

At club level Yashin collected four Soviet Championship and two Cup winner's medals. One last honour was to come: his country's highest award, the Order of Lenin.

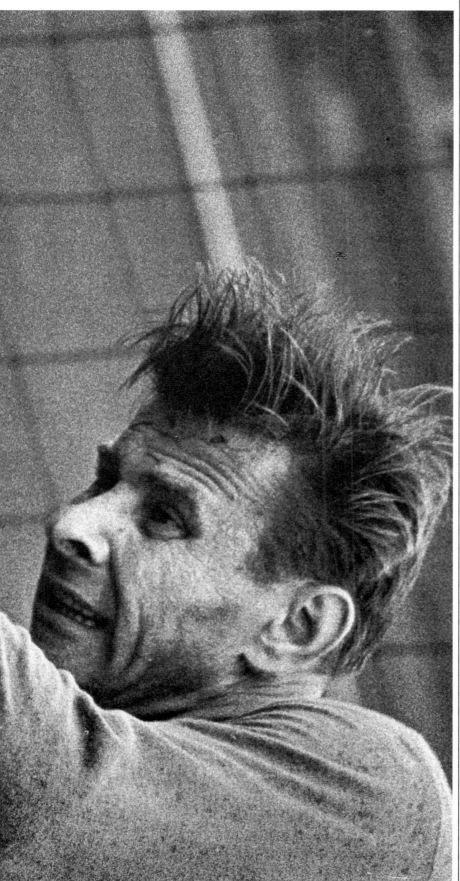

YORK CITY

Founded 1922

Joined League 1929 (Div. 3 N)

Honours Div. 4 Champions 1984

Ground Bootham Crescent

A tradition for stirring deeds in knock-out cups has brought much-needed consolation to York City fans, who have had little to shout about in more than 60 years of League life. A two-season sojourn in the Second Division during the mid 1970s has been the only highlight of an otherwise disappointing history in the bread-and-butter competition. The 'Minstermen's' finest hour came in 1955 when they beat Blackpool (complete with Matthews, Mortensen et al) and Spurs on their way to an FA Cup semi-final against eventual winners Newcastle United, going out only in a replay. Stars of this heroic campaign included goalkeeper Tom Forgan and marksmen Arthur Bottom and Norman Wilkinson. Among other exhilarating exploits was a run to the quarter-final of the 1962 League Cup.

Influential figures have included managers Tom Johnston, who led the club into the Second Division, and Wilf McGuinness, who couldn't keep them there. In fairness, with most Yorkshire supporters favouring the bigger clubs, the task of bringing regular top-level soccer to Bootham Crescent was, and is, little short of Herculean.

YOUNG, George

1922 Born in Grangemouth, Scotland

1941 Joins Rangers from Kirkintilloch Rob Roy

1943 Plays at right-back for Scotland against England in a wartime international

1948 First captains Scotland

1953 Completes run of 34 consecutive Scotland appearances (a record until Kenny Dalglish)

1957 Retires from Scottish League football

1959 Takes over as Third Lanark manager (until 1962)

A giant of a man, 6 ft 2 in tall and heavily built, George Young became a giant also in stature and personality during soccer's post-war golden age. He played 53 Scotland internationals (plus two unofficial wartime games) and 22 times for the Scottish League. He captained Rangers to six Scottish League Championships, four Scottish Cup triumphs and two League Cup wins. In 1948/49 Rangers won all three major Scottish competitions, their success founded on a strong defence in which Young was outstanding.

Young, who captained Scotland a record 48 times, developed a close working relationship with Scottish FA secretary George Graham. In Young's era there was no Scotland manager – except for a brief period during the 1954 World Cup when Andy Beattie was in charge – so he became as much a player-manager as a captain. He captained Scotland eight times against England, and although never on the winning side at Hampden against the 'auld enemy,' he led the Scots to famous Wembley victories in 1949 and 1951.arrying around a lucky champagne cork from a Rangers Cup win he was nicknamed 'Corky' Young. Scottish Player of the Year in 1955, he was still an international when he retired from playing.

Z

ZICO

Zico: another Brazilian, another nickname. The fondness of that country for bestowing two-syllable handles on their favourite players is of great relief to television commentators and fans alike. Zico's career illustrates another tradition – the purchase of South American players by European clubs after an impressive World Cup showing. There's nothing new in it; players have switched continents since the 1930s and even earlier. The few who come to Britain, however, don't seem to stay long, undoubtedly owing to a combination of our climate and native footballing style. The obvious exceptions were the Tottenham pair from Argentina, Osvaldo Ardiles and Ricardo Villa. Those that play on the continent of Europe seem to fare a little better, although Maradona's departure from Naples was a very unfortunate advertisement for soccer. In this shot from the 1982 World Cup, Ardiles *(right)* arrives too late to prevent Zico from unleashing a powerful shot. Brazil won the game 3-1.

1977 Wins UEFA Cup medal, on away goals v Atletic Bilbao

1978 Plays in World Cup – fourth place

1982 Captains Italy to win World Cup, 3-1 v West Germany

1988 Appointed coach of Italian Olympic team; becomes Juventus coach

Zoff, in terms of honours, is one of the most successful footballers of all time. Capped 112 times by his country, he gained World Cup and European Championship winner's medals and, at club level,

ZICO

1953 Born in Rio de Janeiro, Brazil

1968 Joins Flamengo

1969 First-team debut

1975 Scores on Brazil debut, v Uruguay

1977 South American Footballer of the Year

1978 Brazil take third place in World Cup

1979 Scores 89 goals in one season

1981 South American Footballer of the Year...

1982 ...and again

1983 Transferred to Udinese, Italy, for £2.5 million

1985 Returns to Flamengo

1986 Plays in World Cup

quarter-finals

It is one of the injustices of football that Brazil failed to win the World Cup in Zico's time. But by the same token, it was injuries to the midfielder/striker that almost certainly denied his country the prize. In 1978 and 1986 he carried wounds that restricted his appearances, while in 1982 a marvellous Brazilian team was undermined only by the eccentricities of its defence.

By 1983, when Zico went to Italy, he had won three Brazilian titles and South American and World Club

Championships with Flamengo. In his first season with Udinese he was top scorer, with 19 goals. Zico always appeared to be an injury ready to happen, however, and after a second year largely on the sidelines he returned to his former club.

At the age of 33 he played in his third World Cup, but it summed up rather than crowned his career. In the opening group games he played only 22 faultless minutes against Northern Ireland; he then came on as a late substitute against Poland, and missed a crucial penalty against France. A great player whose reputation survived bad fortune, yet one whose memory will evoke frustration as well as delight.

ZOFF, Dino

1942 Born in Mariano del Friuli, Italy

1961 Concedes five goals in debut for Udinese against Fiorentina

1963 Transferred to Mantova

1965 Relegated to Italian Second Division

1966 Promoted

1967 Transferred to Napoli

1968 Wins first of 112 caps; European Championship win, 2-0 v Yugoslavia

1972 Is transferred to Juventus

1973 Runner-up, European Footballer of the Year

five Italian Championships, two Italian Cups and the UEFA Cup.

Yet until he reached the age of 30, Zoff appeared to be heading for a talented but largely unfulfilled goalkeeping career. Spells with Udinese, Mantova and Naples were fruitless and included two relegations. When he was transferred to Juventus in 1972 for £400,000, however, he embarked on an orgy of conquest of Napoleonic dimensions.

At the same time, his move to Turin cemented a permanent place in the Italian team and, shortly afterwards, the record books. After conceding a goal to Yugoslavia in September that year he was unbeaten in 12 international matches. In the 13th, a 1974 World Cup game against Haiti, he finally conceded a goal a minute after half-time, setting a world record of 1,143 minutes without letting the opposition score. His prowess at club level was such that he also established a national record of 903 unblemished minutes.

Zoff was an agile player whose courage, anticipation and reflexes were honed in the ultra-defensive Italian League where packed penalty areas often give goalkeepers little time to adjust. Supremely talented, it was strength of character and the confidence he inspired in the men in front of him that were his greatest asset. His position in the national team was in jeopardy after he let in two long, searing drives against the Netherlands in the 1978 World Cup, but it was Zoff who was chosen not only as goalkeeper but as captain in Spain four years later. He was presented with the Cup a month later.

DINO ZOFF
Dino Zoff is seen here in World Cup action against West Germany in the 1982 Final as Karl-Heinz Rummenigge, blocked out by Collavati, threatens the Italian goal. Italy were victorious and the 40-year-old Zoff, as captain, had the enviable duty of lifting the trophy. Goalkeepers' careers often last longer than those of outfield players, partly because stamina isn't such an important factor in their craft. Confidence and positional sense increase with experience to compensate for diminishing reflexes. Peter Shilton of England and Pat Jennings of Northern Ireland are two other goalkeepers who represented their countries way past the footballer's average retirement age. The number of clean sheets kept by Zoff as an international is testimony to the efficacy of Italian defences as much as to his goalkeeping ability.

Paul Merson, Arsenal, scoring against Liverpool, 1990

Mark Hughes, Manchester United, 1991

PICTURE CREDITS
The editor is very grateful to
all those who supplied
photographs for this book;
the picture librarians at the
various agencies were, without
exception, efficient, helpful
and obliging. In particular
thanks go to Colorsport who
provided the bulk of pictures
and who helped the project
considerably with their
knowledge of football.

All photographs are courtesy
of **Colorsport** except:
Allsport 10, 32, 34, 60, 81, 82,
83, 85, 126, 128, 131, 132, 139,
143, 150-51, 161, 163, 167,
184-5, 189, 191, 199, 200-1,
201, 206
Peter Robinson 17, 77, 148,
168-9, 198, 208
Syndication International 49,
55, 61, 202-3
Simon Inglis 4, 70, 173, 174
Chris Smith title page,
introduction, 73, 101
Illustrated London News 84,
158
**John Frost Historical
Newspaper Collection** 12-13, 84
Andy Ward 16, 105